TOUCHING

Ashley Montagu

TOUCHING

The Human Significance of the Skin

Third Edition

PERENNIAL LIBRARY

Harper & Row, Publishers, New York
Grand Rapids, Philadelphia, St. Louis, San Francisco
London, Singapore, Sydney, Tokyo, Toronto

Library of Congress Cataloging in Publication Data

Montagu, Ashley, 1905–
    Touching: the human significance of the skin.

    Includes bibliographical references and index.
    1. Touch—Psychological aspects.   2. Skin—Psychological aspects.   3. Touch—Social aspects.   4. Health.
I. Title.
BF275.M66   1986   152.1'82   85-45216
ISBN 0-06-015535-3   86 87 88 89 90 MPC 10 9 8 7 6 5 4 3 2 1
ISBN 0-06-096028-0 (pbk.)   90 MPC 10 9 8 7 6 5 4

To the memory of
James Louis Montrose

CONTENTS

PREFACE
to the First Edition

This book is about the skin as a tactile organ very much involved, not alone physically but also behaviorally, in the growth and development of the organism. The central referent is man, and what happens or fails to happen to him as an infant by way of tactile experience, as affecting his subsequent behavioral development, is my principal concern here. When I first started thinking about this subject in 1944 there was very little experimental evidence available bearing upon these matters. Today a considerable amount of such evidence has been made available by a large variety of investigators, and my lonely paper of 1953, "The Sensory Influences of the Skin" (*Texas Reports on Biology and Medicine,* 2, 1953, pp. 291–301), is no longer alone. This book draws upon many sources of information, and notes citing these sources have been gathered in the Reference section, where they are identified by the numbers of the pages and the line or lines on the pages where references or quotations occur. (This system seemed preferable to using note numbers which interrupt the text. When notes are amplifications, suggestions, or comments, however, rather than simple source citations, they are keyed to asterisks and appear on the same pages as the passages to which they refer.)

The skin as an organ, the largest organ of the body, was very much neglected until quite recently. But it is not as an organ as such that I am here concerned with the skin; rather, in contrast to the psychosomatic or centrifugal approach, I am interested in what may be called the somatopsychic or centripetal approach. In short, I am interested in the manner in which tactile experience or its lack affects the development of behavior; hence, "the mind of the skin."

A.M.

Princeton, N.J.
8 February 1971

PREFACE

to the Second Edition

The first edition of this book has gratifyingly found a large audience. The present edition incorporates much new information concerning the vital importance of touch from birth to old age.

One regret that every writer must have is that there does not exist a word which specifically refers to both sexes. In this edition I first attempted to remedy the situation by employing "it" as a substitute for the customary masculine pronouns. The result was an unacceptable impersonality which, combined with the awkward repetitiveness of "he or she" and "his or hers," rendered the change repellent. I, therefore, have adhered to customary usage. It is, of course, to be understood that in all instances both sexes are implied. This book is about human beings, not objects, and no baby is an "it" to its mother, nor should it be to anyone else.

Most of all, for their bibliographical help, I have to thank Louise Schaeffer of the Biology Library, and Terry Caton and Terry Wiggins of the Psychology Library, all of Princeton University.

I have also to thank Louise Yorke of the Library of the Medical Center, Princeton.

To my friend Dr. Philip Gordon I am indebted for his careful reading of proof.

To Elisabeth Jakab, my editor, many thanks for her sympathetic interest and concern for the continued welfare of this book.

A.M.

Princeton, N.J.
20 September 1977

PREFACE

to the Third Edition

i know that touching was and still is and always will be
the true revolution.

—Nikki Giovanni

We in the Western world are beginning to discover our neglected senses. This growing awareness represents something of
an overdue insurgency against the painful deprivation of sensory experience we have suffered in our technologized world.
The ability of Western man to relate to his fellowman has
lagged far behind his ability to relate to consumer goods and
the unnecessary necessities which hold him in thrall—possessed by his possessions. He can reach out to other planets, but
too often he cannot reach out to his fellowman. His personal
frontiers seldom, if at all, permit the passage of a deeply felt
communication across them. The human dimension is con-
stricted and constrained. Through what other media, indeed,
than our senses can we enter into that healthy tissue of human
contacts, the universe of human existence. We seem to be unaware that it is our senses that frame the body of our reality.

To shut off any one of the senses is to reduce the dimensions of our reality, and to the extent that that occurs we lose
touch with it; we become imprisoned in a world of impersonal
words, sans touch, sans taste, sans flavor. The one-dimension-
ality of the word becomes a substitute for the richness of the
multidimensionality of the senses, and our world grows crass,
flat, and arid in consequence. Words tend to take the place of

experience. Words become a declarative statement rather than a demonstrative involvement, something one can utter in words, rather than act out in a personal sensory relationship.

Above all else, it seems to me that it is our role as human beings always to join learning to loving-kindness. Learning to learn, learning to love, and to be kind are so closely interconnected and so profoundly interwoven, especially with the sense of touch, it would greatly help toward our rehumanization if we would pay closer attention to the need we all have for tactual experience.

The impersonality of life in the Western world has become such that we have produced a race of untouchables. We have become strangers to each other, not only avoiding but even warding off all forms of "unnecessary" physical contact, faceless figures in a crowded landscape, lonely and afraid of intimacy. To the extent that this is so, we are all diminished. Because of our untouchableness we have failed to create a society in which people touch each other in more senses than the physical. With our inauthentic selves, and wearing other people's image of what we should be, it is not surprising that we remain unsure of who we really are. We wear the inauthentic selves that have been imposed upon us as uncomfortably as an ill-fitting garment, ruefully, at times, and unknowing, wondering how we got this way. As Willy Loman says in *Death of a Salesman,* "I still feel kind of temporary."

The world of Western man has come to rely heavily for communication on the "distance senses," sight and hearing, and of the "proximity senses," taste, smell, and touch, has largely tabooed the latter. Two dogs may use all five senses in their communication with one another, but the same can hardly be said of two human beings in our culture. With our increasing sophistication and disengagement from each other, we have come to rely excessively on verbal communication, to the extent of virtually excluding the universe of nonverbal communication from our experience—to our great impoverishment. The languages of the senses, in which all of us can be socialized, are capable of enlarging our appreciation and of deepening our understanding of each other and the world in which we live. Chief among these languages is touching. The communications we transmit through touch constitute the most powerful means of establishing human relationships, the foundation of experience.

Where touching begins, there love and humanity also begin—within the first minutes following birth. It is to make these facts known, and their consequences for each of us and for humanity as a whole, that this book has been written.

The first edition, published in 1971, and the second in 1978 gratifyingly found a large audience at home and abroad. The present third edition has been extensively revised and incorporates much new information concerning the tactile needs and beneficial tactile interactions between human beings, from birth to old age.

A.M.

Princeton, N.J.
19 February 1986

ACKNOWLEDGMENTS

I am most indebted to Louise Yorke of the Library of the Princeton Medical Center, Princeton. I thank also Helen Zimmerberg and Louise Schaeffer of the Biology Library, and Mary Chaikin, as well as Janice Welburn formerly of the Psychology Library, all of Princeton University.

To my editors, Hugh Van Dusen and Janet Goldstein, I owe thanks for many courtesies.

To my wife I am grateful for bearing with me during the long gestation of this third edition and for her great help in reading the copyedited manuscript and proofs.

And many thanks to Donna Swanson for permission to reprint her moving poem *Minnie Remembers*.

Finally, I should like to draw attention to Dr. Jules Older's book, *Touching Is Healing* (New York: Stein & Day, 1983), which is full of new insights and admirably serves to complement the present volume.

1 The Mind of the Skin

The greatest sense in our body is our touch sense. It is
probably the chief sense in the processes of sleeping and
waking; it gives us our knowledge of depth or thickness
and form; we feel, we love and hate, are touchy and are
touched, through the touch corpuscles of our skin.

—J. Lionel Tayler, *The Stages of Human Life,*
1921, p. 157.

There is but one temple in the universe, and that is the
Body of Man. Nothing is holier than that high form.
Bending before man is a reverence done to this
Revelation in the Flesh. We touch heaven when we lay
our hands on a human body.

—Novalis
(pen name of Frederich von Hardenberg),
1772. Quoted in Thomas Carlyle's
Miscellaneous Essays, vol. II.

The skin, the flexible, continuous caparison of our bodies, like
a cloak covers us all over. It is the oldest and the most sensitive
of our organs, our first medium of communication, and our
most efficient protector. The whole body is covered by skin.
Even the transparent cornea of the eye is overlain by a layer of
modified skin. The skin also turns inward to line orifices such
as the mouth, nostrils, and anal canal. In the evolution of the
senses the sense of touch was undoubtedly the first to come into
being. Touch is the parent of our eyes, ears, nose, and mouth. It
is the sense which became differentiated into the others, a fact
that seems to be recognized in the age-old evaluation of touch
as "the mother of the senses." Though it may vary structurally
and functionally with age, touch remains a constant, the foun-

dation upon which all other senses are based. The skin is the largest sensory organ of the body, and the tactile system is the earliest sensory system to become functional in all species thus far studied—human, animal, and bird. Perhaps next to the brain, the skin is the most important of all our organ systems. The sense most closely associated with the skin, the sense of touch, is the earliest to develop in the human embryo. When the embryo is less than an inch long from crown to rump, and less than six weeks old, light stroking of the upper lip or wings of the nose will cause bending of the neck and trunk away from the source of stimulation. At this stage in its development the embryo has neither eyes nor ears. Yet its skin is already highly developed, although in a manner not at all comparable to the development it is still to undergo. At nine fetal weeks, when the palm is touched the fingers will bend as if to grip; at twelve weeks, the fingers and thumb will close. Pressure at the base of the thumb will cause the fetus to open its mouth and move its tongue. Firm touching of the back or sole of the foot will result in toe-curling or fanning-out, as well as the placing reflex— bending of the knee and hip, as if to withdraw from the touch. In the womb, bathed by its mother's amniotic fluid and enveloped by the soft walls of the womb, "rocked in the cradle of the deep," the conceptus* leads an aquatic existence. In this environment its skin must have the capacity to resist the absorption of too much water, the soaking effects of its liquid medium, to respond appropriately to physical, chemical, and neural changes, and to changes in temperature.

The skin in common with the nervous system arises from the outermost of the three embryonic cell layers, the ectoderm. The ectoderm constitutes the general surface covering of the embryonic body. The ectoderm also gives rise to the hair, teeth, and the sense organs of smell, taste, hearing, vision, and touch—everything involved with what goes on outside the or-

*Conceptus, the organism from conception to birth. Embryo, the organism from conception to the end of the eighth week. Fetus, from the beginning of the ninth week to birth.

ganism. The central nervous system, which has as a principal function keeping the organism informed of what is going on outside it, develops as the inturned portion of the general surface of the embryonic body. The rest of the surface covering, after the differentiation of the brain, spinal cord, and all the other parts of the central nervous system, becomes the skin and its derivatives—hair, nails, and teeth. The nervous system is, then, a buried part of the skin, or alternatively the skin may be regarded as an exposed portion of the nervous system. It would, therefore, improve our understanding of these matters if we were to think and speak of the skin as the external nervous system, an organ system which from its earliest differentiation remains in intimate association with the internal or central nervous system. As Frederic Wood Jones, the English anatomist, put it, "He is the wise physician and philosopher who realises that in regarding the external appearance of his fellowmen he is studying the external nervous system and not merely the skin and its appendages." As the most ancient and largest sense organ of the body, the skin enables the organism to learn about its environment. It is the medium, in all its differentiated parts, by which the external world is perceived. The face and the hand as "sense organs" not only convey to the brain a knowledge of the environment, but convey to the environment certain information about the "internal nervous system."

André Virél, anthropologist and neurologist, puts it very well when he writes:

Our skin is a mirror endowed with properties even more wonderful than those of a magic looking glass. The primeval mirror that envelops the ovum splits apart only to be swallowed up within itself. Then it reappears on the other side of the original fissure. The divided mirror that is the skin and nervous system combined thus ends up looking at itself, so to speak, resulting in a confrontation that stimulates a neverending movement of images and the birth of what is aptly referred to as reflexive thought.

Throughout life, this prodigious fabric, the skin, is in a continuous state of renewal by the activity of the cells in its deep layers. Every four hours or so, the skin forms two new layers of cells. Skin and gut cells can apparently divide hundreds and thousands of times during the lifetime of a person. Skin cells shed at the rate of more than a million every hour. In different parts of the body the skin varies in texture, flexibility, color, scent, temperature, innervation, and in other features. Furthermore, the skin, and especially the face, recording the trials and triumphs of a lifetime, carries its own memory of experience.

On our skin, as on a screen, the gamut of life's experiences is projected: emotions surge, sorrows penetrate, and beauty finds its depth. Soft, smooth source of youth's vanity, skin later bears wrinkled witness to the toll of years. Radiant in health, it tingles to the affectionate touch.

The skin's growth and development proceed throughout life, and the development of its sensitivities depends largely upon the kind of environmental stimulation it receives. Interestingly enough, in common with chick, guinea pig, and rat, in the newborn human the relative weight of the skin, expressed as a percentage of the total body weight, is 19.7, nearly the same as in the adult, 17.8, suggesting what should be obvious: the enduring importance of the skin in the life of the organism.

In other animals it has been found that "skin sensitivity is apparently earliest and most completely developed during prenatal life." There is a general embryological law which states that the earlier a function develops, the more fundamental it is likely to be. The fact is that the functional capacities of the skin are among the most basic of the organism.

It is that part of the skin which is most immediately exposed to the environment, its most superficial layer, the epidermis, that houses the tactile system. The free nerve endings in the epidermis are almost entirely concerned with touch, as are the nerve plexuses known as Meissner's corpuscles, but interestingly enough they are absent from the highly tactile lips

The Mind of the Skin 7

and tongue. The average number of Meissner's corpuscles per square millimeter is about 80 in the child of three, 20 in a young adult, and 4 in old age. The larger nerve plexuses, known as Pacinian corpuscles, are the specific end organs that respond to mechanical stimuli of pressure and tension. These are particularly numerous under the digital pads of the fingers. A plexus of free nerve endings distributed among the epidermal cells of each hair follicle renders tactile stimulation through mechanical displacement of the hair a very important mechanism in producing tactile sensations.

The surface area of the skin has an enormous number of sensory receptors receiving stimuli of heat, cold, touch, pressure, and pain. A piece of skin the size of a quarter contains more than 3 million cells, 100 to 340 sweat glands, 50 nerve endings, and 3 feet of blood vessels. It is estimated that there are some 50 receptors per 100 square millimeters, a total of 640,000 sensory receptors. Tactile points vary from 7 to 135 per square centimeter. The number of sensory fibers from the skin entering the spinal cord by the posterior roots is well over half a million.

For the body as a whole, the skin provides millions of cells of different kinds, some 350 different varieties per square centimeter, 2 to 5 million sweat glands, and about 2 million pores. Throughout life there is a steady decrease in the number of these structures.

As birth, the skin is called upon to make many new adaptive responses to an environment even more complex than that to which it was exposed in the womb. Transmitted through the atmospheric environment, in addition to air movements, are gases, particles, parasites, viruses, bacteria, changes in pressure, temperature, humidity, light, radiation, and much else. To all these stimuli the skin is equipped to respond with extraordinary efficiency. By far the largest organ system we present to the world,* about 2,500 square centimeters in the newborn and

*The only organs with a larger surface area are the gastrointestinal tract and the alveoli of the lungs, but these are internal organs.

about 19,000 square centimeters, or approximately 19 square feet, in the adult male, in whom it weighs about 8 pounds, containing some 5 million sensory cells, the skin constitutes some 12 percent of the total body weight. The skin ranges in thickness from 1/10 of a millimeter to 3 or 4 millimeters. It is generally thickest on the palms of the hands and soles of the feet, and usually thicker on extensor than flexor surfaces, and thinnest on the eyelids, which must be light and flexible. In summer the skin is softer, because the pores are wider and because of the greater lubrication. In winter the skin is more compact and firm, and the pores are closer together, hairs are more firmly held and less often shed, facts which have been known to furriers for centuries, for the furs of animals taken in winter have for these reasons been preferred over those taken in summer.

THE FUNCTIONS OF THE SKIN. Knitted together with a variety of sturdy cells, the skin protects the soft tissues within the body. Like a frontier of civilization, it is a bastion, a place at which skirmishes are fought and invaders resisted, our first and final line of defense. The functions of the skin are many: (1) as a base for sensory receptors, the seat of the most delicate of the senses, touch; (2) as an organizer as well as an information source and processor; (3) as a mediator of sensation; (4) as a barrier between organism and environment; (5) as an immunologic source of hormones for protective cell differentiation; (6) as a protector of underlying parts from mechanical and radiation injuries; (7) as a barrier to toxic materials and foreign organisms; (8) as a major role player in regulating blood pressure and the flow of blood; (9) as a regenerative repair organ; (10) as a producer of keratin; (11) as an absorptive organ of noxious and other substances, which are eventually excreted in the body's waste products; (12) as a temperature regulator; (13) as an organ involved in the metabolism and storage of fat, and (14) of water and salt metabolism by perspiration; (15) as a reservoir for food and water; (16) as a respiratory organ and facilitator of the two-way passage of gases through it; (17) as the synthesizer of a number of important compounds, including the anti-rachitic vitamin D; (18) as an acidic barrier that protects against many bacteria; (19) while the sebum from the sebaceous glands lubricates the skin and hair, insulates the body against rain and cold, and probably helps to kill bacteria; (20) as a self-cleanser.

The above are some of the physical functions performed by the skin, and they are of fundamental importance. But while in this book we are concerned with the behavioral influences of the skin, especially in response to the varieties of touch, we shall later discuss some of the remarkable physiological changes that touching or the lack of it produces in animals and humans.

One would have thought that the wondrous versatility of the skin, its tolerance of environmental changes, and its astonishing thermo-regulatory capacities, as well as the singular efficiency of the barrier it presents against the insults and assaults of the environment, would have constituted conditions striking enough to evoke the interest of inquirers into its properties.

Strangely enough, until relatively recent years, this has not been the case. Indeed, most of what we know about the functions of the skin has been learned since the 1940s. Though much knowledge has been acquired, of both the structure, biochemistry, and physical functions of the skin, much more remains to be learned. Today the skin no longer languishes for want of interest. Indeed, since the mid-seventies there has been a remarkable explosion of interest in and research on the functions of the skin, with results both amazing and of the greatest importance.

Somewhat surprisingly, the one repository of so much of the sensitive human spirit in which one might have expected to find a sophisticated insight into the functions of the human skin, namely poetry, is found to be disappointingly barren. Poems have been written in celebration of almost every part of the body, but the skin, unaccountably, appears to have been slighted as if it did not exist. John Horder, English poet and writer, has commented on this very point. In an article entitled

"Hugging Humans," he complains that many of the best thought-of English poets remain encapsulated in their intellects, and as often as not are on extremely bad terms with their physical bodies. As he writes:

> The mind/body split has been with us for as long a time as Christianity, probably for a good deal longer. In practical terms, it results in few poems being written about the delights of warm friendship, touch and hugging. Or if they are written, they have a habit of not always making their way into print.

In prose literature the case is otherwise. There are many references to the skin, perhaps the most notable being Gulliver's mortifying account of the diminutive Lilliputians' animadversions on the unprepossessingness of his skin, with its unsightly blotches, pimples, and other disfigurations.

That the importance in human behavior of the tactile functions of the skin has not gone wholly unrecognized is evident from the many expressions in common parlance in which reference is made to them. We speak of "rubbing" people the wrong way, and "stroking" them the right way; of "abrasive" and "prickly" personalities. We speak of "the personal touch," meaning something more than a perfunctory act, the person's own idiom, essentially his personality expressing itself by "getting in touch." We say of someone that he has "a happy touch," of another that he has "a magic touch," and of another that he has "a human touch," or that he has "a delicate touch," or, praise of praises, that *he* has "a feminine touch," and of still another that he is "a soft touch." In the constant search for human contact we get into "touch" or "contact" with others. Some people are "hard" to deal with, others are "softies." Some people have to be "handled" carefully ("with kid gloves"). We speak of someone who is quick to take offense or oversensitive as "touchy," or "tetchy." Some people are "thick-skinned," others are "thin-skinned"; some get "under one's skin," while others remain only "skin-deep." Others are "out of touch," or have "lost their grip." Things are either "palpably" or "tangibly" so or not. The "feel" of a thing is in many ways important to us. Anything gummy, adhesive, or sticky to the touch is "tacky." Our "feeling" for others embodies much of the kind of experience which we have ourselves undergone through the skin. A deeply felt experience is "touching." A touching experience is "poignant," a word which comes to us from the Middle English directly from the Old French *poindre,* by way of the Latin *pungere,* meaning to prick or to touch. If one thing is certain, it is "the healing touch of Time."

Protected from the weather by a fusion of pressure and temperature, blended with warmth, the skin becomes oily and we feel "snug." We "grapple" with problems, and "cling" to each other in desperation. Pleasure in a work of art gives some of us "goose pimples." We say of some people that they are "tactful," and of others that they are "tactless," that is, either having or not having that delicate sense of what is fitting and proper in dealing with others (see p. 287). Through "feeling" we frequently refer to emotional states, such as happiness, joy, sadness, melancholy, and depression, and by that term often imply a reference to touching. We speak of an "unfeeling," unpitying person as "callous," which is the English for the Latin *callum,* meaning "hard skin," and from which the word both for the unfeelingness and the thickened skin is derived. We speak of a person as having grown so "callused" that he has become insensitive to human feeling.

We are never really secure unless we can "hold on to" something; nor do we really believe that we understand anything until we have "a firm grip on it," or "grasp the point." We say of a riveting story that holds us in its "clasp" that it is "gripping." We "clutch our loved ones to our bosom." In the dark we go "groping" or searching blindly about in the hope that we may succeed in feeling our way to security.

"Touchstone," the word for any test determining genuineness or value, reminds us that all the phrases listed above are metaphors for the security that comes with touch.

When we speak of someone who is removed from reality, we say that he is "out of touch with reality," or someone who is not quite "all there" as "a little bit touched." When we describe the contemporary unrelatedness of people to each other, we speak of them as "disengaged," "out of touch," and "untouchable."

As a metaphor for establishing the reality of an idea or its appositeness, nothing could be more determinate than "putting one's finger on it."

One "keeps one's distance." "We reach out" to others. AT&T urges us to "Reach Out and Touch Someone," by making good use of the telephone, a clever appeal to the distance, the isolation, and the loneliness of so many Americans.

We "pat each other on the back," we are "held" by an appealing performance. A voice makes one's skin "tingle." Fear makes one's skin "creep." The skin, in fact, does creep—it contracts, and as it does so it pushes the hair up, and one's hair "stands on end" (the pilomotor reflex).

It is interesting that the "skin" is almost universally used as a metaphor for survival. In life and death struggles or those metaphorically resembling them, the observers "lose no skin off their backs," the lucky escape "by the skin of their teeth," and the losers are "flayed" alive.

What is very revealing, when we think about it, is that there is something very special about the feeling we have for the word "touch." For example, when we speak of "the feminine touch," or "the individual touch," or "the professional touch," what we are feeling is that special attention is being paid, and when we use the word in such a context it is with a special care, not often bestowed upon other words.

The skin, as André Virél has put it, is a two-sided mirror that performs a triple function. Its outer surface reflects the world of objective reality as well as the living world within the body. Its inner surface reflects the outside world in a way that communicates it to the multifarious cells that comprise our organs. Our skin, therefore, not only receives the signals that come to us from our environment and relays them to centers of the nervous system for deciphering, but also picks up signals from our inner world, all of which are then translated into quantifiable terms. The skin is the mirror of the organism's functioning; its color, texture, moistness, dryness, color, and every one of its other aspects, reflect our state of being, psychological as well as physiological. We blanch with fear and turn red with embarrassment. Our skin tingles with excitement and feels numb with shock; it is a mirror of our passions and emotions.

As for touch, as Bertrand Russell pointed out long ago, it is the sense of touch which gives us our sense of reality: "Not only our geometry and our physics, but our whole conception of what exists outside us, is based on the sense of touch. We carry this even into our metaphors: a good speech is 'solid,' a bad speech is 'gas,' because we feel that a gas is intangible, not quite 'real.' "

Although the skin has constantly occupied the forefront of human consciousness, it is strange that it should have elicited so little attention. Most of us take our skin entirely for granted, except when it burns and peels, or breaks out in pimples, or perspires unpleasantly. When we think of it at other times, it is with a vague wonder at so neat and efficient a covering for our insides: waterproof, dustproof, and miraculously—until we grow old—always the right size. As we grow older we begin to discover qualities of the skin, color, firmness, elasticity, texture, we had failed to notice at all before we began to lose them. With the accumulation of years we are apt to regard our aging skin as a rather dirty trick, a depressing public evidence of aging, and a somewhat unwelcome reminder of the passage of time. No longer the good fit it once was, it grows loose and baggy, and is often thin, wrinkled, dry and leathery, even parchment-like, sallow, splotched, or otherwise disenchanted.

But these are all superficial ways of looking at the skin. As we study the observations of numerous investigators, and put together the findings of physiologists, anatomists, neurologists, psychiatrists, psychologists and other investigators, adding to the brew our own observations and knowledge of human nature, we begin to comprehend that the skin represents something very much more than a mere integument designed to keep the skeleton from falling apart, or merely to provide a mantle for all the other organs, but rather that it is in its own right a complex and fascinating organ. In addition to being the largest organ of the body, the various elements comprising the skin have a very large representation in the brain. In the cortex, for example, it is the postcentral gyrus, or convolution, which receives the tactile impulses from the skin, by way of the sensory ganglia next to the spinal cord, then to the posterior funiculi in the spinal cord and medulla oblongata, to the venteroposterior nuclei in the thalamus, and finally the postcentral gyrus. Nerve fibers conducting tactile impulses are generally of larger size than those associated with the other senses. The sensorimotor areas of the cortex are situated on each side of the central gyrus. The precentral gyrus is largely sensory while the postcentral gyrus is mainly motor. Horizontal connecting fibers across the central fissure connect both gyri. Since it is a general rule of neurology that the size of a particular region or area of the brain is related to the multiplicity of the functions it performs (and to the skill, say, in the use of a muscle or group of muscles), rather than to the size of the organ, the proportions of the cerebral tactile area underscore something of the importance of tactile functions in the development of the person. Figures 1 and 2 are drawings or somatotopic maps of sensory and motor homunculi, or "little men," designed to show the proportionate representations of tactile functions in the cortex. From these figures it will be seen how large is the representation of the hand, especially of the thumb, and the enormous representation of the lips.

Actually there are several tactile senses, which are together subsumed under the term *touch:* these are often difficult to define, as when one's skin "creeps" when looking at an eerie scene in a movie or play, or at a "hair-raising" spectacle. We do, however, know of the elements that enter into touch, such as pressure, pain, pleasure, temperature, muscle movements of the skin, rubbing, and the like; then there is the information we receive from our muscles, through the skin, when we move. The term *haptic* is used to describe that mentally extended sense of touch which comes about through the total experience

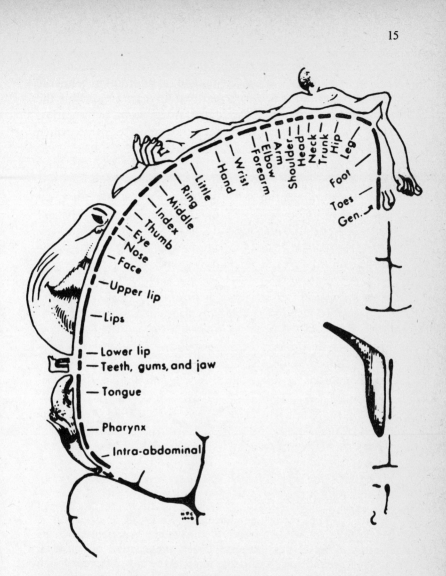

FIGURE 1. The sensory homunculus drawn upon the profile of one hemisphere. The underlying solid lines indicate the extent of cortical representation.

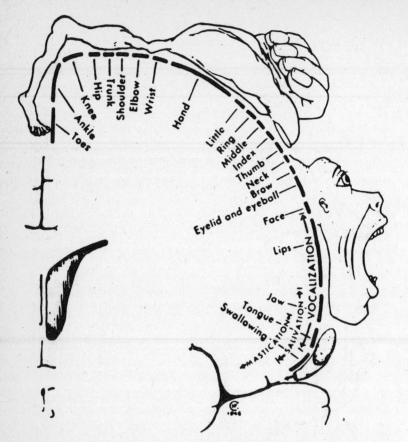

FIGURE 2. The motor homunculus. While there is a close correspondence between sensory and motor representation, the correspondence is not complete. The representation of sensation refers to specific areas and parts, whereas the motor representation refers to the movements of those parts. (From W. Penfield and T. Rasmussen, *The Cerebral Cortex of Man*. New York: Macmillan, 1950, p. 214. By permission.)

of living and acting in space. Our perception of the visual world, for example, in fact blends what we have *felt* in past associations with what we have seen or the scene before us. The haptic is an acquired sense in that it applies to seen objects that have been touched and acted upon. As Greenbie has put it, "Because we experience our earthly environment with all our senses, including smell and sound, the haptic system puts us in imaginative physical contact with places and objects we once touched but now only see, hear, or smell." In the landscape of humanity the haptic sense plays a highly significant role. When we speak of "keeping in touch" we know whereof we speak, that it is not a mere metaphor but a consummation much to be desired.

Consider: as a sensory system the skin is much the most important organ system of the body. A human being can spend his life blind and deaf and completely lacking the senses of smell and taste, but he cannot survive at all without the functions performed by the skin. The experience of Helen Keller, who became deaf and blind in infancy, whose mind was literally created through the stimulation of her skin, shows us that when other senses fail, the skin can to an extraordinary degree compensate for their deficiencies. The first person to have understood this appears to have been Jacob-Rodriguez Pereire (1715–1780), a Spaniard who, working in mid-eighteenth-century France, successfully showed that deaf-mutes could be taught to speak through touch. The method was to have the deaf-mute place his mouth against the ear, the face, or other sensitive part of the body, such as the hand, and for the subject to learn in this way what the meaning was of the various impressions he thus received. "All the senses," Pereire said, "accomplish their functions by virtue of a more or less modified sense of touch."

Among all the senses, touch stands paramount. The sense of pain, mediated from the skin to the brain, provides an essential warning system designed to compel attention. The condition known as *cutaneous alagia,* in which the individual can feel no pain in his skin, is a serious disorder. Those affected by the malady have been known to sustain severe burns and other injuries before becoming aware of any danger. Such persons are in jeopardy of their lives.

The continuous stimulation of the skin by the external environment serves to maintain both sensory and motor tonus. The brain must receive sensory feedback from the skin in order to make such adjustments as may be called for in response to the information it receives. When a leg "falls asleep" or grows numb, the sensory cutoff results in difficulty in initiating leg movement because the impulses from the skin, muscles, and joints are not adequately reaching the postcentral gyrus of the brain. The feedback from skin to brain, even in sleep, is continuous.

As a student and teacher of human anatomy I was, in the course of the years, repeatedly struck by the largeness of the tactile area of the brain as shown, usually in green, in textbook illustrations. No one seemed to have made any significant comment on this. It was not until the middle 1940s, when I commenced to draw together the data bearing on the development of human behavior,* that the recurrence of stray bits of evidence from a large variety of different sources impressed upon me the importance of the skin not only in the development of physical functions, but also in the development of behavioral ones. I delivered a lecture on this subject at the University of Texas Medical School at Galveston in April 1952. This was published in the journal issued by the school in July 1953. The response to the lecture and to the published article encouraged me to proceed with the assembly of the findings which are presented in this book, and which serve, I hope, to throw some light on an aspect of human development that has been largely underappreciated.

What is this aspect? It is quite simply the effect of tactile experience upon human behavioral development.

*Delivered as a course on socialization at Harvard University in the spring term of 1945, and subsequently published in my book, *The Direction of Human Development* (New York: Harper & Bros., 1955; revised edition, New York: Hawthorn Books, 1970).

Our approach to the skin in this book is quite the opposite of that which psychosomatic medicine has so illuminatingly made, the demonstration that what goes on in the mind may express itself in the skin in many different ways. The psychosomatic approach constitutes an invaluable contribution to our understanding concerning the influence of the mind upon the body—for the purposes of discussion we may preserve the artificial separation of mind *and* body—and of the extraordinary sensitivity of the skin in reacting to centrally originating nervous disturbances. That distressing thoughts may break out as boils in the skin, that urticaria, psoriasis, and many other skin disorders may originate in the mind, is no longer the novel idea it was when, in 1927, I read of this relationship in W. J. O'Donovan's pioneering little book, *Dermatological Neuroses.* Since that time considerable progress has been made, much of it admirably set out in Maximillian Obermayer's book of 1955, *Psychocutaneous Medicine,* and many works since. The psychosomatic approach to the study of the skin may be regarded as centrifugal; that is, it proceeds from the mind outwards to the integument. What we shall be concerned with in the present book is the opposite approach, namely from the skin to the mind; in other words, the centripetal approach.

The question we are most concerned to ask and answer in this book is this: What influence do the various kinds of cutaneous experiences which the organism undergoes, especially in early life, have upon its development? Primarily we are concerned to discover: (1) What kinds of skin stimulation are necessary for the healthy development of the organism, both physically and behaviorally? and (2) What are the effects, if any, of the want or insufficiency of particular kinds of skin stimulation?

One of the best ways of discovering whether or not a particular kind of experience is necessary or basic to any particular species and its members, is to determine how widely distributed it is in the class of animals (in the present instance, the mammals) to which the species under investigation belongs; what is phylogenetically basic is likely to be physiologically significant, and significant perhaps in other functional respects as well.

The specific question to which we seek an answer is: Must the member of the species *Homo sapiens* undergo, in the course of early development, certain kinds of tactile experiences in order to develop as a healthy human being? If such experiences are necessary, of what kind are they? For some light on these questions we may first turn to the observations made on other animals.

RATS AND SERENDIPITY. What started me thinking about the skin was the serendipitous reading in 1944, in a totally different connection, of a 1921–1922 paper by the anatomist Frederick S. Hammett, of the Wistar Institute of Anatomy in Philadelphia. Hammett was interested in discovering what would be the effects of total removal of both the thyroid and parathyroid glands from albino rats of the genetically homogeneous Wistar stock. Hammett noted that following the operation some of the animals did not, as they ought to have done, die. It had been thought by many investigators that such a thyroparathyroidectomy must invariably prove fatal, presumably owing to the action of some toxic substance upon the nervous system.

Upon inquiry Hammett found that the rats that had undergone the thyroparathyroidectomies had been drawn from two separate colonies, and that the greater number of the survivors came from what was called the experimental colony. In this colony the animals were customarily petted and gentled. In contrast, the animals exhibiting the higher mortality rate were drawn from what was called the standard stock, a group whose only human contact was that incidental to routine feeding and cage-cleaning by an attendant.These animals were timid, apprehensive, and high-strung. When picked up they were tense and resistant, and frequently exhibited fear and rage by biting. "The picture," as Hammett put it, "as a whole is one of constant high irritability and neuromuscular tension."

The behavior of the gentled rats was strikingly different from that of the standard stock animals. The former had been gentled for five generations. When handled, the gentled animals were relaxed and yielding. They were not easily frightened. As Hammett noted, "They give a uniform picture of placidity. The threshold of the neuromuscular reaction to potentially disturbing stimuli is almost prohibitively high."

With human beings it was very evident that the gentled rats felt secure in the hands not only of those who fondled them, but of everyone. The researcher who had raised them, Dr. Helen King, did so under conditions in which they were frequently handled, stroked, and had kindly sounds uttered to them, and they responded with fearlessness, friendliness, and a complete lack of neuromuscular tension or irritability. The exact opposite was true of the ungentled rats, who had received no attention whatever from human beings, except that involved in feeding and cage-cleaning. These animals were frightened and bewildered, anxious and tense in the presence of people.

Let us see what happened when thyroid and parathyroid glands were removed in the 304 animals operated from both groups. Within forty-eight hours of operation 79 percent of the irritable rats died, while only 13 percent of the gentled rats died—a difference of 66 percent of survivals in favor of the gentled animals. When the parathyroids alone were removed, within forty-eight hours 76 percent of the irritable rats died while only 13 percent of the gentled rats died, a difference of 63 percent.

Standard stock rats, placed at weaning in the experimental colony and gentled, became tame, cooperative and relaxed, and resistant to the effects of the parathyroid gland removal.

In a second series of experiments, Hammett investigated the mortality rate in parathyroidectomized wild Norway rats that had been caged for one or two generations. The wild Norway rat, it is well known, is a notoriously excitable creature. Of a total of 102 wild Norway rats, 92 animals, or 90 percent, died within forty-eight hours, most of the survivors succumbing within two or three weeks of operation.

Hammett concluded that the stability of the nervous system induced in rats by gentling and petting produces in them a marked resistance to the loss of the parathyroid secretion. In excitable rats this loss usually results in death from acute parathyroid tetany in less than forty-eight hours.

Subsequent experience and observation at the Wistar Institute showed that, the more handling and petting rats receive, the better they do in the laboratory situation.

Here, then, was something more than a clue to the understanding of the role played by tactile stimulation in the development of the organism. Gentle handling of rats could make all the difference between life and death following the removal of significant endocrine glands. This discovery was striking enough. But what was equally remarkable was the influence of gentling upon behavioral development. Gentling produced gentle, unexcitable animals; lack of gentling resulted in fearful, agitated animals.

These important findings, it seemed to me, were worth following up. There were innumerable unanswered questions, principally involving the mechanism, the physiology, by which handling or gentling could produce such significant differences in organismal and behavioral responses as Hammett had recorded. Since, apart from the Wistar Institute observations by Hammett and his colleagues, there was literally nothing in print that could throw any light on such questions, I began to make inquiries among animal breeders, among people who had been raised on farms, veterinarians, husbandrymen, and the staffs of zoos—the results were illuminating.

LICKING AND LOVING. Reading the Wistar Institute studies of Hammett, it occurred to me that the "washing" the mammalian mother gives her young, virtually from the moment they are born, in the form of licking, isn't washing at all, but something fundamentally very different and very necessary; that "washing" in the sense of cleaning was not the real function of licking, but that licking served very much more profound purposes. It seemed a reasonable hypothesis that, as Hammett's observations suggested, the proper kind of cutaneous stimulation is essential for the adequate organic and behavioral development of the organism. It seemed likely that the licking mammalian mothers give their newborn, and which they continue for durable periods thereafter, probably serves a basic series of functions, since it is universal among mammals with the exception of man. In that exception, I reasoned, there probably also lay an interesting story, and indeed there does, as we shall later see.

As soon as I commenced my inquiries among persons with long experience of animals I found a remarkable unanimity in the observations they reported. The substance of these observations was that the newborn animal must be licked if it is to survive, that if for some reason it remains unlicked, particularly in the perineal region (the region between the external genitalia and the anus), it is likely to die of a functional failure of the genitourinary system and/or the gastrointestinal system. Breeders of chihuahua dogs were particularly insistent upon this, for according to them the mothers often make little or no attempt to lick their young. Hence there is a high mortality rate among these puppies, caused by failure to eliminate, unless some substitute for maternal licking, such as stroking by the human hand, is provided.

The evidence indicated that the genitourinary system especially simply would not function in the absence of cutaneous stimulation. The most interesting observations on this matter soon became available in the form of an unpremeditated experiment carried out by Professor James A. Reyniers of the Lobund Laboratories of Bacteriology of the University of Notre Dame, Indiana. Professor Reyniers and his colleagues were interested in raising germ-free animals, and in 1946 and 1949 they published their findings in two separate monographs. In the early days of their experiments these workers' labors came to naught because all the experimental animals died of a functional failure of the genitourinary and gastrointestinal tracts. It was not until a former zoo worker brought her own experience to bear upon the solution of this problem, advising the Notre Dame group to stroke the genitals and perineal region of the young animals with a wisp of cotton after each feeding, that urination and defecation occurred. In response to an inquiry, Professor Reyniers wrote me:

> With respect to the constipation problem in hand-reared newborn mammals the following may be of some interest: Rats, mice, rabbits and those mammals depending upon the mother for sustenance in the early days of life apparently have to be taught to defecate and urinate. In the early period of this work we did not know this and consequently lost our animals. The unstimulated handled young die with an occlusion of the ureter and a distended bladder. Although we had for years seen mothers licking their young about the genitals I thought that this was a matter largely of cleanliness. On closer observation, however, it appeared that during such stimulation the young defecated and urinated. Consequently, about twelve years ago, we started to stroke the genitals of the young after each hourly feeding with a wisp of cotton and we were able to elicit elimination. From this point on we have had no trouble with this problem.

Failure of the genitourinary tract to function when newborn mammals were removed, immediately after birth, from contact with their mothers was soon also demonstrated by McCance and Otley. These investigators suggested that normally the licking and other attentions of the mother stimulated an increase in the excretion of urea as a consequence of the change in blood flow to the kidney.

Motherless kittens and other animals have been successfully raised by the appropriate cutaneous stimulation administered by a surrogate "mother." In an engaging account of his rescue of a newborn abandoned kitten from the bushes, Larry Rhine tells how he called up the ASPCA after feeding the kitten from a doll's bottle, and having announced that Moses, as he had named him, was eating quite normally, received the reply, "Of course he is. Your problem is not with the eating. You see, a kitten's first eliminations are stimulated by the mother cat. Now, if you'd like to do the same with a cotton swab dipped in warm water you might be able to . . ." And for the next few days Mr. Rhine was up every two hours, with a cup of warm water and a cotton swab, feeding, swabbing and sleeping—and Moses, who, appropriately enough, had been found in the rushes, flourished.

Observation of the frequency with which the mother licks different parts of the kitten's body reveals a distinct pattern. The region receiving most licking is the genital and perineal region; next in order comes the region around the mouth, then the underbelly, and finally the back and sides. The rate of licking seems to be genetically determined, about three to four licks a second. In albino rats the rate is six to seven licks a second.

Rosenblatt and Lehrman found that, during a fifteen-minute observation session, maternal rats lick their newborn pups for an average of two minutes and ten seconds in the anogenital region and lower abdomen, for about twenty-five seconds to the rear end of the back, about sixteen seconds on the upper abdomen, and about twelve seconds on the back of the head.

Schneirla, Rosenblatt, and Tobach mention, among the criteria defining maternal behavior in the cat, exaggerated licking of self and of young. We shall return to a consideration of the significance of self-licking later. These observers found that between 27 and 53 percent of the time was spent in licking; no other activity approached licking in the amount of time devoted to it.

Rheingold, in reporting her observations on a cocker spaniel, a beagle, and three Shetland sheep dogs (Shelties), states that licking started on the day of birth and occurred infrequently after the forty-second day. The area most commonly licked was the perineal region.

Turning to the order of mammals to which man belongs, the primates, Phyllis Jay reports, on Indian langurs observed in the field under natural conditions, that langur mothers lick their young from the hour of their birth. The same appears to be true of baboons under natural conditions. "Every few minutes she explores the newborn infant's body, parts its fur with her fingers, licks, and nuzzles it."

Interestingly enough, the great apes lick their young immediately after birth, but not much thereafter. The ubiquity of the practice among the mammals testifies to its basic nature.

The self-licking in which many mammals indulge, in the nonpregnant or parturitive state, while having the effect of keeping the animal clean, is probably more specifically designed to keep the sustaining systems of the body—the gastrointestinal, genitourinary, respiratory, circulatory, digestive, reproductive, neuroendocrine, and immunological systems—adequately stimulated. What this means in actual end effects is perhaps best illustrated by the developmental failure which follows any significant restraint of self-licking. A striking behavioral feature of both the pregnant rat and the pregnant cat is intensified self-licking of the genito-abdominal region as pregnancy progresses. The significance of this self-licking may be conjectured as serving to stimulate and improve the functional responses of the organ systems especially involved in the pregnancy during labor, delivery, and parturient periods. It is known that after the birth of the infant or litter, suckling and other stimulation of the genito-abdominal regions of the body serve to maintain lactation and cause the growth of the structures of the breast and mammary glands. There is good evidence that sensory stimulation contributes to mammary development during pregnancy. Drs. Lorraine L. Roth and Jay S. Rosenblatt inquired into this matter experimentally. In a series of ingenious experiments these investigators put neck collars on pregnant rats in such a manner that they were prevented from licking themselves. It was found that the mammary glands of collared rats were about 50 percent less developed than those of control animals.

Since collars would undoubtedly produce some stress effect, other uncollared pregnant rats were subjected to stress effects, while still others were fitted with notched collars which allowed them to lick themselves. In none of these, nor in the normal uncollared groups, was the inhibition of mammary development anywhere nearly as great as in the collared group.

Birch and his collaborators have shown that when the female rat is fitted with a light collar that prevents self-licking of the abdomen and posterior erogenous zone, even though the collar is removed permanently for delivery and thereafter, such females make very poor mothers. They carry materials but fail to build regular nests, spreading the materials around very loosely instead. They do not nurse their young to any extent, but seem to be disturbed when the newborn pups happen to reach them, and tend to move away. The pups would invariably die were it not for artificial interference by the experimenter. Hence, depriving the pregnant female of the self-stimulation of her body, which provides a normal preparation for maternal behavior, seems also to deprive her of orientations that would otherwise promote the fluid-licking, afterbirth-eating, and other activities underlying the transition to the aftercare period.

From such experiments it is clear that cutaneous self-stimulation of the mother's body is an important factor in contributing to the development of the optimum functioning of her sustaining systems, not only before and after pregnancy but equally so during pregnancy. The question immediately arises whether this may not also be the case during these same periods in the human female? It is a question to which the answer seems to be in the affirmative.

It is evident that in mammals generally cutaneous stimulation is important at all stages of development, but particularly important during the early days of the life of the newborn, during pregnancy, during labor, delivery, and during the nursing period. Indeed, the more we learn about the effects of cutaneous stimulation, the more pervasively significant for healthy development do we find it to be. For example, in one of the earliest studies of its kind, it was found that early infantile cutaneous stimulation exerts a highly beneficial influence upon the immunological system, having important consequences for resistance to infectious and other diseases. The study indicated that rats who had been handled in infancy showed a higher serum antibody titre (standard) in every case, after primary and secondary immunization, than those who had not been handled in infancy. Thus the immunological responsivity of the adult appears to be significantly modified by early cutaneous experience. Such immunological competence may be produced through the mechanism of conductor substances and hormones affecting the thymus gland, a gland which is critical in the establishment of immunological function, and also through the mediation of that part of the brain known as the hypothalamus, the between brain.

Indeed, the evidence showing the greater resistance to disease of subjects given early cutaneous stimulation is striking, but is perhaps complicated by the fact that the cutaneously stimulated animal enjoys a great many other correlated advantages, which undoubtedly also play a role in contributing to the higher resistance of the stimulated organism. As many investigators have confirmed, handling or gentling of rats and other animals in their early days results in significantly greater increases in weight, more activity, less fearfulness, greater ability to withstand stress, and greater resistance to physiological damage.

In sheep, although active maternal assistance is not essential in order for the newborn lamb to find the teats and suck for the first time, the process is facilitated by licking and by directional orientation of the ewe toward the lamb. In a series of experiments Alexander and Williams found that it was the combination of the two factors, the licking and the directional orientation—that is, the standing of the ewe facing the kid—that significantly facilitated the progress of the kid toward successful suckling. Neither orientation nor licking alone, which these investigators later refer to as "grooming," facilitated the drive toward suckling to any significant extent. Licking and maternal orientation in every case resulted in substantially greater teat-seeking activity, and also in a tendency towards an earlier increase in weight than in unlicked lambs.

The importance of intercutaneous or reciprocal cutaneous

stimulation, or physical contact, between mother and young, among birds as well as mammals, has been demonstrated by many investigators. Blauvelt has shown that, in goats, if the kid is removed from the mother for only a few hours before she has a chance to lick it and the kid is then restored to her, "she seems to have no behavioral resources to do anything further for the newborn." In sheep Liddell found the same thing, and interestingly enough, Maier observed that the same held true of hens and their chicks. Maier found that when broody hens are prevented from having physical contact with their chicks, even though all other visual cues are left intact, and they are situated in adjacent cages, the hens' broody response quickly disappears. Furthermore, Maier found that hens kept in close physical contact with their chicks and unable to leave them remained broody for a longer period of time than those hens who were free to leave their chicks whenever they chose.

Physical contact, then, appears to act as a principal regulator of broodiness. Stimulation of the skin apparently constitutes an essential condition in causing the pituitary gland to secrete the hormone most important for the initiation and maintenance of broodiness—prolactin. This is the same hormone associated with the initiation and maintenance of nursing in mammals, including the human mother.

Collias showed that, in goats and sheep, mothers establish the identity of their own young immediately after birth, largely by contact, and thereafter vigorously repel any alien young that may approach them. The findings of many independent researchers indicate that there exist certain types of normal species-specific behavior dependent upon particular experiences during critical periods in the life of the individual animal. It has been found that changes in the natural environment at these times often result in the development of abnormal, species-atypical behavior. Hersher, Moore, and Richmond separated twenty-four domestic goats from their newborn kids five to ten minutes immediately following birth, for periods ranging from a half hour to an hour. Two months later these mothers were observed to nurse their own kids less and alien kids more than nonseparated mothers. A most interesting and unforeseen result of this experiment was the appearance of "rejecting" behavior, that is, nursing neither their own nor other kids, among mothers of the nonseparated group. Separation of these highly gregarious animals seems to have influenced the structure of the herd as a whole, "changing the behavior of 'control' animals whose early *postpartum* experiences had not deliberately been disrupted, but whose environment had been affected in turn by abnormal maternal and filial behavior produced in the experimental members of the group."

In an ingenious experiment designed to determine whether the critical period for the development of individual specific maternal behavior could be prolonged in sheep and goats, Hersher, Richmond, and Moore found that this could, indeed, be achieved by enforced contact between dam and young and the prevention of butting behavior.

In the domestic collie, McKinney has shown that, immediately after whelping, removal of the pups for little more than an hour seriously retards the recovery of the mother, a recovery which is accelerated by the rooting, nuzzling, and nursing of the young. McKinney suggested that similar undesirable effects may be produced in human mothers as a consequence of the practice of removing their babies from them at birth without permitting the continued contact that is so urgent a need in the newborn. This suggestion has been fully confirmed by recent research (See Appendix 2, p. 412).

In the rhesus monkey Harry F. Harlow and his co-workers, on the basis of their direct observations, "postulate that contact-clinging is the primary variable that binds mother to infant and infant to mother." Maternal affection, they find, is at a maximum during close bodily face-to-face contacts between mother and infant, and maternal affection appears to wane progressively as this form of bodily interchange decreases.

Maternal affection is defined by these authors as a function of many different conditions, involving external incentive stimulation, different conditions of experience, and many endocrinological factors. External incentives are those relating to the infant, and involve contact-clinging, warmth, suckling, and visual and auditory cues. Experimental factors relating to the maternal behavior probably embrace the mother's entire experience. Here it is probable that her own early experiences are of special importance, as well as her relationships with each individual infant she bears, and her cumulative experiences gained from raising successive infants. Endocrinological factors relate both to pregnancy and parturition, and to the resumption of a normal ovulatory cycle.

Indeed, the mother's early experiences are of considerable importance for the subsequent development of her own offspring, right into adulthood. In a series of elegant experiments, Drs. Victor H. Denenberg and Arthur E. Whimbey showed that the offspring of handled rats, whether in relation to the natural or to a foster mother, exhibited a higher weight at weaning than pups reared by mothers that had not been handled in infancy; they also defecated more and were significantly less active than the offspring of nonhandled mothers.

Ader and Conklin found that the offspring of rats that had been handled during pregnancy, whether they remained with their natural mothers or were cross-fostered to other females, were significantly less excitable than the offspring of unhandled rats.

Werboff and his co-workers found that handling of pregnant mice throughout the gestation period resulted in an increased number of live fetuses and surviving offspring. The decrease in weight these workers observed may, as they suggest, be due to the increased litter size.

Sayler and Salmon found that young mice raised in a communal nest, in which females combined their litters, showed faster rates of growth during the first twenty days than young raised by single females, even when the ratio of mothers to young was the same. The investigators think that the differences in body weight are most likely related to the nutritional benefit of additional and higher-quality milk provided by more than one mother. They also think that tactile stimuli may be operative, as well as thermal ones, the presence of additional littermates and mothers serving to insulate the pups so that more metabolic energy could be devoted to growth. Mice normally spend a great proportion of time in bodily contact with other mice; when isolated from such contact for durable periods of time they show an increased sensitivity to tactile stimuli, but not to photic ones.

Weininger, in 1954, in one of the earliest studies of its kind, found that male rats gentled for three weeks following their weaning at twenty-three days had, at forty-four days, a mean weight 20 grams higher than the ungentled control group; furthermore, the growth of the gentled was greater than that of the ungentled rats. In an open-field test gentled rats ventured significantly closer to the brilliantly lit center of the open-field setup, thus showing more of a tendency to ignore the natural habit of their species to cling to walls and avoid light. Rectal temperatures were significantly greater in the gentled rats, suggesting a possible change in the metabolic rate of these animals.

When exposed to stressful stimuli (immobilization, and total food and water deprivation for forty-eight hours) and autopsied immediately thereafter, the gentled rats showed much less damage to the cardiovascular and gastrointestinal systems than the ungentled rats.

Cardiovascular and other organic damage under prolonged stress, as Hans Selye and others have abundantly demonstrated, may be considered an end product of the action of the adrenocorticotropic hormone (ACTH); that is, one of the hormones secreted by the pituitary gland which acts upon the cortex of the adrenal gland to cause it to secrete cortisone. This interactive relationship is sometimes called the sympathetico-adrenal axis. Weininger suggests that the relative immunity to stress damage exhibited by the gentled animals was probably due to their lesser output of ACTH from the pituitary in response to the same alarming situation with which the ungentled animals were confronted. If this were in fact the case, it would be expected that the adrenal glands of gentled and ungentled rats following stress would show those of the ungentled rats having been stimulated by more ACTH output, to be heavier, and upon examination this was, indeed, found to be the case. "A major change in hypothalamic functioning, involving reduction or inhibition of massive sympathetic discharge in response to an alarming stimulus (and hence decreased ACTH output from the pituitary), is predicted to account for the results mentioned above."

The process is much more complicated than that, but reduced to its essential elements, the relation between the pituitary-adrenal secretions in gentling and stressful situations holds true. Gentled animals respond with an increased functional efficiency in the organization of all systems of the body. Ungentled animals fail to undergo organization expressing itself in functional efficiency, and are therefore in all respects less able to meet the assaults and insults of the environment. Hence, when we speak of "licking and love," or skin (cutaneous tactile) stimulation, we are quite evidently speaking of a fundamental and essential ingredient of affection, and equally clearly of an essential element in the healthy development of every organism.

Fuller found that puppies isolated from all contact shortly after birth, and subsequently stroked and handled by human beings, did better on tests following their emergence from isolation than puppies that had been neither stroked nor handled.

The workers at the Cornell Behavior Farm found that, with no licking at all (although licking for one hour after birth is sufficient) many newborn lambs fail to stand and subsequently die. While it is possible for some lambs to stand without licking, it is notable that when the newborn makes an effort to rise its mother will often keep it down with her foot until she has licked it. Barron found that lambs that had been dried off with a towel (the equivalent of licking) rise on their four feet before lambs who have not been dried off.

The very real effects of early tactile experience have been impressively demonstrated by a series of independent experiments. Karas, for example, found that rats handled during the first five days showed a maximal effect of emotionality, as measured by avoidance conditioning, as compared with animals handled at other times during infancy. Levine and Lewis found that animals handled during days 2 to 5 after birth showed a significant depletion of adrenal ascorbic acid in response to severe cold stress at twelve days of age, as compared with nonhandled animals and animals handled after the first five days, who did not show a significant depletion reaction to stress till the sixteenth day of life. Bell, Reisner, and Linn found that twenty-four hours after electroconvulsive shock, blood sugar level was significantly higher in nonhandled animals and animals handled at times other than the first five days, than in animals handled during the first five days. Denenberg and Karas observed that rats handled during the first ten days of life weighed the most, learned best, and survived longest.

In a study in which rabbits were originally being used as a control group to throw light on the effects of drugs on high-cholesterol diets, Norem and Cornhill serendipitously found that cuddled and played with rabbits showed only half as much evidence of atherosclerosis as rabbits who received the more impersonal, perfunctory care.

The manner in which the young of all mammals snuggle up to and cuddle the body of the mother as well as the bodies of their siblings or of any other introduced animal strongly suggests that cutaneous stimulation is an important biological *need,* for both their physical and behavioral development. Almost every animal enjoys being stroked or otherwise having its skin pleasurably stimulated. Dogs appear to be insatiable in their appetite for stroking, cats will relish it and purr, as will innumerable other animals both domestic and wild, apparently enjoying the stroking at least as much as they do self-licking. The supreme note of confidence offered a human by a cat is to rub itself against your leg.

The touch of a human hand is very much more effective than the application of an impersonal mechanical apparatus, as for example in milking, where it is well known among experts and dairy farmers that hand-milked cows give more and richer terminal milk than machine-milked cows. Hendrix, Van Valck, and Mitchell have reported that horses exposed to human handling immediately after birth developed unusual adult behavior. Among the adult traits observed in these handled horses were responsible behavior in emergencies without loss of cooperative tractability at other times, and inventive behavior for equine-to-human communication in situations of urgency.

Eileen Karsh, of the department of psychology at Temple University (a cat lover who has eleven cats), in studying the socialization of cats, started with 26 kittens three weeks after birth. The kittens were assigned to three treatment groups. The first received handling from three to fourteen weeks of age, the second from seven to fourteen weeks of age, and the third none at all through fourteen weeks of age. The procedure consisted of an experimenter holding a kitten on his or her lap for 15 minutes daily. Each kitten was handled by four experimenters on different days. The three groups were then tested for their friendliness toward people in two ways—first by how long they stayed with an experimenter when not restrained, and then by how long it took them to reach an experimenter.

The group that had been handled from three to fourteen weeks was found to stay twice as long with an experimenter when not restrained as was the group that had not been handled at all. The group that had been handled from seven to fourteen weeks of age stayed a shorter time than the group that had been handled at an earlier age, yet a longer time than the nonhandled group. Similarly, the group that had been handled from three to fourteen weeks took much less time to reach an experimenter than did the nonhandled group. The group that had been handled from seven to fourteen weeks took about the same time to reach an experimenter as did the nonhandled group.

The amount of handling a kitten receives also seems to influence how friendly it is going to become, Karsh found in another experiment. Kittens handled 40 minutes a day in the lab became more sociable than kittens handled 15 minutes a day in the lab, and kittens reared at home were the most sociable of all.

Dolphins, as I know from personal observation, love to be gently stroked. At the Communications Institute in Miami I enjoyed the opportunity of making friends within a few minutes with Elvar, an adult male dolphin who occupied a small tank all to himself. Because Elvar playfully habitually splashed them, visitors were customarily provided with oilskins. Elvar adjusted his splashes to the size of the visitor: small children would receive small splashes, middle-sized children middle-sized splashes, and adults, large ones. For some reason I received no splash at all. Dr. John Lilly, the director, stated that this had never happened before. Approaching Elvar with all the affection, interest, and respect he deserved, I proceeded to stroke the top of his head. This was very much to his liking. During the remainder of the visit Elvar proceeded to expose every part of his body for me to stroke, leaning over sidewards so that I could stroke him under his flippers, which he seemed particularly to enjoy. It is sad to have to record that some months afterwards Elvar caught cold from a human visitor and died.

Dr. A. F. McBride and H. Kritzler of the Duke University Marine Laboratory at Beaufort, North Carolina, have recorded, of a two-year-old female dolphin, that she "became so fond of being caressed by the observer that she would frequently rear cautiously out of the water to rub her chin on the knuckles of his clenched fist." The same observers recorded that "dolphins are very fond of rubbing their bodies on various objects, so a backscratcher, constructed of three stout sweeper's brushes fixed to a slab of rock with the bristles directed upward, was installed in the tank. The young dolphins took to rubbing themselves on these brushes as soon as the adults discovered their purpose."

Similar behavior has been reported in gray whales in the waters of Laguna San Ignacio, west coast Baja California, 430 nautical miles south of the California border. Here a group of friendly whales, and especially an adult female, sought out a group of small boats and their occupants in order to be scratched. They would scratch themselves against the boats and then rise out of the water to be scratched by hand or with a long-handled neck brush. "The pleasure of a touch-stimulus," writes Raymond Gilmore, the author of this fascinating report, "through body-contact is obvious among gray whales." The nine color photos illustrating this speak for themselves.

Quite fascinating is an observation made by Mr. A. Gunner relating to the fleas carried by hedgehogs. He writes:

> I have kept and observed hedgehogs for some fifty or sixty years and am convinced that de-fleaing hedgehogs is not good for them. There is some essential factor which the fleas provide. It may be—and I think it is—a skin circulation stimulus that is missing in an animal unable to nudge, massage, scratch, rub or otherwise stimulate the skin to keep its labyrinth of capillaries properly active.
>
> A zoologist friend assures me that I may be right, as the Australian echidna, some armadillos, and particularly that mammalian curiosity the *pangolin* tolerate insect populations in the overlaps at crevices of their armoured bodies and that the cleaned up and deloused animal does not long survive.

In attempting to follow up this observation I regret to say I could obtain no further information of any kind on the subject, but, like the zoologist friend of Mr. Gunner, I rather suspect that his observation is a sound one. The close (commensal) association of birds with other animals, from crocodiles whose teeth they pick, to sheep on whose backs they often alight, picking debris and insects from their bodies with the obvious approval of their hosts, the "grooming" of monkeys and apes, or the loving embrace—all these forms of behavior indicate that a basic and complex need is involved.

What emerges from the observations and experiments reported here—and there are many more with which we shall deal in subsequent pages—is that cutaneous stimulation in the various forms in which the newborn and young receive it is of prime importance for their healthy physical and behavioral development. It appears probable that for human beings, tactile stimulation is of fundamental significance for the development of healthy emotional or affectional relationships, that "licking," in its actual and in its figurative sense, and love are closely connected; in short, that one learns to love not by instruction but by being loved. As Professor Harry Harlow has put it, from the "intimate attachment of the child to the mother, multiple learned and generalized affectional responses are formed."

In a series of valuable studies Harlow has demonstrated the significance of physical contact between the monkey mother and her infant for the subsequent healthy development of the latter. During the course of his studies Harlow noticed that the laboratory-raised baby monkeys showed a strong attachment to the cloth pads (folded gauze diapers) which were used to cover the hardware-cloth floors and cages. When an attempt was made to remove and replace the pads for sanitary purposes the infants clung to them and engaged in "violent temper tantrums." This is, of course, similar to the "security-blanket" behavior of many small children (see pp. 345–346). It had also been discovered that infants raised on a bare wire-mesh cage floor survive with difficulty, if at all, during the first five days of life. When a wire-mesh cone was introduced, the baby did better; and when this was covered with terry-cloth, husky, healthy babies developed. At this point Harlow decided to build a terry-cloth surrogate mother, with a light bulb behind her which radiated heat. The result was a mother, "soft, warm, and tender, a mother with infinite patience, a mother available twenty-four hours a day, a mother that never scolded her infant and never struck or bit her baby in anger."

A second surrogate mother was built entirely of wire mesh, without the terry-cloth "skin," and hence lacking in contact comfort. The remainder of the story is best told in Harlow's own words. He writes:

In our initial experiment, the dual-mother surrogate condition, a cloth mother and a wire mother were placed in different cubicles attached to the infant's living cage. . . . For four newborn monkeys the cloth mother lactated and the wire mother did not; and for the other four, this condition was reversed. In either condition the infant received all its milk through the mother surrogate as soon as it was able to maintain itself in this way, a capability achieved within two or three days except in the case of very immature infants. Supplementary feedings were given until the milk intake from the mother surrogate was adequate. Thus, the experiment was designed as a test of the relative importance of the variables of contact comfort and nursing comfort. During the first 14 days of life the monkey's cage floor was covered with a heating pad wrapped in a folded gauze diaper, and thereafter the cage floor was bare. The infants were always free to leave the heating pad or cage floor to contact either mother, and the time spent on the surrogate mothers was automatically recorded. Figure 3 shows the total time spent on the cloth and wire mothers under the two conditions of feeding. These data make it obvious that contact comfort is a variable of overwhelming importance in the development of affectional responses, whereas lactation is a variable of negligible importance. With age and opportunity to learn, subjects with the lactating wire mother showed decreasing responsiveness to her and increasing responsiveness to the nonlactating cloth mother, a finding completely contrary to any interpretation of derived drive in which the mother-form becomes conditioned to hunger-thirst reduction. The persistence of these differential responses throughout 165 consecutive days of testing is evident in Figure 4.

We were not surprised [writes Harlow], to discover that contact comfort was an important basic affectional or love variable, but we did not expect it to overshadow so completely the variable of nursing; indeed, the disparity is so great as to suggest that the primary function of nursing as an affectional variable is that of insuring frequent and intimate body contact of the infant with the mother. Certainly, a man cannot live by

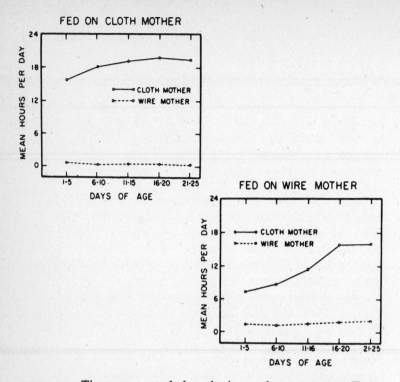

FIGURE 3. Time spent on cloth and wire mother surrogates. (From H. F. Harlow and R. R. Zimmermann, "The Development of Affectional Responses in Infant Monkeys," *Proceedings, American Philosophical Society*, 102:501–509, 1958. By permission.)

milk alone. Love is an emotion that does not need to be bottle- or spoon-fed, and we may be sure that there is nothing to be gained by giving lip service to love.

By far the most important of Harlow's observations was the finding that his infant monkeys valued tactile stimulation more than they did nourishment, for they preferred to cling to "mothers" who provided physical contact without nourishment to wire ones who did supply nourishment. Harlow goes so far as to suggest that the primary purpose of nursing is to ensure

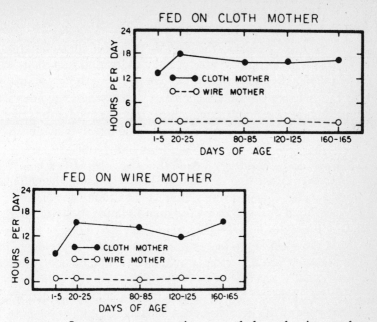

FIGURE 4. Long-term contact time on cloth and wire mother surrogates. (From H. F. Harlow and R. R. Zimmermann, "The Development of Affectional Responses in Infant Monkeys," *Proceedings, American Philosophical Society,* 102:501–509, 1958. By permission.)

frequent body contact between infant and mother. Such contact may not be the primary function of nursing, but it is certainly a fundamentally important one, a matter we shall discuss in greater detail later.

Finally, Harlow concludes:

> We now know that women in the working classes are not needed in the house because of their primary mammalian capabilities; and it is possible that in the foreseeable future neonatal nursing will not be regarded as a necessity, but as a luxury—to use Veblen's term—a form of conspicuous consumption limited perhaps to the upper classes.

As we shall see (pp. 69–95), Harlow thoroughly underesti-mates the importance of breastfeeding in both animals and man, but this does not in the least affect the validity of his con-clusions concerning the value of body contact between mother and infant. As Harlow and his co-workers have shown, in their normal nursing-couple (mother and infant) rhesus monkeys, nutritional and nonnutritional nipple contacts endure for some three months. These nipple contacts undoubtedly play an im-portant role in the development of the individual.

When a baby is born a mother is also born. There is con-siderable evidence that at this time, and for months thereafter, her needs for contact exceed those of the infant. The Harlows observed that during the first few months in the rhesus monkey the mother's need for intimate contact surpassed that of the in-fant, and served to produce maternal protection. In the human mother the need for intimate contact is undoubtedly much greater and considerably more prolonged than it is in other mammals, serving not only important psychological functions, but also many physiological ones, such as arresting of the post-partum hemorrhage, contraction of the uterus, detachment and expulsion of the placenta, improved circulation, etc.

A striking finding of Harlow and his fellow investigators was that when the five utter failures as mothers had their his-tories traced back to their early experiences, it was found that they had been denied the opportunity to develop normal ma-ternal-infant relationships, that they had never known a real monkey mother of their own, and had also been denied normal infant-infant relationships, subsequently having only limited physical association with other monkeys. Two of these mothers were essentially indifferent to their infants, and three were vio-lently abusive. "Failure of normal gratification of contact-clinging in infancy may make it impossible for the adult female to show normal contact relationships with her own infant. Likewise, maternal brutality may stem from inadequate social experience with other infants within the first year of life." Fur-thermore, these investigators found that none of the mother-less-mother animals ever showed normal female sex behavior, such as posturing and responding. They became mothers in spite of themselves. As we shall see, the parallel with such interrelated behaviors in humans is virtually complete, and the significance of these behaviors is virtually identical.

Maternal behavior in mammals is not entirely dependent upon either hormones or learning, but it is more readily and effectively developed by stimulation received by the mother from the young. Roth has shown that maternal behavior is delayed when pups are presented in wire baskets attached to the inside of the female's cage where the female cannot lick or contact them in other ways. Terkel and Rosenblatt found that maternal behavior can be induced more rapidly, in about two days, by confining virgin female rats in narrow cages where they are forced to remain in contact with pups continuously rather than sporadically as in the larger standard cages. Maternal responsiveness to the young varies with the amount of stimulating contact she has with them which permits the various stimuli from the young to exert their effects.

Rosenblatt has proposed the concept of "synchrony" to denote the fact that the mother's behavior is adapted to the needs and behavioral capacities of the young, and that her behavior changes as these capacities develop in the young. *Synchrony,* however, is a term which refers to the simultaneity of events in time, and I would suggest that *interdependence* more accurately describes the relationship and the significance of the reciprocal interstimulation that occurs between mother and offspring in the neonatal period. Of course, there is a marvelous synchrony about these reciprocal changes, but their very reciprocity underscores their interdependence. It is the reciprocal interstimulation between mother and infant that leads to the development in each of the changes, somatic and behavioral, which in the absence of such interstimulation will not occur. Hence, the importance of the interstimulation of the nursing couple can hardly be overestimated.

Harlow and his co-workers comment upon the "extremely powerful social response observed throughout the monkey kingdom," namely that of grooming. This response to their young increased throughout the first thirty days following the birth of the infant, and they suggest that this perhaps represents an intensification of the specific psychological bond between mother and infant.

Phyllis Jay reports that "from the hour of its birth" the mother langur monkey "inspects, licks, grooms, and manipulates the infant. When the newborn is nursing quietly or sleeping, she grooms and strokes it softly without disturbing or waking it. For the first week of life the newborn is never away from its mother or another adult female."

In monkeys, Harlow found that during the first few months after giving birth, the mother's need for intimate contact exceeded that of the infant. This need is, at least in part, therefore productive of the mother's protective behavior. Such contact appears to be as much desired by the human as it is by the monkey mother. In the late 1920s Mary Shirley at Harvard, in an intensive study of twenty-five babies, found: "The earliest signs of affection reported by the mothers were those of patting the breast while nursing and of cuddling down contentedly when held on the mother's shoulder. In the seventh and eighth months the babies demonstrated their affection by patting the mother's face, clasping her around the neck, laying cheek on cheek, turning their faces to be kissed, hugging, and biting." Shirley suggested that while most of these activities were probably learned, the patting and hugging were probably spontaneous. However that may be, it will be noted that all the communicative affectional acts by the babies were tactile. However, there were undoubtedly other communicative acts, such as facial expression, smiling, and laughter.

Tactile communication forms an elaborate medium of communication among primates. Sexual presenting, mounting without sex, lip smacking (ear flattening), embracing, genital/stomach nuzzling, rump nuzzling, mouth/head kissing, rump fingering, hand touching, biting, have been widely observed among primates, and, as Peter Marler, summarizing the evidence, has said, "It would be difficult to overestimate the importance of such tactile signals in maintaining peace and cohesion in primate societies."

The infant primate is virtually in continuous contact with its mother. Its survival depends upon this. Contact and communication with the mother is established and maintained through clinging, suckling, climbing, and vocalizing. As an order, primates are, as Hediger has said, contact animals.

The young are carried on their mothers' bodies for long periods of time. There is much clinging, riding, and contact with other members of the group. Young animals, and often adults, tend to sit and even sleep together in close contact. There is a great deal of touching and, most characteristically, grooming. Primates groom each other. Grooming not only serves to keep the body free of parasites, dirt, and the like, but it constitutes, as Allison Jolly puts it, "the social cement of primates from lemur to chimpanzee." Anthoney has described the development of grooming in the dog-headed baboon, *Papio cynocephalus,* from the infant's suckling, to grasping the specialized suckling fur, to grooming. The reciprocal pleasure enjoyed in this relation is quite probably related to the later pleasure of grooming and being groomed. Throughout life, contact behavior serves to mitigate intense emotional reactions and to keep such disruptive states under a measure of control.

In addition to grooming, primates exhibit a large variety of other contact behaviors, such as patting and nuzzling, especially in greeting behavior. Chimpanzees will not only pat each others' hands, faces, groins, and other parts of the body, but will lay a hand on each others' backs in reassurance, will kiss in affection, and the young especially, in their gluttony for being tickled, will draw the tickler's hand to their bodies.

Grooming with the hands, which is usual among monkeys and apes, or, as among lemurs, with the specialized comblike teeth, presents an interesting seriation for, as Jolly has pointed out, the lemurine form of grooming with the teeth really represents a form of licking. This view of grooming may be extended to the finger-picking variety, and finally to the stroking of human beings. In short, it may well be that there has been an evolutionary development from licking, to tooth-combing (as among lemurs), to finger-grooming, to handstroking or caressing, as in chimpanzee, gorilla, and *Homo sapiens,* and that therefore handstroking is to the young of the human species virtually as important a form of experience as licking is to the young of other mammals. This is a matter into which we shall inquire further. Meanwhile, it would seem evident that one of the elements in the genesis of the ability to live is "licking" or its equivalent in other forms of pleasurable tactile stimulation.

We conclude, then, that the study of mammal, monkey, ape, and human behaviors clearly shows that touch is a *basic behavioral need,* much as breathing is a basic physical need, that the dependent infant is designed to grow and develop socially through contact, tactile behavior, and throughout life to maintain contact with others. Furthermore, that when the need for touch remains unsatisfied, abnormal behavior will result.

2 The Womb of Time

There are many events in the womb of time, which will
be deliver'd.
—Shakespeare, *Othello,* 1, iii.

As we have seen in the preceding chapter, licking, or tooth-
combing, or grooming of the young soon after they are born
and for an appreciable period thereafter, appears to be an indispensably necessary condition for their survival. Such stimulations seem to be equally necessary for the healthy behavioral
development of the young. If this is so, why then is it that
human mothers neither lick, tooth-comb, nor groom their
young?

Human mothers do none of these things. Extensive inquiries over many years yielded only two cultures in which
mothers sometimes washed their young by licking. In regions
in which water is scarce, among the Polar Eskimos and in the
Tibetan highlands, mothers sometimes resort to licking their
older young children as a substitute for washing them with
water drawn from other sources. The fact is that human mothers do not lick their young, though traditional wisdom has
not been insensible to the likeness between what the good
human mother does and what the mammalian mother of other
species does. The parallel is recognized in such phrases as *un
ours mal léché,* "an unlicked cub." The French phrase is often
employed to describe an ill-mannered person, "a boor,"
one who is "gauche," awkward in his relations with others.
Although the notion behind this phrase originally referred to
the belief that the young of some animals were born in so undeveloped a form that they had to be licked into shape by the

mother,* later usage conferred upon the phrase a meaning implicitly recognizing the importance of the mother's gentle ministrations in the development of what might be called "relatability." George Sarton, the distinguished Belgian-American historian of science, for example, wrote in his private journal, "I have now discovered that the first of August is the saint's day of the Spaniard Raymond Nonnatus (1200–1240). He was called Nonnatus because he was 'not-born,' but removed from his mother's womb after her death. My own fate was not very different from his, because my mother died soon after my birth and I never knew her. . . . Many of my shortcomings are due to the fact that I had no mother, and that my good father had no time to bother much about me. I am indeed 'an unlicked bear' (un ours mal léché)."

The question we have to answer here is: What, if any, are the equivalents of "licking" which the human mother gives her child in order to prepare its sustaining systems for adequate functioning?

I suggest that one of the equivalents for "licking" is represented by the long period of labor that the parturient human female undergoes. The average duration of labor with the firstborn is sixteen hours; with subsequent-born children the average duration of labor is eight hours. During this period the contractions of the uterus provide massive stimulations of the fetal skin. These uterine contractions serve much the same functions and end effects that licking of the newborn does in other animals. In the womb the fetus has been constantly stimulated by the amniotic fluid and by the growing pressures of its own body against the walls of the uterus. These stimulations are greatly intensified during the process of labor in order to prepare the sustaining systems for postnatal functioning in ways somewhat different from those which were necessary in the aquatic environment in which the fetus has thus far spent

---

*Pliny the Elder (A.D. 23–79) writes in his *Natural History,* Book VIII, 126, "Bears when first born are shapeless masses of white flesh a little larger than white mice, their claws alone being prominent. The mother then licks them gradually into proper shape."

its life. This intensification of cutaneous stimulations is especially necessary in the human fetus because, contrary to general belief, the period of gestation is not completed when the baby is born. It is only half-completed. It will be necessary for us to discuss this matter further, in order to gain some insight into the precarious condition in which the young of human kind is born, and why it is necessary that the human neonate undergo certain kinds of cutaneous stimulation.

THE MEANING OF NEONATAL AND INFANT IMMATURITY IN HUMANS. Why are human beings born in a state so immature that it takes eight to ten months before the human infant can even crawl, and another four to six months before he can walk and talk? That a good many years will elapse before the human child will cease to depend upon others for his very survival constitutes yet another evidence of the fact that humans are born more immature, and remain immature for a longer period, than any other animal.

The newborn elephant and the fallow deer are able to run with the herd shortly after they are born. By the age of six weeks, the infant seal has been taught by his mother to navigate his watery realm for himself. These animals all have long gestation periods, presumably because animals that give birth to small litters are unable to protect them as efficiently as predatory animals, and must therefore give birth to young who are in a fairly mature state. A long gestation period serves to allow for such maturation.

The elephant, which has a gestation period of 515 to 670 days, gives birth to a single infant. In animals such as the fallow deer, which gives birth to a litter of two or three, the gestation period is 230 days. In the seal, which produces only a single pup at a birth, the gestation period varies from 245 to 350 days. Predatory animals, by contrast, are very efficient in protecting their young, and have a short gestation period. Their litters may vary from three at a birth upwards; the size of the young may be small at birth, and the young may be born in a somewhat immature state. The lion, for example, which generally has a litter of three cubs, has a gestation period of 105 days. Humans have a gestation period of 266½ days, which is distinctly in the class of long gestation periods. Since this is so, what can be the explanation for the extremely immature state in which humans are born? This is a somewhat different question from that which refers to the prolonged immaturity of the young of human kind.

Apes are also born in an immature condition, but remain in that state for a much shorter period than human infants. The average duration of gestation in the gorilla is about 252 days, in the orangutan about 273 days, and in the chimpanzee 231 days. Labor in the apes generally lasts not more than two hours, which contrasts strikingly with the average of sixteen hours for the firstborn and eight hours for the subsequent born in the human female. Like humans, the apes are monotocous, that is, one infant is usually conceived and born at term, but compared with that of humans the development of the young ape is somewhat more rapid, so that the infant ape takes about one-third to two-thirds of the time the human infant does to develop such traits as lifting the head, rolling, worming along, sitting alone, standing, and walking. Ape mothers tenderly care for their young for several years, and it is not uncommon for breastfeeding to continue for three or more years. Human immaturity in infancy, therefore, may be regarded as an extension of the basic infant immaturity characteristic of all anthropoid forms, characteristic, that is, of the great apes and probably earlier forms of humankind. Among anthropoids the care, feeding, and protection of the young fall exclusively to the females. Only when the females and the young are endangered do the males act to protect them.

While the length of the gestation period lies within the same range in anthropoids and in humans (see Table 1), there is a marked difference in the growth of the fetus in the two groups. This is seen in the great acceleration in the rate of growth of the human fetus, as compared with the anthropoid fetus, towards the end of the gestation period. This is most strikingly seen in the increase in size of the human fetal brain,

Table 1. LENGTH OF GESTATION, POSTNATAL GROWTH
PERIODS, AND LIFE SPAN IN APE AND HUMAN

GENUS	GESTATION (DAYS)	MENARCHE (YEARS)	ERUPTION OF FIRST AND LAST PERMANENT TEETH (YEARS)	COMPLETION OF GENERAL GROWTH (YEARS)	LIFE SPAN (YEARS)
Gibbon	210	8.5	?–8.5	9	30
Orangutan	273	?	3.0–9.8	11	30
Chimpanzee	231	8.8	2.9–10.2	11	35
Gorilla	252	9.0	3.0–10.5	11	35
Human	266½	13.5	6.2–20.5	20	75

which by the time of birth has acquired a volume of between
375 and 400 cubic centimeters. Total body weight of the
human newborn averages 7 pounds. In the chimpanzee total
body weight of the neonate is, on the average, 4.33 pounds
(1,800 grams), and the brain volume is about 200 cubic centimeters. In the gorilla the total body weight of the newborn is
about 4.75 pounds (1,980 grams), and the brain size at birth
would appear to be not much more than in the chimpanzee.
The smaller size of the anthropoid newborn is probably correlated to some extent with the shorter duration of labor in the
anthropoid female. In humans, however, the large body size,
and especially the large size of the head at 266½ days of fetal
age, necessitate the birth of the child at that time. If it were not
born then and it continued to grow at the rate at which it is
geared to grow, it could not be born at all—with lethal consequences for the continuation of the human species.

As a result of the evolution of the erect posture in humans,
the pelvis has undergone major rearrangement in all its parts.
Among these changes has been a narrowing of the pelvic outlet. During parturition the pelvic outlet enlarges somewhat
with the relaxation of the pelvic ligaments, enough to permit
the head of the child, with a certain amount of molding and
compression, to pass through the birth canal. In adaptation to
this situation the skull bones of the human infant, in relation to
the membranes in which these bones develop, grow more slowly
than those of the ape infant of the same gestation age. Thus the

human infant's skull bones allow for a considerable amount of movement and overlapping in adaptation to the compressive forces that will act upon them during the process of birth. The human infant, then, is born when it is because it must be born at that time; for as we have seen, the rapid growth of its brain during the last trimester would make birth impossible. The brain growth of the anthropoid infant presents no such problems, particularly in view of the mother's generous pelvic arrangements.

Not only does the prolonged period of behavioral immaturity of the human infant reveal how undeveloped and dependent it is at birth, so too does its biochemical and physiological immaturity. For example, a variety of enzymes remain undeveloped in the newborn human. In this the human shares a trait common to a number of other mammals, except that in the human infant, unlike most other mammalian infants thus far investigated, most of these enzymes are not present at all. In guinea pigs and mice, for example, the liver enzymes develop during the first week of life, but require some eight weeks for full development. It appears that in all mammals some factor is present in the uterine environment which represses the formation of liver enzymes in the fetus. In the human infant some liver and duodenal enzymes (amylase) do not appear until several weeks or months have passed. Gastric enzymes are present which are fully capable of dealing with the ingested colostrum and milk from the maternal breast, but these enzymes cannot effectively metabolize foods normally consumed by older children.

All the evidence indicates that, while the duration of the gestation period in humans differs by only a week or two from that of the great apes, a large number of other factors, all combining to lead to the considerably more prolonged development of the human infant, cause it to be born before what is generally believed to be its gestation has been completed. One would think that a creature developing at the rate of the human fetus in the later stages of uterine development and during childhood, should, developmentally, enjoy a much longer period of gestation within the womb. In humans, as compared with apes, every one of the developmental periods—infancy, early childhood, later childhood, adolescence, young adulthood, later adulthood or maturity, and terminal age—with the exception of the developmental period within the womb, is greatly extended in duration. Why not also the period of gestation?

The explanation seems to be that the fetus must be born when its head has reached the maximum size compatible with its passage through the birth canal. This transmigration constitutes no mean accomplishment. Indeed, the passage through the 4 inches of the birth canal is the most hazardous journey a human being ever takes. The evidence suggests that the human fetus is born before its gestation is completed. The rate of growth of the brain is proceeding at such a pace during the last month of pregnancy that its continuation within the womb would render birth impossible. Hence, the survival of the fetus and the mother requires the termination of gestation within the womb when the limit of head size compatible with birth has been attained, and long before maturation occurs.

The process of evolution by which the increase in the length of human developmental periods has been accomplished is known as *neoteny*. The term refers to the process whereby the functional and structural features of the young (fetal or juvenile) of ancestral forms are retained in the developmental stages of the maturing individual, from infancy to adulthood. Man's large head, flat face, roundheadedness, small face and teeth, absence of brow ridges, thinness of skull bones, late suture closure, relative hairlessness, thin nails, prolonged period of educability, playfulness, love of fun, and many other traits all constitute evidence of neoteny.*

The gestation period, then, is also greatly extended in humans, except that its latter half is completed outside the womb. Gestation, as we have usually understood it, is not it would seem completed at birth, but is continued from gestation

*For a detailed exposition of neoteny see Ashley Montagu, *Growing Young* (New York: McGraw-Hill, 1981).

within the womb, *uterogestation,* to gestation outside the womb, *exterogestation.* Bostock has suggested that the limit of exterogestation be set at the stage of the beginning of effective crawling on all fours, a suggestion which has considerable merit. Interestingly enough, the average duration of exterogestation, taking its limit here to be when the infant commences to crawl, lasts, on the average, exactly the same time as uterogestation—namely, 266½ days. In this connection it is also of interest to note that while the mother continues to nurse her infant, pregnancy will be delayed for some time. Nursing the child at the breast causes the suppression of ovulation for variable periods of time, and thus constitutes a natural, although not altogether dependable method of child spacing. It also suppresses menstrual bleeding. Menstrual bleeding tends to be heavier and longer-lasting when the mother does not breast-feed, and, as a consequence of the heavier bleeding, the mother's reserve energies tend to be somewhat depleted. The premature cessation of breastfeeding would, then, result in distinct disadvantages, especially when a mother already has other children who require her attention. Hence breastfeeding confers benefits not only upon the baby but also upon the mother, and therefore upon the group. This is to mention only the physical benefits of breastfeeding. Even more important are the psychological advantages which are reciprocally conferred upon infant and mother in the nursing situation, especially in a species in which the mother is symbiotically designed to continue the gestation of her child outside the womb.

To learn what the child must learn in order to function as an adequate human being, he must, then, possess a large warehouse in which to store all the necessary information—a brain, in short, of considerable storage and retrieval capacity. It is a striking fact that by the time the human child has attained its third birthday it has virtually achieved full adult brain size. The average brain volume of the human three-year-old is 960 cubic centimeters, while the brain volume of the human adult, attained at the age of twenty years, is 1,200 cubic centimeters;

that is to say, after the end of its third year the human brain will grow by only another 240 cubic centimeters to attain its full size, and that 240 cubic centimeters will accumulate by small increments over the next seventeen years. In other words, at the end of three years of age the human child has achieved 90 percent of its brain growth. Significantly, the infant brain more than doubles in volume by the end of its first year to about 750 cubic centimeters, or 60 percent of its adult size. Almost two-thirds of the total growth of the brain is achieved by the end of the first year. It will take an additional two years to add almost another third to the volume attained at the end of the third year (see Table 2). In its first year, therefore, the infant's brain grows more than it ever will again in any one year.

It is important that most of the brain growth be accomplished during the first year, when the infant has so much to learn and do. Indeed, the first year of life requires a great deal

Table 2. GROWTH IN BRAIN AND CRANIAL CAPACITY IN HUMANS (BOTH SEXES)

AGE	WEIGHT (GRAMS)	VOLUME (CUBIC CENTIMETERS)	CRANIAL CAPACITY (CUBIC CENTIMETERS)
Birth	350	330	350
3 months	526	500	600
6 months	654	600	775
9 months	750	675	925
1 year	825	750	1,000
2 years	1,010	900	1,100
3 years	1,115	960	1,225
4 years	1,180	1,000	1,300
6 years	1,250	1,060	1,350
9 years	1,307	1,100	1,400
12 years	1,338	1,150	1,450
15 years	1,358	1,150	1,450
18 years	1,371	1,175	1,475
20 years	1,378	1,200	1,500

SOURCE: *Growth and Development of the Child, Part II,* White House Conference (New York: Century Co., 1933), p. 110.

of unobtrusive packing for a journey that will continue for the rest of the traveler's life. To perform this packing safely, the infant must possess a brain much larger than 375 to 400 cubic centimeters, but quite clearly he cannot wait until he has grown a brain of 750 cubic centimeters before being born. Hence, he must be born with the maximum-sized brain possible, and do the remainder of his brain growing after birth. Since the human fetus must be born when its brain has reached the limit of size congruent with its admission into and extrusion through the birth canal, such maturation or further development as other mammals complete before birth, the human mammal will have to complete after birth. In other words, the gestation period will have to be extended after birth.

When the uterogestation period is extended beyond the expected date of delivery for more than two weeks, the pregnancy is said to be postmature. Some 12 percent of births are delayed two weeks beyond the due date, and some 4 percent are delayed three weeks. All the evidence indicates that postmaturity is increasingly unfavorable for the fetus, as well as for its postnatal development. The perinatal mortality rate is more than twice as high for postterm infants as it is for term infants, and the incidence of primary cesarean section done because of head-pelvis disproportion is double that in term infants; severe congenital abnormalities occur in about a third more of these postterm children, and they are generally characterized by a reduced capacity to adapt. All of which underscores the importance of being born at term.

The human infant is almost, if not quite, as immature at birth as the little marsupial which, born in an extremely immature state, finds its way into its mother's pouch, there to continue its gestation until it is sufficiently matured. The human infant remains immature much longer than the infant kangaroo or opossum, but whereas the marsupial infant enjoys the protection of its mother's pouch during its period of immaturity, the human infant is afforded no such advantage. However, the human infant comprises part of a symbiotic unit; the mother, having given it shelter and sustenance within the womb, is elaborately prepared throughout the period of pregnancy to continue to do so, once the baby is born, outside the womb, considerably more efficiently than the marsupial mother. The biological unity, the symbiotic relationship, maintained by mother and conceptus throughout pregnancy does not cease at birth; indeed, it is naturally designed to become even more intensively functional and mutually involving after birth than during gestation in the uterus.

If this interpretation of the gestation period is correct, then it would follow more than ever that we are not at present meeting the needs, in anything approaching an adequate manner, of the newborn and infant young, who are so precariously dependent upon their new environment for survival and development. Although it is customary to regard the gestation period as terminating at birth, I suggest that this is quite as erroneous a view as that which regards the life of the individual as beginning at birth. Birth no more constitutes the beginning of the life of the individual than it does the end of gestation. Birth represents a complex and highly important series of functional changes which serve to prepare the newborn for the passage across the bridge between gestation within the womb and gestation continued outside the womb.

Because the human infant is born in so precariously immature a condition, it is especially necessary for the parental generation of the human species fully to understand what the immaturity of its infants really signifies: namely, that with all the modifications initiated by the birth process, the infant is still continuing its gestation period, passing, by the avenue of birth, from uterogestation to exterogestation in a continuing and ever more complex interactive relationship with the mother, the one person in the world who is best equipped to meet its needs. Among the most important of the newborn infant's needs are the signals it receives through the skin, its first medium of communication with the outside world. In preparation for its functioning in the postnatal world, the massive contractions of the uterus upon the body of the fetus play an important role. It is this that we have now to consider.

ON BEING STROKED THE RIGHT WAY. The relatively short labor experienced by nonhuman mammals is usually insufficient to activate such sustaining systems as the genitourinary and gastrointestinal systems, and in part the respiratory system; hence mothers must activate them by licking their young. This they are designed to accomplish by an inbuilt series of reactive behaviors to odors, wetness, touch, temperature, early experience, and the like. Such inborn reactive responses are feeble in human mothers. The human mother's responses to her newborn will to a large extent depend on her own early experience as an infant and child and to some extent upon learning and maturation. If the mother has not enjoyed such experience or learned how to behave as a mother she is very likely to prove inadequate, endangering the continued survival of her baby.* Hence, a basic assurance that the baby will be adequately prepared for postnatal functioning must be physiologically automatic. This basic assurance must not be dependent upon any postnatal behavior such as "licking," necessary as that may be for further development in other species. This insurance in the human species is secured by the prolonged contractions of the uterus upon the body of the fetus. The stimulations thus received activate, or tone up, the sustaining systems for the functions they will be called upon to perform immediately after birth. In short, it is here being suggested that in the human species the prolonged uterine contractions during labor represent, in addition to their other vital functions, a series of massive cutaneous stimulations calculated to activate and ensure the proper functioning of the sustaining systems.

When we ask what the function is of the ordinary uncomplicated process of labor and birth, the answer is: preparation for postnatal functioning. The process of preparation takes some time, for there are many changes which must be induced in the fetus about to be born if he is successfully to negotiate the brave new world of his immediate postnatal existence. The

*For a further discussion of this subject see A. Montagu, *The Reproductive Development of the Female* (Littleton, Mass: PSG Publishing Co., 1978).

bridge the process of birth forms between prenatal and postnatal life constitutes part of the continuum of individual development. The initiation of the birth process is associated with a fall in oxygen saturation of the placenta and of the fetal circulation, followed by the onset of labor; that is to say, the beginning uterine contractions which average about one a minute, and the breaking of "the bag of waters." All this, and much more that is involved in these bare words, means that a baby is to be born, to which must be added that it is to be born prepared to adjust successfully to the next series of events in the developing continuum of its life. That series of events cannot be broadly subsumed under the words "postnatal existence," for "postnatal existence" refers to the whole of life outside the womb, and clearly no newborn is ever prepared to deal with the whole of that postnatal life over which, only after many years, if at all, it will achieve some sort of mastery. What the fetus must be prepared to deal with during the birth process is the *immediate* neonatal period of the first few hours, then days, weeks, and months of gradual adjustment and habituation to the requirements of early postnatal existence. Towards this end the neonate must be readied with all its sustaining systems, as well as its muscular system, prepared to function.

The sustaining systems are the *respiratory* system, which controls the intake of oxygen as well as the utilization and elimination of carbon dioxide; the *circulatory* system, which conveys the oxygen through the blood vessels to the capillaries to supply the cells, and, in turn, to take up the gaseous waste products and return them to the lungs; the *digestive* system, which is concerned with the ingestion and chemical breakdown of solid foods and liquids; the *eliminative* systems, which carry the waste products from the alimentary tract, from the urinary tract, and from the skin through the sweat glands; the *nervous* system, which enables the organism to make the appropriate response to the stimuli it receives through that system; and the *endocrine* system, which, in addition to the important role it plays in growth and development and in behavior, assists in the functioning of all these systems. The response of the respiratory center to the biochemical changes induced by the lack of oxygen and the accumulation of carbon dioxide initiates the whole complicated process of respiration. The circulation becomes autonomous, the foramen ovale in the septum between the two atria of the heart which, in the fetus, permits blood to pass directly from the right into the left atrium, begins to close, and the ductus arteriosus, which connects the aorta with the pulmonary trunk directly below, begins to undergo occlusion. Blood is now carried by the pulmonary arteries to the lungs, there to be aerated, and returned to the heart by the pulmonary veins, and then from the left ventricle through the aorta into the general circulation. This is a very different arrangement from that which existed in the fetus. It now involves the functioning of the muscles of the chest and abdomen, the diaphragm, and the heart, as well as such organs as the lungs, and the whole of the upper respiratory tract in quite novel ways. In addition, the temperature regulation of the body now begins to be taken over by the newborn, the experience of birth initiating the stimulation of the temperature-regulating centers.

Contraction of the uterus upon the body of the fetus stimulates the peripheral sensory nerves in the skin. The nervous impulses thus initiated are conducted to the central nervous system where, at the proper levels, they are mediated through the vegetative (autonomic) nervous system to the various organs which they innervate. When the skin has not been adequately stimulated, the peripheral and autonomic nervous systems are also inadequately stimulated, and a failure of activation occurs in the principal organ systems.

It has been an age-old observation that when the newborn infant fails to breathe, a hearty slap or two on the buttocks will generally be sufficient to induce breathing. The profound physiological significance of this remarkable fact appears to have escaped attention. Reasoning from the physiological relations already indicated, it seemed to me likely that under similar conditions, that is, when the baby failed to breathe immediately after birth, stimulation of the respiratory center and the respiratory organs could perhaps be achieved by subjecting the baby to immersion, alternately, in hot and cold baths. Upon inquiry I found that this was, indeed, an old-established practice. In such cases it would seem reasonable to assume that it is the cutaneous stimulation which activates the autonomic nervous system, with the autonomic nervous system acting in turn upon the respiratory centers and viscera. The effect of a sudden cold shower upon respiration is well known, and is indicative of a similar series of events.

The short, intermittent stimulations of the skin over a prolonged period of time that are produced by the contractions of the uterus upon the body of the fetus thus appear to be perfectly designed to prepare it for postnatal functioning.

How can we be sure that this is in fact one of the functions of the prolonged cutaneous stimulation? One of the things we can do is to inquire into what happens when there is inadequate cutaneous stimulation of the fetus, as in the case of precipitately born children. This often occurs in prematurity, and also in the case of many cesarean-delivered infants. In such cases what we should expect to find, according to our theory, would be disturbances in the gastrointestinal, genitourinary, and respiratory functions. Investigations made without any knowledge of or reference to our theory, but which are directly relevant to it, substantially support the theory. For example, Dr. C. M. Drillien studied the records of many thousands of prematures and found that during the early years of postnatal life they exhibited a significantly higher incidence of nasopharyngeal and respiratory disorders and diseases than normally born children. This difference was especially marked during the first year.

In 1939, Mary Shirley published the results of a study on premature children of nursery school and kindergarten age conducted at the Harvard Child Study Center in Boston. Shirley found that premature children exhibit a significantly higher sensory acuity than term children, and in comparison are somewhat retarded in lingual and manual control, as well as in postural and locomotor control. Control of bowel and bladder sphincters, significantly enough, was found to be achieved later and with difficulty in the premature children. The attention span is short; such children are inclined to be highly emotional, jumpy, anxious, and usually shy. Summarizing her findings, Shirley observed that in the preschool period, the prematures present significantly more behavior problems than full-term children. These problems include hyperactivity, later acquisition of bowel and bladder control, enuresis, excessive distractibility, shyness, thumb-sucking, negativism and hypersensitivity to sound. In interpreting this prematurity-syndrome Shirley pointed out that

> premature births often are cataclysmic; unduly prolonged or precipitant, both of which conditions subject the baby to birth trauma. . . . Thus, it seems possible that, through a less favorable prenatal environment or through the too early loss of intrauterine media, or through the lack of adequate time for the birth preparatory responses, or through birth injuries that are sometimes so slight as to be unrecognized or through a combination of these factors, the premature may be predisposed toward the development of a higher degree of nervous irritability than the term child.

The "lack of adequate time for the birth preparatory responses" is the critical passage here, and the finding of the later and more difficult learning of control of bowel and bladder sphincters the significant observation.

Cesarean-delivered babies suffer from a number of disadvantages from the moment they are born. Their mortality rate, to begin with, is two to three times as great as that which follows vaginal delivery. At full term the rate is twice as great in cesarean-delivered babies as in vaginally delivered ones. In elective cesarean deliveries, that is to say, in nonemergency cesareans, the mortality rate is 2 percent higher than for vaginally delivered babies. In the emergency cesareans the mortality rate is 19 percent higher than in vaginal deliveries.

Death from the respiratory disorder known as hyaline membrane disease is ten times more frequent in cesarean-delivered than in vaginally delivered babies.

It may be conjectured that the disadvantages, among other things, from which cesarean-delivered babies suffer, compared with vaginally delivered babies, are to a significant extent related to the failure of adequate cutaneous stimulation which they have suffered.

Pediatricians have noted that cesarean babies tend to be characterized by greater lethargy, decreased reactivity, and less frequent crying than the vaginally delivered.

In the hope of throwing some light on the developmental history of the cesarean-delivered infant, Dr. Gilbert W. Meier of the National Institutes of Health conducted a series of experiments on macaque monkeys (*Macaca mulatta*). He compared thirteen cesarean-delivered with thirteen vaginally delivered infants for the first five days of their lives. He found that the vaginally delivered infants "were more active, more responsive to the situation, and more responsive to additional stimulation within that situation." Vocalizations, avoidance responses—the beginnings of true learning responses—and activity counts were on the average about three times more frequent in the vaginally delivered than in the cesarean-delivered infants.

Quite possibly, had the cesarean-delivered babies been given an adequate amount of caressing for some days after they were born, a significant change might have been observed in their behavioral and physical development. All the evidence clearly points in that direction.

Drs. Sydney Segal and Josephine Chu of the University of British Columbia studied twenty-six vaginally delivered and thirty-six cesarean-delivered babies, and found that the latter showed a smaller crying vital capacity than the former, a difference that persisted for the six days of their stay in the baby nursery.

A number of biochemical differences have been found between cesarean-delivered and normally delivered babies, such as higher acidosis, lower serum proteins, lower serum calcium, and higher potassium in the cesarean-delivered.

A most significant finding relates to the production of

sugar in newborn infants. Normally when a small amount of glucagon, a substance thought to be secreted by the pancreas, is introduced into the digestive system, the system responds by producing sugar. In cesarean-delivered infants the amount of sugar produced in response to this glucagon factor is much less than in vaginally delivered infants, *in the absence of labor.* When, however, labor occurs before cesarean delivery, this difference is obliterated. The basic importance of labor in the preparation of the infant for postnatal functioning is thus strikingly confirmed.

In contrast, in their studies of rats, Grota, Denenberg, and Zarrow found no differences between cesarean-delivered and vaginally delivered young in survival until weaning, or in weaning, weight, and open-field activity.

Both Shirley and Drillien observed that prematures, as children, presented more frequent and greater feeding problems than children born at term. Such observations, abundantly confirmed by other observers, suggest the possibility that inadequate cutaneous stimulation plays a role here, and, in some cases at least, results in a greater susceptibility to infection and disorder of the respiratory, gastrointestinal, and genitourinary systems. Further contributory evidence is to be seen in the meconium plug syndrome. This is the condition in which a plug formed of loose cells, intestinal gland secretions, and amniotic fluid produces intestinal obstruction, resulting in a marked delay in the emptying of the stomach and the passage of food through the intestines. In such cases there is an apparent failure of the pancreas to secrete the protein-splitting enzyme trypsin, leading to inadequate peristaltic action of the intestines. Hence there is both a failure and a breakdown in the movement of the meconium. The whole syndrome strongly indicates a failure of action of the necessary substances upon the gastrointestinal tract.

Dr. William J. Pieper and his colleagues studied the case data from the files of a state child-guidance clinic, which enabled them to compare 188 pairs of normally delivered and cesarean-delivered children matched for age, sex, ethnic group, ordinal position, and father's occupational level. Comparisons were made in 76 variables. In most of these variables these two groups of children were indistinguishably similar, but in a small number they were significantly different. Thus, cesarean-delivered males and all cesareans eight years of age or older were more likely to have a speech defect, to have a speech defect at the time of the diagnostic examination, and to have a mother rated as behaving inconsistently in the mother-child relationship. The other six differences were as follows: normally born males were found to have more unspecified somatic complaints; cesarean-delivered males were more likely to be rated by the psychologist as showing evidence of organic involvement; cesareans under eight years of age were more likely to present the symptoms of fear of school and various other personality difficulties; and cesareans over eight years of age were more likely to present the symptoms of restlessness and temper.

Clearly, the differences found by Pieper and his colleagues between cesarean-delivered and normally delivered children were largely of an emotional nature, the cesarean-delivered children being somewhat significantly more emotionally disturbed than the normally delivered children. It would be difficult to attribute such differences to the absence or inadequacy of a single factor in the development of these cesarean children, but as we shall see, it is quite probable that inadequate cutaneous stimulation during the perinatal period—that is, the period shortly before and shortly after birth—may have been one of the factors involved.

Dr. M. Straker found a significantly higher frequency of emotional disturbance and anxiety in cesarean-delivered individuals than in normally delivered ones. Liberson and Frazier found that the electroencephalographic patterns in cesarean newborns show evidence of greater physiological stability than in the normally born. This finding, however, is difficult to evaluate as an evidence of greater or lesser general physiological stability. It is referred to here simply to make it clear that the evidence does not all point in the same direction. One would hardly expect it to.

That postpartum cutaneous stimulation can to some extent compensate for a lack of skin stimulation during the birth process is supported by Dr. Donald H. Barron's observation of twin kids delivered without the occurrence of labor, by cesarean section. If one newborn kid is left wet in a warm room, while the other is completely dried off with a towel, cleaning it well, the kid that has been dried gets up before the other. This difference in response, Barron remarks, points to the great survival value of cutaneous stimulation. "I have the impression," he states, "that the drying, licking, and the grooming are important in raising the general level of neural excitability in the kid, and thereby hasten his ability to rise on his knees, to orient himself, and to stand."

Since the head of the human term fetus is, within the womb, larger than it has ever been, and since it lies in the head-down position in the narrowest part of the womb, the stimulations received from the contracting uterus by the face, nose, lips, and remainder of the head are very considerable. This facial stimulation corresponds to the licking of the muzzle and oral region given by other animals to their young, and presumably produces much the same effect, namely, the initiation of sensory discharge into the central nervous system and the raising of the excitability of the respiratory center. As Barron has shown, there is a rise in the oxygen content of the blood associated with licking and grooming, in the newborn of goats: "Raising the excitability of the respiratory center in turn increases the depth of the respiratory effort, increases the level of oxygenation of the blood, and so enhances the capacity for further muscular movement and strength."

Insofar as the higher oxygenation of the blood is concerned, these observations have been confirmed in the normally newborn human, as compared with the cesarean-delivered and the premature. McCance and Otley have shown that when the newborn rat is removed from its mother immediately after birth, its kidneys remain relatively functionless for the first twenty-four hours of its life. They suggest that normally the attentions of the mother cause an increase in the excretion of urea owing to some reflex change in the blood flow to the kidney.

The skin and the gastrointestinal tract meet not only at the lips and mouth, but also at the anal region. Hence it is scarcely surprising, in the light of what we have already learned, not only that gastrointestinal function will be activated by stimulating this region, but that respiratory function will also often be activated by such stimulation. This method of inducing respiration in the newborn often works when other methods fail.

That the skin and the gastrointestinal tract are often interactive has been suggested in clinical reports for many years. Disorders and diseases simultaneously affecting both the gastrointestinal tract and integument have been observed in many cases.

That the benefits of maternal-infant cutaneous contacts are reciprocal is evident from the fact that when the newborn is placed in contact with its mother's body, the uterus will be stimulated to contract. This fact constituted part of the folk wisdom of many peoples for centuries. It is, for example, reported from Brunswick, in Germany, that it is the custom not to allow the child, during the first twenty-four hours after its birth, to lie by its mother's side, "otherwise the uterus can find no rest and scratches about in the woman's body, like a large mouse." Folk wisdom, while recognizing the fact, failed when it came to drawing the correct conclusion from it—namely, that the contractions of the uterus were beneficial to the mother.

The evidence surveyed in the preceding pages, sparse as it is, nevertheless lends strong support to the hypothesis that an important function of the prolonged labor and especially the contractions of the uterus, in the human female, is to serve much the same purpose that licking and grooming of the newborn serve in other animals. This purpose is to further the infant's development for optimum postnatal functioning of its sustaining systems. We have seen that in all animals cutaneous stimulation of the infant's body is in most cases an indispensably necessary condition for the survival of the young. We have suggested that in a species such as *Homo sapiens,* in which gestation is only half-completed at birth, and in which maternal behavior is dependent upon learning rather than upon instinct, the selective advantage would lie with a reflex initiation and maintenance of uterine contractions functioning for the fetus as an automatic, physiologically massive stimulation of its skin, and through its skin of its organ systems. The evidence, as we have seen, tends to support this hypothesis, that the uterine contractions of labor constitute the beginning caressing of the baby in the right way—a caressing which should be continued in very special ways in the period immediately following birth and for a considerable time thereafter. This we may proceed to discuss in the next chapter.

3 Breastfeeding

I will lift up mine eyes unto the hills,
from whence cometh my help.
                        —Psalms 121.1.

Whether or not we accept the psychoanalytic view that life in
the womb is normally a supremely pleasurable experience, a
blissful state rudely shattered by the ordeal of birth, there can
be little doubt that the process of birth is a disturbing one to the
birthling. Having spent its prenatal life in a supporting aquatic
environment, within a medium in which the second law of
thermodynamics is perfectly satisfied by the constancy of the
temperature and the pressure, that is to say, within the amniotic fluid surrounded by the amniotic sac, the fetus is said to
live a Nirvana-like existence. This blissful existence is rudely
interrupted largely owing to a fall in the levels of the preg-
nancy-maintaining hormone progesterone in the mother's
bloodstream, resulting in the turbulent series of changes which
the fetus begins to experience as the birth process. The contractions of the uterus in labor act as compressive forces upon
its body, so that it is pushed against the birth canal where the
repeated thrusts of its head against the maternal bony pelvis
produce the protective swelling beneath its scalp known as the
caput succedaneum. It is doubtful whether the fetus quite ap-
preciates that this apparently gratuitous assault upon its person
is designed entirely for its benefit. Providentially, the oxygen
available to it at this time is gradually undergoing reduction, so
that such consciousness, such awareness of pain as it may be
capable of, is probably reduced. This may well be the function
of the anoxia or hypoxia, as this reduced state of oxygenation is
called. The contracting uterus completes its parturitive func-

tions with the expulsion of the fetus from the uterus. With birth, the newborn moves into a wholly new zone of experience and adaptation, from an aquatic solitary existence into an atmospheric and social environment.

At birth, atmospheric air immediately rushes into the lungs of the newborn, inflating them and causing them to press against and to produce gradual rotation of the heart. There is, as it were, a competition for space between the heart and the lungs. The *ductus arteriosus* between the arch of the aorta and the upper surface of the pulmonary trunk, which in the fetus made it possible to bypass the systemic circulation involving the lungs, begins to contract and close. The cupolae of the diaphragm begin to rise eccentrically up and down, the chest wall to expand, all of which could hardly be described as contributing to a pleasant experience for the newborn. Ushered into the world with what appear to be, as Laurence Sterne put it, "squalls of disapprobation at the journey he was compelled to perform," what the newborn is looking forward to, and has every right to expect, is a continuation of the life he enjoyed in the womb—in other words, a womb with a view—before it was so unseemly interrupted by the birth process. Instead, what he receives in our highly sophisticated Western societies is a rather dusty answer.

The moment he is born, the cord is usually cut or clamped, and until recently, the child was exhibited to his mother and then was taken away by a nurse to a baby room called the nursery, so called presumably because the one thing that was not done in it was the nursing of the baby. Here he was weighed, measured, his physical and any other traits recorded, a number put around his wrist, and then put in a crib to howl away to his heart's discontent.

The two people who need each other at this time, more than they ever will at any other in their lives, are separated from one another, prevented from continuing the development of that symbiotic relationship which is so critically important for the further development of both.

During the whole of pregnancy the mother has been elaborately prepared, in every possible way, for the continuation of the symbiotic union between herself and her child, to minister to his dependent needs in the manner for which she alone is best prepared. It is not simply that the baby needs her, but that each needs the other. The mother needs the baby quite as much as the baby needs the mother. The biological unity, the symbiotic relationship, maintained by mother and conceptus throughout pregnancy does not cease at birth but becomes— indeed, is naturally designed to become—even more intensified and interoperative than during uterogestation. As Kulka, Fry, and Goldstein have said:

> Contact needs are probably gratified fully in intrauterine life, and a gradual transition in the postnatal period is mandatory for healthy development. Much of the earliest kinesthetic satisfactions must be supplied to the infant by the environment—cuddling, rocking, being kept warm, etc.

Giving birth to her child, the mother's interest and involvement in its welfare is deepened and reinforced. Her whole organism has been readied to minister to her infant's needs, to caress and make loving communications to her baby at the breast. From the breast the baby will not only take in the wondrous colostrum, the lemony-yellowish fluid which confers such immunological and other physiological benefits upon the child, but the child will also, by suckling, confer vital benefits upon the mother. The psychophysiological benefits which mother and child, the nursing couple, reciprocally confer upon one another in the continuing symbiotic relationship are vitally important for their further development. This is a fact which is only very slowly coming to be recognized in our highly sophisticated, technologized, dehumanized, cubistically dilapidated Western world, a world in which breastfeeding has been considered by many to be beneath human dignity. As one expensively educated young woman indignantly exclaimed when I asked her, sometime during the fifties, whether she was going to breastfeed her baby, "Why, only animals do that. None of my friends do." It was a world in which 96 percent of new mothers were bottlefeeding their babies, a world in which pediatricians assured mothers that bottlefeeding was every bit as good as breastfeeding, and often even better. Indeed, as James Croxton has remarked, "Humans are the only mammals that raise their infants as though they were not mammals."

It was, and to some extent still is, a world in which the place for breastfeeding was in private. Breastfeeding in public is still considered indecent. In May 1975 the Associated Press reported an incident from Miami, Florida, involving three young mothers who were ordered by a ranger to leave a public park. They were told they could no longer use the park for picnics because, as the mayor later explained, such conduct violated the city's decency ordinance, and the sight of women breastfeeding their babies was inappropriate, "especially in a public park where kids play." One of the breastfeeding mothers happened to be a leader of the La Leche League in Florida (the international organization which has been largely instrumental in encouraging a return to breastfeeding). When she and the president of the league appeared on a well-known TV show in June 1975, they were greeted with a surprising amount of hostility from some women in the audience who felt that nursing should only be done in private.

We live in the logical denouement of the Machine Age, when things are increasingly produced by machine, and human beings, who are turned out to be as machinelike as we can make them, see little wrong in dealing with others in a similarly mechanical manner; an age in which it is considered a mark of progress when whatever was formerly done by human beings is taken out of their hands and done by machine. It has been reckoned an advance when a bottle formula could be made to substitute for the contents of the human breast and the infant's enjoyment of the experience, especially in an age when many women were unhappily to take over the values of the masculine world.

In the widely read official manual *Infant Care*, issued by the U.S. Children's Bureau of the Department of Health, Education and Welfare, a work mainly edited by women, the 1963 edition refers to an apparently not uncommon negative attitude toward the tactile experience of breastfeeding. "You may feel," the editors write, "some resistance to the idea of such intimacy with an infant who, at first, seems like a stranger. To some mothers it seems better to keep the baby at arm's length, so to speak, by feeding plans which are not so close."

These sentences reflect a widespread failure to understand the meaning and importance of the intimacy which should exist, from the moment of birth, between mother and infant.

During the birth process mother and infant have had a somewhat trying time. At birth each clearly requires the reassurance of the other's presence. The reassurance for the mother lies in the sight of her baby, its first cry, and in its closeness to her body. For the baby it consists in the contact with and warmth of the mother's body, the support in her cradled arms, the caressing, the cutaneous stimulation it receives, and the suckling at her breast, the welcome into "the bosom of the family." These are words, but they refer to very real psychophysiological conditions.

The benefits to the mother of immediate breastfeeding are innumerable—not the least of which, after the weariness of labor and pain, is the emotional gratification, the feeling of strength, of power, the composure, and the sense of fulfillment that comes with the handling and suckling of the baby.

Within a few minutes after the baby is born the third stage of labor should be completed; that is, the placenta should be detached and ejected. The bleeding from the torn vessels of the uterus should begin to be arrested, and the uterus should commence its return to normal size. When the baby is put to nurse at the mother's breast immediately after birth, and even before the cord is clamped, if the cord is long enough, the baby's suckling will serve to accelerate all three processes. By suckling at the breast the baby sets up major changes in the mother; its suckling increases the secretion of oxytocin from the pituitary gland, producing massive contractions of the uterus, with the consequence that: (1) the uterine muscle fibers contract upon the uterine vessels; (2) the uterine vessels undergo constriction at the same time; (3) the uterus begins to undergo reduction in size; (4) the placenta becomes detached from the uterine wall; and (5) is ejected by the contracting expulsive uterus. In addition, the secretory functions of the breast are greatly augmented by the induced secretion of prolactin from the pituitary gland. Physiologically, the nursing of her babe at the breast produces in the mother an intensification of her "motherliness," the pleasurable care of her child. Psychologically, this intensification serves further to consolidate the symbiotic bond between herself and her child. In this bonding between mother and child the first few minutes after birth are important. This is the beginning of that time when mother and baby are literally getting in touch with one another. For the newborn, among other things, the breast is the substitute for and functions as the umbilical cord and placenta.

For the newborn, what better reassurance can there be than the support of its mother and the satisfaction of suckling at her breast, what better promise of good things to come? The cutaneous stimulation the baby receives from the mother's caressing, from the contact with her body, its warmth, and especially the perioral stimulations—that is, the stimulations received during suckling about the face, lips, nose, tongue, mouth—are important in improving the respiratory functions and through this means the oxygenation of the blood. As an assistance in suckling, the newborn is equipped with a median papilla on its upper lip which enables it to gain a firm hold on the breast. At the same time, at the breast the baby is ingesting the valuable colostrum, the best of all the substances it could possibly imbibe. The colostrum lasts about ten days and, among other things, acts as a laxative; it is the only substance that can effectively clean out the meconium in the baby's gastrointestinal tract. Colostrum constitutes the most powerful insurance against the baby's development of diarrhea. Babies ingesting colostrum do not develop diarrhea. The fact, indeed, is that the only known successful treatment for diarrhea in babies is breastfeeding. Colostrum is richer than true milk in lactoglobulin, which carries the factors that immunize the baby against a number of diseases.

It is interesting to note here that the colostrum of mothers of premature babies is about three times more powerful than that of mothers of term babies, a finding which suggests that prematures should be fed their mother's colostrum, whether they are able to suckle or not.

Years ago Dr. Theobald Smith of New York showed that colostrum conferred upon calves immunity to colon bacillus septicemia. In 1934 Dr. J. A. Toomey demonstrated that similar immunizing factors against this bacillus were present in human colostrum, as well as immunizing factors against other bacteria that infect the gastrointestinal tract. Colostrum encourages the growth of desirable bacteria and discourages the growth of undesirable bacteria in the gastrointestinal tract of the newborn. Since that time colostrum has been shown to contain a vastly greater number of substances beneficial to the baby.

In many ways the newborn calf is more mature than the human newborn. Like the calf, the human newborn has an undeveloped immunological capacity at birth; that is, it has no antibodies and little ability to make its own as defenses against foreign invaders. The antibody-rich colostrum from its mother's breast, which is some fifteen to twenty times richer in gamma globulin than maternal serum, provides the newborn with such antibodies, and confers a passive immunity upon him for the next six months, by which time he will gradually have acquired his own antibodies.

Thus breastfeeding provides a number of correlated benefits for the newborn, immunological, neural, psychological, and organic. Over the four or more million years of human evolution, and as a consequence of seventy-five million years of mammalian evolution, breastfeeding has constituted the most successful means of ministering to the needs of the dependent, precariously born human neonate. Breastfeeding is the primary mode of nurturance.

While I am in this book principally concerned with the stimulation of the skin as an important factor in the development of the individual, and not with the immunological and nutritive properties of the substances ingested during breast-feeding, it is fundamentally important for us to understand that the colostrum which postnatally lasts for some ten days, the transitional milk which lasts for some eight days, and the permanent milk which comes in about the eighteenth day, are all designed to meet the gradually developing metabolic needs of the infant in adjustment to its developing abilities to deal with the various substances it ingests. The baby's enzyme systems take some days to develop sufficiently to be able to deal with these substances, mostly proteins. The colostrum, transitional, and permanent milk, coming in as gradually as they do, are perfectly timed and adjusted to the physiological development of the infant's gastrointestinal system.

The facts, indeed, indicate that breastfeeding constitutes a fundamental requirement for the human newborn. Not that the newborn cannot survive in the absence of breastfeeding, but that he will not develop in as healthy a manner as the breastfed baby, and finally, that the breastfed baby, at any rate, will get a much better start toward healthy development than the nonbreastfed baby.

The *development* of colostrum and of transitional milk will occur in the absence of a suckling baby, but the *giving* of these substances to the baby will depend upon the suckling of the baby. The link between *making* milk and *giving* milk is called the *letdown reflex*. When the baby begins to suckle at the breast, the cutaneous stimulation the mother receives initiates nervous impulses that travel along neural circuits to the pituitary gland, which then releases the hormone oxytocin into the bloodstream. The oxytocin, reaching the glandular structures of the breast, stimulates the basket cells that surround the alveoli and milk ducts, resulting in expansion of the ducts. This, in turn, results in a greater flow of milk down into the sinuses behind the nipple, and from thirty to ninety seconds after the baby has begun to suckle the letdown reflex is completed, and the flow into the baby of the rich substances in the mother's breast will continue as long as she perseveres in breastfeeding.

I feel strongly that no mother who really loved her baby and was aware of the differences between her own milk and cow's milk would prefer to bottlefeed her infant. The differences between the two milks would take volumes to describe; suffice it to say that those differences are considerable, in amounts and proportions of fats, proteins, sugars, gamma globulins, lysozyme, taurine (important in brain development), lactoferrin, and many other important constituents, all just right and indispensable for the healthy growth and development of the infant, while cow's milk is quite wrong for him.

Whenever possible, the baby should be put in his mother's arms immediately after birth, and in most cases it *is* possible. Those who separate the baby from the mother, and resort to such procedures as cutting and tying the cord immediately after birth, or holding the baby in a tub of water, thereby declare themselves insufficiently aware of the newborn's needs, and may do him considerable harm. Babies need to breathe following birth, and to breathe deeply. The best way to initiate and stimulate deep breathing in the baby is to put him to suckle at his mother's breast, and for her to caress and cuddle him. This will bring important reflex mechanisms into action, and help in the establishment of that deeper inspiration, which may otherwise remain shallow, a condition many people go through life with without being aware of it until some serious respiratory condition strikes. In the absence of such stimulation, the baby may be forced to rely upon his inner breathing. Such fetal breathing draws upon the oxygen carried by the red blood cells in the baby's liver, which is a blood-forming organ before birth receiving oxygenated blood from the placenta. The diaphragm, which arches over the liver, exerts an upward suction on the blood supply. This assists the flow of blood toward the baby's lungs and brain. The baby's movements of the torso, and the familiar wriggling before and after birth, augment diaphragmatic functions.

Sometimes the baby's fetal breathing persists, and if it

continues, a state of inanition may result. The two sources of oxygen available to the newborn are the outer air and his own tissues, but since the latter source is meager and fast diminishing, he cannot rely too long on the latter. He must begin to take in deep inspirations of oxygenated air. Not only this, as Margaret Ribble has pointed out:

> The calibre of developing blood vessels may not become sufficient for the irrigation of nerve cells; the myelin sheaths which protect and nourish the nerve fibers may not complete themselves; brain metabolism itself may become established on a poor basis. Such handicaps as these can make an individual biologically unfit to meet the stress and strain of later life. . . . The importance of mothering in helping the child to breathe at this time can hardly be stressed too greatly.

Indeed, nothing could be better devised for the initiation of efficient breathing than suckling at the mother's breast. From what we know of the neurophysiology of suckling, the evidence suggests that when babies are born in some respiratory distress, being put to nurse at the mother's breast, by stimulating their respiratory system, will relieve their distress. Anderson has shown this to be so in lambs, and two nurse-midwives, Kathy Higgins and Linda Van Art, have confirmed this on depressed babies. In the depressed baby suckling is facilitated by flexing its knees against the abdomen and by placing the adult's fingertip in the baby's palm to be grasped. The baby begins to suckle and "pinks up" immediately.

That mother and child are designed for maximum contact in the early development of the infant has been convincingly shown by Blurton Jones. He cites such evidence as Ben Shaul's studies on the composition of milk in relation to feeding schedules in different species. In rabbits and hares, for example, feeding occurs every twenty-four hours, and they have milk with very high protein and fat content. The tree shrew, *Tupaia belangeri,* which feeds every forty-eight hours, has an even higher protein-fat milk content. Apes and humans, on the other hand, who have continuous access to the breast, have very low protein-fat milk content. The rule is that wide-spaced scheduled feeders have high protein-fat milk content, whereas short-spaced, on demand, almost continuous feeders have low protein-fat milk content. This indicates that the human mother, like the ape mother, is designed to carry her baby with her wherever she goes.

Ape and monkey babies who are so carried and fed on demand seldom or never vomit or burp. When, however, they are reared by hand and fed on a two-hour schedule, they frequently do so. So the evidence suggests that frequent breastfeeding of the infant has more than a nutritional purpose, that it has the additional important purpose of bringing mother and child into as continuous physical contact as possible.

Albrecht Peiper has remarked that among civilized peoples the breastfed infant becomes a crib infant who, if he is breastfed at all, returns to his mother's body only at feeding times. He points out that among nonliterate peoples mothers carry their children around with them on their bodies, as monkey mothers do. "It is an unnatural achievement," he writes, "for the human baby to have to spend his life in a crib. He is in no way adjusted to the crib; rather, his wish to be carried around becomes clearly evident again and again. Calming by rocking or pacifiers is reminiscent of the time when mother and child were physically more closely associated."

It is from the breast that "the milk of human kindness" flows.

While breastfeeding is maintained, pregnancy will not usually occur for at least ten weeks after the birth of the child, and often much longer, depending upon the intensity of the breastfeeding—the greater the frequency, the longer the contraceptive effect lasts. This is largely due to the anovulatory effect of prolactin which is released from the pituitary gland as a result of suckling. Thus during the breastfeeding period a kind of natural birth control will be in effect. The advantages of breastfeeding to the baby are enormous. In one pilot study of

173 children followed from birth to the age of ten years, including both breastfed and nonbreastfed children, it was found that the children who had not been breastfed had four times as many respiratory infections, twenty times more diarrhea, twenty-two more miscellaneous infections, eight times as much eczema, twenty-one times more asthma, and twenty-seven times more hay fever.

Similarly, Drs. C. Hoefer and M. C. Hardy in a study of 383 Chicago children found that breastfed children were physically and mentally superior to those who were artificially fed, and that those fed from four to nine months were in these respects more advanced than those breastfed for three months or less. The artificially fed ranked lowest in all the physical traits measured. They were nutritionally the poorest, the most susceptible to the diseases of childhood, and slowest in learning to walk and talk.

Drs. S. Goldberg and M. Lewis found that girl babies are more likely to be breastfed than boy babies, and to be nursed for longer periods. Mothers touch and hold their daughters more than their sons. At one year of age they found more attachment behavior toward their mothers in girls than in boys. The authors think that the differences are probably due to the difference in the amount and quality of the tactile interaction girls received, as contrasted with that received by the boys.

Early weaning is a subject on which we have no data for the human species. But we do have some data on rats. Dr. Jiri Krecek of the Institute of Physiology of Prague, at an international symposium held at Liblice, Czechoslovakia, on "The Postnatal Development of the Phenotype," stated the thesis that the period of weaning in mammals is a critical one, inasmuch as several basic physiological processes are being reorganized at this time, particularly those involving salt balance, general nutrition, and fat intake. Defining weaning as withdrawal from breastfeeding at sixteen days of age, other workers reported that rats who were weaned early displayed a conditioned reflex less rapidly than those weaned at thirty days of age, and also that the adult of these animals showed deficiencies in ribonucleic acid, a basic constituent of all cells. It was also found that the principal electrolyte-regulating steroid was detrimentally affected by early weaning, and that even the male hormones, the androgens, are adversely affected. At the same symposium Dr. S. Kazda described a pilot study of human adults indicating that reproduction and certain kinds of pathology may be affected by early weaning.

The advantages of breastfeeding during the first year of life on subsequent development and into adulthood have been demonstrated by a number of investigators. The evidence indicates that the infant should be breastfed for at least twelve months, and terminated only when the infant is ready for it, by gradual steps in which solid foods, which can begin at six months, commence to serve as *substitutes* for the breast. The mother will generally sense when the baby is ready for weaning.

In many indigenous, so-called primitive cultures, breastfeeding is carried on for some four years, and often more, even though the breastfeeding is after some months supplemented with other foods. It is interesting to note that breastfeeding in some parts, at least, of Europe, was in former times continued for some years. H. E. Bates, the English novelist, in his autobiography, *The Vanished World,* writing of his native Northamptonshire, tells how the women invaded the fields in autumn to harvest the hay, and adds: "I have heard my grandfather say of these women that it was no uncommon sight to see a woman suddenly unbutton her blouse in the harvest-field, take out a milky breast, and suckle a child old enough to stand and reach the nipple."

In contemporary America prolonged breastfeeding is no longer as uncommon as it was not so long ago. It should always be remembered that it is not merely the nutritional and immunological advantages of breastfeeding, important as they are, that are involved in breastfeeding, but the humanizing interacting experiences of the nursing couple, and the fulfillment of their emotional and psychological needs. As Benedek suggested long ago, motherliness cannot be developed via bottle-feeding.

SUCKLING, *NOT* SUCKING, AND TOUCH. It is hardly credible that an event which has occurred within human experience so many millions of times and been observed as frequently as breast-feeding should be so little understood, not only from the nutritional point of view, but from the standpoint of what the baby actually does when suckling. In the literature generally, "sucking" and "suckling" are not distinguished, the terms being used indiscriminately and interchangeably to refer to "suckling." The baby is said to "suck" its mother's nipple. The baby knows better than to do anything so foolish, for were he to suck the nipple all he would for the most part succeed in achieving would be to produce a partial vacuum in his mouth and fail to develop the ability to suckle properly. A baby sucks at the nozzle on the top of a bottle, but at the mother's breast a baby suckles. It is only when the milk is flowing very freely and the baby does not have to work at obtaining it that he will be content with the nipple alone resting in his mouth.

The full suckling reflex is triggered off not only by stimulation of the lips, but also by touch receptors deep in the mouth. For this reason the baby must draw an appreciable amount of the breast into the mouth. There is a short critical period for the establishment of the suckling reflex; hence the importance of putting the baby to nurse at its mother's breast as soon after birth as possible.

Suckling is an altogether different form of behavior from sucking. Contrary to the general belief, in suckling it is not the nipple that is the part of the breast that is grasped, but the areolar region. It is against the collecting sinuses situated under the areola that the lips and gums of the baby press to express the milk. The nipple is drawn to the back of the mouth and compressed between the upper gum and the tip of the tongue resting on the lower gum. The tongue is applied to the lower surface of the nipple and drawn from before backward while compressing it against the hard palate. Suckling, by inducing the secretion of prolactin and oxytocin from the pituitary, with the first hormone initiates the reflex concerned with the maintenance of milk secretion, and with the second the milk ejection or "letdown" reflex. The nipple and the areola are drawn into the mouth and sealed by the lips and buccinator muscles. The richly vascularized spongy lips of the newborn are highly sensitive to touch, while the upper lip is equipped with a median papilla that ensures a firm grip on the roughened surface of the areola. This roughened surface is due to the numerous elevations produced by the underlying areolar glands that secrete the fatty material that lubricates and protects the areola and nipple during nursing.

A breastfeeding mother holds the child at alternate breasts for feedings, thereby giving equal stimulation and exercise to both sides of the infant's face and head, as well as other parts of the body. On the contrary, the bottlefeeding mother tends to hold the child in whatever position is comfortable, and it has been generally observed that this tends to be almost always in the same position on the left side. Holding the infant on one side most of the time may not be altogether to the advantage of the child. But this is a mere speculation, and requires research. With the bottle instead of the breast, and with toys rather than its mother's caressing hands, the infant is encouraged to manipulate things rather than to "handle" people. As Philip Slater says, in his book *Earthwalk,* such training is useful for mastering and relating to machines, rather than for interrelating warmly with others.

Sometimes a baby, when put to nurse at the mother's breast, will fail to suckle and appear unable to take the nipple into the mouth. This usually occurs when the baby is wrapped in a towel or some other material. When it is removed and the baby's skin allowed to come into contact with the mother's skin, the baby will usually begin to suckle.

Suckling, it should be noted, is usually preceded by more or less prolonged licking of the nipple and areola, lasting several minutes. The licking serves to ready the breast for suckling, to familiarize the baby with the pleasures of a nourishing new world.

The baby uses very different muscles in suckling from those he used when sucking in the womb. For this reason to vary breastfeeding with bottlefeeding is not to be recommended, because it may confuse the baby, and he may have trouble adjusting.

In suckling, the suctorial pads situated in the baby's cheeks, which give them their rounded form, are primarily responsible for setting up the negative pressure that draws the milk into the oral cavity. This is probably assisted by the narrow fold of erectile tissue, frequently present on both the lower and upper gums and extending between the eyetooth buds in each jaw. They are credited with assisting the sealing off of the oral cavity around the nipple and areola, the suckling cone. For this reason, Robin and Magitot, who first described these structures in 1860, called them the "labium tertium," the pair of assisting third lips. The third lips disappear between the third and sixth months. Stimulated by the baby's suckling the membranes become quite swollen, and in addition to acting as an accessory organ of sensation, they assist in sealing the areola and nipple more hermetically into the mouth. It is in this manner that the relevant structures of the infant's face and mouth serve to create the "oral pump" that milks the mother's breast.

These arrangements constitute a beautiful example of morphological and functional maternal-infant reciprocity in the breastfeeding situation. Within the mouth the baby's various structures, and especially the tongue, receive a very different exercise in the breastfed from that undergone, or rather not undergone, by the bottlefed infant. It should therefore be hardly surprising that the later development of facial morphology, of the jaws, eruption and occlusion of the teeth, as well as the development of speech, should differ in the breastfed as contrasted with the bottlefed.

For example, in a study of 327 children, F. M. Pottenger, Jr., and Bernard Krohn found that facial and dental development in those who had been breastfed for more than three months was better than those who had been breastfed for less than three months or not at all. They conclude their report with the following words. "These findings in our 327 cases indicate that it is advisable to nurse a child at least 3 months, and preferably 6 months. This will stimulate optimal malar [cheekbone] development. We have also observed that patients who were well nursed had better developed dental arches, palates, and other facial structures than patients who were not nursed."

Bertrand, who measured the mesiodistal relationship of the dental arches in 1200 Rhodesian Bantu-speaking children from five to sixteen years of age who had experienced some three to four years of breastfeeding, found that 99.6 percent were normal, and only 0.3 percent had a prognathic overbite. The percentage of 99.6 normal in the Bantu children contrasts sharply with the percentage of 70 for normally developed jaws in whites, and 27 percent underdeveloped mandibles and 3 percent prognathic overbites in whites. Bertrand concludes that "The lack of breastfeeding and a soft diet produces underdeveloped jaws with consequent orthodontic problems (e.g., in Caucasian children)."

What has come to be known as the "nursing-bottle syndrome," rampant decay of the upper four incisors in children under four, has been found in 8 percent of London children, and in the United States Nizel has estimated that the average child of four has 2.5 decayed or filled teeth, as compared with 10 percent or more with the nursing-bottle syndrome.

Suckling involves continuing positional mechanisms of pharynx and mouth, with participation of pharynx and larynx in respiration. Together these mechanisms form a composite of rhythmic processes or "phrases," consisting of one or more suckles, a swallow, and a respiration. The infant's suckling phrase is repeated throughout the period of established feeding. During suckling the oral structures are distinctively coordinated. The tongue, lower lip, mandible, and hyoid (the U-shaped bone above the thyroid cartilage which is at the base of and supports the tongue) move together as a unified "oral motor organ."

The amount and quality of exercise that the oral and pharyngeal structures undergo during the process of suckling appear to be associated with a speedier development of clarity of speech than is the case in bottlefed babies. Frances Broad, in two studies embracing 319 white children, five to six years of age, found that the breastfed children were in all respects of speech development, clarity of articulation, tonal quality, and also reading ability and general confidence, superior to the bottlefed. Girls have clearer speech than boys of the same age. The superiority was especially marked in the breastfed as com-- pared with the bottlefed boys.

These findings are not surprising, for as Broad points out, the organs of suckling and articulation are much the same; hence, it might be expected that conditions influencing the development of the suckling response would have an effect on the structures required for speech. Another factor, she suggests, may be the fact that since the incidence of infections in infancy is reduced by breastfeeding, and since the ability to speak is adversely affected by infections of the respiratory tract, the latter leading quite often to infections of the auditory apparatus, and since the ability to speak depends upon the ability to hear, this may explain the greater incidence of defective speech qualities in the bottlefed as compared with the breastfed. In which case, the solution, she suggests, is a rapid return to breastfeeding.

BREASTFEEDING AND SPEECH. In breastfeeding it is important for the mother to do what she is naturally impelled to do: speak to the baby.

In a longitudinal study of 28 working-class women, 14 of whom were given one hour of extra postpartum contact with their infants in the first three months after birth, and fifteen hours additional in the first three days of life, Ringler, Trause, Klaus, and Kennell found that how mothers speak to their two-year-olds is associated with the children's speech and language comprehension at five, but only among pairs who experienced no more than the amount of contact which was routine in hospitals at the time: a glimpse of the baby at birth, a brief contact for identification at six to eight hours, and then visits of twenty to thirty minutes for feedings every four hours.

It would appear that maternal speech is associated with children's later speech and language comprehension. Among these mother-child pairs, the richer the mother's speech to her two-year-old, as reflected in the number of adjectives she used, the higher was the child's IQ at five. The more words she used in a sentence, the better the child understood complex phrases. By contrast, the simpler and more telegraphic her speech, the poorer the five-year-old's ability to express himself. These relationships occurred only among mother-child pairs who experienced extra contact in the postpartum period.

"One must infer" the authors write, "that among these lower class young women, extra contact enhanced their relationships with their infants." Being more involved with each other and susceptible to each other's influence, in both preverbal and verbal stages of interaction, they did better on the whole than mother-child pairs who were less involved.

While these observations are not specifically related by the authors to maternal speech at breastfeeding, it seems likely that the breastfeeding mother's speech to her baby would have a valuable effect on its speech development.

It has been vaguely known for some time that there is a close interrelationship between the development of speech and that of the hand. Adolescents and adults often use gestures of the hand as an auxiliary language in virtually every form of speech. It seems to me that in the development of the infant's speech this is a subject which has been quite inadequately investigated, particularly in connection with the tactile stimulation of the child.

Géber, in her study of 308 Uganda children, found an all-around advance of development in motor coordination, in adaptivity, language, and personal/social relationships over European children. The attitudes of the Ganda mothers toward their children seemed to be largely responsible for the differences. Before the child is weaned, the mother's whole interest is focused on him. By comparison, Ganda children who came from higher classes, whose families had become somewhat Westernized, tended to show considerably less precocity. Similar observations were made by Ainsworth about Ganda children.

When the functions of the breast are discussed it is usually its nutritional capacities that are emphasized, and very properly so, but should not be to the exclusion of everything else. For the process of breastfeeding involves a great deal more than providing physical nourishment for the child. That great deal more is a psychocultural environment that is of the first order of importance for the growth and development of the child's ability to function as a mentally healthy human being. Breastfeeding involves a large number of complex variables, so that studies that treat it as if it were a fairly simple form of behavior are not likely to throw much light on its relation to later forms of behavior.

Breastfeeding and bottlefeeding are very broad terms for a host of different patterns of maternal-infant interaction. Overfeeding, underfeeding, scheduling, demand, pacing of rate of baby's intake, handling, arbitrary feedings, amount of physical contact, mother's acceptance of the baby, mother's stability, marital adjustment, and many other factors are involved in the feeding situation.

In the matter of thumbsucking, it may be suggested that far from being a diagnostic sign of insufficient sucking, satisfaction, or disturbed emotional development, thumbsucking is in many cases, if not in all, an act designed to perpetuate the pleasure the child has experienced in suckling or sucking. And further, that instead of being discouraged, thumbsucking should be treated as a perfectly normal behavior and be allowed to run its natural course.

More than 400 years ago William Painter wrote of the breast as "that most sacred fountaine of the body, the educatour of mankind." From many sources, the evidence such as it is supports Painter's view of breastfeeding. In short, what happens between mother and infant in the breastfeeding relationship, from the first minutes following birth and thereafter, constitutes the foundational experiences upon which the human behavioral capacities are developed. It is within the first thirty minutes that the primary bonding is initiated between mother and infant, and this can only occur when the baby is put to nurse at the mother's breast. The physiological benefits that mother and infant reciprocally confer upon each other during that interchange are so fundamental that there can be not the least doubt that they were designed to continue in this manner the symbiotic relationship they had maintained throughout pregnancy. All through pregnancy the mother has been elaborately prepared to minister to the dependent needs of her child from the moment it is born. Indeed, the nursing couple are in every way quite indispensable to each other, an indispensability that, in the Western world, is generally not understood by the very persons who have been elected the experts or authorities on the requirements of mother and child in childbirth and thereafter. It is as if there were a conspiracy against both mother and child to deprive them of their inalienable constitutional rights to human development.

Much else could be said on the advantages of breastfeeding accruing to both mother and child; the aim is, of course, to give the child something rather more than an adequate diet, to provide it, in sum, with an emotional environment of security and love in which the whole creature can thrive. Breastfeeding alone will not secure this. It is the mother's total relatedness to her child that makes breastfeeding significant.

The experience of breast and touch can be seen, within the framework of a concept drawn from gestalt psychology, as a figure-ground perception, with body always there as ground, and reaching for the breast as figured stimulus. This figure-ground experience initiates not only the letdown reflex, but the ongoing process of socialization of two human beings.

It is highly probable that the development of the skin itself as an organ is greatly benefitted by the experience at the breast. While I know of no experimental data on this, there does exist some evidence from other sources and on other animals tending to support this view. For example, Truby King, the distinguished New Zealand pediatrician, was much impressed with the statements on this subject made to him by a merchant dealing in wool and hides. The piece is worth quoting in its entirety. Truby King had spoken to the merchant of the advantages of breastfeeding, and the latter replied: "I don't need convincing as to what mother's milk must mean for the child—I know it already from my own business. *Why, I can tell you how your boots were fed!*" He then proceeded to elaborate.

> In the trade we know the highest grade of calf-skins as Paris Calf. That is because calves reared on their mother's milk to provide the finest veal for Paris, have also incidentally set the standard for the whole world as to what is best in the way of calf-skins for tanning.
>
> Suppose the hair has not been removed, it is smooth and glossy, not harsh or dry, and it all lies the right way. Or take the leather, it isn't patchy. The whole hide is more or less uniform, smooth and fine-grained. When you feel and handle it you find that it has a certain body and firmness, and yet it is pliable and elastic. It's nice to touch and handle—there is a kindly feeling about it. Why [pausing to think of an illustration] it's like the face of a sleek child that is doing well, compared with one that's not flourishing.

"What about the other kind?" Truby King inquired. To which the merchant replied:

> Oh, you mean the "bucket-feds." Of course there is every grade and degree; but speaking generally, the hide is patchy—it's not all over alike. It tends to be harsh and dry, and has a more or less dead feeling. There is not the same body in it, and it hasn't the fine grain and pliancy of Paris Calf. It's not kindly to the touch. Why, look here, when handling a first-rate calf-skin we say to one another in the trade: "By Jove, that's a good piece of stuff—why, that's milk-fed."

While there can be small doubt that the "kindliness" of the milk-fed skin is in large part due to the nutrients ingested by the calf from its mother's milk, some of its quality, we will not,

I am sure, be far wrong in concluding, is probably also due to the cutaneous stimulation received by the calf from the mother.

The observation on "the face of a sleek child that is doing well, compared with one that's not flourishing," is significant, for while I know of no observations bearing on the matter, there can be little doubt that the character of the skin of a breastfed infant differs in many ways from that of a bottlefed infant.

The quality of the tactile stimulation received stands in direct relation to the qualitative development of the organism in all its organ systems. As we have already noted, since the introduction of the mechanical milking of cows, it has been observed that hand-milked cows give more and richer terminal milk than machine-milked cows. This appears to be true also in the lactating human female. Usually, as we know, the tactile stimulation provided by the baby's suckling at the nipple initiates the letdown reflex and the full flow of milk. But in cases in which the breastmilk is for some reason insufficient, systematic massage, starting at the abdomen and carried up to the breasts, is generally sufficient to stimulate an abundant flow of milk.

Sir Truby King states:

> The value of massage of the breasts, and sponging them twice a day with hot and cold water alternately, has been abundantly demonstrated for some years at the Karitane Harris Hospital, New Zealand. It is found that these simple measures, along with an abundance of fresh air, bathing, daily exercise, due rest and sleep, regular habits, suitable feeding and drinking of extra water, rarely fails to re-establish breastfeeding in cases where the supply has been falling off—indeed where suckling has been entirely given up for days or even for weeks.

It is known that in the absence of suckling stimulation the hormone which initiates the secretion of milk, namely prolactin, will not continue to be produced by the anterior pituitary gland in adequate quantities, and ovulation, failing to be inhibited, will resume. In order to test whether the production of prolactin would continue in the absence of suckling, but in the sight, sound, and body contact with the young, Moltz, Levin, and Leon surgically removed the nipples from female rats who were subsequently impregnated and allowed to give birth normally. When compared with unoperated control groups from whom the young had been removed twelve hours after birth, it was found that the control females began to ovulate after an average of seven days, a sham-operated group ovulated at sixteen days, while the experimental group ovulated at twenty days. The exteroceptive stimuli of sight, sound, odor, and perhaps "feel" of the young, this investigation suggests, even in the absence of suckling, are able to promote the output of prolactin in amounts sufficient to inhibit ovulation for sixteen to twenty days.

The intercutaneous stimulation of the nursing couple has evolved quite clearly as a reciprocating developmental arrangement designed to activate and to keep tonally at their optimum the various bodily functions of both mother and child. The areola and the nipple possess very sensitive reflexogenic capacities. When uterine irritability is at its maximum, during and shortly after labor, stimulation of the nipple causes pronounced, often violent, contractions. The center of this reflexogenic mechanism is believed to be in the hypothalamus, which stimulates the release of the hormone oxytocin from the posterior pituitary gland. It is this hormone that is involved in the onset of labor, and together with various other conditions, in the onset of the birth itself. As we have already seen, oxytocin is also the hormone which is released in abundance as a result of the baby's suckling at the breast, a reflex activity resulting in the letdown reflex and the flow of milk.

We see, then, how beautifully designed the suckling of the baby at the mother's breast is, especially in the immediate postpartum period, to serve the most immediate needs of both, and from this to grow and develop in the service of all their reciprocal needs. What is established in the breastfeeding relationship constitutes the foundation for the development of all human social relationships, and the communications the infant receives through the warmth of the mother's skin constitute the first of the socializing experiences of his life.

It is quite remarkable that in a pre-Freudian age, Erasmus Darwin—Charles Darwin's grandfather—in an extraordinary book entitled *Zoonomia, or the Laws of Organic Life,* first published in 1794, should have suggested a relationship between breastfeeding and subsequent behavioral development. In his book, Darwin wrote as follows:

> All these various kinds of pleasure at length become associated with the form of the mother's breast; which the infant embraces with its hands, presses with its lips, and watches with its eyes and thus acquires more accurate ideas of the form of its mother's bosom, than of the odor and flavor of warmth, which it perceives by its other senses. And hence at our maturer years, when any object of vision is presented to us, which by its waving or spiral lines bears any similitude to the form of the female bosom, whether it is found in a landscape with soft gradations of rising and descending surface, or in the forms of some antique vases, or in other works of the pencil or chisel, we feel a general glow of delight, which seems to influence all our senses; and if the object be not too large, we experience an attraction to embrace it with our arms, and to salute it with our lips, as we did in our early infancy the bosom of our mother.

It may well be that the psalmist who wrote the words, "I will lift up mine eyes unto the hills, from whence cometh my help," was responding to the influence of such early experiences. One thing is certain: he could not possibly have been a bottlefed baby.

Erasmus Darwin traces the origin of the smile to the experience of the infant at its mother's breast. He writes:

> In the action of sucking, the lips of the infant are closed around the nipple of his mother, till he has filled his stomach, and the pleasure occasioned by the stimulus of this grateful food succeeds. Then the sphincter of the mouth, fatigued by

the continued action of sucking, is relaxed; and the antagonist muscles of the face gently acting, produce the smile of pleasure: as cannot but be seen by all who are conversant with children.

Hence this smile during our lives is associated with gentle pleasure; it is visible on kittens, and puppies, when they are played with, and tickled; but more particularly marks the human features. For in children this expression of pleasure is much encouraged, by their imitation of their parents, or friends; who generally address them with a smiling countenance: hence some nations are more remarkable for the gaiety, and others for the gravity of their looks.

It is as good a theory of the origin of smiling as any that has been offered, and it is to be noted that it does not escape Darwin's attention that the readiness with which people smile is to a large extent culturally conditioned. The fact that the smile universally constitutes an evidence of pleasure, of friendliness, may at least partly be due to the origins of smiling in the infant's oral-tactile pleasures at the maternal breast.

The meaning of skin contact with the mother, especially at her breast, is recalled most beautifully by Kabongo, a Kikiyu chief of East Africa. He was eighty years of age when he spoke these words:

My early years are connected in my mind with my mother. At first she was always there; I can remember the comforting feel of her body as she carried me on her back and the smell of her skin in the hot sun. Everything came from her. When I was hungry or thirsty she would swing me round to where I could reach her full breasts; now when I shut my eyes I feel again with gratitude the sense of well-being that I had when I buried my head in their softness and drank the sweet milk that they gave. At night when there was no sun to warm me, her arms, her body, took its place; and as I grew older and more interested in other things, from my safe place on her back I could watch without fear as I wanted and when sleep overcame me I had only to close my eyes.

"Everything came from her." These are the key words. They imply warmth, support, security, satisfaction of thirst and hunger, comfort, well-being, the very satisfactions that every child must experience at its mother's breast.

ANOTHER REASON WHY BABIES ENJOY THE BREAST. It is not commonly known that among the mammals, human milk is the sweetest of all, containing 7 percent of milk sugar, compared with 4 percent in cow's milk. It is of interest to note that there is good evidence that not only the human newborn, but also the human fetus, relish the sweet taste of fluids they swallow and prefer them to rather less exciting ones. Years ago Dr. Karl de Snoo showed that the fetus in utero has a strong appetite for saccharine injected into the amniotic sac. Later authors have since found that a sucrose solution administered through a specially designed device causes the newborn to suck more slowly, accompanied by a higher heart rate. The sweeter the solution the slower was the sucking rate and the higher the heart rate. The investigators, Crook and Lipsitt, suggest that the decrease in sucking speed may reflect a primitive form of savoring and, together with the accelerated heart rate, a hedonic experience.

That suckling is an absorbingly pleasurable experience for the infant is evident from its responses to it. Even nonnutritive sucking is enthralling to the infant. Field and Goldston have found that infants on a pacifier during heelstick procedures exhibit less behavior distress and less severe postnatal complications.

It is through body contact with the mother that the child makes its first contact with the world, through which he is enfolded in a new dimension of experience, the experience of the world of the other. It is this bodily contact with the other that provides the essential source of comfort, security, warmth, and increasing aptitude for new experiences, the fountain of which begins with breastfeeding, from which all benisons flow and the promise of good things to come.

4 Tender, Loving Care

The paved highway of belief through touch
And sight leads straightest into the human heart
And the precincts of the mind.
— Lucretius (c. 60 B.C.), *De Rerum Natura,*
V, 105–107.

From early days,
Beginning not long after that first time
In which, a Babe, by intercourse of touch,
I held mute dialogues with my Mother's heart
I have endeavour'd to display the means
Whereby this infant sensibility,
Great birthright of our Being, was in me
Augmented and sustain'd.
— William Wordsworth,
The Prelude, 1850,
II, 1. 265–272.

In that seminal book of 1948, *Psychosocial Medicine: A Study of the Sick Society,* the psychiatrist James L. Halliday writes:

As the first few months following birth may be regarded as a direct continuation of the intrauterine state, there is need for continuance of close body contact with the mother to satisfy the requirements of the kinesthetic and muscle sense. This requires that the baby be held firmly, nursed at intervals, rocked, stroked, talked to, and reassured. With the disappearance of the "shaley wife" and the introduction of the perambulator the need for adequate body contact is often forgotten. How readily the infant reacts to the absence of the contact is seen when a baby is laid on a flat surface such as a table without support. Immediately it reacts with a startle and a cry. Mothers who are anxious (from whatever cause) tend when holding a child to hold it loosely or insecurely instead of firmly and confidently, and this to some extent explains the saying that "anxious mothers produce anxious babies," the insecurity of the mother being, as it were, sensed by the child. The absence of accustomed mother contact has a bearing on the problem of "fretting" such as is seen when an infant is removed from a hospital. Many of us who have been resident medical officers in a fever hospital used to be somewhat skeptical of the importance of fretting, but recent observations have shown its reality and its practical importance, in that infants deprived of their accustomed maternal body contact may develop a profound depression with lack of appetite, wasting, and even marasmus leading to death. As a result of these findings volunteer women now attend some of the children's hospitals to provide infants that are fretting with periods of handling, caressing, rocking, etc. (The results are said to be dramatic.)

The results are, indeed, dramatic—and thereby hangs a fascinating tale.

During the nineteenth century more than half the infants in their first year of life regularly died from a disease called *marasmus,* a Greek word meaning "wasting away." The disease was also known as infantile atrophy or debility. As late as the second decade of the twentieth century the death rate for infants under one year of age in various foundling institutions throughout the United States was nearly 100 percent. It was in 1915 that Dr. Henry Dwight Chapin, the distinguished New York pediatrician, in a report on children's institutions in ten different cities made the staggering disclosure that in all but one institution every infant under two years of age died. The various discussants of Dr. Chapin's report, at the Philadelphia meeting of the American Pediatric Society, fully corroborated his findings from their own experience. Dr. R. Hamil remarked, with grim irony, "I had the honor to be connected with an institution in this city of Philadelphia in which the mortality among infants under one year of age, when admitted to the institution and retained there for any length of time, was

100 percent." Dr. R. T. Southworth added, "I can give an instance from an institution in New York City that no longer exists in which, on account of the very considerable mortality among the infants admitted, it was customary to enter the condition of every infant on the admission card as hopeless. That covered all subsequent happenings." Finally, Dr. J. M. Knox described a study he had made in Baltimore. Of two hundred infants admitted to various institutions, almost 90 percent died within a year. The 10 percent that survived, he stated, did so apparently because they were taken from the institutions for short times and placed in care of foster parents or relatives.

Recognizing the emotional aridity of children's institutions, Dr. Chapin introduced the system of boarding out babies instead of leaving them in the charnel houses the institutions had become. It was, however, Dr. Fritz Talbot of Boston who brought the idea of "Tender, Loving Care," not in so many words but in practice, back with him from Germany, where he had visited before World War I. While in Germany Dr. Talbot called at the Children's Clinic in Dusseldorf, where he was shown over the wards by Dr. Arthur Schlossmann, the director. The wards were very neat and tidy, but what piqued Dr. Talbot's curiosity was the sight of a fat old woman who was carrying a very measly baby on her hip. "Who's that?" inquired Dr. Talbot. "Oh, that," replied Schlossmann, "is Old Anna. When we have done everything we can medically for a baby, and it is still not doing well, we turn it over to Old Anna, and she is always successful."

America, however, was massively under the influence of the dogmatic teachings of Luther Emmett Holt, Sr., Professor of Pediatrics at New York Polyclinic and Columbia University. Holt was the author of a booklet, *The Care and Feeding of Children,* which was first published in 1894 and was in its 15th edition in 1935. During its long reign it became the supreme household authority on the subject, the "Dr. Spock" of its time. It was in this work that the author recommended the abolition of the cradle, not picking the baby up when it cried, feeding it by the clock, and not spoiling it with too much handling, and, while breastfeeding was the regimen of choice, bottlefeeding was not discounted. In such a climate the idea of tender, loving care would have been considered quite "unscientific," so that it wasn't even mentioned, although, as we have seen, in places like the Children's Clinic in Dusseldorf, it had already received some recognition as early as the first decade of the twentieth century. It was not until after World War II, when studies were undertaken to discover the cause of marasmus, that it was found to occur quite often among babies in the "best" homes, hospitals, and institutions, among babies apparently receiving the "best" and most careful physical attention. It became apparent that babies in the poorest homes, with a good mother, despite the lack of hygienic physical conditions, often overcame the physical handicaps and flourished. What was wanting in the sterilized environment of the babies of the first class and was generously supplied to babies of the second class was mother love. Recognizing this in the late twenties, several hospital pediatricians began to introduce a regular regimen of mothering in their wards. Dr. J. Brennemann, who for a time had attended an old-fashioned foundling home where "the mortality was nearer 100 percent than 50 percent," established the rule in his hospital that every baby should be picked up, carried around, and "mothered" several times a day. At Bellevue Hospital in New York, following the institution of "mothering" on the pediatric wards, the mortality rates for infants under one year fell from 30 to 35 percent to less than 10 percent by 1938.

What the child requires if it is to prosper, it was found, is to be handled, and carried, and caressed, and cuddled, and cooed to, even if it isn't breastfed. It is the handling, the carrying, the caressing, the caregiving, and the cuddling that we would here emphasize, for it would seem that even in the absence of a great deal else, these are the reassuringly basic experiences the infant must enjoy if it is to survive in some semblance of health. Extreme sensory deprivation in other respects, such as light and sound, can be survived, as long as the sensory experiences at the skin are maintained.

Cases capable of throwing considerable light on the importance of cutaneous stimulation in the absence of other kinds of stimulation are represented by those few instances in which either the loss of such senses as vision and hearing occurred at or shortly after birth, or where the child has been kept in a dark room with a deaf-mute mother. The most dramatic instances of the first sort are the cases of Laura Bridgman and Helen Keller. Their stories are too well known to be retold here, except to draw attention to the fact that, having lost both vision and hearing, these two children were, after much effort, reached through the skin and eventually learned to embrace the whole of the human world and to communicate with it upon the highest levels entirely through the skin. Until each of these children had learned the finger alphabet—in other words, communication through the skin—they were cut off virtually completely from interactive social relations with other human beings. They were isolated, and the world in which they lived held little meaning for them; they were almost completely unsocialized. But after the patient efforts of their teachers had succeeded in enabling them to learn the finger alphabet, the world of symbolic communication was opened to them, and their development as social human beings proceeded apace.

Equally interesting is the case of Isabelle. She was an illegitimate child, and for that reason she and her mother were secluded from the rest of the mother's family in a dark room where they spent most of their time together. Born in Ohio in April 1932, Isabelle was discovered by the authorities in November 1938. She was then six and a half years of age. Lack of sunshine and poor nutrition had produced severe rickets. As a result Isabelle's legs were so bowed that when she stood erect the soles of her shoes came nearly flat together, and she moved about with a skittering gait. When found, she resembled a wild animal more than anything else, mute and idiot-like. She was at once diagnosed by a psychologist as genetically inferior.

However, a specialist in child speech, Dr. Marie K. Mason, put her through an intensive and systematic training in speech, and in spite of all prognostications to the contrary succeeded not only in teaching her to speak normally, but to achieve with speech all the usual associated abilities. In two years she covered the stages of learning that normally require six years. She did very well at school, participating normally in all school activities.

The case of Isabelle conforms to the type picture of the isolated child with malnutrition, idiocy, and muteness, who nevertheless, under intensive training, became a thoroughly normal socialized being. Malnutrition did not do any noticeable damage to the nerve cells of her brain, and her development to perfectly normal social adjustment strongly suggests that she probably received a great deal of attention from her mother, mostly of a tactile nature, during the years of their isolation together.

Today tactile programs for the improvement of the speech of the congenitally deaf hold out great promise.

Laura Bridgman and Helen Keller communicated through the sense of touch. We are told that Isabelle also communicated with her mother in this manner and by gesture. Isabelle's disabilities and her nonsocialization were entirely due to her prolonged isolation. Her ability to recover from its effects was almost certainly due to the fact that she had been adequately loved by her mother, handled, held, caressed, and fondled.

It is recorded of Frederick II (1194–1250), Emperor of Germany, in his own time called *stupor mundi,* "wonder of the world," but referred to by his enemies in less flattering terms, that

> he wanted to find out what kind of speech and what manner of speech children would have when they grew up if they spoke to no one beforehand. So he bade foster mothers and nurses to suckle the children, to bathe and wash them, but in no way to prattle with them, for he wanted to learn whether they would speak the Hebrew language, which was the oldest, or Greek, or Latin, or Arabic, or perhaps the language of their

parents, of whom they had been born. But he laboured in vain because the children all died. For they could not live without the petting and joyful faces and loving words of their foster mothers. And so the songs are called 'swaddling songs' which a woman sings while she is rocking the cradle, to put a child to sleep, and without them a child sleeps badly and has no rest.

These are the words of the thirteenth-century historian Salimbene.

"For they could not live without the petting . . ." This observation constitutes the earliest known pronouncement on the importance of cutaneous stimulation for the development of the child. Undoubtedly awareness of the value of caressing the child is much older than that.

As Dr. Harry Bakwin, among the earliest pediatricians to recognize the importance of mothering the hospital child, has written, "Most important to the young baby appear to be the skin sensations and the kinesthetic sense. Babies are readily soothed by patting and by warmth, and they cry in response to painful stimuli and to cold. The quieting effect of keeping babies outdoors may be due, in part, to the movement of the air on the skin."

The reference to warmth and to air points to some very important influences in the immediate postpartum experience of the newborn. The baby's temperature *in utero* is probably about the same as its mother's, but during the birth process and in the perinatal period the baby's temperature is somewhat higher than the mother's, varying between 97.5° and 102.0° Fahrenheit with a mean of about 100°. Temporary exposure to cold air will stimulate the baby to cry, but is in no way damaging unless the exposure to cold is prolonged. Babies respond pleasurably to warmth and with distress to cold. Neonatal cold injury can lead to death. Normally the warmth of the mother's body flowing through to the baby will comfort him, and the absence of the warmth will distress him. When, in later life, we speak of the "warmth" of a person, as compared with those who are "cold," these are not, we may suspect, mere figures of speech. As Otto Fenichel has said:

Temperature eroticism in particular is often combined with early oral eroticism and forms an essential part of primitive receptive sexuality. To have cutaneous contact with the partner and to feel the warmth of his body remains an essential component of all love relationships. In archaic forms of love, where objects serve rather as mere instruments for gaining satisfaction, this is especially marked. Intense pleasure in warmth, frequently manifested in neurotic bathing habits, is usually encountered in persons who simultaneously show other signs of a passive-receptive orientation, particularly in regard to the regulation of their self-esteem. For such persons, "to get affection" means "to get warmth." They are "frozen" personalities who "thaw" in a "warm" atmosphere, who can sit for hours in a warm bath or on a radiator.

The human newborn, even if he is born before term, has considerable ability to regulate his own temperature, but the range of thermal environment in which he remains comfortable, his range of thermal neutrality, is of lesser amplitude than in the adult, because he has the disadvantages of a relatively large surface area from which to exchange heat and a small body mass to act as a heat sink (a mass which absorbs heat). Hey and O'Connell have examined the neutral thermal zone in clothed babies, and concluded that a draught-free environment of 75° F is necessary to provide neutral thermal conditions for most cot-nursed babies in the first month of life. Brück has shown that for the newborn, whose internal heat has been overtaxed, ambient temperatures below 73–77° F will result in cooling much more quickly than in the adult.

The clothed baby is at an advantage over the naked baby. The bare face and head, and especially the face, will not only provide the important sweating areas for the dissipation of heat, when that becomes necessary, but will also serve to receive the cool air which will act as a stimulus to respiration. Glass and his co-workers have shown that blanketing symptom-free low birthweight infants not only simplifies their management, but also enhances their immediate and long-term ability to resist acute cold stress.

A source of warmth, as Dr. J. W. Scopes has remarked, not often considered in our sophisticated society is the baby's mother. Swaddling the baby against the mother's bare skin provides a warm and thermostatically controlled microclimate.

The newborn baby produces its own heat from a series of sites distributed over various parts of its body. These sites are associated with a brown adipose tissue and occur on the back between the shoulder blades, in the posterior triangle of the neck and around the muscles of the neck extending under the collar bones to the armpits, in islands around the trachea, esophagus, and the large vessels between the two lungs and the arteries accompanying the ribs and the internal mammary arteries. In the abdomen the largest collection of brown adipose tissue is situated around the adrenal glands and kidneys, with smaller masses around the aorta. Blood draining from the interscapular pad into the vertebral plexus of veins around the spinal cord may play an important role in the temperature regulation of the newborn baby.

In newborns with respiratory deficiency leading to oxygen deficiency (hypoxia) or excess carbon dioxide in the blood (hypercapnia), or who have suffered birth trauma, these conditions may contribute to the rapid development of low temperature (hypothermia). It is believed that the extra heat production of brown adipose tissue is especially vulnerable to hypoxia.

There is reason to believe that there exist two systems of temperature sensitivity, one for warmth and one for cold, and to these the newborn is particularly sensitive. Like adults, the infant tolerates high external temperatures better than he does low ones, and prefers warmth to cold, but precisely what role the early experience of differences in temperature plays in his subsequent development, except in the matter of cold injury, we do not know; we may surmise that it is not inconsiderable.

The temperature sense or senses present many complexities which are far from being well understood. The metabolic response to sudden changes in temperature can be very threat-

ening. For example, as Hey and his co-workers have shown,
while a baby may be born into a draught-free room warmed to
a temperature of 82–86° F, when an exchange transfusion is
performed under these conditions, the deep body temperature
of the baby will fall progressively unless active steps are taken
to warm the donor's blood. There is good reason to believe, as
these investigators suggest, that the use of cold blood could
precipitate circulatory collapse during exchange transfusion.
The same is often true when it is necessary to give adults a
rapid transfusion of stored blood.

Cold has a constricting effect upon the blood vessels and
also tends to slow the flow of blood, with resulting accumulation of deoxygenated blood in the capillaries, leading to cyano-
sis, that is, blueness of the skin. This is greatly affected by
temperature, being accelerated by warmth and decelerated by
cold.

The practice of bathing babies shortly after they are born
often exposes them to heat loss and cold, especially when the
cheeselike coating, the *vernix caseosa* as it is called, is removed.
The vernix caseosa is composed of sebum secreted from the
baby's own skin glands and shed epithelial cells from its skin.
In the liquid medium of the womb, this serves as an insulating
layer which protects the baby's skin from maceration. Following birth, the vernix caseosa serves as an insulation against loss
of heat and the penetration of cold. For this reason the practice
of washing away this cheeselike substance is considered undesirable by some authorities. This would be particularly true
where the surrounding temperature is less than 80° F. In general, it might be a good idea to leave this substance undisturbed
and the baby placed with the mother until she is ready to nurse
it.*

The baby's suckling pressure at the breast is lower at 90° F
than at 80° F, according to the findings of Elder on twenty-
seven full-term healthy infants. Cooke found that caloric in-

---

*Since the vernix caseosa tends to dry rapidly upon exposure to air, it
presents no particular problems.

take in infants decreased as environmental temperature increased from 80° F to 90° F, and that caloric intake increased when temperature decreased from 91° F to 80° F. Such findings suggest that the common hospital practice of heavily wrapping infants at feeding time might benefit from review.

In a study of eighteen babies over the first month of life, Peter Wolff found that temperature and humidity both have important effects on the amount of time babies sleep, and also on their behavior and crying. Babies kept at 80–90 degrees cried less and slept more than when kept at 78 degrees.

Responses to nakedness and skin contact were interesting. From the third day on, seven out of these eighteen babies began to cry when they were undressed, crying that increased in vigor over the second and third weeks. Covering them with a blanket was not enough to soothe these babies. What worked was swaddling or providing cloth contact for chest or abdomen, such as toweling and blanketing, the texture of the cloth being soft and gentling.

The obvious efforts of mothers among the mammals to keep their young warm, and broody behavior among birds sufficiently testify to the great importance of warmth for the development of the young. The strong drive of the young to huddle together in the absence of a broody or warming mother further serves to underscore the importance of a necessary condition which can best be produced in the young through body contact.

The suggestion has been made that the basic factor in changes induced by handling may be temperature. Schaefer and his co-workers, for example, found that rats whose temperature had been lowered showed the same drop in ascorbic acid in the blood as handled rats. The conclusions of these investigators have been criticized on various methodological grounds, without denying that temperature may be a variable in producing manifold effects in different animals.

The touch of a cold hand is not pleasant—the touch of a warm one is, an observation which brings us to the consideration that cutaneous sensation cannot be a matter simply of touch or pressure, but must in part be a response to temperature. Caressing with an ice-cold hand would scarcely be received by the recipient as comforting, but rather as an unpleasant, if not outright painful experience. "Cold comfort" is something less than comforting. Clearly, it is the quality of cutaneous stimulation that conveys the message, and this is made up of a complex of different factors. A sharp, painful slap conveys a very different message from a tender, gentle caress, and differences in skin pressure may make all the difference between a painful and a pleasurable sensation. It is probably in something of this manner, by the evaluation of such factors as pressure, intensity, rhythm, duration, firmness, and the like, that infants are able to discriminate between those who, when holding them, care for them and those who do not.

It is the messages the infant picks up through its own muscle-joint receptors from the manner in which it is held, rather than mere pressure on the skin, that tell the infant what the holder "feels" about it. The skin belongs to the class of organs called *exteroceptors* because they pick up sensations from outside the body. Receptors that are stimulated principally by the actions of the body itself are called *proprioceptors*. It is both through its skin and the proprioceptors that the infant receives the messages from the muscle-joint-ligament behavior of the person holding it.

The infant makes the proper discriminations in much the same way that adults do when they draw inferences about the character of a person from the quality of his handshake. At least, those individuals who have not been desensitized in their capacity to do so are able to draw such conclusions with a high degree of accuracy. Every baby is clearly born with this kinesthetic sense, and the evidence we have—experimental, observational, experiential, and anecdotal—all tends to support the view that, just as we learn to speak by being spoken to, and will speak as we have been spoken to, so we learn to respond to exteroceptive skin stimulation and proprioceptive muscle-joint stimulation largely as a function of our early experience or conditioning in these senses.

It is quite probable that something of the manner in which the individual comes to carry himself, to hold his head, his shoulders, and to move his limbs and torso, is related to his early conditioning experiences. It is well known, for example, that the anxious individual, whether infant, child, or adult, tends to rigidify his movements, to tense his muscles, to over-elevate his shoulders, and even to glare with his eyes. These conditions are not infrequently associated with pallor and dry-ness of the skin, not to mention other cutaneous disorders. In anxiety and fear states skin temperature will tend to drop, pre-sumably as a consequence of the constriction of the blood ves-sels supplying it. In embarrassment and pleasurable states the opposite effect is likely to occur; the skin temperature rises, and in blushing the enlargement of the blood vessels produces a reddening of the skin. One student of biofeedback reports that when he was listening at a scientific meeting to two participants engaged in argument, his skin temperature dropped, but re-turned to normal immediately after the arguers sat down.

Thoughts and feelings are often communicated in nonver-bal ways, through movements of the body. The study of this subject is known as *kinesics*. Kinesics is concerned with the ex-ploration of the various adjustments, without their necessarily being aware of the fact that they are making them, in which human beings are constantly engaged in relation to the pres-ence and activities of other human beings. Our leading student of kinesics, Ray L. Birdwhistell, is convinced that kinesic be-havior is learned, systematic, and analyzable. "This," he writes, "does not deny the biological base in the behavior but places the emphasis on the *interpersonal* rather than the *expressional* aspects of kinesic behavior."

It is in the interpersonal relationship with the mother, ex-teroceptively and proprioceptively, as well as *interoceptively,* especially involving the receptors of the gastrointestinal tract—and this is very important—that the child establishes its first communicative relationships. Quite probably, during this period conditioning conducive to the formation of hypertensive habits takes place. These hypertensive habits later show up in hypertensive conditions affecting the gastrointestinal tract in the form of colitis, hypermotility, ulcers, and the like, affecting the cardiovascular system in the form of psychogenic cardiovascular disturbances, affecting the respiratory system in the form of asthmatoid conditions, and, of course, affecting the skin in a large variety of disorders.

Dr. P. Lacombe has described a remarkable case of a severely neurotic female patient who manifested depressive violent behavior and neurodermatosis. The grandmother of the patient gave the latter's mother minimal tactile attention as a child, and the patient's own mother failed her in this respect also. Lacombe sees this patient's disorder as the expression of a loss of the infant-mother attachment resulting in a fixation on the mother. Loss of the mother equals loss of ego, and loss of maternal skin as point of contact reappears in the patient as weeping skin areas. The patient's pet dog also suffered from skin problems, which Lacombe interprets as due to the identification of the dog with its mistress. The ego, says Lacombe, "is the perception of the bodily self, and what one feels and knows of the body is the skin."

A striking example of specific cutaneous conditioning during the first two weeks of life, and subsequent regression to this very early age level, is illustrated by a case of trichotillomania, pathological hair pulling, reported by Dr. Philip R. Durham Seitz in a child under three years of age.

A 2½ year-old white, female child was referred for psychiatric study by a dermatologist because of scalp hair loss of one year's duration. Dermatologic examinations had failed to reveal an organic basis for the alopecia. The scalp exhibited an over-all thinning and shortness of hair, more marked on the right side.

During the initial psychiatric interview, it was observed that the child cuddled herself in the arms of her mother and sucked milk from a nursing bottle. While sucking the nipple of the nursing bottle, which was held in the left hand, she searched her scalp with the right hand for remaining hairs. When a hair or group of hairs was found, she pulled these out with a twisting motion of her fingers. The hairs were then carried in her fingers to her upper lip, where she rolled them against her lip and nose. This process was continued as long as she nursed from the bottle, but ceased promptly when the nipple was removed from her mouth. The mother pointed out that the child pulled her hair only when sucking from the nursing bottle, and that invariably sucking was accompanied by hair pulling and nose tickling. The author went to the home of this family in order to observe the child, and also observed her during play in his office. Hair pulling and nose tickling were found to occur only, and then invariably, when the child sucked milk from a nursing bottle.

Further interviews with the mother elicited the following information: The girl was the first and only child of lower middle-class parents, both of whom exhibited somewhat precarious emotional adjustments. The father was a Salvation Army musician, and both parents were devoutly religious. They had been married for five years, considered themselves entirely compatible marital partners, and had both wanted the child at the time she was conceived. However, because of the difficulty they had experienced with her, they employed contraceptives to avoid further pregnancies. The girl was born at term, delivery being uneventful. For the first two weeks the mother nursed her baby at her breast, but discontinued this abruptly during the third week because she believed her lactation to be insufficient. The child's growth and development during the first year and one-half appeared to be normal. She sat at three months, stood at seven months, walked at ten months, began to talk at eighteen months. She was weaned from the bottle when she was one year old, after which she ate solid foods and drank liquids from a cup.

When the child was eighteen months old, a punitive program of toilet training was instituted, which involved scoldings and spankings whenever she soiled herself. In retrospect, the mother realized it was following onset of this toilet training program that the child began to refuse solid foods, insist upon milk from a nursing bottle, and pull out her hair and tickle her nose while sucking. In addition, she had become difficult to manage, resisted all efforts to teach her toilet habits, and cried a great deal, would not mind, and demonstrated a desire to splash water on herself.

From observation of the child Dr. Seitz reasoned that her refusal to eat solid foods and her continued nursing from a bottle suggested an unconscious desire to return to an earlier suckling stage. Her hair pulling and nose tickling suggested that somehow she wished in some way to duplicate the original suckling situation. This raised a question: Was her nose tickled while she was at the breast? The nose tickling suggested that hair on the mother's breast might have been responsible. With this in mind the mother's breasts were examined and revealed "a ring of long, coarse hairs surrounding each nipple."

In order to test the hypothesis suggested by this association, a nipple was constructed with a ring of coarse human hairs projecting around its base. This arrangement provided an automatic tickling of the child's nose whenever the nipple was held in the mouth. When sucking at the nipple she would slowly turn the bottle, brushing the upright hairs against her nose and upper lip. Hair pulling did not occur. The automatic nose tickling apparently satisfied the need to regress to the early experience at the breast.

The importance of this fascinating case lies in its demonstration of early psychocutaneous conditioning, within the first two weeks of life. Nursed at the hairy breast of her mother for two weeks, and then abruptly withdrawn from it, this little girl attempted to reinstate the conditions at the breast by providing herself with hair from her own head with which to stroke her nose and lip while sucking at a rubber nipple at the end of a glass bottle.

"To what other neurotic traits," asks Dr. Seitz, "and psychosomatic reactions may an individual be predisposed in later life by specific cutaneous conditioning of this type? Psychocutaneous disorders of the nose? Nose picking? Hay fever, or allergic rhinitis?" These are good questions.

NOSING, NURSING, AND BREATHING. Psychocutaneous disorders of the nose should be a fertile field for exploration, but I know of no significant studies in this area. Yet it is clear from the many different ways in which people treat their noses that early conditioning may very well have played a part in determining or influencing their kinesic behavior towards this part of their anatomy. People pull at their noses, stroke them, flatten them, compress them, wrinkle them, put their bent fingers under them, place their index finger against them, scratch them, rub them, massage them, breathe heavily or lightly through them, or flare their nostrils. It would hardly be warranted to attribute all such habits to early conditioning, but there can be little doubt that in many cases such habits are in some way related to early cutaneous conditioning. The nose, it has been said, is the gateway to life and death. This, of course, refers to its respiratory functions. As we have already seen, it is probable that the proper development of the respiratory function is to some extent dependent upon the amount and kind of cutaneous stimulation the infant experiences. It is not unlikely that persons who have received inadequate cutaneous stimulation in infancy develop as shallow breathers, and become more susceptible to upper respiratory tract and pulmonary disorders than those who have received adequate cutaneous stimulation. There is some reason to believe that certain types of asthmas are, at least in part, due to a lack of early tactile stimulation.

There is a high incidence of asthma among persons who as young children were separated from their mothers. Putting one's arm around an asthmatic while he is having an attack may abort or alleviate it.

Margaret Ribble has pointed out the importance of tactile experience in breathing.

Respiration [she writes], which is characteristically shallow, unstable and inadequate in the first weeks after birth is definitely stimulated reflexly through sucking and through physical contact with the mother. Infants who do not suck vigorously do not breathe deeply and those who are not held in the arms sufficiently, particularly if they are bottle-fed babies, in addition to breathing disturbances often develop gastrointestinal disorders. They become air-swallowers and develop what is popularly known as colic. They have trouble with elimination or they may vomit. It seems that the tone of the gastrointestinal tract in this early period depends in some special way on reflex stimulation from the periphery. Thus, the touch of the mother has a definite biological implication in the regulation of the breathing and nutritive functions of the child.

Forty-four years after this passage was written, wholly unaware of it, Dr. Bruce Taubman, a pediatrician in private practice in Philadelphia, hypothesized that continuous crying in the colicky baby occurs when parents inadvertently fail to respond to the baby's needs. This suggested to him that the amount of crying might be reduced by helping the parents develop a more appropriate reponse to their infants. The experimental group of mothers were counseled not to let their babies cry whenever they could, to pick them up, hold them, and feed them on demand or whenever they wished to "suck." Infants so handled showed a 70 percent decrease in the amount of crying compared to the untreated colicky infants, who showed no decrease in crying, and cried 2½ times as much as normal control infants.

Colic is described as a troublesome condition of unknown cause which affects many infants, usually under three months of age. The manner of crying is frequently suggestive of abdominal pain, often associated with gas. Whatever the cause it would seem that Taubman's observations tend to confirm Ribble's statement that "the tone of the gastrointestinal tract in this early period depends in some special way on reflex stimulation from the periphery," and that "the touch of the mother has a definite biological implication in the regulation of the breathing and nutritive functions of the child."

To continue with the subject of breathing for a moment,

before returning to the nose through which that breathing mainly takes place, it has already been pointed out that immediately following upon exposure to atmospheric air, the newborn's previously unexpanded lungs fill with air and the various changes in pressure which occur at the moment of birth help to initiate the postnatal type of respiratory movements that continue throughout the life of the person. The need to breathe is so compelling that a three-minute denial of it is often sufficient to cause death. The urge to breathe is the most imperative of all man's basic urges, and the most automatic. The process of learning to breathe is an anxious one. Every breath we take, even as adults, is preceded by a faint phobic stir. Under conditions of stress many persons go into labored breathing reminiscent of breathing at birth. Under such conditions the person often regresses to fetalized activities and assumes fetal positions. In fear or anxiety one of the first functions to be affected is breathing. Yet, in spite of its automaticity, breathing or respiration is under voluntary control and under conscious control for short periods of time, as any person who has ever taken singing lessons knows, and for very durable periods of time, as every Yogi knows. This control is actually exerted during the ordinary activities of everyday life, such as speaking, swallowing, laughing, blowing, coughing, and sucking. Breathing, indeed, is not simply a physiological process, but a part of the way in which an organism behaves.

That many of the elements of breathing are learned is evident from the fact that there are significant class differences in the manner of breathing. Heavy or stertorous breathing, like noisy soup- or coffee-sipping, occurs very much more frequently among members of the lower classes than among members of the upper classes. Differences in the rate of breathing and oxygen-combining capacity of the lungs, as Dill has shown, are closely correlated with occupational status. Inadequate, shallow breathing, associated with chronic feelings of fatigue in later life, as compared with healthy deep breathing, are also for the most part learned habits, and may well have some connection with early cutaneous experiences.

To return to the nose: It could be that the various forms of handling the nose in later life, including nose picking, may be related to early experiences in the feeding situation, especially the breastfeeding situation. In nursing at the breast the baby's nose is frequently in contact with the mother's breast, and it is quite possible that the rhinal experiences there enjoyed or unenjoyed may have something to do with these various later manipulations of the nose. Most monkeys and apes pick their noses, and often eat the debris they remove therefrom. Some small children do likewise, and even adults have been known to do so. The association of picking one's nose and eating in such cases suggests the possibility of some form of early conditioning, and that nose picking alone may be a form of self-gratification regressive to such an early period of experience. "The private life is above everything ... just sitting at home and even picking your nose, and looking at the sunset," wrote V. V. Rozanov, the Russian writer.

Allowing for the fact that most people carry bacteria of various sorts in their noses and that these are often irritating, and therefore induce a great deal of handling of the nose, nevertheless nose handling and especially nose picking can scarcely be altogether attributed to pruriginous bacteria. It would be a matter well worth further investigation.

As the prominent peninsula it is, the nose affords a convenient piece of the main upon which to make a landfall with one's hand, and to which one can cling stroking or otherwise manipulating it with that reassured feeling that comes from being able to establish contact, even though it be only with oneself. The nose seems to be a particularly favored part of the body, for purposes of reassurance. We often recognize this kind of manipulation as a nervous gesture in others without being conscious of it in ourselves.

Why should "making a nose at" or "thumbing one's nose at" another be regarded as gestures of disdain?

From fish to humans the oral region is the earliest part of the body to become sensitive to cutaneous stimulation. The lips are established as erogenous zones, that is, as pleasure-giving structures, long before the baby is born. Fetuses at five months and earlier have been observed in the womb sucking their thumbs. The experience at the breast or the bottle, very different as it is in each case, further reinforces the erogenicity of the lips. Suckling is the major activity of the baby during the first year of his life, and his lips, presenting the externally furled extension of mucous membrane that lines his mouth, constitute the instruments with which he makes his first most sensitive contacts, and incorporates so much that is vital to him of the external world. It is therefore not surprising that the lips should be more fully supplied with sensory nerve endings than any other part of the body, with the possible exception of the fingertips. Indeed, the representation of the lips in the brain exceeds that devoted to sensory inputs from the entire torso. Lips, mouth, tongue, the sense of smell, vision, and hearing, are all intimately bound up with each other and the experience of suckling. If it is at the breast, it constitutes suckling; if it is at the rubber nipple of a bottle, it is sucking—two very different kinds of experiences. Research findings are sometimes contradictory concerning the advantages of breastfeeding as compared with bottlefeeding and the effects of each kind of regimen upon subsequent behavior. What is, however, quite clear is that it is not alone the type of feeding that is important for subsequent behavior, but also the overall behavior of the mother during the feeding. Cold mothers who breastfeed do not do as well in influencing the later behavior of their children as warm mothers who bottlefeed. Such, for example, were the findings in a study conducted by Dr. Martin I. Heinstein on some 252 Berkeley, California, children.

As we have already had occasion to see, the infant very quickly responds to the mother's behavior towards it, and what is most important to its own behavioral development is not so much the material with which it is fed, as the manner in which it is fed. It is precisely this kind of experience that will be picked up by the skin and the specialized mucous membranous structure we call the lips. Whether children who have had cold mothers or inadequate nursing will seek further gratification in lip stimulation, and will exhibit more of it than those who have had warm mothers and have been adequately nursed, is a question for which I know of no research answers. The variability in this, as in other matters, is undoubtedly considerable and probably quite complex. Many children do spend a great deal of time manipulating their lips with their fingers, often while making a humming-murmuring sound to accompany the manually stimulated lip movements. They obviously enjoy doing this. I suggest that in thumb-sucking or finger-sucking it is not simply the sucking that is gratifying, but that a certain amount of satisfaction is also obtained from the stimulation of the lips. The hand of the baby often rests on its mother's breast during suckling or upon the bottle during artificial feeding; the baby's eyes follow every movement of its mother's eyes and face, and it grows accustomed, as well, to the sounds that both she and it make in the nursing situation. It is not difficult to understand how all these factors become closely integrated in a developing neuropsychic complex. Hence, when in later life the individual becomes a victim of the smoking habit, he may, again at least in part, be conjectured to have become so addicted as a regression to the complex of similar pleasures he experienced during the earliest period of his life. The sucking, the lip stimulation, the handling of the cigarette, cigar, or pipe, the pleasure of blowing and seeing the smoke, of inhaling it, of smelling and tasting it, is all very gratifying—even though the long-term effects may be lethal. Part of the pleasure of chewing gum is probably derived from the constant oral-lip stimulation.

Many writers on the subject have considered that the early experiences at the lips and mouth constitute the gateway to much of our understanding of later developments. The distinguished American psychologist G. Stanley Hall believed the first center of psychic life to be the mouth and the sense of taste, accompanied by a "tactile pleasure truly aesthetic which arises from bringing smooth things to the lips and hard things to the toothless gums."

Freud makes the activity of the infant's lips at the breast a foundation stone of his theory of sexuality. He writes:

It was a child's first and most vital activity, his sucking at his mother's breast, or at substitutes for it, that must have familiarized him with this pleasure [of rhythmic sucking]. The child's lips ... behave like an erotogenic zone, and no doubt stimulation by the warm flow of milk is the cause of the pleasurable sensation. The satisfaction of the erotogenic zone is associated, in the first instance, with the satisfaction of the need for nourishment. ... No one who has seen a baby sinking back satiated from the breast and falling asleep with flushed cheeks and a blissful smile can escape the reflection that this picture persists as a prototype of the expression of sexual satisfaction in later life. The need for repeating the sexual satisfaction now becomes detached from the need for taking nourishment—a separation which becomes inevitable when the teeth appear and food is no longer taken by sucking. ...

Though much that has been attributed to the oral phase of development has not been adequately investigated, there can be not the least doubt of the existence of a profound relationship between oral experiences in infancy and later sexual competencies. Nor can there be any doubt of the intimate connection between the skin and all its appendages, including hair, glands, neural elements, and sexual behavior. A French wit has remarked that love is the harmony of two souls and the contact of two epidermes.* And indeed, it is in the sexual act that, next to the perinatal experience of labor, the individual experiences his most massive cutaneous stimulations, with the lips and tongue and mouth usually actively involved. Nor can there be any doubt that eating and love become closely interwoven in such a manner that in later life eating often becomes a substitute satisfaction for love, obesity frequently constituting an evidence of a failure to obtain love. The offering of food is often more than a perfunctory evidence of the tendering of love.

* A variation of Chamfort's "Love as it exists in society is merely the mingling of two fantasies and the contact of two skins." S. R. N. Chamfort, *Products of the Perfected Civilization* (New York: Macmillan, 1969), p. 170.

Gorillas and chimpanzees will take food between their lips and offer it to their infants directly. Two-year-olds beg their mothers for food by presenting their pursed lips to them; the mothers will then gently push the food directly into the young ones' mouths. In addition, chimp mothers gently press their lips into various parts of their infants' bodies, up to the end of the first year. An infant's hand will be taken and the palm touched with the lips. The lips remain close to the teeth with the mouth open. Adults touch each other in the same way, pressing their lips to an arm or shoulder, at times to their own hands. A worried child touches its mother in this way, or even an adult male chimp while he is copulating. In this way the kiss of greeting among chimpanzees could have originated from the rather groping contact of the lips.

Mouth-to-mouth feeding of infants is very common among indigenous peoples. It is, therefore, not difficult to see how touching with the lips as a demonstration of affection may have been reinforced among humans.

The psychoanalyst Sandor Rado has suggested that an important element in early sucking lies in the achievement of a pleasant feeling of satiety and a diffuse feeling of sensual pleasure in which the whole organism participates, and he describes this as an "alimentary orgasm."

That the mother experiences something akin to sexual stimulation by the baby's suckling is well known, and that the baby experiences sensations which, endowed with meanings, later become perceptions of something resembling sexual gratification, is highly probable. We have already noted that inadequate mothering may seriously affect the subsequent sexual behavior of the offspring. The Harlows, to whom we owe this observation, have also shown that while rhesus monkeys raised by live mothers were more advanced in social and sexual behavior than those raised by surrogate mothers constructed of terry-cloth-covered wire, the surrogate-raised infants developed perfectly normal social and sexual behavior if they were permitted each day to play in the stimulating environment of other infant monkeys. The Harlows rightly pointed out that the

role played by infant-infant relationships as determiners of adolescent and adult adjustments should not be underestimated.
It is more than possible, the Harlows suggest, that the infant-
infant affectional system "is essential if the animal is to respond positively to sheer physical contact with a peer, and it is
through the operation of this system, probably both in monkey
and man, that sexual roles become identified and, usually, acceptable."

It is indeed possible, even probable, as the Harlows suggest, that infant-infant contacts are necessary for the full development of social and sexual competence, but that, in the
absence of any kind of mother at all, such behavior would,
even in the presence of other-infant contacts, not develop as
well as in mothered infants. Certainly it is clear that, in
humans, good mothering without peer contacts has not
seriously detrimentally affected the social and sexual development of innumerable individuals. Indeed, there exists an extensive literature showing how enormously important the
mother's behavior is for her infant's subsequent social and sexual development. We may be reasonably sure, when all the
evidence is in, that however valuable the infant-infant affectional relation may prove to be, it will never equal the influence of the affectional relationship that exists between the
nursing couple, always with the understanding that the mother
is genuinely affectionate. There can be little doubt that peer interaction in the social growth and development of the child is
of considerable importance, for it is in the give and take between peers that children try out and learn many of the modu-
lations of interpersonal behavior.

As Yarrow, in an excellent survey of the evidence, puts it,
"The mother as a social stimulus provides sensory stimulations
to the infant through tactile, visual, and auditory media, i.e.,
through handling, cuddling, talking and playing with the child,
as well as by simply being visually present." Deprivation of
such sensory stimulations from the mother are serious in their
effects.

There is a clear relation between a lack of touching in infancy and childhood and the awkwardness and roughness in "play" that characterizes such individuals in childhood and in later life—individuals who are unable to establish contact without colliding.

It is in the region surrounding the mouth that the human embryo first responds to tactile stimulation. It is not surprising, therefore, to find that the first communications with the outside world are established by the infant through the lips, and this very gradually. It has been shown that stimulation of the newborn in the lip region triggers the oral orientation reflex—that is, opening of the mouth and rotation of the head in the direction of the stimulus. This will occur when only one lip is unilaterally stimulated. When both lips are simultaneously stimulated the grasping or prehension of the stimulus will occur, the orienting rotation ceases, and the suckling movements begin. This stimulus is normally the nipple and then the areola of the mother's breast. This rooting, as it is known—that is, digging with the nose and mouth to find the breast—will occur thereafter whenever the baby is brought into contact with the mother's body or anything resembling the breast. These two reflex activities, oral orientation and lip grasping, are two distinct stages in the development of rooting behavior. The integration of these two reflexes into "oral grasping" in suckling represents one of the first developmental advances made by the newborn toward grasping the world, in general as well as in particular. In other terms, these two reflexes are known as the *searching pattern* on the one hand, and the *orienting* or *suckling pattern* on the other. The clinging behavior of the lips around the nipple and areola, and later the kneading, clinging, and resting of hands and fingers on the breast, represent, as Spitz has pointed out, the precursors and prototypes of object relations.

Rooting, or the *rooting reflex,* as it is usually defined—namely, head-turning and mouth movements in an infant when the cheek or mouth region is touched, and possibly also in response to the odor of the mother's breast—will do well enough, if it is remembered that developmentally rooting consists of two reflexes, the *oral orientation reflex* and the *pre-hension of the stimulus* by the lips.

There is one very important consequence that follows from our understanding of the rooting reflex, and it is the error often made in initiating breastfeeding. As Aldrich long ago (1942) pointed out, when the hand of the mother or nurse is placed on the infant's cheek, and the head is pushed toward the breast, the baby tries to turn his head toward the pressing hand instead of the breast. As a result, it is erroneously concluded that the baby is averse to the breast. Instead of the hand, the baby's cheek should be allowed to touch the breast. Drugs given the mother during parturition may wholly abolish the rooting reflex for three or four days after birth.

"To smack one's lips" represents an old expression for satisfaction. It is interesting that lip smacking should be used by mother baboons to pacify their young as well as others. "The mother," writes Irven DeVore, "makes almost no sound except that resulting from soft lip smacking as she grooms her infant. Lip smacking, initiated at birth by the mother, is one of the most frequent and important of all baboon gestures. For both sexes at all ages this gesture serves to reduce tension and promote tranquility in social interactions." Ordinarily the direct approach of an adult male is very frightening to other members of the troop; it is therefore of great interest to observe that when an adult male approaches an infant who is with its mother, he will do so with vigorous lip smacking. To call the infant, who may have climbed a tree, the mother will stare intently in its direction and smack her lips loudly.

Human mothers will often make pacifying sounds to their babies in similar ways or by pursing their lips and producing a variety of sounds. Babies almost invariably respond with pleasure to such pacifying sounds. Making such sounds to babies, especially soft lip-sucking ones, constitutes one of the most effective means of inducing them to laugh through their tears, even to the point of hiccups. At six weeks or even earlier an infant's attention will be immediately arrested by such sounds, and in the absence of all else will exercise a tranquilizing effect upon him. This strongly suggests that the infant identifies the sounds and the lips from which they emerge with pleasurable experiences.

The mother's caressing, comforting, and bestowal of affection through kisses with the lips constitute experiences in which the infant is repeatedly conditioned. By the age of two the average child will have learned to hug and kiss. Failure to do so, according to Sally Provence of the Yale Child Study Center, may be a symptom which requires further investigation. Delay in kissing, in her experience, may indicate a neurological problem that interferes with the use of facial muscles, or it may indicate a disorder such as autism, characterized by a lack of self-awareness, or it may simply indicate a lack of affection at home. But not all well-nurtured children are kissing bugs. Each individual has his own style of showing affection, and in early childhood, Provence points out, many children play hard to get. "The only real question is whether the child understands kissing as a means of communication. When he chooses to, can he?"

Raven Lang's observation that mothers usually speak to their babies in a high-pitched voice has drawn attention to the fact that babies prefer sounds in the high-frequency range, and female voices to those of males.

TOUCHING AND FEELING. The baby's rooting behavior is exploratory, scanning, and has for its purpose and consummation the finding and engaging of the nipple and areola between the lips. While rooting will soon be abandoned for visual scanning, the rooting is nonetheless important in that it constitutes, among other things, a reverification and a reaffirmation of the existence of a pleasure-giving other, pleasure-giving by virtue of nothing more than the other's existence, her tangibility. Her tangibility is the ultimate reassurance, for in the final analysis we do not believe in the reality of anything unless we can touch it; we must have *tangible* evidence. Even faith rests ultimately upon a belief in the *substance* of things to come or of past events experienced. What we perceive through the other senses as reality we actually take to be nothing more than a good hypothesis, subject to the confirmation of touch. Observe how often people will respond to a sign reading "Wet Paint." Quite frequently they will approach and test the surface with their fingers for themselves. The sign acts upon them as a signal to touch, to verify. As the old saying has it, "Seeing is believing, but feeling is the truth." In art galleries I have, on occasion, observed a woman approach a painting, gaze at it, and then pass her fingers over a part of it, as if to get its tactile import.

Seeing is a form of touching at a distance, but touching provides the verification and confirmation of reality. That is the reason why eye *contact* is the perfect example of touching at a distance. Depending upon the context of the situation, touching any person with the eyes is considered an affront or as a declaration of interest. Rubbing one's eyes in disbelief—as if the rubbing were done in order *palpably* to verify that what one is seeing is in fact so is a not uncommon experience. The rubbing with one's fingers of one's closed eyes (the "palpebrae"), metaphorically and physically removes the film that may be over one's eyes, and at the same time proves that one's eyes are still there and are seeing what they see—palpably.

Touch attests to "objective reality" in the sense of something outside that is not myself. As Walter Ong has written, "And yet, by the very fact that it attests the not-me more than any other sense, touch involves my own subjectivity more than any other sense. When I feel this objective something 'out there,' beyond the bounds of my body, I also at the same instant experience my own self. I feel other and self simultaneously." Dr. Abraham Levitsky has pointed out that by its very nature, "touch is close and sight is far. We permit contact with those things and people we trust and enjoy. We withdraw from contact with what we don't trust and what we fear."

Withdrawing from what we do not trust and from the things we fear reminds us that the dark often possesses a tangibility and an eeriness which the light never has. The very idea of a ghost or a monster during daylight is laughable, but with the loss of contact that ensues with darkness the world becomes the scene of possible improbabilities. The ghosts we deride in daylight provoke our skins to creep at night. The imagination renders the intangible tangible, and we draw the bedclothes over us to keep the phantoms out.

As further evidence of touch in communication and verification is the observation repeatedly made of monkeys and apes who, when confronted with the image of themselves in a mirror, touch, stroke, or kiss the reflection, and then reach around the mirror in order to touch the creature they believe to be behind it. Robert Yerkes remarks on this in connection with his observation of Congo, a female gorilla: "Peculiarly significant is the gorilla's tactual exploration and search where visual might have been expected to predominate. Important also are the degree of her persistence in examining the mirror image and trying to locate its original, and her utter unwillingness to let the mirror go." Since Yerkes' report there have been many similar ones on the great apes and monkeys.

"It is clear," observes Ortega y Gasset, "that the decisive form of our intercourse with things is in fact touch. And if this is so, touch and contact are necessarily the most conclusive factor in determining the structure of our world." And Ortega goes on to point out that touch differs from all the other senses in that it always involves the presence, at once and inseparably, of the body that we touch and our body with which we touch it. Unlike vision or hearing, in contact we feel things inside us, inside our bodies. In tasting and smelling the experiences are limited to the surfaces of the nasal cavity and palate. Thus, it comes about that our world is composed of presences, of things that are bodies. And this they are because they come into contact with the closest of all things to us, to the "I" that each of us is, namely, our body.

From the tangible evidence of the mother's body, the clinging of the lips, of hands and fingers to the breast, with the world at his fingertips in a very real sense, the infant will develop an awareness of his own and his mother's body which will constitute his first object relations. And what cannot be too often emphasized here is that, while much else is involved, it is through the primacy of the skin in his experience that the infant gropes his way to this establishment of object relations.

It is in large part the stimulation of his skin by touch which enables the child to emerge from his own skin. Those who have been failed in such stimulation remain, as it were, imprisoned within their skin, and then act as if the skin were a barrier that shuts them in, and being touched becomes for them an assault upon their integrity.

Around suckling, as the cutaneous or tactile composite of experiences, the earliest perceptions are organized. As Ribble has remarked, "As a result of mothering the child gradually combines and coordinates sucking, or food intake, with sense intake—looking, listening, and grasping—and thus a fairly complicated behavior complex is established." Movements of the lips upon the mother's breast, the developing scanning of her face and eyes, hand and finger movements in relation to the mother's body, the feeling tone associated with these experiences, enable the infant to establish in its mind a code by means of which it can reconstitute and reduplicate all these and the associated experiences, and by making the proper signals, as figure upon the ground of the maternal body, evoke the appropriate responses. What it has learned by the exploration of the mother's body, through skin, lips, tongue, hands, and eyes, the infant utilizes as a basis for further learning about its own body, exploring it mostly with its hands. Indeed, the earliest strivings toward the reintegration of self are commenced through the oral experiences at the mother's breast. In these the tongue plays a prominent role, for the tongue is a significant tactile organ; in addition the newborn is as capable as the adult of clear-cut taste discriminations.

What is the meaning of sticking one's tongue out at another as a gesture of defiance? Can it be a signal of disappointed rejection, meaning "I don't love you," or "I don't care for you," the very opposite of the feelings enjoyed through one's tongue at one's mother's breast? Oral-genital contacts, however, would seem to replicate the breastfeeding experience.

It is of interest to note that in the brain the area devoted to the lips, on the central gyrus of the cortex, is disproportionately large by comparison with that devoted to other related structures. (See Figure 1.) This is equally true of each of the four fingers and the thumb, which brings us to the consideration of the hand and fingers in the development of the sense of touch. The very phrase "the sense of touch" has come to mean, almost exclusively, feeling with the fingers or hand. Indeed, when one considers the various ways in which the word "touch" is employed in speech, it becomes apparent that the variety of meanings are for the most part extensions of the meaning "to touch with the hand or a finger or fingers."

The evolution of the hand as a sensorimotor organ in the primates, the order of mammals to which humankind belongs, has played a major role in the success of that group of about 150 living species. This is especially true of humankind. As one surveys the order from lorises, lemurs, monkeys of the New and Old World, through the apes to humankind, we perceive an increasing capacity to manipulate, explore, and differentiate by touch objects and surfaces that are within reach.

The philosopher Immanuel Kant (1724–1804) called the hand the human outer brain, and the psychologist G. Revesz noted that the hand is frequently more intelligent and endowed with greater creative energy than the head. Among animals, he further noted, there appears to be some correlation between mental ability and manual dexterity. In humans, he observed, there was a clear reciprocal relationship between the hand and the development of the intellect. "The working hand," he said, "is the tool of the eye." The hand, he added, represents the symbol and model of all our important tools. Similar ideas had already been expressed by Sir Charles Bell (1774–1842), the great physiologist and anatomist, in his Bridgewater treatise on *The Hand.* I think it was Frederic Wood Jones who, in 1920, in his superb work on the hand, first drew attention to the hand as an organ.

As the instrument of touch, the hand is by far the most informative of all our organs, with the possible exception, *on oc-*

casion, of the brain. Interestingly enough, when one consults a dictionary for the various meanings of the word, one finds that the entry under "touch" is likely to represent the most extensive in the volume. It is by far the longest entry—fourteen full columns—in the magnificent *Oxford English Dictionary.* This in itself constitutes some sort of testimony to the influence which the tactile experience of hand and fingers has had upon our imagery and our speech.

Originally derived from the Old French *touche,* the word is defined by the *Oxford English Dictionary* as "the action or an act of touching (with the hand, finger, or other part of the body); exercise of the faculty of feeling upon a material object." *Touching* is defined as "the action, or an act, of feeling something with the hand, etc." The operative word is *feeling.* Although touch is not itself an emotion, its sensory elements induce those neural, glandular, muscular, and mental changes which in combination we call an emotion. Hence touch is not experienced as a simple physical modality, as sensation, but affectively, as emotion. When we speak of being touched, especially by some act of beauty or sympathy, it is the state of being emotionally moved that we wish to describe. And when we describe someone as being "touched to the quick," it is another kind of emotion that we have in mind. The verb "to touch" comes to mean to be sensitive to human feeling. To be "touchy" means to be oversensitive. "To keep in touch" means that however far we may be removed we remain in communication. That is what language was originally designed to do, to put and to keep human in touch with human. The experiences the infant undergoes in contact with his mother's body constitute his primary and basic means of communication, his first language, his first entering into touch with another human being, the genesis of "the human touch."

Of "touch" the *Oxford English Dictionary* says that it is "the most general of the bodily senses, diffused through all parts of the skin, but (in man) specially developed in the tips of the fingers and the lips." It is through the lips that the infant grasps reality, as well as the body-building substances that he ingests. It is for a time the only means of judgment the infant has. That is why, as soon as he is able, he puts things to his lips in order to judge them, and continues to do so long after he has arrived at other means of perception and judgment. The other means of perception and judgment at which the infant ultimately arrives are through the tips of his fingers and the palms of the hand, a hand that has rested upon the mother's palpably and recurringly reassuring breast. At birth none of the infant's senses are as well developed as the sense of touch. While all his senses are operative and play an increasingly significant role in his perception and communication with the external world, especially with the mother, none are as basic as touch. It is the sense of touch upon which the infant depends: lips, and generalized body contact, and then fingertips to whole hand.

The beginning development of self commences with the responses to the conditions of life which the infant experiences. When, as he does, he takes action at the breast to get what he wants, this constitutes a decisively critical experience in his development. He feels encouraged to act on his own, knowing that he will continue to reach his goal with the encouragement of the (m)other. As Bruno Bettelheim has pointed out, it is for this reason so potentially destructive to schedule feedings by the clock, not merely because they mechanize and routinize the experience of feeding, but because they deprive the infant of the feeling that it was his own signals that resulted in the satisfaction of his hunger. Disregard of his signals discourages, and he tends to lose the impulse to develop the mental and emotional techniques for handling the environment, and thus for the adequate development of self and personality. The signal, the gesture, the communication that goes unanswered at any age can be a painful experience. At an early age it is especially so, and may result in a virtually complete cessation of the attempt to communicate.

The baby who is adequately satisfied receives the feeling that the world is his for the asking. At the breast the world is at his fingertips, and while it may be an exaggeration to say, as Bettelheim does, that all his later ability to do things on his own may be the consequence of this early conviction, it is probably near enough, for all practical purposes, to the truth. Reva Rubin, chairman of the department of obstetrical nursing at the University of Pittsburgh, found a definite progression and an orderly sequence in the nature and amount of contact a mother makes with her baby. She found that from small areas of contact the mother gradually moves to more extensive ones, at first using only her fingertips, then her hands including palms, and then much later her arms as an extension of her whole body.

> The initial contacts made by the mother with her child are exploratory in nature. Fingertips are used also, but somewhat stiffly. This is not necessarily a graceless gesture. At this point, the mother will usually run one fingertip over the baby's hair, rather than her hand, to discover that his hair is silky. She will trace his profile and contours with her fingertip. If she turns his head toward food, she uses her fingertips; if she has to support his head in bathing, she uses the index finger and thumb (no palm); if she has to turn him over, she seems to contact parts of him with her fingertips. She does use her arms and her hands to passively receive him, but her arms are not active participators in touch at this stage. Later, her arms will hold firmly, but just now she carries the baby as though he were a bouquet of flowers, in arms held so stiffly that she becomes fatigued.

In fingertip exploration, Reva Rubin points out, involvement is tenuous. As in courtship, in making contact one is not sure how one will be received. This is true in the courtship stage of tentative advances, before the hand-holding stage of reciprocal confidence and commitment has been established. In maternal touch, the fingertip stage precedes that of commitment.

Commitment seems to await some personally evocative response of the infant. Sometimes it is a burp, more often it is the particular way he cuddles or, still more often, the way he expresses unbounded pleasure (three months later). This response must come from the baby, no one else, if the sense of partnership, of mutuality, in this kind of relationship is to progress. The particular sign that satisfies the mother's requirements may vary. It should also be pointed out that she is very vulnerable at this time to signs of rejection. But if the young mother has an essentially strong ego, she will search out, somewhat optimistically, positive signs of mutuality for a progressive relationship.

The next stage of maternal touch arrives gradually and is superimposed on the earlier stage. The whole hand is now used for maximal contact with the infant's body. The mother is more likely to support the infant's buttocks with the palm of her hand. The hand on its back will be in full contact with it. Both hands will be relaxed and comfortable, coinciding with her feeling about her child, a message which the baby receives with the sense of security that is thus conveyed to it as its responsiveness to her firm comforting support creates a feeling it obtains through touch and the interoceptive sensations it experiences in this feedback relationship.

It is sometime between the third and fifth days that the mother will advance from fingertips to the whole cupped hand to stroke her baby's head. Her own body language progresses gradually from bathing its anogenital region at fingertip distance—that is, from the exploratory information-seeking phase to that of a more intimate involvement in the use of her whole hand.

Recalling here our discussion of cutaneous stimulation in mammals in the perinatal period as contributing to the improved maternal abilities of nonhuman mammals (pp. 30–31), Reva Rubin's remarks, following, are of the greatest interest.

Mothers who have had a very recent experience of appropriate and meaningful bodily touch from a ministering person, as during labor, delivery, or the postpartum period, use their own hands more effectively. This is true of both . . . firsttime mothers and . . . mothers who have had more than one child. Conversely, if the mother's most recent experiences of contact in relation to her own body have been of a remote and impersonal nature, she seems to stay longer at this stage in her own activities with the baby.

These are most important observations, which should lead us to consider seriously whether it would not be a good idea to institute the practice of regular body caressing by the husband of his wife during pregnancy, labor, and after the birth of the baby. On purely theoretical grounds this would appear to be advisable. We have in addition the experimental evidence and the backing of such observations as Reva Rubin's to suggest not only that such stimulation should be given by the husband to his wife, but that this might become standard obstetrical practice.

At a round-table meeting held in October 1974, Ms. Raven Lang, lay midwife from Vancouver, said that she teaches the husbands of pregnant women during delivery to massage the mother's perineum. This method she has found very effective in avoiding perineal tearing and the need for episiotomies.

In parenthesis it is interesting to learn what young nursing students think of touching the skin of pregnant women. Reva Rubin tells us that in most cases the students felt that touching the body of another constituted an intrusion into areas that were not to be violated. Their inability to time the contractions of the mother in labor was due to their reluctance to apply more than their fingertips to the mother's abdomen. Nothing that the women in labor themselves or their instructors tried helped thaw the students' hands, which were, according to Professor Rubin, "stiff, awkward, cold, and useless." Skin, the students told her, is a strange thing; "it is soft and rubbery; smooth and firm like marble, only warm."

But with unhampered growth and experience beginning nurses, like beginning mothers, will develop their skills of gathering information through touch as a means of discriminating diagnosis and a vehicle of personally meaningful communication.

They will be able to read and recognize, through touch, the amount of body heat produced by a local or general body task; the kinds of perspiration produced by physical or psychological work. They will discern skin textures and recognize change, favorable or unfavorable. They will recognize another's appeal for contact, controls, or guidance, and be able to provide appropriate dosages for touch for each of these. And since touch is always individualized, the interpersonal communications effected through touch will tend to be significant in a way that verbal language cannot achieve.

Klaus and his co-workers studied maternal behavior in twelve normal mothers at the first postnatal contact with their normal full-term undressed infants one half hour to thirteen and a half hours after birth, and in nine other mothers during their first three tactile contacts with their premature infants. An orderly progression was observed in the mothers of full-term infants. They commenced with fingertip touching of the infants' extremities and proceeded in four to eight minutes to massaging, and encompassing palm contact on the trunk. The rapid progression from fingertip to palm-encompassing contact within a period of ten minutes does not quite agree with Rubin's observation to the effect that palm and close contact develop only after several days. In the first three minutes fingertip contact was 52 percent, with 28 percent palm contact. In the last three minutes of observation fingertip contact decreased to 26 percent and palm contact increased to 62 percent. An intense interest in eye-to-eye contact was observed at first contact.

The mothers of normal infants permitted to touch them in the first three to five days of life followed a similar sequence, but at a much slower rate.

Dr. H. Papoušek has stated that mothers who did not want their pregnancy, touch more and longer with the fingertips, and this correlates with the amount of crying in their babies. In wanted pregnancies the mothers choose more palm contact and the babies are calmer in the first days.

The observations of Rubin, Klaus, Kennell, and others suggest that there exists a species-specific behavior in human mothers at first contact with their infants. "Because this period of life appears so critical," write Klaus et al., "modern social and hospital practices which now separate the mother from her sick or premature infant for prolonged periods require a very thorough re-evaluation." Indeed, while some progress has been made such reevaluation is long overdue, for the evidence now available renders it clear that separation is damaging to the premature and full-term infant as well as to the mother. Such separations have long-lasting effects.

There is now abundant evidence that premature babies do much better when their mothers are allowed to handle them, after proper instruction in handwashing, masking, and gowning. Barnett and his co-workers at the Stanford University School of Medicine encouraged forty-one mothers to handle their premature infants at any time of the day or night, with considerable benefit to everyone involved: infants, mothers, nurses, and doctors. There was no increase in the much-feared infections and no complications of any sort. Similar observations have been made by other observers. In commenting upon these findings, an editorial in the *British Medical Journal* (June 6, 1970) observes:

> It may well be that the immediate postpartum period is the most important time for the initial contact between mother and child, as it is in animals. Many (but certainly not all) mothers feel the urge to have skin contact with the baby immediately he has been born; they think that it is important that they should be fully conscious, and not under an anaesthetic at the time of delivery; and they want to put the baby to the breast immediately.

The editorial then proceeds to make the following incredible comments:

> No one has proved that it is desirable for the mother or the premature baby that this close contact should be established immediately after birth or later during the period in hospital or that absence of contact does any harm. One cannot prove everything, and not everything is worth trying to prove. Great

expenditure of time and effort may go into trying to prove something for the sake of proving it: something which, though important in itself, is not worth trying to prove, perhaps because the answer seems obvious. There are occasions when one has to make medical decisions on the basis of common sense and on what seems natural and normal.

Enlightening in this connection is a report, published in 1975, on 614 drug-induced labors, all of which were unnecessary, and most of which resulted in untoward effects either upon infant or mother or both. Sheila Kitzinger, who wrote the report, states:

> It was not only the sight or sound of the baby, but physical contact, which was a clear signal in the bonding that took place between mother and neonate, and which in those accounts which described the meeting-through-touch of mother and baby obviously initiated a rush of feeling. A mother who had had a cesarian section woke up to find the baby waiting to be put in her arms, and holding her baby, "washed him in tears of joy." Another woman said, "I didn't feel any emotion when I first saw Catherine lifted out and heard her cry, but as soon as they gave her to me to hold a few seconds later I thought she was fantastic." The mothers themselves often wanted touch most of all: "I did so want to cuddle and touch her before she was wrapped." Denial of the opportunity for this seemed not only the greatest hardship, but was interpreted as an aggressive act on the part of authority. Women described how they tried to put the baby to the breast, for example, but how it was "grabbed" or "snatched away," or how the midwife "did not believe in it" or "was shocked," or took the baby away because she must not do it as it would "make the baby sick," or took the baby away because she said it was necessary to weigh, bathe, Apgar-rate, clothe it, put it under a heater, or give it to the paediatrician. Other mothers said they were not permitted to hold their babies immediately because "they were too busy with the placenta." These mothers clearly surrendered their babies reluctantly, and some experienced helpless anger.

Sostek, Scanlon, and Abramson, in a study of thirty-four mothers and their normal first-born, found that mothers whose babies had been separated for at least twenty-four hours due to elevated maternal temperatures without other symptoms showed reduced confidence and higher anxiety levels during the neonatal period than mothers whose babies had not been separated. These changes were, however, transient. Infant development after one year did not differ in the separated babies. Their study confirms the findings of enhanced maternal confidence following extended postpartum contact.

As a result of the drugs administered, especially analgesics which are injected into the epidural space in the lower back, the mother frequently does not feel the cutaneous contact between herself and the baby as it is being born. The child is "delivered," born, and experienced in an unfeeling way, so that it is not to be wondered at that the mother often fails to develop any feeling for the child. As more than one woman has remarked under such conditions, "If the baby hadn't been brought back to me, I wouldn't have missed him." A quite frequent remark heard from such mothers when the baby is first returned to them, after an absence of twenty-four hours in the "nursery," is, "Hello, little stranger."

Klaus and Kennell have observed that when the newborn is separated from its mother, the mother frequently tends to be noticeably hesitant and clumsy when she begins to take on the infant's care. It takes her several visits to learn the simple mothering tasks of feeding and diapering that most mothers pick up rapidly. "When the separation is prolonged," they write, "mothers report that they sometimes forget momentarily that they even have a baby. After a premature baby has gone home it is striking to hear how often the mother reports that, although she is fond of her baby, she still thinks of him as belonging to someone else—the head nurse in the nursery or the physician—rather than to herself."

The maternal sensitive period, as Klaus and Kennell have termed the period shortly after birth, is important but not crucial for the bonding which ties not only mother and child together, but would also do so for mother, father, child, and other children together, if they were but given the opportunity to participate in welcoming the new member into the bosom of the family. As things used to be in hospital deliveries, the baby was separated from the mother, the father was not permitted to participate in the birth of his child, and such emotions as the mother was left with she all too frequently projected upon the obstetrician or whatever other helpful figure may have been present . . . or else was left grievously frustrated, a candidate for the development of postpartum blues. It is reported that well over 80 percent of women delivered of babies in hospital suffer from postpartum blues. The position of helplessness in which the mother is put when the baby is separated from her is exceedingly depressing, especially when all her drives are readied to make her the most active participant in the continuing sustenance of the child outside the womb that she was to it inside the womb. When she is denied this, the mothering of her infant, she may come to look upon him as a foreign body, or even, as Dr. E. Furman has stated, to maltreat him because his demands interfere with the fulfillment of her own needs.

Dr. Marjorie J. Seashore and her colleagues investigated the effects of denial of early mother-infant interaction on maternal confidence in the context of the premature birth situation. One group of twenty-one mothers of prematures were denied physical interaction with their infants in the first two weeks following birth, and a contact group of twenty-two mothers were allowed to care for their premature infants in the hospital nursery during this period. Separation resulted in lower self-confidence for primiparous mothers, but not for multiparous mothers; however, even in their case separation had a negative effect on those who were initially low in self-confidence.

A year later it was found that mothers who had not been separated touched their infants more than separated mothers touched theirs. Mothers of nonseparated male infants laughed with, smiled, and talked to their infants more than mothers in other corresponding groups. Mothers of separated female infants behaved like the mothers of nonseparated male infants. Primiparous mothers spent much more time with their infants in nonspecific play and distal attachment behaviors such as looking, talking, smiling, and laughing. Proximal attachment behaviors such as touching and holding were primarily affected by the sex of the infant. Mothers touched their male infants more, but female infants were held a greater amount of the time.

Klaus and Kennell have summarized the findings of seventeen studies on the amount of contact between mothers and their newborn infants, and of seven other studies of a similar sort, as well as a number of others. The conclusion drawn from all these studies is that the groups with early contact, usually within the first thirty minutes, showed significantly more attachment behaviors. Typically, De Chateau in Umea, Sweden, found that in the early contact group three months later mothers fed their babies twice as long as did the controls (after thirty minutes); they also spent more time looking face to face at their infants, whereas the control mothers were more often involved in cleaning them. As Klaus and Kennell remark, "The two groups appear to focus on different ends of the baby. One group was busy cleaning up whereas the other was giving love." Early contact infants cried less and smiled and laughed more than control group infants. Breastfeeding in the early contacts was 175 days, in the later contacts 108 days.

In an endeavor to understand how the normal mother-infant relationship works, Dr. Myron A. Hofer of the department of psychiatry, Montefiore Hospital, and Albert Einstein College of Medicine, Bronx, New York, studied the effects of maternal separation in two-week-old rats, when survival without the mother is possible. After one day those that have been separated show clear differences from those that have been normally mothered. The separated infants show less locomotor and self-grooming behavior and are generally less active, and their body temperatures have fallen $1-2°C$ below normal levels. When heat is supplied they become more active; indeed, they show more locomotor, exploratory, self-grooming, defecation, and urination, and are slower to fall asleep than normally mothered littermates. It would seem that the separation experience in an unfamiliar environment leads to a state of increased excitability, which normal mothering tends to regulate.

Over the first twelve to eighteen hours, cardiac and respiratory rates led to 40 percent reductions in the separated rats. These rates could be returned to normal levels by strong tactile stimulation, a tail pinch, for example. The rates could also be maintained at normal levels in the absence of the mother for some twenty-four hours if enough milk was given to produce normal weight gain. Subsequent work supports the view that at this developmental age the central nervous system is "informed" of the amount of nutrient in the gut and regulates cardiac rate accordingly.

"What," asks Dr. Hofer, "does this tell us about the transfer of information within the mother-infant relationship?" And he answers, "Apparently the mother functions as an external physiological regulatory agent for the infant, through the milk she supplies." The mother maintains a certain level of responsiveness in the tone of the heart by the milk she supplies, of behavioral responsiveness by her thermal input, and also tends to reduce long-term levels of excitability by tactile and olfactory stimulation. Dr. Hofer concludes that the effects of early separation from the mother are the effects of sudden loss of information. From these studies it is clear that functional organization depends on certain kinds of specific sensory stimulation early in life, the chief of these being tactile and olfactory.

Finally, in a most important statement, Dr. Hofer emphasizes that insofar as the long-term effects of early experience are concerned, we would do well to recognize the coexistence of several discrete behavioral and physiological processes set in motion by the early experience, each of which interacts with subsequent developmental processes. Because of the different developmental schedules followed by individual behavioral and physiological subsystems, the resulting pattern responses may be very different at different ages.

Much research remains to be done on the nature of the physiological changes that occur in mother and infant during various periods, the sensitive periods, of their reciprocal development. But whether premature or full term, it is clear that the mother needs her baby immediately after birth quite as much as the baby needs her. Each is primed to develop a full set of potentialities—the maternal role in the one case, that of developing human in the other. The earlier the interaction, the better for both infant and mother. Any interruption in the physical contact between them in the neonatal period—that is, the first two or three weeks—detrimentally affects both. Physiologically, the physical interaction between mother and child activates and enhances those essential hormonal and other changes in each which contribute to their optimum functioning. Psychologically, the involvement in each other is profoundly deepened. The presence of each to the other constitutes a continuous reenforcement of their mutual strengths, their reciprocal involvement.

Nonetheless, a large proportion of obstetricians, the hospitals with which they are associated, and pediatricians, seem to be unaware of these facts. During a roundtable discussion held in 1974 on maternal attachment, one of the women participants (Ms. Suzanne Arms) "expressed exasperation with the general reluctance to accept the importance and benefits of early mother-infant contact. Dr. Klaus agreed that obstetricians had not accepted it, and Dr. Quilligan added that pediatricians have, in fact, enhanced separation. "The first thing the pediatrician does is to put the baby in an isolette and get it out of the delivery room." Happily, there has been some progress since 1974.

There is clearly urgently important work to be done in reforming the attitudes of obstetricians and pediatricians towards the care of mother and child.

Among the things we need to understand more fully than we have yet done is that the baby takes its cues from the mother's behavior towards it. Bateson and Mead, writing of Bali, state:

The Balinese child is carried either loosely on the hip, as in most of the plains villages, or in a sling, as in Bajoeng Gede, but even where the hand of the mother is substituted for the sling, the child's adaptation is the same, passive, adjusting itself by complete limpness to the movements of the mother's body. It may even sleep with head wobbling to the timing of the mother's rice pestle. The baby receives its cues as to whether the outside world is to be trusted or feared directly from contact with the mother's body, and though the mother may have schooled herself to smile and utter courtesy phrases to the stranger and the high-caste, and may display no timorousness in her artificially grimacing face, the screaming baby in her arms betrays the inward panic.

The kinesic means which enable the child to respond to its mother's inward states, no matter what her outward ones may appear to be, have already been discussed. The observation is universally confirmed that the child is able to do so in response to the messages he receives from his mother's muscle-joint behavior.

While much has now been written on the bonding between mother and newborn, and between parents and the newborn, it is important to recognize that bonding between siblings and the newborn is quite as valuable in the development of family and sibling relationships. Those who have witnessed the bonding which occurs between a sibling as young as twenty months and the newborn, the amazement, delight, and interest displayed in this new phenomenon, have little doubt that the quality of the relationship that subsequently develops between them is related to this early bonding. As one mother writes, "Jeremy and Heather have a fascinating relationship—completely the opposite of that which many would anticipate between a toddler and usurping newborn. I believe the tenderness and concern he shows toward her, and the fascination with which she looks into his eyes, can be partially attributed to their bonding at birth. Jeremy loves to hold and stroke her and never objects to sharing his 'milky' with her. They even sleep together in a bed attached to our bed."

GRASPING AND LEARNING. It is evident from the child's exploratory movements with its hands that they play an important role in discovering the lineaments and boundaries of the world in which it lives. Also fascinating to observe is the way young infants will clap the palms of their hands together, at first very much as a reflex, later in obvious enjoyment. It is possible that this constitutes the origin of later clapping in pleasure or approval.*

During the first two or three months, the infant's grasping is largely reflex. It is not until about twenty weeks of age that it is voluntarily able to grasp an object, and even that grasping has to develop through several stages, from the ulnar grasp (on the little-finger side) in the early months to the radial grasp (on the thumb side), and then to the finger-thumb grasp at about nine months of age. At six months the infant transfers objects from hand to hand. It plays with its toes and, as it were by way of validation, everything goes to its mouth, an activity which it abandons at about the end of its first year. After that the child's progress is one of increase in manipulatory precision so that by the time it is three years old it can fully dress and undress itself.

These are skills achieved principally by means of the learning that has gone on through the skin and joint-muscle senses in the feedback interaction between mother and child and the associated experiences she provides. Learning is defined as the increase in the strength of any act through repetition, the child being constantly reinforced by the pleasurable rewards it receives in relation to its mother; the greater the satisfaction, the greater the strengthening of the bond between the stimulus and the response. The opposite is also true, namely, the greater the discomfort, the greater the weakening of the bond.

The manner of learning through these senses is illuminatingly described by Margaret Mead in her account of the Balinese child. In Bali the child spends most of its first two years

*For a discussion of the problem thus raised see M. Mead and F. C. Macgregor, *Growth and Culture* (New York: Putnam, 1951), pp. 24–25.

first within the arms and then on the hip of another human being who is lightly conscious of its presence. The baby is carried very loosely wrapped in a cloth that is sometimes laid over its face when it is carried indoors, and suspended in a sling around the shoulder of mother or father or of a young adolescent. Sleeping and waking occur without the baby moving out of the arms of its mother. At about two months of age, still in the sling, the infant is set astride the hip, now securely fastened to the carrier's body. The mother feels free to pound her rice without further attention to the infant, and the latter learns to adjust to her every movement. If it falls asleep it may be laid down on a bed-platform inside the house, but when it awakens it is immediately picked up. Practically the only occasion when a child under five or six months is out of someone's arms is when it is bathed. Since the child is almost invariably carried on the left hip its right arm is pinioned under the carrier's arm or extended around the carrier's back, so that when it reaches out with the left hand for something offered it, the carrier pulls the left hand back—for it is forbidden to receive things in the left hand—and pulls the right hand out. In this manner the child's reaching behavior occurs in a supervised, culturally patterned situation. In the course of its first year the child is carried by all sorts of people, male and female, young and old, skilled and unskilled. The child enjoys a rather varied experience of the human world, of different skin surfaces, different odors, different tempos, different ways of being held, and a correspondingly narrow experience of objects. The only objects that it habitually touches are its own ornaments: a beaded necklace with a little silver box attached, on which it teethes, and its own silver bracelets and anklets.

"So the child learns life within human arms. It learns to eat, with the exception of the experience of being fed in its bath, to laugh, to play, to listen, to watch, to dance, to feel frightened or relaxed, in human arms." The child urinates in the arms of its carrier, and feels the urination disregarded. It defecates, and feels the low concern with which a dog is called to tidy up the scene, the baby, the sling, and the body of the carrier. The child is relaxed and the carrier habitually inattentive. Since the infant spends many hours on the mother's hip while she is pounding rice, it is of great interest to learn that Colin McPhee, the leading authority on Balinese music, found that the basic tempo of Balinese music is the same as the tempo of the women's rice pounding. Ethnomusicologists do not appear to have concerned themselves with the possible relation between childhood experiences and the character of a particular culture's music. But clearly this would appear to be a promising field of inquiry. Recently John Chernoff has made an approach to the subject in his study of the music of African peoples. His book is very much worth reading.

The early conditioning the Balinese child receives in relation to its mother's body is apparently connected with the ease with which older children fall asleep leaning against other people. Some people fall asleep while standing in the midst of a tightly packed audience at a theatrical performance, relaxed and slightly swaying. The expected environment for sleep is the close proximity of other bodies. During ceremonies of various sorts people may be crowded together in a space no larger than a double bed, sitting, sleeping, dozing.

Clothing for the child means something that binds the child and its mother together. This is quite different from the meaning clothing has in the Western world, where it is used to separate child and mother. In Bali the mother's shawl serves as a sling, a wrapper for the infant, a diaper, and a pillow folded under its head. When it is frightened the mother draws the cloth over the child's face; she may also do this when it sleeps. The child is attached to its carrier by a cloth that is neither distinctively its own nor the carrier's, and since children are neither dressed nor undressed at routine times each day, neither clothes nor sleeping habits differentiate night from day for the Balinese. They develop no internalized time pattern, waking and sleeping at any hour, as impulse or interest dictates.

During infancy the child is fed in the bath, and mother and father often splash and manipulate the genitals of the male baby; thus the bath becomes a situation of heightened bodily pleasure. It is, however, a mixed kind of pleasure during which the child is manipulated as if it were a puppet capable of obstructive but not of human movement, an attitude which contrasts strongly with the closer contactual relationship with the carrier in suckling and eating snacks in the arms. When, significantly enough, the child is old enough to walk to the spring, he bathes himself, and bathing becomes from then on a solitary pleasure, performed in company but in a withdrawn manner.

In this account of the early cutaneous experiences of the Balinese child we may see, as it were in high relief, the effects of certain kinds of experiences, for which the skin represents a most important sensory receptor, upon the later behavior of the individual, even to the act of sleeping in bodily contact with another. In this connection the question may here be raised whether the increasing modern practice of husband and wife occupying separate beds may not be related to the decreasing tactile relationships between the modern mother and her child.

Separating mother and baby, dressing the baby in clothes, and similar dissociative practices certainly serve to reduce the amount of intercutaneous contact and communication between mother and infant. Instead of sleeping in another human being's arms, as the Balinese infant does, the infant of the Western world spends the greater part of its waking hours and all of its sleeping hours alone and apart from others. One will spend the whole of one's sleeping life before marriage in a bed by oneself, and when married may find it impossible to adjust to sleeping in the same bed with another, except for the purposes of making love. Hence, the popularity of twin beds may be positively correlated with childrearing habits in which from an early age the child is conditioned to "go" to sleep alone. It "goes" to sleep. Its separation contributes to a later feeling of separateness, and to the separateness of each of the members of the family.* As Professor Jerome Singer has said, "The pleasures of the marital bed for both women and men go far be-

---

*For an early discussion of this subject see A. Montagu, "Some Factors in Family Cohesion," *Psychiatry,* 7 (1944), pp. 349–352.

yond the actual sexual satisfactions and erotic stimulation to reflect a great deal of the quality of security and closeness to a companion that we see early manifested in the bedtime rituals of children."

To be tender, loving, and caring, human beings must be tenderly loved and cared for in their earliest years, from the moment they are born. Held in the arms of their mothers, caressed, cuddled, and comforted, the familiar human environment, to which Balinese children can always return, is found in "the known arms of parents and siblings, where fright and comfort, interest and sleep, have already been experienced. Bodies are always there, other people's bodies to lean against, to huddle together with, to sleep beside."

The close contacts and the rhythmic tactual stimulation accompanying the carrier's bodily movements, the patting, stroking, and caressing the child receives in this way or from the hands or other parts of the body of the carrier, are soothing, assuring, and comforting. The rhythm of this kind of tactual stimulation that the mother conveys to the child in her arms is almost universally reproduced in the lullabies sung or hummed to lull children to sleep. Children who are unhappy, frightened, or otherwise disturbed may usually be soothed and restored to a sense of security when taken up in the arms of a comforter. To put one's arms around another is to communicate love to the other, for which another word is security. To rhythmically rock the body when emotionally disturbed is comforting.

MOTHER-HUGGERS, MOTHER, AND OTHER CARRIERS. Ape babies remain in constant contact with the mother's body during the first four or five months after birth. Unlike mammals that come into the world relatively undeveloped and stay within the nest or home prepared by the mother, the so-called nest-huggers (nidicolous) or nest-fleers (nidifugous) who are born so well developed they can follow the parent or even live by themselves, baby apes are mother-huggers. All monkeys and apes are mother-huggers. Under conditions of danger, survival depends upon being able to cling to one's mother's fur, so that she can carry the infant with her on her flight. Under conditions of fear or anxiety, this behavior persists into old age. Adult males look around for a friendly comrade to embrace or take by the hand.

Like other primate infants, the human infant is a mother-hugger, and should be carried continuously in contact with the mother's body during the early days of its life. As Dr. Wolfgang Wickler, the distinguished ethologist of the University of Munich, points out, the entire behavior repertory of the baby is adapted for this. The baby clings to the mother, especially to her hair. The baby becomes helpless only when it is separated from the mother. As Wickler says, "It is not biological to place our babies in cribs. Symptomatic of this is that the babies cry out of loneliness with abnormal frequency in our culture, while one scarcely even finds this among primitive people."

To put a baby in a crib is to consign to solitary confinement this most social of all contact creatures. The jail of the crib is no substitute for the snugness of the cradle, that admirable invention thousands of years old, which sophisticated societies have discarded. Why? The answer to this question constitutes a case history in itself. It serves to illustrate how our ignorance of the most elementary facts concerning the needs of infants permits us, in the name of progress, to abandon the most valuable of practices and substitute the worst for them. The answer will also serve to shed some additional light on the functional activities of the skin in maintaining physical and mental health.

THE NATURAL HISTORY OF THE CRADLE AND THE SKIN. The story of the decline and fall of the cradle is a typical one of fads, fashions, fallacies, and of ill-informed and misguided authoritarianism. During the 1880s the view developed among physicians and nurses that there was danger in overindulging the child. It was thought that many of the complaints from which babies suffered were due to the well-meant interference of fond parents. It soon came to be "authoritatively" held that the clearest and first evidence of this spoiling of the baby was the cradle. Hence the cradle had to go. Dr. John Zahovsky of St. Louis, recalling this period, writes:

> I had the opportunity to follow this attack on the cradle during my early professional career. It seemed to me then that the greatest influence emanated from the babies' hospitals in New York, Philadelphia, and Chicago, since many of the writers in the prominent women's magazines had received their training there. In the nineties all these magazines published numerous articles on the care of the baby. Many of these contained vicious attacks on the use of the cradle.

The well-known educator of nurses, Lisbeth D. Price, in her textbook on nursing published in 1892, emphasized (in italics) that the baby *"should never be rocked nor hushed on the nurse's neck."* And this, of course, meant that mothers especially should desist from such practices also.

In America during the 1890s the attack on the cradle was widely extended through articles on child care, for the most part published in the leading women's magazines of the day. The greatest influence in the campaign against the cradle was exercised by the pediatrician to whom reference has already been made in a similar connection, namely Dr. Luther Emmett Holt. For more than a generation, Dr. Holt kept up his attack on the cradle. In the first edition of his widely used textbook on pediatrics (1897), Holt wrote: "To induce sleep, rocking and all other habits of this sort are useless and may be harmful. I have known of an instance where the habit of rocking during sleep was continued until the child was two years old; the moment the rocking stopped the infant would awake."

It was Holt who was responsible for writing what became the most popular guide to the rearing of children for almost fifty years. This was entitled *The Care and Feeding of Children: A Catechism for the Use of Mothers and Children's Nurses,* and was first issued in 1894. This booklet was read by millions of mothers and mothers-to-be. In it, replying to the question, "Is rocking necessary?", Holt wrote, "By no means. It is a habit easily acquired, but hard to break and a very useless and sometimes injurious one." Again, writing in 1916, Holt advised that the crib should be one that does not rock in order that "the unnecessary and vicious practice may not be carried on." One does not have to imagine the effect that the word *vicious* had upon so many mothers.*

This sustained attack on the cradle, led by one of the most influential pediatricians of his day, eventually succeeded in rendering the cradle obsolete, and the outmoded model was turned in for the new one: the stationary, dangerous prisonlike crib. The very fact that, from the earliest days of human history, mothers had rocked their babies to sleep in their arms was taken to mean that the practice was archaic, and that rocking babies in cradles was equally antiquated, certainly not "modern." Alas, in the headlong rush to be "modern," worthwhile institutions and ancient virtues may be abandoned and lost. With so many authoritative voices raised against the cradle as "habit-forming," "unnecessary and vicious," "spoiling," and even ruinous of the child's health, no mother who genuinely loved her child could conscientiously disregard the injunction to discontinue so "detrimental" a practice.

All this was made easier for the mother to accomplish because it was during this period (from 1916 to the 1930s) that the newest and most influential psychology of the day was beginning to make itself felt. This was the "Behaviorism" of John

---

*The reader who may wish to know what manner of man could have entertained such ideas may be referred to a profile written by one of his last assistants together with another pediatrician: Edwards A. Park and Howard H. Mason, "Luther Emmett Holt (1855–1924)," in B. S. Veeder (ed.), *Pediatric Profiles* (St. Louis, Missouri: Mosby, 1957). A few excerpts may be quoted. "His manner was more than serious, it was earnest. There was nothing about him which could be called impressive, due perhaps to the absence of any outstanding feature; rather he appeared a highly efficient, perfectly coordinated human machine. He seemed to us austere and unapproachable." He is not known to have said "good morning" to his secretary in the many years she worked for him, nor is he known ever to have praised anyone or anything (p. 58). Finally, of *The Care and Feeding of Children,* the writers remark, "It is only fair to point out that in recent years some pediatricians have felt that through its rigid philosophy of upbringing the booklet had had a harmful influence" (p. 53).

Broadus Watson, professor of psychology at Johns Hopkins University. "Behaviorism" held that the only sound approach to the study of the child was through its behavior. The basic contention was that only the objectively observable can constitute the data of science. What could not be observed—the child's wishes, needs, and feelings—was excluded from the behaviorist's interest and was therefore treated as if it did not exist. The behaviorists insisted on treating children as if they were mechanical objects that could be wound up any which way one pleased; children were at the mercy of their environment, and parents could by their own behavior make them into anything they desired. Sentimentality was to be avoided, because any show of love or close physical contact made the child too dependent upon its parents. What one should aim for, urged the behaviorists, was the encouragement of independence, self-reliance, and the avoidance of any dependence upon the affections of others. One must not spoil children with affection.

It was through his book *Psychological Care of Infant and Child,* published in 1928, in which he pays unbounded tribute to Holt, that Watson and his disciples were able to reinforce and compound the errors of Luther Emmett Holt. Mothers were enjoined to keep their emotional distance from the child, to desist from kissing, coddling, or fondling it. They were not to respond too readily to their children's cries for food or attention. Their capacities, Watson said, should be trained toward conquering the world. In order to do so, children must be taught to master their feeding schedules, toilet training, and other tasks, according to a strict regimen. It is the problem-solving techniques and boundless absorption in activity with which the child must be prepared that will enable him to cope with the demands of American society. Such a child will be "as free as possible of sensitivities to people and one who, almost from birth, is relatively independent of the family situation."

"There is," Watson wrote, "a sensible way of treating children. . . . Never hug and kiss them, never let them sit in your lap. If you must, kiss them once on the forehead when they say good night. Shake hands with them in the morning. Give them a pat on the head if they have made an extraordinarily good job of a difficult task. Try it out. In a week's time you will find how easy it is to be perfectly objective with your child and at the same time kindly. You will be utterly ashamed of the mawkish, sentimental way you have been handling it." And so the learned psychologist proceeds nonsensically and disastrously on; Bertrand Russell approved the book, *Parents Magazine* hailed it as one that should be on "every intelligent mother's shelf," and the *Atlantic Monthly* referred to it as "a godsend to parents."

This unsentimental, mechanistic approach to childrearing greatly influenced psychology for a time and exercised a profound effect upon pediatric thinking and practice. Pediatricians advised parents to maintain a sophisticated aloofness from their children, keeping them at arm's length, and managing them on a schedule characterized by both objectivity and regularity. They were to be fed by the clock, *not* on demand, and only at definite and regular times. If they cried during the intervals of three or four hours between feedings, they were to be allowed to do so until the clock announced the next feeding time. During such intervals of crying they were not to be picked up, since if one yielded to such weak impulses the child would be spoiled, and thereafter every time he desired something he would cry. And so millions of mothers sat and cried along with their babies, and, as genuinely loving mothers obedient to the best thinking on the subject, bravely resisted the "animal impulse" to pick them up and comfort them in their arms. Most mothers felt that this could not be right, but who were they to argue with the authorities? No one ever told them that an "authority" is one who *should* know.

An anguished mother poignantly recalled those days in the following verses:

> *They told me babies should not be held;*
> *It would spoil them and make them cry.*
> *I wished to do what is best for them,*
> *And the years went swiftly by.*

Now empty are my yearning arms;
No more that thrill sublime.
If I had my babies back again,
I'd hold them all the time!

As for so-called authorities and experts, it is especially important to understand that it is the mark of an educated person that he never finally makes up his mind on any matter of first importance, and that an educated person is one who has overcome the deficiencies of the educational system.

Giving the child too much attention, it was repeatedly emphasized, was calculated to spoil it, while the practice of rocking the baby to sleep, either in a cradle or in one's arms, was considered to belong to the Dark Ages of child rearing. And so the cradle was finally banished to the attic or lumber room and the baby consigned to a crib. In this way, it was felt, at one stroke was eliminated an old-fashioned way of caring for babies and an "archaic" piece of furniture. Mothers were resolved to be modern and unsentimental. It is sad to have to record that wherever other nations have "gone modern" they, too, have discarded the cradle.

In India and in Pakistan, for example, where the most "enlightened" people have begun to introduce Western ways, the cradle is also beginning to be considered "old-fashioned," and is being threatened with a fate similar to that which it suffered in the Western world. Dr. Brock Chisholm, the distinguished psychiatrist and former director of the World Health Organization, tells of an occasion where he was being shown over a large general hospital in Pakistan. He writes:

As we were going along a corridor which was a sort of balcony on the side of the building, we passed the screened door of a ward. Suddenly someone pointed out to me, with great enthusiasm, something away off on the horizon in the opposite direction. Now, to any old Army inspecting officer, the situation was perfectly clear; there was something nearby they didn't want me to see. Therefore I was quite sure that whatever was hidden behind this screened door I should see. If you see only what people want you to see you will never find out anything.

So I insisted, at some risk of offense, on seeing this ward, and when I insisted, my guides began apologizing, saying that I really wouldn't like to see it at all. It was of a very old pattern; they were ashamed of it; they hoped to get it changed; they hoped that the World Health Organization might help them get the money to adopt modern and new patterns for this particular ward, because it was very bad indeed. It was a pattern hundreds of years old.

However, I still insisted that even as an antiquity I would like to see it. I went in to see this ward, with the reluctant accompaniment of the train of people with me, and I saw the best maternity ward I have ever seen in any country, far better than I have ever seen in North America. Here was a big maternity ward with beds down both sides. The foot posts of each bed were extended up about three feet or so, and slung between the foot posts was a cradle. The baby was in the cradle, and I noticed as I looked down the ward that one squeak out of the baby and up would come the mother's foot, and with her toe she would rock the cradle. On the second squeak, which showed that the baby was really awake, she would reach into the cradle and take the baby into her arms, where a baby is supposed to be most of the time.

Dr. Chisholm adds:

They wanted to get rid of that perfectly beautiful arrangement, to put their babies under glass the way we do, and to keep them in inspection wards where they can be seen at a distance by their loving fathers whenever they visit, and taken to their mother if she is good and does as the nurse tells her! They wanted to do all that because we Westerners had given them the impression that all our methods are superior to theirs.

This is a sad story, for in their drive toward the achievement of Western "progress" and "advancement," the peoples of the East and other technologically developing countries, who until

recently had preserved many of their ancient virtues, are slav-
ishly bent on catching up with us, even to the extent of imitat-
ing our worst errors.

Among ourselves the cradle went out of existence when the
notion became fashionable that to fondle a child, to caress or to
rock it was to endanger its development as an unspoiled independent person. To rock it in a cradle came to be regarded as
especially backward and reprehensible.

Unsound as this kind of thinking is, and damaging as it has
been to millions of children, many of whom later grew up into
disturbed persons, the behavioristic, mechanistic approach to
childrearing is still largely with us. Hospital "deliveries," the
technologization of obstetrics, the removal of babies from their
mothers at birth, the failure to breastfeed them soon after they
are born, the elimination of breastfeeding and the substitution
and encouragement of bottlefeeding, the demotion of the pacifier, and so on, constitute some of the melancholy evidences of
the dehumanizing approach to the making of people, as op-
posed to the making of human beings.

Having spent the whole of his preceding life snugly en-
sconced in his mother's womb, the baby would certainly feel
more comfortable cosily tucked into a cradle than abandoned
to a large crib in which he lies, either on his front or on his
back, exposed to the dull and uninteresting flat white surface of
the sheet or the ceiling, with only the prison bars at the side of
the crib to break the monotony of this bleak, one-dimensional
landscape. As Sylvester has said,

> Small infants raised in oversized cribs are frequently very
> frightened infants because they are too far removed from
> sheltering surfaces. They often appear inhibited in their
> courage to experiment and explore. Infants disturbed by
> new situations or by the prodrome [a premonitory symptom]
> of physical illness often draw closer to protective shelter
> (the mother's arms, the sides of the crib), giving spatial ex-
> pression to their need to constrict the boundaries of their
> pre-ego protectively.

One cannot help wondering whether the unexplained occurrence of "crib death," or "sudden infant death syndrome"—that is, the finding dead in its cot of a baby who has been perfectly healthy and for whose death no cause can be found—may not, at least in part, be due to inadequate sensory stimulation, particularly tactile stimulation. Inadequate sensory stimulation may not be the only factor involved in crib deaths, but it may well be a predisposing factor. It is rare for a child over one year to be found dead unexpectedly. Most crib deaths occur in infants between one and six months. It would be interesting to know what the incidence of sudden infant death would be in cradle-raised compared with crib-raised babies.*

SUDDEN INFANT DEATH SYNDROME, PRENATAL BREATHING, AND MATERNAL CARE. The sudden infant death syndrome (or crib death) is characterized principally by the cessation of breathing after one or more apneic (nonbreathing) episodes. Thus far, after many investigations, autopsies, anatomical, physiological, biochemical, and other tissue and organ studies, the causes, or cause, of SIDS remain unclear. I can claim no particular expertise regarding the problem, but in the course of reading and thinking about touching in its many forms, as a factor in human development, it became clear to me that tactile stimulation, among much else, plays an important role in the development of postnatal breathing.

It has been known for centuries that babies who are not breathing at birth may be stimulated to do so by cutaneous stimulation of one form or another. This is also true of infants during an apneic episode. All mammals, with the exception of

*A reader of this paragraph sent me an account from her local newspaper of a nurse who, recognizing the symptoms of sudden infant death in her own seven-month-old girl, wired her to an alarm that monitors her heartbeat. When her heart stops the alarm goes off, and the mother simply by touching the little girl starts her breathing again—"About People," *The Sacramento Bee,* 15 January 1974. This type of alarm has since been widely adopted.

humans, lick their infants following birth. This serves the function of stimulating the gastrointestinal and genitourinary, as well as the respiratory tracts.

In utero the fetus breathes through the oxygen it receives from the placenta and its liver. At birth the infant has to adapt itself to a new form of breathing, very different from its prenatal breathing. In this, as in most other functions, human infants exhibit a great deal of variability.

The human fetus normally receives a great deal of cutaneous stimulation during labor and parturition, and since humans are born in a highly immature condition compared to most mammals, the evidence is now overwhelming that they continue to require a great deal of tactile stimulation. This their mothers are normally abundantly able to provide, by cuddling, caressing, breastfeeding, and the like. The satisfaction of these basic needs are beneficial both for infant and mother.

At birth the infant is a prenatal breather and must adapt himself to the pressures of an atmospheric environment, a process which the mother is designed to assist. The evidence strongly suggests that should she fail to do so the infant will not in many cases learn to breathe properly, and so will remain a shallow breather. It is suggested that this shallow breathing is a factor, in some cases, in the causation of apneic episodes, some of which may lead to death.

This is, of course, not what happens to all infants who have been inadequately mothered, but that it does occur in a proportion of presumably vulnerable infants, especially those who have failed to make the transition from prenatal-influenced shallow breathing to deep postnatal breathing, seems likely.

It is here suggested that the two factors critical, in many cases of SIDS, are (1) inadequate maternal care and (2) the resulting failure of adaptation to postnatal breathing. For the first factor the best and most convincing evidence comes from an investigation carried out by Dr. Arno Gruen. In this study Dr. Gruen reported the results of interviews with the parents of infants who had died of SIDS. To summarize in his own words

Dr. Gruen found that "the neurophysiological antecedents of SID reside in a mothering that reinforces REM* sleep, diminishes arousal through the thwarting of expected expectations and weakened sucking, and makes the infant's dream state too preoccupying. Under such conditions the occurrence of apnea can lead to death."

It will be some time before Dr. Gruen's study will be published, but when it is it should be read by everyone interested in SIDS, for a brief summary cannot do it justice. The essence of Dr. Gruen's observations lies in the repeated confirmation that the failure of mothering is the principal factor in producing the conditions which lead to SIDS, especially in the period between six and nine months. Those conditions, the evidence suggests, are the appropriate development of the many anatomical and physiological changes from the fetal to the complex postnatal respiratory system.

In a crib the baby is weighed down by a set of coverings tucked in at the sides and foot of the crib, and thus left partially surrounded by air; this is not quite what it wants or needs. What it does want and need is the supporting contact of a snugly comforting environment, as reassurance and security that it is still in contact with the world and not airily suspended in it. The baby assures itself that all is well largely through the messages it receives from the skin. The supports it receives in the enveloping environment of the cradle are very reassuring to it, for the cradle affords it something of a replication, a continuation, of the life it led so long in the womb, and this is good and comforting. When the baby feels uncomfortable or insecure it may whimper and if its mother or anyone else rocks the cradle this will have a soothing effect. Rocking reassures the baby, for in its mother's womb it was naturally rocked by the normal motions of her body. To be comfortable means to be comforted, and for the infant this comfort is largely derived from the signals he receives from the skin. The greatest of all comforts is to be cradled in the mother's arms or lap or sup-

*REM=Rapid Eye Movement.

ported on her back. There is, as Peiper has remarked, "no better sedative." As he says, "It is necessary to rock a healthy young infant in his cradle or in the arms or baby carriage only once when he is on the verge of crying: He immediately quiets down and starts to cry again as soon as the movement stops momentarily. He will surely not cry if it is done right."

It is absurd to suggest that the cradle is harmful because the infant will develop the habit of having to be rocked before it will be able to fall asleep. If cradle rocking is habit-forming, so is breastfeeding or bottlefeeding. Yet children are weaned from breast or bottle, unless it is done too suddenly, without any serious difficulty or after effects. Millions of babies who had been rocked to sleep in cradles grew up to be adults who were able to fall asleep without needing to be rocked. Children outgrow the cradle as well as they do their baby clothes.

Rocking chairs are still popular among older folks, especially in unsophisticated rural areas, where "modernity" has not made such complete inroads as it has in the more worldly-wise urban areas. It is strange that no one has ever suggested that the rocking chair is "unnecessary and vicious" in adults, or that adults will be unable to relax unless they can do so with the assistance of a rocking chair. Rocking chairs, in fact, for adults, and especially the aging, are to be highly recommended for reasons similar to those which make the cradle so highly recommendable for babies. Rocking, in both babies and adults, increases cardiac output and is helpful to the circulation; it promotes respiration and discourages lung congestion; it stimulates muscle tone; and not least important, it maintains the feeling of relatedness. A baby, especially, that is rocked, knows that it is not alone. A general cellular and visceral stimulation results from the rocking. Again, especially in babies, the rocking motion helps to develop the efficient functioning of the baby's gastrointestinal tract. The intestine is loosely attached by folds of peritoneum to the back wall of the abdominal cavity. The rocking assists the movements of the intestine like a pendulum and thus serves to improve its tone. The intestine always contains liquid chyle and gas. The rocking movement causes the chyle to move backward and forward over the intestinal mucosa. The general distribution of chyle over the whole of the intestine undoubtedly aids digestion and probably absorption. Writing in 1934, Zahovsky stated that "young infants who are rocked after nursing as a rule have less colic, less enterospasm [intestinal spasm] and become happier babies than those who are laid in the crib without rocking. In fact, I have several times availed myself of this physical therapy even in recent years to relieve the dyspeptic young baby.... I firmly believe that the cradle assists maternal nursing." Dr. Zahovsky concludes with the words, "Someday, I believe, it will be no disgrace to rear the young baby in a cradle and even sing him to sleep by a lullaby."

Regrettably many years have had to elapse before anyone could be found to echo Dr. Zahovsky's words. The cradle should be restored to the infant. It should never have been discarded in the first place. The reasons that were given for its banishment were completely unsound and wholly unjustified, based as they were on misconceptions concerning the nature and needs of the child and the ludicrous notion that cradle rocking is detrimental to the child.

The benefits of rocking are considerable. When the infant is too warm the rocking has a cooling effect, hastening evaporation from the skin. When the infant is too cold the rocking helps to warm him. The warming has a hypnotic effect on the infant, and it is soothing to his nervous system. Above all, the rocking motion produces a gentle stimulation of almost every area of his skin, with consequential beneficial physiological effects of every kind.

As a first step in the ultimately possible, and much to be desired restoration of the cradle to its rightful place,* rocking chairs have been introduced into some hospitals. For example, at Riverside Hospital, Toledo, Ohio, rocking chairs have been

---

*For those who are handy with simple tools cradle patterns may be ordered from Craft Patterns, Dept. L, Elmhurst, Illinois, 60126.

in use as a regular part of the infant-care program. In 1957 a mahogany rocking chair was introduced as a Christmas gift from Riverside nurse aides, who pooled money to buy what they voted as "most needed new equipment" at the hospital. In each of the three nurseries a rocking chair is available, including one for premature infants. Ms. Herbert Mercurio, obstetrical supervisor, states that the old rocking chairs are always used by nurses and aides at infant feeding time. "It's the best way to feed a baby and put him to sleep at the same time. It's relaxing for the nurse, too." The rocking chairs are used to pacify crying babies. Ms. Mercurio feels strongly that rocking chairs are useful and practical and encourages their use at home. "A rocking chair," she remarked, "won't spoil a child. This is something they enjoy, but outgrow rapidly."

Quite possibly the rocking chair used in this manner has some advantages over the cradle. I think both might well become standard equipment in the home with a small infant—in this manner at once satisfying the need for rocking of both infant and adult.*

Studies on the effects of rocking on human infants indicate their considerable benefits. Neal studied the effects of rocking on two- to three-month prematures. These were rocked for the number of days they were premature, and it was found that the rocked prematures were significantly superior to the nonrocked prematures in the development of tracking behavior to visual and auditory stimulation, head lifting, crawling, muscle tone, strength of grasping, and weight gain. In addition no edema ever developed in the rocked prematures, whereas it did in some of the nonrocked ones. Ms. Neal suggests that rocking stimulation provided by the mother during pregnancy constitutes an important sensory input for normal development, and

---

*On the advantages of the rocking chair see R. C. Swan, "The Therapeutic Value of the Rocking Chair," *The Lancet,* vol. 2 (1960), p. 1441; J. Yahuda, "The Rocking Chair," *The Lancet,* vol. 1 (1961), p. 109. For an amusing account of a club devoted to the cultivation of the rocking chair see T. E. Saxe, Jr., *Sittin' Starin' 'n' Rockin'* (New York: Hawthorn Books, 1969).

that prematures are unduly handicapped, following deprivation stimulation, by their premature birth.

Woodcock observed the effects of rocking newborn female
babies in a mechanical bassinet for one hour a day for six days.
On the sixth day they were tested for heart-rate response to a
buzzer as a measure of reactivity. It was found that the rocked
babies had significantly fewer responses and took a shorter
time to finish their acceleration response than the unrocked
newborns. The decreased heart-rate and acceleration responses
in the rocked infants suggest an increased maturational development.

A fascinating account of the serendipitous discovery of the
benefits of rocking for seriously disturbed mental patients is
reported by Dr. Joseph C. Solomon. Dr. Solomon observed
that patients taken from their rooms in hospital for transfer to
another town by train, though they had earlier needed to be restrained in straitjackets and muffs, became very quiet and calm
as soon as the train was in motion. Solomon reasoned that,
since in the womb the child is subjected to considerable passive
motion, part of the human contact these patients may have
missed as children was the active rocking in the mother's arms
which would, among other things, stimulate the vestibular apparatus. Purposive active motions, Solomon suggests, develop
with facility and pleasure when the passive motion imparted by
the mother has been satisfactorily internalized as an integrated
inner function.

> Conversely, when there is little chance for the internalization
> of the passive movements derived from the mother, the active
> rocking becomes a habitual device for self-containment. It is a
> method of defending the formative ego against the feeling of
> being abandoned. This follows the principle of Newton's Sec-
> ond Law. If you actively push against something, it is as
> though something is pushing against you. In this way the in-
> fant accomplishes the goal of not feeling completely alone. It
> is as though somebody is always there. As such it is another
> self-containment device similar to thumbsucking, the secu-
> rity-blanket, nail-biting, or masturbation.

Dr. William Greene, Jr., in the course of studying a group of patients suffering diseases of the lymphatic and blood vessels, found that a large proportion of them had developed their illness following a loss, usually of the mother or mother substitute. The association of vascular ills with the loss of maternal support suggested to Dr. Greene that the fetus, far from being a passive recipient of nourishment, was really a working member of a going partnership. Within the uterus, Greene suggests, the fetus may feel and respond to "vibrations, pressures and sounds provided by the mother's vascular pulses, and emanating chiefly from the aorta, and perhaps other abdominal blood vessels." The growing fetus, stimulated by the mother's internal functions, may be aware of the presence or absence of these, their constancy and change. Intrauterine activity, for the fetus, may constitute the "outside environment," just as, somewhat later, the functioning of its own digestive system will constitute, for the newborn, its outside environment. Within the womb the fetus may perceive the mother's internal functions as a kind of outside object, and become aware of itself as a being separate from such stimuli. Dr. Greene suggests that the infant, separated from the mother at birth, is "exposed to new stimuli . . . different, less persistent, exotic, and, most important, relatively random." The change, however, need not be total. The rocking and patting a mother gives her newborn may provide it with "a kind of object perception which bridges birth and . . . is the model of all those perceptions to come later." Rocking "tends towards synchrony with the mother's and/or baby's respiratory rate," while patting "approximates the mother's and/or baby's cardiac rate." The mother, in other words, who rocks and pats her baby may in some measure re-create the stimuli of her breathing and pulse rhythms, rhythms that were significant to it before birth, and thus give the baby the reassurance of a familiar environment that it so much needs.

HANDLING PREMATURES. In this connection, the findings on premature babies are extremely interesting. For example,

Freedman, Boverman, and Freedman in a study of five co-twin control cases found that the rocked twin, after an upward weight trend was established some seven to ten days after birth, gained weight at a greater rate per day than the unrocked controlled twin in every instance, although the advantage of the rocked group was only a temporary one. The experimental twin was rocked for thirty minutes twice daily.

A variety of deficits is likely to be exhibited by many prematurely born infants in later life. However, one factor that has received insufficient attention in previous research is the possibility that sensory deprivation may contribute to such impairments. The possible adverse effects of life in the controlled, monotonous environment of an isolette where the premature infant remains, receiving minimal emotional and tactile stimulation for several weeks, have been the subject of a pilot study by Sokoloff, Yaffe, Weintraub, and Blase. These investigators studied four boys and one girl of low birth weight and compared them with a similar group. The experimental group were stroked five minutes every hour of the day for ten days, while the control group were provided with routine nursery care. The handled infants were found to be more active, regained their initial birth weight faster, appeared to cry less, and after seven to eight months were found to be more active and healthier as measured by growth and motor development. Though the sample is very small these findings agree with those of Hasselmeyer, who found that premature infants who received increased sensory, tactile, and kinesthetic stimulation were significantly more quiescent, especially before feedings, than unstimulated controls.

Tiffany Field, Saul Schanberg, and their co-workers carried out an admirably controlled study of the effects of tactile-kinesthetic stimulation provided to twenty-eight prematures of thirty-one weeks mean gestation age and mean body weight of 1,288 grams, during transition care in the intensive care unit. The stimulation consisted of body stroking and passive movements of the limbs for three fifteen-minute periods a day for an eighteen-day period. It was found that compared to an unstimulated matched control group, the stimulated prematures averaged a 47 percent greater weight gain per day (mean = 25 versus 17 grams), were more active and alert during sleep-wake behavior observations, and showed more mature habituation, orientation, and range of state behavior on the Brazelton scale, which looks at the infant's capabilities most important for developing social relationships. Finally, the investigators underscore the fact that the stimulated prematures spent six days less in hospital than the unstimulated, yielding a cost saving of $3,000 per infant. "These data," they conclude, "suggest that tactile/kinesthetic stimulation may be a cost effective way of facilitating growth and behavioral organization even in very small preterm neonates."

Klaus and Kennell on the basis of their own studies and a thorough examination of the work of others have concluded that early contact between mother and premature is vitally important for both. Mothers who early touched and explored the bodies of their infants showed increased commitment to the infant, greater confidence in their mothering abilities, and greater stimulating and caretaking skills, as compared with the mothers who did not have early contact with their infants. In fact, the studies had to be discontinued because the nurses found them too painful, observing as they did how unfavorable the outcome was for the later contact couples as compared with the early contact ones.

When the children reached age three and a half, mothers who had had early contact with their prematures spent more time looking at them during feeding, and the children had significantly higher IQs, 99 as compared with 85 for late contact children.

The studies revealed that if a small premature is either touched, rocked, fondled, or cuddled daily during his stay in the nursery, he has fewer nonbreathing (apneic) periods, enjoys an increased weight gain, as well as advances in central nervous system functioning.

Over many years of observation Klaus and Kennell gained the distinct impression that the earlier the mother comes to the premature unit and touches her baby, the more rapid is her recovery from the pregnancy and birth. Their survey of the subject thoroughly confirms that impression impressively. The importance of the father's participation in these close contacts with the premature should be given greater attention than it has yet received, for it is at this time that a profound bonding is initiated between infant and father, the value of which cannot be overestimated.

What is most needed, indeed, in all our hospitals, as Dr. A. J. Solnit has put it, is "a warm, receptive, flexible environment that is people centered rather than technique centered."

The self-rocking commonly seen among patients in mental hospitals has often been remarked, and is frequently observed as an act of self-comfort in grief among individuals who do not otherwise rock. Among many Semitic-language-speaking peoples, including orthodox Jews, body-rocking often accompanies prayer, grief, and study. It is quite clearly a form of comforting behavior.

The behavior and motivations of all mammalian infants are directed towards maintaining contact with the mother. Contact-seeking is the foundation upon which all subsequent behavior develops. When such contact-seeking is frustrated, the infant resorts to such behaviors as self-clasping, finger-sucking, rocking, or swaying. These behaviors constitute a regression to the passive movement-stimulation experienced in the womb, the swaying, rocking motions, and the sucking of fingers with forearms pressed against the body. Self-rocking and similar repetitive activities represent substitutes for passive movement-stimulation, just as self-clasping and finger-sucking substitute self-stimulation for social stimulation. Dr. William A. Mason and his colleague Dr. Gershon Berkson, then at the Delta Regional Primate Research Center of Tulane University, New Orleans, tested the presumed relationship between self-rocking and the quality of maternal stimulation. They compared two groups of rhesus monkeys, both separated from their mothers at birth. One group was reared with a cloth-covered social substitute that moved freely about the cage on an irregular schedule; the other group was reared with a device identical to the moving dummy, except that it was stationary. The three monkeys reared with stationary dummies all developed stereotyped rocking as a persistent pattern, whereas those reared with the moving robots showed no evidence of such behavior.

Thus it would seem probable that self-rocking represents a form of substitute satisfaction of the need for passive movement-stimulation which would normally be obtained from a mother to whom one could cling or who carried one in contact with her body.

Solomon's view that the rocking motion stimulates the vestibular apparatus is undoubtedly sound, but misses the point that, in rocking, the skin itself undergoes a complex series of motions, not to mention the motions of proprioceptors and interoceptors, and the motions of internal organs. All of this is eroticizing. Rocking or swaying represents a kind of self-caressing, a self-comforting, and as such it is often observed in grief and mourning. It is significant that the region of America in which the rocking chair remains most popular should be New England—the land of the cod and the seemingly cold fish.

For breastfeeding, the rocking chair is an excellent device not only for the baby, but also for the mother. Rocking chairs are comfortable and relaxing for both. As the mother gently rocks, she improves the circulation in her legs. The to-and-fro motion stimulates the vestibular apparatus in the baby's inner ears, contributing to his better control of balance and position. With each change of position, as the baby is laid on his abdomen across his mother's lap, he becomes aware of the different movements. With the security of his mother's presence as background, he learns to interpret and to use the sensations produced in his vestibular apparatus. Later this ability to interpret these sensations will help him develop and maintain the balance he will need as he learns to stand and walk. The early stimulation provided by the gentle movements of the rocking chair will make it easier for him to learn to balance on his own two feet.

PREMATURES, TOUCH, AND THE VESTIBULAR SYSTEM. Dr. Anneliese Korner and her collaborators at Stanford University Medical Center in a pilot study found that placing premature infants on gently oscillating head-to-foot waterbeds significantly reduced the number of temporary breathing interruptions (apneic spells), especially when the prematures were placed on the waterbed during the first four postnatal days. The rationale behind this experiment was that compensatory vestibular-proprioceptive stimulation resembling that prevailing in the womb may benefit the infant. These investigators also found that very small prematures with severe skin problems or prematures recovering from surgery or receiving parenteral nutrition (other than through the alimentary canal) also appear to derive benefits from waterbed flotation.

Dr. Korner, hoping to offset certain deficits within the environment in which prematures are raised, and to compensate for forms of stimulation that are prevalent *in utero* but are minimally provided in premature infant care, set up a series of experiments designed to assist prematures to accelerate their development. It has long been known that one of the most effective ways of soothing a crying newborn is to pick him up and put him to the shoulder. In several earlier studies Korner and her co-workers unanticipatedly found that such intervention, in addition to soothing the infants, made them bright-eyed and alert, and inclined to scan the environment. Because such visual exploration is most conducive to the earliest forms of learning, by means of which the motorically helpless infant is most apt to become acquainted with his environment, including his mother, the question arose whether it was the contact or the stimulation of the vestibular system and the activation of the antigravity reflexes that produced this effect. Experiment showed that it was the vestibular stimulation that evoked significantly more visual alertness than contact. Furthermore, it was not the upright position as such that improved the infant's visual behavior, and only when the infant was moved, either vertically or horizontally, was his visual tracking performance significantly enhanced.

It occurred to Dr. Korner that prematures might benefit from lying on an oscillating waterbed (corresponding to the mother's respirations), specially designed for them as a stimulus which by its contribution to their movement would also provide a number of clinical benefits. The waterbed, it was thought, would help preserve the fragile skin of very small infants and the soft head support of the mattress might reduce the incidence of asymmetrically shaped heads and intracranial bleeds. It was further postulated that waterbed flotation would reduce the infant's need to cope prematurely with the full impact of gravity, thus conserving energy, and that the incidence of apneic episodes would be reduced.

Prematures ranging in age from twenty-seven to thirty-four weeks were randomly assigned to experimental and control groups. The experimental group was placed on the oscillating waterbed before the sixth postnatal day. The experimental group remained on the waterbed for seven days and nights. The oscillations were from head to foot. The control group was placed on nonoscillating waterbeds. The experimental group received gentle, hardly visible, twelve to thirteen oscillations per minute, with thirty minutes of oscillations and sixty minutes of quiescence. It was found that apnea (announced by the ringing of a bell 20 seconds after its onset) was significantly reduced in oscillating prematures as compared with the nonoscillating group. The nonoscillating waterbed has been found to be clinically useful for prematures suffering from all sorts of conditions, including recent surgery.

In another group who were never on the waterbed, there was a highly significant difference in the number of apneic incidents as compared with the nonoscillating waterbed prematures. Six out of seven prematures had less apnea on the oscillating waterbed compared with those on a standard foam rubber mattress.

What is of great interest in Korner's work is not only the light it throws on the role played by the vestibular system, but that the latter plays an important part in what is often attributed exclusively to tactile stimulation alone, something most important to remember in the care of the infant. What is equally interesting is that the developmental advances reported among infants of indigenous peoples, as compared with infants of the same age in the Western world, are almost certainly due to the manner in which they are carried by their mothers, on back or front or even swaddled on cradleboards. The growing fashion among Western mothers, and some fathers, of carrying their infants in such ways should result in more advanced behavioral development resulting from the effects of tactile, vestibular, and social stimulation such infants receive.

We digress here for a moment to define the forms of touch, for their understanding is important in the approach to prematures. Three forms of touch are distinguished, mainly by the roles they play in behavior. *Social touch* fosters social bonds, attachment, and emotional integrity, the effects of touching in social situations, social stimulation, and social deprivation thus constituting the broadest area of our interest. In *passive touch* the organism is touched; contact with the subject's skin is effected by some external agent, such as a rough surface moved over the stationary fingers. This contrasts with *active touch,* in which the organism touches, and refers to the subject's initiation and performance of the acts required to effect skin-object contact, exploration and manipulative use of the skin, and hence stimulation of receptor systems in the muscles, tendons, and joints—the kinesthetic system.

The term *haptic* refers to touch in its widest sense, and is often used to indicate exploratory and manipulative touch in contrast to tactile sensations resulting from stimulation of passive receptors.

Quite independently of Korner's work Drs. Jerry White and Richard Labarra found that tactile and kinesthetic stimulation of the relatively large premature infant during the first two weeks of life extended over ten days resulted in accelerated weight gain, with a 10 percent advantage over unstimulated controls. The stimulated infants were described as eager eaters who retained their feedings well, and were more active and alert. In view of their findings, as well as those of others, the authors suggest that considering the subdued, relatively monotonous environment of the premature nursery, sensory, perceptual, and possibly motoric deprivations suffered by prematures in such environments could be avoided, to the advantage of the premature, if positive, practical methods of intervention were to be incorporated into nursery routines to alleviate such conditions. Increased stimulation, they suggest, could be carried out by mothers while the infant is still in the nursery ward, and beyond that by parents at home. Instruction in such practical methods could become part of the workshop training of expectant parents.

"Increased stimulation" of prematures would, however, need to be carefully researched, for there is some evidence that it is easily possible to overstimulate the premature infant. Dr. Peter Gorski of Mount Zion Hospital and Medical Center in San Francisco has drawn attention to the fact that some prematures are detrimentally affected by noise, light, and social touch. He found that apnea and bradycardia (slowing of heartbeat) often preceded social touching. Fragile preterm infants, Dr. Gorski suggests, "are exquisitely sensitive to, and perhaps easily overwhelmed by, tactile intervention."

Apparently social interaction can easily overburden the nervous system of the preterm infant. In talking about the problem with parents, Gorski puts things in a positive way, while explaining why an exciting stimulus may overburden a baby with low energy levels. "We don't want parents to feel that they're bad for the child or that the child is rejecting them, and we don't want them to be afraid to approach the baby at all. They simply need to understand how taxing social interaction can be for a weak infant."

Is the special care unit the best place for prematures? In England, where many births still take place at home, it was shown long ago that survival rates are higher for prematures born at home than for those born in hospital.

Dr. Allen Gottfried of California State University at Fullerton has commented on the possible inadequacies of the intensive and convalescent care units for prematures. In a study of prematures in such units, Gottfried concluded that touch appears to be most important in regulating behavior and development. He also found that while prematures in such units receive some seventy contacts a day in the intensive care unit, and some forty-two in the convalescent care unit, what they receive is mostly describable as nonsocial touching. Responses to the infants' crying during contacts occurred in approximately 21 percent of cases, but the caregivers attempted to soothe in less than half those occasions. When they did try it was usually by talking to the infant and seldom by touching. Gottfried observes that since, as Speidel has suggested, failure to respond soothingly to the infant's crying is associated with a fall in oxygen levels in the blood (hypoxemia), Gottfried suggests that changes in premature intensive and convalescent units are indicated. He also makes the point that lack of responsiveness to infants' cries may serve to delay development of infant potentialities and social reactions. He concludes that his findings, at any rate, "indicate that the nature of the tactile environment of infants in special care units may not be conducive to optimal development."

It is clear from a study of the many investigations, only a small fraction of which could be cited here, that prematures greatly benefit from gentle social touching, but that in many forms of behavior involving social touching, such as hugging, cuddling, picking up and shouldering, cradling, rocking, carrying, and the like, additional benefits accrue as a result of wholly unconscious proprioceptive-vestibular stimulation. The same holds true for the preambulatory infant. For the latter it is recommended that carrying devices, cradles, games, amusements, and the like that stimulate the proprioceptive-vestibular apparatus should be arranged without overstimulating the child.

ROCKING, MUSIC, AND THE DANCE.

> *But O for the touch of a vanish'd hand*
> *And the sound of a voice that is still!*

Was Tennyson, when he wrote those poignant words, unconsciously or consciously recalling his early experiences of his mother? It has been said that music utters the things that cannot be spoken. In much music there is a very pervasive tactile quality. Wagner's *Liebestod* is said to represent a musical version of coitus leading to orgasm and postcoital subsidence. Debussy's *L'Après-Midi d'un Faune* conveys the most tactile of sexual nuances. In the "rock" music of our day, so aptly named, for the first time in the history of the dance in the Western world the participating couples no longer touch each other at any time but remain separated throughout the dance, dancing most of the time to deafeningly loud music of which the lyrics, usually addressed to one's parents, or generally to the older generation, only too often say, "You do not understand," "Where were you when I needed you?" or words to that effect.

As Lawrence H. Fuchs has noted, these songs are sharply critical of the older generation, they stress the hypocrisy of society, the loneliness of the good in an unloving world, and the evils of its social injustice. "They constituted not just a manifesto of rebellion but an admission of loneliness and confusion, as in Dylan's words when he tells us that his existence is tied to 'confusion boats.'"

Sounds of various sorts may be experienced and appreciated for their tactile qualities, as, for example, when one says of someone's voice that it is "smooth," like "velvet," or "caressing." Music may be similarly experienced. Sally Carrighar, in her autobiography, tells us that when at the age of six she heard a distinguished violinist play, she "seemed to receive this magnificent sound through not my ears alone but through the skin all over my body."

"Singers," Edmund Carpenter tells us, "determine pitch by feel. The experience is not unlike rock music which one feels, often through the entire body."

Lawrence K. Frank, in a brilliant paper on tactile communication, writes: "The potency of music, with its rhythmical patterning and varying intensities of sounds, depends in large measure upon the provision of an auditory surrogate for the primary tactile experiences in which ... rhythmic patting, is peculiarly effective in soothing the baby."

Can it be that dances like the Twist and later ones of the same rock variety, together with rock music, represent, at least in part, reactions to a lack of early tactile stimulation, to a deprivation suffered in the antiseptic, dehumanized environments created by obstetricians and hospitals? Where but in such a setting should we enact this most important of all dramatic events: the birth and welcoming of a new member into "the bosom of the family"?

The most involved and the larger part of the constituency of the rock groups are adolescents. This is not surprising. For it is they who remain closest to the conditions they are protesting through their music, their dances, and their other forms of expression. Under the circumstances it is highly desirable that the young should protest in these ways against the conditions they find so intolerable. But unfortunately the young are not always clear as to the nature of all the things that need to be changed. This would be too much to expect. However, in the areas in which they are most perceptive, childrearing, education, and human relations, they often see far beyond their elders. *Love* is a word which has come to be meaningful to them, to signify a great deal more than it does to most adults, and if they will demonstratively act it out, they may yet succeed in remaking the world.

It is interesting that, in February 1974, George Thiess, president of Arthur Murray, Inc., commenting on the 20 to 35 percent increased enrollment in his dance studios, said that men were no longer embarrassed about dancing. Couples were doing things together. Hostile dancing—his term for rock dancing—"doesn't work anymore, because couples are relating to each other differently than in the sixties." He referred to his dance groups as "touch-go-theques."

The contemporary public wiggling by uncoupled couples which passes for dance is clearly sexual, suggesting an inverse awkwardness which prevents the dyad from indulging in the closeness of tactile dancing where one body touches the other.

The contortionist form of contemporary dancing seems like a narcissistic statement of being alone together.

In many indigenous cultures, and some Christian sects, dance during trance serves to communicate a sense of contact with the supernaturals.

The tactual sensitivity with which the baby is born has already undergone much preparatory development in the womb. We know that the fetus is capable of responding both to pressure and to sound, and that the beating of its own heart at about 140 beats per minute and the beating of its mother's heart, with a frequency of 70, provides it with something of a syncopated world of sound. Given the knowledge that the baby is laved by the amniotic fluid to the symphonic beat of two hearts, it is not surprising to learn that the soothing effect of rhythmical sounds has been connected, in the hypotheses of some researchers, with the feeling of well-being assumed to exist *in utero* in relation to the mother's heartbeat.

Dr. Lee Salk has shown that, both in monkeys and in the human species, the mother has a marked preference for holding her infant on the left side. Because the apex of the heart is more exposed on the left side, it is reasoned that the preference which these primate mothers show for holding the baby's head against that side is related to the need of the baby to continue to hear the solacing rhythm of its mother's heartbeat. Since, however, most mothers are right-handed, they are most likely to hold the infant in the left arm, thus leaving the right hand free and putting the infant's head opposite the apex of the heart. This may be the real explanation for the manner in which most mothers hold the infant on the left side.

On the assumption that exposure to a normal heartbeat sound immediately following birth would tend to buffer the trauma of birth by providing the infant with the continuity of a familiar security-giving stimulus, Dr. Salk exposed a number of babies in a hospital nursery to the tape recording of normal authentic heartbeat sounds at 72 paired beats per minute. The results were most interesting. A significantly larger number, 69.6 percent of babies who were exposed to the heartbeat sounds, gained weight after the first twenty-four hours of age, whereas only 33 percent of the unexposed group gained weight. One or more babies were crying 38.4 percent of the time during the heartbeat phase of the experiment, but 59.8 percent of the time when the sound was not present. Breathing was deeper and more regular among the heartbeat babies than among the controls. Respiratory and gastrointestinal difficulties decreased during the heartbeat period.

Dr. Salk concluded that the sound of a normal heartbeat during the early days and weeks of its postnatal life may well contribute to the infant's better emotional adjustment later in life. Because of its deep-rooted biological significance as the first sound, the constant security-giving sound, the sound experienced when closest to the mother, the heartbeat sound or its equivalent later succeeds in allaying fear where all else might fail.

In that luminous poem, *The Prelude,* Wordsworth recalls "that first time/ In which, a Babe, by intercourse of touch,/ I held mute dialogues with my Mother's heart."

What connection, if any, does the mother's heartbeat and that of the fetus have to the beat and rhythms of music? *Zwei Herzen in Dreiviertel Takt—Two Hearts in Three-Quarter Time* was a highly successful film in the early thirties. Its theme song, from which the film took its title, was a waltz written, as are all waltzes, in three-quarter time, 1. 2. 3—the baby's heart having beaten, most of its time *in utero,* twice for every one beat of the mother's heart. Is it possible that such a juxtaposition of meanings represents a reverberation of uterine or infantile experiences? Dr. Joost Meerloo thinks it likely.

> Every mother [he writes] intuitively knows that in order to put her baby to sleep she has to rock it, thereby repeating the nirvanic dance [of the fetus in the womb]. The lullaby "Rock-a-bye Baby" unobtrusively takes the child's memory back to the world it has just left. Rock 'n' Roll does the same for older children. It is just as simple as that! Rhythm and whirling around take each of us back to reminiscences of nirvanic equanimity.

But listen well. This does not imply that the dance means no more than a regressive reminiscing, even though in many of us syncopated rhythms, music and counterpoint at regular intervals cause a deep oceanic yearning and a longing for maternal protection, which once was the happy world we lived in.

Dr. Meerloo also draws attention to what he calls "The Milk Dance," the rhythmic interaction between mother and child during the baby's suckling at the mother's breast. The kind of experience the infant has had at the breast, Dr. Meerloo believes, will influence the individual's later rhythmic interests and moods. Nursing deprivations, being brought too late to the breast or getting no breastfeeding at all, may cause the repressed rhythms to come to the fore inappropriately. "As a result of this so-called early oral frustration these children may withdraw desolately in a corner, spontaneously showing the milk dance, while rocking and rolling in a void. These are the children whom doctors give the sophisticated label of being early schizophrenics. Indeed, some of these children can remain such dancing zombies for the rest of their lives, always searching, in a frozen rhythm and unrest, for the lost Nirvana."

Dr. Meerloo considers it important to describe these early biological roots of the dance, because in his clinical practice he has met "many a dance student who used her or his dance aspirations not only to create beauty of gesture and movement, but also as a means to return unobtrusively to frustrated, desperate moods carried over from childhood."

"The charm," he adds, "and the seduction imposed on us by these vibrant reminiscences can drag us into the despair of continuous repetition of sad memories just as easily as they can lead us into the highest triumph of freely creating a new counter-gesture: the dance. From then on our movements become lighter than air, ethereal gestures into space, away from all heaviness."

In the dance, Dr. Meerloo thinks, man's earliest existence is revealed. "Whenever rhythm, cadence, syncopation reach ear and eye man is unobtrusively dragged back into the very beginning of his existence; together with others he undergoes a common regression. The clue of mental contagion is the inadvertent common regression *all* people undergo when special sounds and rhythms reach their ears. That is the reason why tapping, rhythmic calling, musical shouting, jazz, etc., are so infectious."

The disposition to respond to rhythmic stimuli seems to be genetically based, but the manner in which the responses are expressed are culturally determined. For example, keeping time to music by tapping with the foot is a culturally learned activity, mostly as a result of unconscious imitation. Most of us are unaware that we are beating time in this way to the music. Apropos of this point I remember, many years ago, reading the autobiography of the great Hungarian philologist Arminius Vambery. Vambery was an extraordinarily gifted linguist. His Arabic was perfect. This enabled him, in disguise as an Arab, to make the pilgrimage to Mecca when that was still a forbidden city to infidels like him. In Mecca he was honored with a feast by one of the local chieftains, as a visiting Arab dignitary from distant parts. While music was being played the chieftain approached Vambery, and good-humoredly said to him, "You are a European." Vambery was astonished. "How did you find out?" he inquired. "I observed," the chieftain replied, "that during the playing of the music you beat time with your foot. No Arab ever does that."*

There does appear to be a natural predisposition for rhythmic movement in man. The manner of that movement is, however, culturally conditioned. The body contact characteristic of ballroom dancing represented a formalized closeness in rhythm which would not in other situations be permitted except between husband and wife or parents and children. Then in the twenties in America, cheek leaning was added to body contact in dancing. Again, this was a formalized act which

---

*I quote the story from memory. It will be found in Arminius Vambery, *The Story of My Struggles* (London: Fisher Unwin, 1904).

would not otherwise have been allowed except between relatives. Did this cheek leaning represent an attempt to achieve
the cutaneous contact that had been denied the cheek leaners
earlier in life? May it not also be that rock 'n' roll and other
popular contemporary varieties of music and the dance represent a like response? At least in part, but in a very fundamental
way, may not these forms derive from a periphrastic response
to an early insufficient experience of comforting, rocking, rolling, and cutaneous stimulation?

In the cradle-rockingless, lullabyless, strife-torn world of
the twentieth century, rock 'n' roll music and plaintive lullabies, sometimes beautiful, usually stridently percussive, possibly represent compensatory effects for the lack of solicitude
which parents have in the past exhibited for their children's
tactile needs, a cry for affection. Ignorance concerning the experience of such needs is widespread. But this does not mean
that it is uncorrectable. The music of a segment of the population and of a period may sometimes bear a direct relation to
the kind of early conditioning experiences, or lack of them, the
individual has undergone in early life. Whether or not this is
true in the present instance, in relation to the skin, cannot be
decided until a great deal more research has been done on this
engaging subject. It is an interesting conjecture, and it is worth
pursuing if only for the light it might throw on the micro-me-
chanics of human development, which is to say the light it
might throw on yet another aspect of human nature.

The use of touch in trance events around the world as a
way of communicating a sense of contact with the phenomenal
world is widespread, as is its use for communicating with the
world of supernaturals. In each case the dancer is taken out of
the normal patterns of contact with the members of his community. Haitian, Balinese, Bushman, and Pentecostal dances
are good examples of what may well be universally true.

In community dancing, and as in the Ghost Dance of
North American Indians, it is the closeness of the dancers that
conveys their unity and the security that they find in proximity
to each other.

CLOTHES AND THE SKIN. Our discussion has considered the possible relation of the kinds of experiences of early cutaneous stimulation and the kinds of music and dance that may develop, especially in response to the lack of adequate rocking and cutaneous stimulation. This brings us to another interesting question—namely, the relationships of clothes, skin, and behavior.

Irwin and Weiss have found that activity was significantly less in infants when they were clothed than when they were unclothed. This raised the question whether the reduced activity was due to mechanical restraint by the clothes or possibly the elimination of self-stimulation, or perhaps the alleviation of hunger contractions, or finally, whether the clothing perhaps reduced or offered insulation against incoming stimuli.

The correct answer to these questions is probably that all four factors are operative, but that the last is the most important—the insulation that clothing produces against incoming stimuli.

It is difficult to say whether or not the habit of dressing the infant in clothes early in his life bears any relation to the development of behavioral differences, distinguishing those behaviors from behaviors found in cultures in which neither children nor adults wear clothes. Clothes, and different kinds of clothes, probably affect the skin differently enough to result in behavior directly traceable to the effects exercised through the skin. It may be conjectured that the remarkable innovations in dress worn by young people, and such phenomena as long hair, beards, and other hispid facial embellishments in the male, have some connection with early kinds of tactile or lack of tactile experiences. Hair is an important appendage of the skin, and indeed constitutes the avenue through which much of its stimulation is initiated. Possibly the hair that young men began to sport on their heads and faces in the late 1960s in some measure represents an expression of the need for love which was earlier denied them because of the stroking and patting and caressing they failed to receive in infancy. The highly successful musical play *Hair* was emphatically, among other things, devoted to long hair and, for a bit, to nudity. Perhaps it would not be putting too great a strain on the imagination to offer the exegesis that what the play was pleading for is more love, for being stroked the right way rather than being rubbed the wrong.

During World War I, when women began to bob their hair and shorten their skirts, Eric Gill, the distinguished English type designer, typographer, and sculptor, penned the following quatrain:

> *If skirts should get much shorter*
> *Said the flapper with a sob,*
> *There'll be two more cheeks to powder*
> *And one more place to bob.*

One wonders what he would have thought of miniskirts, topless waitresses, see-through blouses, and bikinis.

Allowing for the demise of Anthony Comstock, Mrs. Grundy, and the Censor, as well as for the increasing amplitude of our enlarging freedoms, it may be that the massive exposure of the skin and its integumentary specializations is related to the need for cutaneous satisfaction of those who in their earlier lives failed to receive such satisfactions.

The increasing popularity of "skinny dipping" and "nude beaches" may not be altogether unrelated to this. The waterbed, which in recent years has enjoyed some popularity, appeals, presumably, because of its "cuddly" sensual qualities. Instead of the statically "indifferent" qualities of the ordinary bed, it provides a constantly stimulating series of hugs and caresses as one moves in its embrace, and an encompassing support when one sleeps in it reminiscent of that time we fell asleep on our mother's body. Many young couples with an infant or two have spoken enthusiastically of the virtues of the waterbed. In addition to making a fine bed, it also makes a good rocker-cradle. The waterbed has to be filled nearly to capacity and set within a frame, in order to save stress on the seams. Because the infant may manage to find his way between the bed and the frame, he should never be left unattended on the waterbed. Padding and bedclothes help to protect the bed from puncture. Parents can sleep together with their infants on the bed in comfort, and with much less interruption than when the infant is in a crib. Infants and their siblings love to run and jump about on a waterbed, and one never has to worry about spills ruining the mattress. Failing a waterbed, a regular bed can be lowered to a safe level or the mattress placed on the floor as a safety precaution to keep young ones from tumbling out.

Clothes largely cut off the experience of pleasurable sensations from the skin; hence, the actual or symbolic shedding of clothes may represent attempts to enjoy experiences that had been earlier denied. Natural skin stimulation, the play of air, sun, and wind upon the body, can be very pleasurable. Flügel, who conducted an inquiry into the matter, found that such natural skin stimulation was often described in "glowing" terms, as "heavenly," "perfectly delightful," "like breathing in happiness," and in similar expressions of pleasure. The growth of the nudist movement almost certainly reflects the desire for more freedom of communication through the skin.*

This, interestingly enough, takes the form of visual communication through the inspection of the nude body. All nudists agree that this greatly reduces sexual tension, and is of general therapeutic value. Touching, even between husband and wife, was strictly forbidden in all nudist camps, but that rule is today tending to be somewhat relaxed. Hartman, who has made a serious study of nudists, expresses his pleasure in seeing "nudists engaged in various games involving physical contact but not involving any suggestive activities. I had heard so much about the no-touch rule but had been warmly embraced by both males and females during the period of the research and found that such cordiality had nothing to do with

*One of the earliest serious discussions of nudism and the disadvantages of clothes is to be found in Maurice Parmalee, *The New Gymnosophy* (New York: Hitchcock, 1927). See also the book that introduced nudism to America, by F. Merrill and M. Merrill, *Among the Nudists* (New York: Garden City Publishing Co., 1931).

sexual arousal. This contact was one of the more pleasurable experiences of the research." Hartman points out that American culture has been regarded as a no-touch one. His observations on nudists lead him to believe that nudists may unwittingly have aggravated the situation. "I believe," he writes, "that much more personal growth would take place among individuals where there is some kind of affectionate touch contact, especially with closely related individuals and generally between all persons. It was my observation that the no-touch rule is on its way out."

The association of nudity with sex is, of course, so strong that where touching of the clothed body is permissible, the same part of the body is taboo to touch when it is unclothed. This rule, however, does not apply to parents and their small children. As the children grow older, physical contact becomes more restrained, and by adolescence is completely terminated, so that adolescents who touch each other while clothed cease to do so when in the nude in camps.

One of the consequences of the habit of wearing clothes from early infancy is that the skin fails to develop the sensitivity it would have done had clothes not been habitually worn. It has been observed, for example, that among nonliterate peoples the skin is very much more responsive to stimuli than it is among Europeans. Kilton Stewart, in his book *Pygmies and Dream Giants,* reports of the Philippine Negritos that they "are very sensitive to creeping things, and were amazed that an ant could crawl up my leg without my being aware of it."

The differences between individuals in skin sensitivity are quite remarkable. There are some who when they touch another feel "a sort of electrical current" passing between them, whereas others experience nothing of the sort. It is also of interest to note that while some individuals retain this sensitivity into old age, others tend to lose it in middle age. Quite possibly in these latter cases hormonal changes may be involved.

The "electricity" that is often, metaphorically speaking, said to pass between people when touching one another may be something more than a mere metaphor. The skin is an especially good electrical conductor. Electrical changes may be measured at the skin surface in a variety of ways, one of the best known of these being the psychogalvanometer or, as it is commonly miscalled, "the lie detector." Emotional changes acting through the autonomic nervous system usually produce an increase in the electrical conductance of the skin (a decrease in resistance) across the palms of the hands or feet. There can be little doubt that in tactile stimulation electrical changes are transmitted from one individual to the other.

Finally, it is worth noting that the skin usually contains little moisture, and that cold dry skin is a good insulator and constitutes the principal protection against electric shock.

MATERNAL AVERSIVE BEHAVIOR. Not all women who become pregnant want children and after the children are born not infrequently exhibit aversive behavior toward them. Dr. Louise Biggar has reported on these situations most interestingly. She found that just as monkeys who are rejected by their mothers strive all the more strongly to approach or cling to them, the human child behaves in much the same manner; and just as the monkey mother repels and at some level simultaneously attracts the infant, so do many human mothers. This results in a double-bind situation similar to that described by Bateson and his collaborators for schizophrenia. Conflicting signals of repulsion and approach from the mother put the infant in a double bind. Accordingly, it would be expected that infants caught in such a bind would exhibit certain behavioral reactions, such as anger, conflict, and aggression.

Studies of three independent samples of infants and mothers confirmed the theory. It was found that the greater the mother's aversion to physical contact with the infant during the first three months, the more anger seemed to direct the infant's mood and activities nine months later. In addition, it was found that "the more the mother had shown an early aversion to physical contact with the infant, the more frequently the infant struck or angrily threatened to strike the mother in relatively stress-free situations." The degree of security of the children studied was assessed at six years of age during a three-minute reunion with the parent after an hour of separation. It was found that the children who at one year of age had been called very secure initiated conversation with the parent in a personal way, and were highly responsive conversationally, initiating some physical contact as well.

The six-year-olds who had been very insecure as infants showed three main patterns of behavior. One group was linguistically avoidant, responding minimally to questions, and talked about things rather than about themselves, and tended to avoid ventral orientation with the parent by crossing the room or moving away. Another group was rejecting of the parent, saying "Don't bother me," or "Why don't you go sit over there." The third pattern, which was rare, was called inappropriate caregiving. This consisted in children of this group behaving parentally toward their parents, reflecting another kind of organization of attachment. From the time that the human infant has reached the stage of forming attachments to caregivers, Biggar wisely observes the physical and tactual accessibility of certain persons is continually monitored by the infant, and becomes an organizing principle in its behavior.

Biggar's work once again gives strong support to the fundamental importance of touch during early development, and underscores once more the serious consequences of default on the part of attachment figures.

EFFECTS UPON THE MOTHER OF MATERNAL-INFANT SEPARATION. Much has been written on the effects of separation from the mother upon the infant, but until recently little had been written on the effects upon the mother. There are now many studies showing that separation of the infant from the mother shortly after birth for about twenty-four hours or less is likely to produce a decline in maternal confidence, accompanied by anxiety. Sostek, Scanlon, and Abramson have reported on this and have surveyed the literature. Psychologically, both mother and infant are much advantaged in every way by close contact as immediately after birth as possible. What does not seem to have been given sufficient attention has been the physiological effects upon the mother of infant separation. Midwives have known for centuries that simply leaving the newborn and mother in skin contact causes the uterus to undergo contractions, and thus speeds it on its way to return to normal size. The only time I had seen a discussion of this subject was in a communication to *Child-Family Digest* in 1954 by Mrs. Betsy Marvin McKinney (to which reference has already been made on an earlier page). The importance of Mrs. McKinney's communication is such that it is reprinted in full in Appendix 2. The custom of separating mother and infant after birth still goes on in many hospitals, though it is good to say that the trend is now in the opposite direction, and that in many institutions family birth centers have been created as part of the hospital or have been founded by well-trained laypersons.

If only for the fundamental reason that the first language of communication between newborn and mother is through the skin, by touch, the newborn and mother should not be separated, except when the one or the other needs to rest or sleep, or during maternal infection. Any obstetrical practice which disregards that dictum should be discouraged.

Among all mammals thus far investigated, and there have been many, separation of newborn and mother even for as little as an hour will lead to indifference to and even rejection of the infant by the mother.

"DERMO-OPTICAL PERCEPTION." Some persons claim to possess skins so sensitive that they are able to "see" with them. Since the skin is derived from the same embryological ectodermal layer as the eyes, several investigators have maintained that in such individuals the skin has retained some primitive optical properties, and it is this that enables them to see with the skin. This view was forcibly argued by the French novelist Jules Romains in 1919 in his book, *Vision Extra-Rétinienne.* At regular intervals the idea makes its appearance in the press, when some individual is reported with "eyeless sight," or as being able to see from the socket from which his eye was removed, or through his fingers, or through the skin of the face following a thorough sealing of the eyes.

There is, in fact, no evidence whatever that will withstand a moment's critical examination that anyone has ever been able to see with the skin. What appear to be impressive performances are usually due to trickery. Martin Gardner has discussed many alleged cases of dermo-optical perception, and thoroughly disposed of them. The sensory capacities of the skin are remarkable enough to render the making of exaggerated claims for it quite unnecessary. The ability of blind persons like Laura Bridgman and Helen Keller, and Madame de Staël, who used to pass her hands over the faces of her visitors in order to gain some idea of what they looked like, are a matter of record. But no one ever claimed that these ladies were seeing through their skin. We all have stereognostic ability—that is, the ability to perceive objects or forms by touch—and in a metaphoric sense most human beings can almost "see" the form of the object they have touched. The tips of the fingers are the parts of the body that are characterized by the greatest sensitivity in "reading," that is in stereognizing, the form of objects by touch. The Braille alphabet, three dots high and three dots wide, makes it possible for blind people to read the most complex works in any language. In Braille the reader does not "see," but interprets the dots in the brain as read through the fingertips. This code was the invention of a blind boy of fifteen, Louis Braille (1809–1852).

If any evidence were required to demonstrate the mind of the skin, it could rest on the sensory capacities of the fingertips alone. Those capacities, in the form of sensory receptors that pick up the stimuli, in turn transmit them to the brain in the form of complex nervous impulses. Through repetition, that is by learning, capacities become abilities enabling the individual to make the fine discriminations that endow the particular sensations with particular meanings. An ability is a trained capacity, and every human being has to learn how to make such fine discriminations. Just as he has to learn the ability of stereognosis, so too he learns to develop the sensitivities inherent in his skin, or he does not. That particular variety of learning is almost entirely determined by the cutaneous and related experiences he has undergone during infancy and childhood.

DERMOGRAPHIA. *Dermographia* or *dermatographia* is skin writing or the raising of wheals by pressure, usually on the broad expanse of the back. One may write on the skin with a blunt instrument. When the wheals show up red, hyperreactivity of the vagus nerve (vagotonia) is involved; when the wheals are predominantly white, the sympathetic nervous system is involved. The wheals themselves are produced by oozing of fluid from capillaries into the surrounding tissue, the oozing in turn, apparently, resulting from local dilation of the blood vessels. Everyone's skin will wheal if stroked sufficiently often or struck sufficiently hard, but in the abnormal cases mild stroking is sufficient to produce dermographia. Whether or not dermographia has any relation whatever to early childhood cutaneous experience is at present quite unknown.

Children have for generations played at tracing letters on each other's backs, competing with each other for the highest number of correct identifications. Adults, too, can play this game with varying degrees of competence. The brain, clearly, is capable of translating patterns of stimulated touch receptors into letters and simple images. No one, so far as I know, has ever studied the variability in translating such dermatographic messages in different individuals. It would not, I think, be too rash to predict that significant correlations would be found between such dermatographic skills and early cutaneous experience.

Drs. Paul Bach-y-Rita and Carter C. Collins of the Smith-Kettlewell Institute of Visual Sciences of the University of the Pacific Graduate School of Medical Sciences in San Francisco, basing themselves on the knowledge of the ability of the brain to translate dermal messages, have found that such translation also occurs when the stimuli come from arrays of electrodes or vibrating points connected to a camera. After a few hours of training, blind subjects can recognize geometric figures and objects like chairs and telephones. Additional training produces the ability to judge distance and even to recognize faces.

The skin and the retina of the eye are unique in that their sensory receptors are laid out in a pattern. This enables both the retina and the skin to pick up regularities and patterns of stimuli and to convert them readily into images in the brain. Using an array of electrodes mounted in an elastic matrix, which can be worn on the back or abdomen, under regular clothes, a camera is mounted on the blind person's head like a miner's lamp. This camera can transmit to the electrodes the information it picks up, which the electrodes in turn transmit to the skin. The information is then translated in the brain for what it is. During the course of this research, it was found that the abdominal skin "sees" better than that of the back or forearms.

The spatio-temporal perceptive capacities of the skin are quite remarkable. Time is handled almost as well by the skin as by the ear. The skin can pick up a break of about 10 thousandths of a second in a steady mechanical pressure or tactile buzz. Eye discriminations are about 25–35 thousandths of a second. The skin picks up the location of distances on its surface very much more efficiently than the ear is able to locate sounds at a distance. Utilizing this information, Dr. Frank A. Geldard of the Cutaneous Communication Laboratory at Princeton University has worked out an opthohapt alphabet which can be flashed to the skin rapidly and vividly. The symbols are easy to learn and read, in a language that may be called "body English." Geldard has shown that Rousseau's envisionment, in 1762, in his treatise on education, *Émile,* of the possibility of communicating through the skin was indeed a remarkable piece of prescience. The skin, Geldard has demonstrated, is capable of receiving and reading rapid and sophisticated messages. "There is every likelihood," he says, "that skin languages of great subtlety and speed can be devised and used."

In 1907 Maria Montessori showed that children appeared to learn more readily when they could feel the letters as well as observe them. It has recently been suggested that if congenitally blind children can feel "visualizations," then perhaps the transfer from feeling a pattern to recognizing its visual image is a natural process. Unfortunately, the facts do not support the suggestion, since for the congenitally blind things have no spatial remoteness, and so they are unable to judge distance. Even after they have recovered their sight, they are for some time unable to visualize distance. For the congenitally blind there is no such thing as "tactual space." When they become sighted, everything is a complete novelty, and they are quite unable to recognize visually any objects from their experience of their tactual shape.

A dramatic and illuminating account of the inability of a sightless person to visually recognize objects with which she was tactually familiar before she became sighted is told by Sheila Hocken in her book *Emma and I.*

Dermo-optical perception is a myth, but perception through the skin by means of its other properties is a reality. The skin possesses the ability to respond to a large variety of modalities. Already electronic devices are available which vibrate in an outline identical to the letters of the alphabet, enabling a blind person, after a little practice, to see. In addition to vibrotactile communication, research is proceeding on coding alphabets through electropulses. B. von Haller Gilmer and Lee W. Gregg of the Carnegie Institute of Technology have been pursuing this approach. They point out that the skin is rarely if ever "busy," a fact which enables it to learn, to become habituated to codes that cannot be interfered with under any conditions. The vibrotactile or electrotactile signal cannot be shut out. Nor can the skin close its eyes; it cannot even hold its ears—in this respect it more closely resembles the ear than the eye. Von Haller Gilmer and Gregg postulate that by its very nature, the skin is not handicapped with excess verbiage, as is the written and spoken word. Perhaps the skin has possibilities of codes, they suggest, even superior to other channels because of its "simplicity." The skin may be unique in combining the spatio-temporal dimensions of hearing and vision, the ear being best in the temporal, and the eye in the spatial dimension.

With an apparatus designed by J. F. Hahn to deliver and measure square wave pulses to the skin and its resistance, von Haller Gilmer and Gregg have made exploratory studies on both normal and blind subjects. Given areas of the skin may be stimulated at the rate of one pulse per second, with a duration of one millisecond, for up to two hours without report of pain. A pulse language, therefore, becomes possible once the pulses for the code have been worked out. Such an artificial language, the elements of which are defined by cutaneous sensations, has remarkable possibilities. Placing the cutaneous sensations in one-to-one correspondence with the elemental sounds of speech (phonemes), these investigators will be using a programmed computer (the code interpreter) as an analog to the human communications receptor. With the aid of this computer they hope to construct a system that may yield the necessary information upon which a good code can be based.

Touch as interval has never been properly investigated. By an *interval* in music is meant the difference in pitch between any two notes. The great variety of intervals experienced in touch carries the signals to the brain, which gives them meaning. As in music, so also in tactile experience, intervals can be either concordant or discordant. The psychophysics of the subject has yet to be explored.

ITCHING AND SCRATCHING. Itching is an irritating cutaneous sensation which provokes the desire to scratch or rub the skin. Scratching, the usual means of relieving itching, is done by scraping with the fingernails. The psychosomatics of itching and scratching are well known. That distinguished polymath William Shakespeare put it this way in *Coriolanus* (I. i. 162), where he makes Caius Marcius say:

> *What's the matter, you dissentious rogues,*
> *That, rubbing the poor itch of your opinion,*
> *Make yourselves scabs?*

An "itch" in the mind, as it were, will often express itself as an itch in the skin. Musaph, who has written a fascinating monograph on the subject of itching and scratching, describes these as "derived" activities—that is to say, as activities which are derived from the "sparking over" or transduction into a skin response of experiences related to and prepared by the individual's early life. For example, in frustrating situations angry emotions may be converted infra-symbolically into itching and scratching. The various forms of psychosomatic pruritis—that is, functionally induced itching of the skin— often represent the unconscious striving to obtain the attention that was denied in early life, especially the attention that was denied to the skin. Unexpressed feelings of frustration, rage, and guilt, as well as the strong repressed need for love, may find symptomatic expression in the form of scratching even in the absence of itching.

Seitz has drawn attention to the clandestine scratching of many persons who feel ashamed because the practice causes them to experience pleasurable sensations of an erotic quality. For example, Martin Berezin has described the case of a woman of forty-eight who suffered from a severe pruritis ani, so severe that she induced excoriations of the perineum by scratching. During the course of psychotherapy it was discovered that the scratching of her anus represented a masturbatory equivalent, a discovery confirmed when she shifted her scratching to her external genitalia. With the resolution of her conflict, the pruritis disappeared altogether.

The erotic quality of much scratching is fairly obvious. An old proverb has it, " 'Tis better than riches to scratch where it itches." Montaigne, in his essay "Of Experience," writes, "Scratching is one of nature's sweetest gratifications, and nearest at hand." While no less a person than James I of England declared that "No one but kings and princes should have the itch, for the sensation of scratching is so delightful." And that choleric character Thomas Carlyle went so far as to say, "The height of human happiness is to scratch the part that itches." The relief from emotional tension offered by scratching has been portrayed by Samuel Butler (1612–1680) in *Hudibras*,

> *He could raise scruples dark and nice,*
> *And after solve 'em in a trice:*
> *As if Divinity had catch'd*
> *The itch, on purpose to be scratched. (I. I. 163)*

Ogden Nash sums it all up succinctly in his quatrain, "Taboo to Boot,"

> *One bliss for which*
> *There is no match*
> *Is when you itch*
> *To up and scratch.*

Brian Russell points out that deprivation of love often results in itching, an itch to be loved. "The patient with widespread eczema whose skin relapses on the very suggestion of discharge from the hospital, regresses to an infantile stage of dependency with the mute appeal, 'I am helpless; you must care for me.' "

Scratching may be simultaneously a source of pleasure and of displeasure, expressing guilt and a tendency toward self-punishment. Disturbances in sexuality and hostility are almost always present in patients with pruritis.

The reciprocal benefits implied in the old saying, "You scratch my back, and I'll scratch yours," convey something more than a metaphor.

In August 1971 closed-circuit TV was installed in the Tribune Tower in Chicago in order to protect the offices against would-be thieves. But before word got around of the existence of the TV monitors, they revealed, writes Clarence Petersen, "something very significant about human nature. The nature of the human is, more than anything else, to itch. It is simply astonishing how many people itch and, of course, that is counting only those who are uninhibited enough to scratch." Indeed, itching and scratching are forms of behavior so often indulged that almost all of us would be astonished were we to become aware of the frequency with which we resort to them.

The pleasures of back scratching are phylogentically very old; even invertebrates are soothed by gentle back rubbing, and it is well known that all mammals enjoy it. Also, like man, other mammals enjoy back scratching in the absence of itching even more than in its presence. The instrument known as a back scratcher or scratch-back is a very ancient device; the latest electric models are advertised as being "better than a friend, with a hand that jiggles up and down like the real thing." Thus, the sheer pleasure-giving qualities of the appropriately stimulated skin testify to its need for pleasurable stimulation. In this sense almost every kind of cutaneous stimulation that is not intended to be injurious is characterized by an erotic component. Under the appropriate circumstances, even a touch on the hand can be sexually exciting. It is highly probable that the differences in the degree of cutaneous sensitivity that different individuals exhibit to the pleasures derivable from stimulation of the skin in all states and conditions of being are largely influenced by early experiences of cutaneous stimulation. Certainly the experiments of the Harlows and others abundantly testify to that fact in monkeys, apes, and other mammals, while psychiatric research fully supports the relationship in humans.

BATHING AND THE SKIN. The delight that infants take in a warm bath, their joyful splashing and gurgling, and their great reluctance to leave the water testify to the pleasure they derive from this hydrous stimulation of the skin. It is perhaps not surprising, therefore, that the bathroom has become the temple of the American household, and the daily bath a ritual celebration of the hymn to self-laving. Women find the bath relaxing; men find the shower stimulating. And both men and women often spend considerably more time in the bath than one would think necessary for the mere purposes of cleanliness. Can it be that in addition to enjoying the pleasures derived from the cutaneous stimulation which each sex obtains in its own way, these pleasures in part represent a ritual revival of pleasures originally enjoyed in the aquatic environment of the mother's womb, and in the early experiences of bathing during infancy?

It is of great interest that men, and sometimes women, who seldom otherwise sing will break out into song in the bathtub or under the shower. What can be the explanation of this? Also, a high proportion of masturbatory activities take place in the bath or shower. Why? Clearly the stimulation of the skin by the water is very different in the shower from what it is in the tub. The sudden and continuing stimulation of the skin by the shower water induces active respiratory changes which in the appropriate subject are likely to result in song. This is much less likely to happen under the more gentle stimulation of the water in the tub. In both cases, however, the rubbing of the skin is likely to induce erotic sensations leading to masturbatory activities.

The heightened pleasure derived from tactile stimulation in water is a serendipitous discovery that many a couple of lovers has made. In water the skin appears to assume new properties, it becomes excitingly smooth, much more pleasant to the touch, and greatly enhances the pleasures of sexual communication.

The enormous increase in the number of private swimming pools, and the rush to the beaches in summer, with bathing incidental to exposure to sun and gentle breezes, further serves to testify to the great pleasure taken in the sensory excitements provided by shedding one's clothes and exposing one's skin to the elements. Years ago Dr. C. W. Saleeby in his book entitled *Sunlight and Health* made eloquent comment on this. Referring to the skin, he wrote:

This admirable organ, the natural clothing of the body, which grows continually throughout life, which has at least four distinct sets of sensory nerves distributed to it, which is essential in the regulation of the temperature, which is waterproof from without inwards, but allows the excretory sweat to escape freely, which, when unbroken, is microbe-proof, and which can readily absorb sunlight—this most beautiful, versatile, and wonderful organ is, for the most part, smothered, blanched, and blinded in clothes and can only gradually be restored to the air and light which are its natural surroundings. Then and only then we learn what it is capable of.

Virtually everyone, from the time of Plato to the present day, who has ever written on the subject has sung the praises of nudity over the clothed body; but contemporary man, and especially woman, quite fail to understand the needs of the skin, and from this ignorance often do themselves great and irreparable damage. The sun worship in which increasing numbers of people indulge today not only results in drying, wrinkling, and other damage to the skin, but in many cases initiates the development of skin cancer. Most visible signs of skin damage attributed to aging, as Dr. John M. Knox has pointed out, are actually a result of sunlight exposure. Moderate exposure to sunlight is not only desirable but necessary. Immoderate exposure to sunlight is not only unnecessary but dangerous. It is a rather sad reflection on human folly when one thinks of the billions of dollars women spend on the cosmetic care of their skin in the form of lotions, balms, creams, and the like, while at the same time overexposing their skins to the very worst of possible damaging influences, excessive sunlight. Twenty minutes of exposure to the midday summer sun can result in sunburned redness of the skin. Most people will spend hours on a beach exposed to the sun, an exposure which may result in painful blistering sunburn. It is interesting that the notion of tanning as a sign of health came into being in the 1920s. This corresponds to the period when the heavy-handed teachings of the behaviorists were causing parents to approach their children as if they were automata, and caressing and other forms of cutaneous stimulation of the child were being reduced to a minimum. Possibly, here, too, there is a connection. The tanning may symbolically mean, "You see, the sun has continued to smile upon me, and I have basked freely and uninhibitedly in its embracing rays. I have been well and warmly loved."

SKIN AND SLEEP. The skin remains the most alert of the senses in sleep, and is the first to recover on awakening. Sense organs in the skin and the deeper interoceptive sense organs appear to be involved in bringing about the movements of sleep. Skin that is lain on for too long becomes overheated through lack of ventilation, and as a result messages which result in a change of position are communicated to the appropriate centers. Analysis of heartbeat records in normal sleep have shown that some six minutes before the sleeper stirs his heart begins to beat faster. With the change in sleeping position, the heartbeat slowly returns to its normal rate.

Anna Freud has commented on the close interrelation between the needs for sleep and for cutaneous contact, "falling asleep being rendered more difficult for the infant who is kept strictly separated from the mother's body warmth." Ms. Freud also draws attention to interrelation between sleep and passive body movement—that is, rocking. The relaxed child sleeps, the troubled child suffers from disturbed sleep. Normal sleep is a stimulus barrier. Disturbed sleep is a condition of vulnerability to internally originating excitements. Children who have been briefly separated from their mothers will, during the period of separation, suffer from disturbed sleep. As Heinicke and Westheimer state in their book on the subject, "We find that not only is the most intense fretting for the parents concomitant with the maximum sleep disturbance, but ... disturbances in sleep are directly connected with longing for the parents." After the third day there would be a pronounced decline in the sleep disturbances of these children, but difficulties in falling asleep and fear of being left alone were noticeably frequent. Furthermore, "more of the children had persistent sleeping difficulties during the period following reunion (or its equivalent) than did those who had not been separated." The separations of these two-year-old children lasted from two to twenty weeks. At some point during the first twenty weeks after reunion, seven of the ten children who had experienced separation had noticeable difficulty in falling asleep or remaining asleep, or both. The duration of the sleeping difficulties persisted from one to twenty-one weeks, with the median at four weeks.

Such findings strongly suggest that early interference with the normal mothering process, not only after the infant has made strong identifications with the mother, but even before, may seriously affect the individual's ability to fall asleep or remain asleep. And that, in early infancy especially, the mother's holding, carrying, cuddling, and rocking of the infant constitute acts which play a significant role in the development of later sleep patterns that may persist throughout life.

Deprivation of the tactile need, like deprivation of any other need, causes the infant distress, a separation anxiety. It will therefore sound the distress signal designed to compel attention to its need, by crying. Aldrich and his co-workers found that among the less generally recognized causes of crying in infants is the need for fondling and rhythmic motion. These investigators found a constant relationship between the amount and frequency of crying and the amount and frequency of nursing care: the more care, the less crying. Infants will continue to cry even when they see that they are being approached or when the mother calls to them. Such infants, however, will cease crying immediately when picked up and fondled. Affectionate tactile stimulation is clearly, then, a primary need, a need which must be satisfied if the infant is to develop as a healthy human being.

And what is a healthy human being? One who is able to love, to work, to play, and to think critically and unprejudicedly.

5 The Physiological Effects of Touching

A Province packed up in two yards of skin.
—John Donne, *The Seconde Anniversarie*, 1612.

Surveying the research studies on animal and human responses to touching, one is impressed by how frequent are the marked advantages in health, alertness, and responsiveness of those who have been "handled" as compared with those who have received minimal or no handling. Weininger, in an early unpublished study of ten infants beginning at ten weeks of age, whose mothers were taught to stroke their infants' backs, reported that at six months of age these infants had fewer sniffles, colds, vomiting, and diarrhea than the infants in the control group, whose mothers had not been taught to stroke their infants. What is becoming increasingly evident is that underlying these and many other differences are significant changes in the structure and interrelated functions of the nervous and immunological systems.

The mounting evidence that the skin has an immunologic function has recently been confirmed by a number of independent investigators. The skin, it has been found, more particularly its most superficial layer, the epidermis, produces a substance immunochemically indistinguishable from thymopoietin, the hormone of the thymus gland active in producing T-cell differentiation. T-cells are responsible for cellular immunity. They are called T-cells because, following their origin in the embryo from lymphocytic stem cells in bone marrow, they migrate (at least half of them do) to the thymus gland, where they are processed to become T-cells. In some way not yet understood, the thymus confers *immunologic competence* upon the

T-cells, the ability to differentiate into cells capable of performing specific immune functions. There are thousands of such individually different T-cells, each able to react to a specific antigen and destroy it.

That tactile stimulation has profound effects, both physiological and behavioral, upon the organism, has only recently become known, but exactly how those effects are produced physiologically and biochemically was unknown. It is only in recent years that the subject has begun to receive attention, and in what follows some recent investigations, of a type which will increasingly serve to enlarge our knowledge concerning the manner in which touching or the lack of it produces its manifold effects, will be briefly discussed.

Dr. Martin Reite and his colleagues of the Developmental Psychobiology Research Group at the University of Colorado Medical Center have found that infant bonnet monkeys (*Macaca radiata*), upon separation from their mothers for two weeks, suffer from suppressed immunological functioning. On being restored to their mothers after the fourteen-day separation, their bodies return to a normal lymphocyte proliferation.

A similar depression of lymphocyte response was observed in a pair of pigtailed monkeys (*Macaca nemestrina*) who had been raised together until, at seventeen weeks, they were separated for an eleven-day period, and then reunited, when their lymphocyte response returned to normal.

Drs. Stephen Butler and Saul Schanberg of Duke University Medical School have shown that ornithine decarboxylase (ODB), the enzyme necessary for the biosynthesis of the polyamines putrescine and spermine, the end products of the enzyme being intimately involved in the regulation of protein and nucleic acid synthesis, as well as an important regulator of growth and differentiation, is affected by hormones in the preweanling rat and thought to play a role in stress. In the ten-day-old rat pups, it was found that when separated from their mothers for as little as one hour, there was a significant decline in ODB. The effect peaked at two to four hours of maternal deprivation, at which time the brain ODB was 60 percent below that of equally handled littermate controls. Return to the mother rapidly reversed the deprivation-induced decline in all brain regions and also in the heart. There can be little doubt that similar effects are produced in human infants who have been more or less maternally deprived.

In another series of experiments, Kuhn, Evoniuk, and Schanberg found that maternal deprivation was associated with a specific suppression of tissue response to the growth-promoting peptide hormones, growth hormone, and placental lactogen. When the rat pups of the experiment were restored to their mothers, there was a rapid return to normal.

The investigators concluded that some subtle mother-pup interaction was responsible for the reversal of the untoward effects in maternally deprived preweanling pups; they suspected that tactile experience might be a principal factor. To test this hypothesis, the following experiments were performed: eight-day-old preweanling pups were removed from their mothers to a comfortable nest, and in one group they were subjected to ten to twenty short, fairly heavy strokings on back and head areas every five minutes with a one-inch camelhair brush softened lightly with water. In other experiments, two different forms of stimulation were tested: slower, more gentle stroking of the same number and duration, or a single pinch on the tail was administered. Deprived pups not experimentally treated in these ways were kept in a separate container in the same incubator and not handled at all except at the beginning and end of the experiments.

In the first experiments brain, heart, and liver ODC activity was compared after five different experimental manipulations: control pups left with the mother for two hours, pups that were maternally deprived for two hours, and maternally deprived pups that were handled by heavy stroking, light stroking, and tail pinching. The brain, heart, and liver activity in maternally deprived rat pups that were not handled decreased to levels significantly below control activity. Similarly, ODC activity in pups handled by pinching or light stroking also was significantly below control levels. Neither of these two forms of stimulation produced a significant increase in ODC activity over that of maternally deprived littermates. In contrast, brain, heart, and liver ODC activity in maternally deprived pups that were heavily stroked remained at or above control ODC levels.

In another experiment, similar results were obtained for growth hormone (GH), and in a third experiment the possibility was investigated that tactile stimulation would raise the ODC activity and serum GH levels already lowered by maternal deprivation. Brain, heart, and liver ODC activity and serum GH levels in pups deprived for four hours were compared to those of pups that were deprived for two hours, and then stroked heavily for two hours. Serum GH and ODC levels in brain and heart in pups that were stroked were not significantly different from controls. In contrast, both ODC activity and serum GH in pups that were maternally deprived and not handled at all for four hours were significantly lower than those of control animals. Liver ODC activity in stroked pups also was significantly elevated above that of maternally deprived, unstimulated pups, although activity did not return to the level of control littermates.

Schanberg and his co-workers recently thoroughly confirmed their original findings, and showed that the decline in ODC following maternal separation occurs even before the innervation of peripheral tissues in their rat pups. Commenting on the significance of their findings, the investigators point to the striking similarity in the symptoms they produced in their animals to the retardation of growth and behavioral development in children known as "psychosocial dwarfism." The separated rat pups exhibited much the same phenotypic effects as separated monkeys and children. There can be little doubt that those effects involve similar physiological or psychoneuroimmunological mechanisms.

The findings of these and other investigators provide the experimental evidence for what has long been suspected—namely, that there are significant biochemical differences between humans who have enjoyed adequate tactile stimulation and those who have not, a statement that will probably be found to hold true throughout life: that the unloved person, taken at any age, is likely to be a very different biochemical entity from those who have been adequately loved. For many years certain forms of "failure to grow or thrive," often characterized by varying degrees of mental retardation, were diagnosed as due to pituitary hormone insufficiency, particularly the growth hormone, until it was discovered the pituitary inadequacy, so-called idiopathic hypopituitarism, and the condition it produced, was actually due to inadequate love on the part of one or the other parent, especially the mother. The condition is now called "psychosocial dwarfism," or "maternal deprivation dwarfism," or "reversible hyposomatotropinism."

Dr. Elsie M. Widdowson of Cambridge University in 1951 seems to have been the first to show that an unpleasant environment could affect the growth of children, weight being affected as well as height. The cause of the unpleasant environment was a stern and forbidding woman superintendent who ruled the orphanage with a rod of iron, compared with the children of neighboring orphanages who were cared for by women who were genuinely fond of children.

Drs. G. F. Powell, J. A. Brasel, and R. M. Blizzard of the department of pediatrics at Johns Hopkins University Medical School were the first to recognize that so-called idiopathic hypopituitarism was not due to malfunction of the pituitary gland, but the result of unfavorable psychosocial conditions. Of the thirteen children they studied, all had unsatisfactory home backgrounds. The adverse environment was associated with bizarre behavior, speech defects, mental retardation, decreased weight and height, and endocrinologic and physiologic deficits.

In another typical case a female fraternal twin, who had severe growth retardation beginning in her seventh year, began to recover after entrance into a school environment. Physical, psychological, and social growth was reversed so that, at age thirteen, she was approximately equal to her twin brother in all respects. Retrospectively it was found that this child had been intermittently separated from her home, was difficult, disliked by her parents, and considered to be permanently retarded both physically and mentally by them. Furthermore, "she was a rapid eater and did not appear to enjoy cuddling"—a very significant remark, for it is the general rule that unloved children tend to substitute eating for the love they fail to receive, and are at first awkward about cuddling since they are so unused to it, and don't know how to respond. These latter are my observations and not those of the authors.

The classic works on the separated child of Margaret Ribble, René Spitz, Anna Freud and Dorothy Burlingham, William Goldfarb, Ashley Montagu, John Bowlby, James Robertson, all published between 1943 and 1957, drew attention to the untoward effects of maternal deprivation, and although in most cases there was hardly a reference to touching, it is quite clear from each of these studies that a principal component in producing the ill effects upon the children was the lack of contact with their mothers.*

*The list of these works will be found on pp. 451–452.

6 Skin and Sex

For touch,
Touch, by the holy powers of the Gods!
Is the sense of the body; whether it be
When something from without makes its way in,
Or when a thing, which in the body had birth,
Hurts it, or gives it pleasure issuing forth
To perform the generative deeds of Venus.

—Lucretius (c. 96 B.C.–c. 53 B.C.),
De Rerum Natura, II, 434.

The true language of sex is primarily nonverbal. Our words and images are poor imitations of the deep and complicated feelings within us. Unsure of touching as a way of sharing with others, we have allowed our fears and discomforts to limit the rich possibilities for nonverbal communication. Sexual expression has a power most of us are still beginning to explore.

The French wit (quoted in an earlier chapter), who defined sexual intercourse as the harmony of two souls and the contact of two epidermes, elegantly emphasized a basic truth: the massive involvement of the skin in sexual congress. The truth is that in no other relationship is the skin so totally involved as in sexual intercourse. Sex, indeed, has been called the highest form of touch. In the profoundest sense touch is the true language of sex. It is principally through stimulation of the skin that both male and female are brought to orgasm in coitus, in the case of the male largely through the sensory receptors in the penis, and in the female through the sensory receptors in the vagina and circumvaginal areas of the skin. Both in the male and in the female the pubic and suprapubic areas, which are covered with hair, are highly sensitive, the *mons veneris,* however, being much more sensitive in the female than the corresponding area in the male. In correlation with this it is interesting to note that in the female the hair of the suprapubic region tends to be crinkly, forming a pad, in contrast to the male, in whom the hair tends to be longish and uncurled. Also the *mons veneris* is more abundantly padded with fatty tissue than the suprapubic region in the male. These differences are probably adaptive in response to the male's assumption of the prone horizontal position atop the female in intercourse in relation to the latter's supine horizontal position.

Several functions are served by these anatomical arrangements. In both sexes chafing or bruising of the skin is thus avoided as well as excessive pressure on the bony pubis, while sexual excitement is enhanced. The suprapubic hairs at their bases, when stimulated, serve to produce those chemo-conductor changes in the nerve endings which, together with the nerve endings directly supplying the skin, induce a heightening of sexual excitement. The perineal region, that is the region extending from the base of the external genitalia to and including the anus, is also supplied with hair and sensory nerves that are highly erotogenic. Indeed, the anogenital region in both sexes is supplied with the most highly innervated tactile sensitive hair follicles of almost any part of the body. The nipples in both sexes are similarly highly sensitive, as are the lips. Stimulation of the nipples is sexually exciting. Both in nonpregnant and in pregnant women, as also in men, stimulation produces a significant increase in secretion of the pituitary hormone prolactin, the hormone that maintains lactation and inhibits ovulation. The lips and the external genitalia are especially well supplied with concave, disclike branched sensory nerve endings, each in contact with a single enlarged epithelial cell. Such nerve endings are scarce in hairy skin. In the female, orgasm may be produced by rubbing the *mons veneris*. A similar effect is seldom achievable in the male by rubbing the suprapubic region. Thus, the female may masturbate without stimulating the vagina directly, whereas the male masturbates by direct stimulation of the penis.

For both sexes the most urgently sexually arousing stimuli

are tactile. In sexual foreplay, as well as during intercourse, manual and oral stimulation of erogenic zones greatly intensifies the sexual experience. A little reflection will suggest that there may be some relation between such sexual experiences and those we spent—or did not spend—at our mother's breast. This is especially true of the exploration of the body which the infant makes through its fingers. Interestingly enough, the fingertips themselves are erogenous. Reciprocal stimulation of the fingertips between two mutually sexually interested persons can be sexually quite arousing. During coitus breathing is deepened, and this has the effect of washing the CO_2 from the blood; this, in turn, changes the ionic balance of the body fluids, with a resulting increase in nerve excitability, expressed in a tingling of the skin, especially at the fingertips.

The question we have to ask is: Do individuals who are maternally adequately cared for differ from those who are not, in the manner in which they respond to cutaneous stimulation in sex relations, in petting, and coitus? The answer is that the evidence is now abundant which shows that those individuals who have been adequately mothered are clearly superior in all tactile relationships to those who have not. It will be recalled that none of the Harlows' motherless mother-animals ever showed normal female sex posturing and responding. "They were impregnated, not through their own effort, but because of the patience, persistence, and perspicacity of our breeding males." Apparently adequate mothering is necessary for the development of healthy sexual behavior. And what, in our present connection, "adequate mothering" means is the complex of cutaneous stimulations, among other things, which activates the tactile response systems of the infant, and thus early in its life experience prepares it for later adequate functioning in all situations involving tactility. This appears to be especially true of sexual behavior. Just as the individual learns his or her gender role, so, too, each learns or fails to learn the behavioral responses one makes as a result of conditioning originally initiated through the skin.

René Spitz, in a film he made of the nursing couple,

showed how the nursing mother communicates a kind of vital sex education to the infant as it feeds at the breast. This is seen best in the way in which she gives the breast to the infant, the quality and amount of direct intimate contact she encourages between herself and the child, the presence or absence of restless, frigid, or irritated behavior during the feeding or other care of the child, all of which constitute the first preverbal lessons in sex education. Nursing mothers will frequently describe the breastfeeding experience as "sexy," and the quality of this "sexiness" it may be conjectured is not without its lasting influence upon the erotic development of the individual.

"At the beginning of life," writes Anna Freud,

> being stroked, cuddled, and soothed by touch libidinizes the various parts of the child's body, helps to build up a healthy body image and body ego, increases its cathexis with narcissistic libido, and simultaneously promotes the development of object love by cementing the bond between child and mother. There is no doubt that, at this period, the surface of the skin in its role as erotogenic zone fulfills a multiple function in the child's growth.

The mother's holding and cuddling of the child plays a very effective and important role in the child's subsequent sexual development. A mother who loves her child enfolds it. She draws the child to her in a close embrace and, male or female, this is what as adults they will later want and be able to do with anyone they love. Children who have been inadequately held and fondled will suffer, as adolescents and adults, from an affect-hunger for such attention. Dr. Marc H. Hollender of the department of psychiatry of the Vanderbilt School of Medicine, Nashville, Tennessee, has reported, as part of a larger study on the need for body contact, on thirty-nine women with relatively acute psychiatric disorders, the most common of which was neurotic depression. In the larger study, Dr. Hollender and his collaborators found that the need to be held and cuddled, like other needs, varies in intensity from person to person and in the same person from time to time. For most women, it was found, body contact is pleasant but not indispensable. However, at one extreme they found women who considered body contact disagreeable and even repugnant, while at the other extreme were women who experienced it as a desire so compelling that it resembled an addiction.

The need for body contact, like oral needs, may become intensified during periods of stress. But while oral longings may be readily satisfied alone, with food, tobacco, alcohol, or the like, body-contact longings can scarcely be satisfied without the participation of another person.

Of the group of thirty-nine women patients, twenty-one, or slightly more than one-half, had used sex to entice a male to hold them. Twenty-six of the women had made direct requests to be held. Nine women who had made a direct request had not used sex, and four women who had used sex had not made a direct request.

Clearly, then, such women may offer men sex when their real desire is to be held or cuddled. As one of these women put it, in describing her desire to be held, "It's a kind of an ache. ... It's not like an emotional longing for some person who isn't there; it's a physical feeling."

Hollender quotes a former call girl who said, "In a way, I used sex to be held." The resort to sexual intercourse as a means of obtaining body contact has been referred to by Blinder in a discussion of depressive disorders. "At best," he writes, "the sexual experiences of these intensely unhappy people seem more an attempt to make some sort of human contact, however incomplete, than to achieve physical satisfaction." Malmquist and his co-workers, in reporting on twenty women who had three or more illegitimate pregnancies, state: "Eight of the 20 reported that they were consciously aware that sexual activity for them was a price to be paid for being cuddled and held. Pregenital activity was described by these eight as more pleasurable than intercourse itself, which was merely something to be tolerated." Similar observations have been made by other investigators.

Hollender and his co-workers comment, "The desire to be

cuddled and held is acceptable to most people as long as it is regarded as a component part of adult sexuality. The wish to be cuddled and held in a maternal manner is felt to be too childish; to avoid embarrassment or shame, women convert it into the longing to be held by a man as part of an adult activity, sexual intercourse."

If one asks why being held by women would not be even more desirable for these patients, the answer is that they do often use various devices to persuade women friends to hold them, but when this is achieved they quickly become uncomfortable and draw away, a withdrawal reaction that never occurs with men. Most of these women linked their desire for being held with "adult" sexuality, as unequivocally unrelated to anything suggesting homosexuality. Overtly, at any rate, they do not want to be taken for lesbians. One woman stated that when she was held by a woman her face reddened and she became afraid that whoever might see her would think she was a homosexual. A third woman said, "I don't want any woman to touch me. I think of lesbians."

Hollender and his co-workers believe that for some women, the need to be held or cuddled is a major determinant of promiscuity. It may well be that such women often have a strong unconscious drive to be held by women, who represent the mother, a need which has been repressed and causes them to seek body contact with men and women on a heterosexual basis, paying the men with their disinterested sexuality, and withdrawing from too close contact with the women for fear that their true motives may be discovered even to themselves. The face-reddening of the one woman is perhaps significant in this connection. Some of the patients in this study were so averse to sexual intercourse with their husbands or anyone else that they would forego the strong desire to be held rather than submit to intercourse.

What is being observed in the great longing of these women to be held and cuddled is a response to a need which was largely left unsatisfied in infancy and childhood. This is made evident in cases in which women as young girls had turned to their fathers in the hope of receiving the warmth and love they failed to receive from their mothers. They turned to their father not as a father, but as a mother substitute. As women, they used sex as a means of obtaining maternal gratifications. In many of these women the nonverbal message is: being held is being loved. It is Hollender's view that the more intense the wish to be held, the more likely it is to stem from the seeking of security, a response conditioned in infancy.

In a further study, in which the original group of 39 women participating in the first project was enlarged to 112, all between the ages of eighteen and fifty-nine, information was gathered on the correlations between the wish to be held and various behavioral patterns and subjective reactions. It was found that a strong desire to be held or cuddled correlated with a general leaning towards openness in emotional expression. Such women were interested in and derived much pleasure from orality, they were comfortable with or accepting of sexuality, felt free to feel and express hostility, responded in a friendly or affectionate manner after imbibing alcohol, responded positively to another form of body contact, ballroom dancing, and found pleasure in tactile behavior of other kinds.

In a study of the wish to be held during pregnancy Hollender and McGhee found the variability rather interesting. In many cases there was a distinct increase in the need to be held; this was associated with a need for reassurance and security. In some women, who felt themselves physically unattractive, there was a decrease in the need to be held. Such women, the investigators suggest, may be expressing an actual diminution of that need, or they may be reacting against an underlying wish that they either cannot accept or cannot expect to have gratified. The latter might be the case in women who have no regular partners or who regard themselves as very unattractive. The wish may then be blocked before reaching awareness or it may be denied.

How do the sexes compare in the desire to be held and the wish to hold? Hollender and Mercer investigated this question. The subjects were thirty men and forty-five women ranging in age from eighteen to fifty-four. They were patients in two small psychiatric units or were seen as outpatients in the same institutional settings. It was found that quite a significant number of men long to be held, and some don't even have sex in mind; while others feel that it is more masculine to hold than to be held. Apparently, while men can acknowledge their longing to be held, the need either does not reach the intensity it reaches in some women or, if it does, is not reported.

VERY EARLY ADOLESCENT PREGNANCY. In the United States well over a million adolescent girls become pregnant every year. The most rapid rate of increase in pregnancies is among girls under fifteen years of age, children who are neither physiologically, socially, or psychologically prepared for the role of motherhood. There have been all sorts of explanations for this epidemic of teenage pregnancies, and no doubt there are many conditions, varying with different individuals, which are responsible. It does not appear to have occurred to anyone that a lack of pleasurable tactility in later childhood might be one of those conditions.

Dr. Elizabeth McAnarney, who has had much experience with teenage pregnant girls, has raised the question whether coitus in ten- to fourteen-year-old girls might not represent behavior for nonsexual purposes, and whether early adolescents who engage in coitus prematurely are seeking closeness and cuddling from another human being, rather than sexual pleasure. She notes that at a time when the adolescent's need for touching has increased, it has been largely, if not entirely, terminated. Such adolescents may use their newly acquired genital capacity and coitus to meet the need for touching, for being held.

As Dr. McAnarney writes:

As sexual impulses reemerge at adolescence . . . the adolescent begins to recognize that the opposite-sex parent cannot be the adult love object. In addition, the incest taboo prohibits the adolescent and the opposite-sex parent from becoming emotionally or physically too close. The combination of the emotional distancing that occurs when the young person surrenders the opposite-sex parent and the incest taboo may be the major theoretical reasons that adolescents and their parents do not engage in touching.

Ann Landers, whose newspaper column has approximately seventy million readers from all walks of life, asked them to reply to the following question, "Would you be content to be held close and treated tenderly and forget about 'the act'? Answer Yes or No." Within four days over 100,000 replies poured in. Of the respondents 72 percent said "Yes," they would be content just to be held close and treated tenderly and forget about sex. Of those 72 percent, 40 percent were under forty years of age.

Ann Landers concluded from her survey that the almost two-thirds of the women who voted "Yes" were saying that they wanted to be valued, to feel cared about, that tender words and loving embraces are more rewarding than "an orgasm produced by a silent, mechanical, self-involved male."

In order to discover what role, if any, cultural differences might play in influencing the desire to be held among women, Drs. L.T. Huang, R. Phares, and M.H. Hollender investigated the matter among five groups of Asian women living in Kuala Lumpur, Malaysia. Altogether 190 women were investigated:

24 Chinese-educated Chinese
65 English-educated Chinese
25 Malay-educated Malays
34 English-educated Malays
42 English-educated Indians.

All subjects were married, most in their twenties and thirties. The findings are striking. The Chinese-educated Chinese showed the least desire to be held, and regarded the wish as something to be kept secret. At the opposite extreme were the liberated English-educated Chinese, who preferred to be held and were not inclined to keep their wish secret. English education does not have a similar effect on the Malay women among whom, if anything, the effect is opposite, for the Malay-educated women express the need to be held and are less inclined than the English-educated Malay women to deny the wish. These findings appear to be consistent with the greater relative freedom to express sensual feelings and to enjoy sex among the Malay-educated. The authors conclude that their study demonstrates that cultural factors as well as psychological ones exert a profound influence on the wish to be held. The influence, they add, is similar to that of culture on sexual responsiveness.

Lowen has published a number of case histories of women who suffered a lack of tactile stimulation in infancy, and who in later life engaged in sexual activities in a desperate attempt to gain some contact with their own bodies. "This compulsive activity," writes Lowen, "may give the impression that these persons are oversexed. They are, if anything, undersexed, for the activity stems from a need for erotic stimulation rather than from a feeling of sexual charge or excitement. Sexual activity of this kind never leads to orgastic satisfaction or fulfillment, but leaves the person empty and disappointed."

These are important points, for they draw attention to the fact that in the Western world it is highly probable that sexual activity, indeed the frenetic preoccupation with sex that characterizes Western culture, is in many cases not the expression of a sexual interest at all, but rather a search for the satisfaction of the need for contact. As Lowen remarks, "An ego that is not grounded in the reality of body feeling becomes desperate."

It is significant that almost universally there is a close identification between touch and sex. In the special case of members of the English-speaking world, as Bruce Maliver has said of most Americans (unable to feel comfortable about touch as a friendly or affectionate statement), they see physical contact between adults almost exclusively as a prelude to sex, and hence, subject to the usual range of sexual taboos. Intimations of sexual interest are readily communicated by a touch of the hand or a limb, by a gentle squeeze of hand, arm, or shoulder. And without intercourse each may bring the other to orgasm by the gentle touching, caressing, or stroking, of loving hands. Intercourse should mean what the word once implied: communication between two people in which coitus plays a part, and does not constitute the whole of the experience of making love. Without tactile communication—what the body feels and says nonverbally—the experience of sex can only be at most incomplete.

Strictly speaking, as Freud pointed out, the whole body is an erotogenic zone, and as Fenichel has stated, touch erotism is comparable to the sexual pleasure derivable from looking (scopophilia). Both are brought about by sensory stimuli of a specific kind in particular situations. In the development from pregenital oral and anal satisfactions to genital primacy, in which sexual excitations become genitally oriented and dominant over the extragenital erogenous zones, the sensory stimulations normally "function as instigators of excitement and play a corresponding part in forepleasure. If they have been warded off during childhood they remain isolated, demanding full gratification on their own account and thus disturbing sexual integration."

The authors of the chapter on "Sexuality" in that admirable book *Our Bodies, Our Selves* quote a woman in a group discussion who remarked that although she didn't want intercourse, she did want to be physically close to someone and be held and touched, and she felt "they all go together."

While the need to be held may be experienced as something quite apart from intercourse, nevertheless it is almost always a major component of the need for sex, and in many cases, as we have seen, may be even more compelling. As the authors referred to above say, "From the moment we were born we all began making ourselves feel good by touching and playing with our bodies. Some of these experiences were explicitly sexual." It is these early tactile experiences and the pleasure they have given that we seek to experience, to re-experience, with a chosen other, throughout life.

A tragic example of the search for physical contact through sex as a reassurance of love and alleviation of anxiety is the case of the late popular singer Janis Joplin. Myra Friedman, in her biography of the singer, tells it all.

> Janis breathed, thought, felt, acted at a primitive level that was nearly absolute. Even in her twenties, she was still like a hurt and pleading child who wants exactly that very love complete in the physical embrace, and sex, in a way, was a valid synonym for what she was in search of. It wasn't love as an adult knows it: no sharing, no interest, no commitment, no giving, none of those things at all. But it really was love to *her*. In her hunger for affection, she was nearly amok. Her constant pursuit of physical contact resonated with echoes of infant longing, and frustration of such a need could not help but produce an unbearable anxiety. In that sense, sex was a palliative, an escape from tension that could not be endured, thus making sexual relief of inordinate, overbearing importance.

In Hollender's and in Lowen's women, the need for being held was almost certainly warded off, and has therefore remained isolated and pressing and quite separated from their disturbed and unintegrated need for sexual relations. The only real need they know is the pregenital one of being held and cuddled, and principally loved in this manner. The high intercorrelation between maternal behavior and later child behavior in other variables renders a causal connection between early parental failure and the later longing to be held highly probable.

As Jurgen Ruesch has written:

> We know that to secure healthy development any person has to be supplied with the right kind of stimulus at the right time and in the right amount. This is particularly true of children. Quantitatively inappropriate responses of the parents to the infants' primitive messages, such as "I am cold," "I am wet," "I am tired," or "I have had enough" establish deviant feedback circuits. . . . Qualitatively inappropriate responses can produce disturbances which are in no way different from those produced by the quantitatively inappropriate responses.

To offer food when thirst is prominent, to offer fluids when excessive cold has to be managed, are self-explanatory examples.

The warding off or separation between the need to be held and the need for sexual satisfaction in Hollender's women may be accounted for by the recognition (made as long ago as 1898 by Albert Moll) of the sexual impulse as divisible into two components, the one limited to bodily and mental approximation to another individual, the *contrectation impulse* (from *contrectare*, "to touch," "to think about"), and the other insofar as it was confined to the peripheral organs, as the *detumescence impulse* (from *detumescere*, "to stop swelling," "to subside"). Moll makes it quite clear that each impulse at first operates quite independently of the other, as we may observe in children who are highly tactile but who have no accompanying sexual interest in others until further development has occurred. Should failure to develop contrectation occur as a consequence of inadequate tactile experience, the individual may become fixated on the satisfaction of this need, with consequent exclusion of the development of the need for detumescence.

TOUCH AND COMMUNICATION. It has been remarked that in the final analysis every tragedy is a failure of communication. And what the child receiving inadequate cutaneous stimulation suffers from is a failure of integrative development as a human being, a failure in the communication of the experience of love. By being stroked, and caressed, and carried, and cuddled, comforted, and cooed to, by being loved, the child learns to stroke and caress and cuddle, comfort and coo, and to love others. In this sense love is sexual in the healthiest sense of that word. It implies involvement, concern, responsibility, tenderness, and awareness of the needs, sensibilities, and vulnerabilities of the other. All this is communicated to the infant through the skin in the early months of his life, and gradually reinforced by feeding, sound, and visual cues as the infant develops. The primacy of the infant's first perceptions of reality through the skin can no longer be doubted. The messages he receives through that organ must be security-giving, assuring, and pleasurable if the infant is to thrive. Even in food intake, as Brody has shown in her excellent study of mothering, "save under conditions of body security and comfort no infant, however hungry, appeared to enjoy his feeding."

Such evidence as we possess strongly suggests that inadequate communication with the baby through the skin is likely to result in inadequate development of later sexual functions.

Freud's view of the skin as an erotogenic zone differentiated into sense organs and special erogenic zones such as the anal, oral, and genital really refers to erogenized tactile zones, and what he calls infantile sexuality appears to be, as Lawrence Frank has observed, largely tactuality. As growth and development proceed, this tactile sensitivity is gradually transformed into interpersonal relations, autoerotic activities, and eventually into sexual activities. It is to be regretted that in Freud's emphasis, some would say overemphasis, on the erotogenic character of the skin it should have come to be seen principally and almost exclusively as significant for sexual development alone. This erotogenic view of the skin has somewhat hindered the recognition of its role in the development of other behavioral traits.

In this area it would be foolish to pretend to more knowledge than we possess, for while thousands of monographs, books, and articles have been written on virtually every aspect of sex, the role of early cutaneous experience in the mothering situation has been largely neglected. Brody raises the question of "whether earliest skin and muscle erotism has received less than due recognition for the part it plays in gratifications derived from oral erotism and feeling in the first months of life" (p. 338). The answer is that it has, indeed. Hence we are dependent here to a large extent upon conjecture and inference rather than upon the solid ground of research.

The fact that males have projecting external genitalia, penis and scrotum and gonads, makes their handling by the mother, the infant itself, and others, a great deal more inviting and easier than is the case in the female. It is therefore likely that male infants in all cultures undergo considerably more genital stimulation than females. This difference in sexual anatomy may also, at least in part, explain the greater frequency of masturbation—self-gratification through skin stimulation—in boys than in girls. The early stimulation of the external genitalia in boys by the mother, or other persons, or both, may have all sorts of later developmental behavioral effects.

"It is notable," wrote Lawrence Frank,

> that in our discussions of personality development in children and of sexuality, so little attention has been given to the tactual cutaneous experiences of the infant. Like all young mammals who are licked, nuzzled, cuddled and kept close to the mother, the human infant likewise has apparently a similar need for close bodily contacts, for patting and caressing, for tactual soothing which calms him and restores his equilibrium when hurt, frightened, or angry.

This tactual sensitivity is especially acute in the genitals.

> This infantile tactuality, like his other organic needs, is gradually transformed as the child learns to accept mother's voice as a surrogate, her reassuring words and tones of voice giving him an equivalent for his close physical contacts, or her angry scolding voice serving as punishment and making him cry as if hit. Caressing becomes the chief form of intimacy and expression of affection, with appropriate words and tones of voice. All physical contacts become meaningful and colored by emotion.

Frank then goes on to point out that during the so-called latency period—the period from about four or five years to about twelve during which interest in sex is sublimated—girls and especially boys are less likely to seek and receive tactual contacts from parents. Tactual sensitivity, however, reappears more strongly than ever at puberty or shortly thereafter, and becomes a major need-objective, to touch and to be touched, not merely as an impersonal sensory stimulation, but as a symbolic fulfillment of the search for intimacy, acceptance, reassurance, and comforting or, in some who have been failed, a continual avoidance of such contacts.

With further development, the need for tactuality

> ... becomes one of the chief components in sexual approaches and intercourse, where the individual's early infantile experiences of adequate tactuality or deprivation may govern his or her capacity for response. The tactual-cutaneous sensitivity of the genitals at puberty becomes more acute and in the male becomes the major focus of his sexuality, while the female seems to retain more of the larger overall tactuality of infancy while exhibiting especial sensitivity in breasts, labiae and clitoris. Auto-erotic practices may serve as both vicarious fulfillments and/or preparation for coitus.

The enormous variety of meanings which sex may have for different individuals, a language which has the kinds of things to say to the other that can be said in no other way, an exchange of love, a means of hurting or exploiting others, a mode of defense, a bargaining point, a way of self-denial or self-assertion, an affirmation or a rejection of masculinity or femininity, and so on, not to mention the abnormal or pathological expressions which sex may take, all, more or less, are influenced by early tactile experience.

In the Western world in particular countless numbers of us were brought up to believe that sensual pleasures were bad; indeed, all pleasures of the body were wrong and worse. Hence, such pleasures were strongly discouraged. Babies had their thumbs withdrawn from their mouths, and if as infants they persisted they were punished or had their arms immobilized. Fondling their genitals or happily feeling their bodies was similarly discouraged. As Gay Luce has pointed out, this is a destructive message, implying that something is wrong with one's body and with feeling good about oneself.

Not only may the destructiveness affect the feeling the child develops about itself, but the parental prohibitions and punishments may seriously affect parent-child feelings, and especially the way the child feels about the repressive parent. The result will be a serious and wholly unnecessary diminishment for both.

As Lowen points out,

> The quality of the physical intimacy between mother and child reflects the mother's feelings about the intimacy of sex. If the act of sex is viewed with disgust, all intimate body contact is tainted with this feeling. If a woman is ashamed of her body, she cannot offer it graciously to the nursing infant. If she is repelled by the lower half of her body, she will feel some revulsion in handling this part of the child's body. Each contact with the child is an opportunity for the child to experience the pleasure of intimacy or to be repulsed by the shame and fear of it. When a mother is afraid of intimacy, the child will sense the fear and interpret it as a rejection. The child of a woman who is afraid of intimacy will develop a feeling of shame about its own body.

Dr. Andrew Barclay of Michigan State University has drawn attention to the fact that at birth, among the ways in which boys and girls differ from each other are: (1) Boys keep their eyes open more than girls; (2) boys move more; and (3) girls stop crying when picked up. As a consequence boys are held more during the first six months, and since they do not stop crying when picked up they are walked and rocked for longer periods. After six months the girls are held more since they are not so active and are receptive to holding and cuddling when boys are more likely to resist this in favor of moving about on their own. These differences may serve to explain why males are more easily aroused by visual stimuli and females by tactile ones. Barclay concludes that the changeover from being held to not being held in boys, and from not being held to being held in girls, leads to differences in gender roles.

During the first six months, as Erikson has pointed out, the child is learning about trust and mistrust, and changes in the sequence in patterns of holding male and female infants may influence trust-mistrust in ways which influence and shape gender roles. Since boys are relatively deprived in passing from being held to being less held, males should tend to be more mistrustful of others. Girls are relatively enhanced by being held more over time, thus females should be more trusting of people in general. Everyday experience confirms this.

Among the myths with which parents in the Western world have endeavored to condition their children are: (1) "Little men don't cry," and (2) "Nice girls don't do that." By hearing the first myth often enough, males learn that to deny their feelings is to be "grown up." By subscribing to this myth we have been producing adults who have denied their feelings for so long that they no longer know what they are feeling, who they are, and therefore are not sure how they should behave. These people require extreme stimulation, such as the explicit sex movies or the "football frenzy," to really feel anything.

Persuading girls to believe that "Nice girls don't do that" is to train them to deny their sexuality. "Nice" girls don't touch themselves, or let boys touch them, and so on. Some females after years of travail manage to free themselves from such early conditionings; some, alas, never do.

Any display of physical affection or contact tends to be interpreted as sexual. This in itself is highly significant because tactility is in fact closely related to the development of sexual behavior and almost always retains something of that character. However, in the tactile-deprived individual the sexual component of tactility remains confused and anxiety-ridden. Hence, such individuals tend to avoid touching others and resent being touched, except under special conditions.

Early deprivations of tactile experience may lead to behavior calculated to provide substitutes for such tactile deprivations in the form of self-manipulation of various kinds, masturbation and toe-, finger-, or thumb-sucking, pulling or fingering the ears, nose, or hair. It is an interesting fact that among nonliterate peoples who generally give their children all the tactile stimulation they require, finger-sucking or thumb-sucking seldom occurs. Moloney, for example, writes: "My observations in Africa, Tahiti, and the islands around Tahiti, the Fiji Islands, Islands in the Caribbean, Japan, Mexico and Okinawa confirmed for me the fact that most babies in these areas are breast fed and carried on the person of the mother. In these areas I noted that thumbsucking was practically non-existent."

Moloney believes that the thumb becomes a substitute for the mother, just as the pellets of paper do, which schizoid or shizophrenic children so often roll between their fingers. As Lowenfeld has put it, the fingers act like antennae or feelers which probe the surroundings for ensuing motor activities.

The oft-heard complaint directed by women at the clumsiness, crassness, and incompetence of men in their sexual approaches and in sexual intercourse itself, men's lack of skill in foreplay and their failure to understand its meaning, almost certainly substantially reflects the lack of tactile experience that such males have suffered in childhood. The roughness with which many men will handle women and children constitutes yet another evidence of their having been failed in early tactile experience, for it is difficult to conceive of anyone who had been tenderly loved and caressed in infancy not learning to approach a woman or a child with especial tenderness. The very word *tenderness* implies softness, delicacy of touch, caring for. The gorilla, that gentle creature, is the most frequently slandered animal when women wish to describe the sexual approaches of the average male. Sex seems to be regarded as a tension releaser rather than as a profoundly meaningful act of communication in a deeply involving human relationship. In many of its elements the sexual relationship reproduces the loving mother-child relationship. As Lawrence Frank has put it:

Tactile communication in adult mating, both as foreplay and in intercourse, has been elaborated and refined by some cultures into the most amazing array of erotic patterns which through a variety of tactual stimulation of various parts of the body serve to arouse, prolong, intensify, and evoke communication. Here we see tactile communication, reinforced and elaborated by motor activities and language, by concomitant stimulation, visual, auditory, olfactory, gustatory, and the deeper muscle senses, combined to provide an organic-personality relationship which may be one of the most intense human experiences. It is, or can be, considered an esthetic experience in that there may be little or no instrumental, purposive, or cognitive elements, with greater or less loss of space-time orientation. But the elementary sexual processes of the human organism may be transformed and focused into an interpersonal love relationship with an identified person to whom each is seeking to communicate, using sex not for procreation, as in the mating of a female in heat ready to be fertilized, but as "another language," for interpersonal communication. Here we see how the primary tactile mode of communication, which has been largely overlaid and superseded by auditory and visual signs and symbols, is reinstated to function with elementary organic intensity, provided the individuals have not lost the capacity for communication with the self through tactile experiences.

It may well be asked, If men are affected in this manner by lack of early tactual experience, how are women affected? The answer to that question is: Much in the same manner as the women discussed earlier in this chapter, who longed to be held and cuddled. These women were affected by more or less frigidity, a condition which they could easily conceal by pretending to excitements they did not feel, or by a seeming nymphomania which actually craves tactual satisfactions. Once again it must be emphasized that it is not being suggested that such conditions are entirely the results of tactual deprivations in early life, but only that they may, in part, be so.

Women have always in great numbers complained of the male's lack of tenderness sexually and in general. May not this deficiency have become rather more epidemic in the recent period as a consequence, again at least in part, of the abandonment of breastfeeding and the reduction in the tactual experiences of the child?

Many mothers early begin to reject demonstrations of love

by their sons in the mistaken belief that unless they do so they will cause their sons to become too deeply attached to them. There are many fathers who reject their sons' embraces because, as one such father, a physician, remarked to me, "I don't want him to become one of those" (meaning a homosexual). The appalling ignorance revealed in such attitudes is very damaging, and the effects would serve to reinforce the male's inability to relate himself tactually to another human being.

TACTILE DEPRIVATION AND EXCESSIVE MASTURBATION IN CHILDREN. The relationship between tactile deprivation in infancy and childhood and sex is clearly evident in the many reported cases of early excessive masturbation in children. In the absence or withdrawal of warm tactile stimulation, the child sometimes turns to its own body for gratification. Dr. Glen McCray, in a report of five cases, four girls and one boy, found that excessive masturbation may be produced by actual or fantasized withdrawal of parental affection and may also appear with the birth of a new sibling, prolonged absence of a parent, or actual loss by divorce or death. In each of Dr. McCray's cases excessive masturbation ceased when parental attitudes changed and the parents were able to reinstitute appropriate tactile stimulation. Touching, holding, patting, wrestling, or any other game which involved a good deal of body contact was encouraged and carried out by those parents able to subdue their own erotic feelings in deference to the child's need for physical contact.

TACTILE DEPRIVATION AND VIOLENCE. The Harlows, in a well-known experiment, reported on the adult behavior of a group of five rhesus female monkeys who had never known a real mother of their own. As mothers these monkeys were utterly hopeless—two were essentially indifferent to their young, and three were so violently abusive to their infants they had frequently to be separated. Normally appropriate cues offered by the infants for eliciting maternal behavior resulted in repulsion and rejection, and otherwise brutal behavior. The Harlows suggest that "failure of normal gratification of contact-clinging in infancy may make it impossible for the adult female to show normal contact relationships with her own infant," would be an oversimplified explanation for such behavior, and we agree. They believe, on the contrary, that "maternal affection in the monkey is a highly integrated, global system, not a series of isolated components that vary independently ... depending more upon general social experience than upon specific experiences." Tactile experience is fundamental, but it is not the only experience necessary for the adequate social development of animals and humans. Be that as it may, there is a striking parallel between the motherless monkey's behavior toward her young, and that of the human mother who has been massively failed in mothering experience during her own infancy. As Drs. Brandt F. Steele and C. B. Pollock of the University of Colorado found when they studied the parents of abused children in three generations of families, such parents were invariably deprived of physical affection themselves during their childhood. In addition, their adult sex life was extremely poor. The women never experienced orgasm, and the men's sex life was unsatisfying.

The parallel between the motherless monkey's adult behavior and that of the parental disasters suffered by the adult child batterers as children is deadly. Dr. James H. Prescott, a developmental neuropsychologist at the National Institute of Child Health and Human Development, at Bethesda, Maryland, believes that a principal cause of human violence stems from a lack of bodily pleasure during the formative periods of life. "Recent research," he writes, "supports the view that the deprivation of physical pleasure is a major ingredient in the expression of physical violence. The common association of sex with violence provides a clue to understanding physical violence in terms of deprivation of physical pleasure." He goes on to point out that unlike violence, people cannot seem to get enough of pleasure, for which they are constantly in search of new forms that ultimately seem to be substitutes for the natural sensory pleasures of touching. Laboratory experiments have convinced Dr. Prescott that deprivation of sensory pleasure is the principal root cause of violence. There is a reciprocal relationship between them; *the presence of one inhibits the other.* Rage is not possible in the presence of pleasure. A raging, violent animal will calm down when electrodes stimulate the pleasure centers of its brain. Dr. Prescott suggests that during development certain sensory experiences will create a neuropsychological disposition for either violence-seeking or pleasure-seeking behavior later in life. Writes Dr. Prescott:

> I am convinced that various abnormal social and emotional behaviors resulting from what psychologists call "maternal-social" deprivation, that is, a lack of tender, loving care, are caused by a unique type of sensory deprivation, *somatosensory* deprivation. Derived from the Greek word for "body," the term refers to the sensations of touch and body movement which differ from the senses of sight, hearing, smell, and taste. I believe that the deprivation of body touch, contact, and movement are the basic causes of a number of emotional disturbances which include depressive and autistic behaviors, hyperactivity, sexual aberration, drug abuse, violence, and aggression.

Dr. Prescott may be claiming a bit too much for the effects of somatosensory deprivation, but if his claims are in the least excessive they are in the right direction and for the most part, as the evidence abundantly testifies, worthy of more attention than they have thus far received. As Prescott has said, numerous studies of juvenile delinquents and criminals have revealed a background of broken homes, neglectful or abusive parents. Take almost any violent individual and inquire into his history as a child, and it can be predicted with confidence that he will be discovered to have had a lacklove childhood, to have suffered a failure of tender, loving care.* It should, however, be made quite clear that there are a number of cases on record of

---

*For a detailed discussion of this see A. Montagu, *The Direction of Human Development* (revised edition, New York: Hawthorn Books, 1970).

persons who suffered a lacklove infancy and who somehow emerged mentally quite healthy.*

In passing it may be observed that many rapists, who are almost invariably men, are not so much driven by the need for sex, as by the need to commit brutal acts against women. It may be that, among other things, the child equates tactual deprivation with maternal rejection, an experience which in later life will cause him to resort to sexual violence against women. It may also be that a similar mechanism is involved in the general oppression that women have suffered at the hands of men.

There is some evidence that in incest the driving force is rarely the need for sex, but rather a need for closeness, warmth, and caring.

To be roughly handled has been considered by many women, especially women of the working classes, an incontestable token of love. There is, for example, the well-known feminine Cockney supplication to her man: "If yer loves us, chuck us abaht." The sexual element was very evident in the flagellation epidemics of medieval times, as a penance which the church at first approved and then forbade, when it realized the sensuality involved. That the participants in such flagellation episodes were more than anxious to receive the caresses of the whip suggests that a great many infants in medieval times received an inadequate amount and quality of tactile stimulation.

Slapping children, with whatever intention, as a form of discipline or for any other reason, turns the skin into an organ of pain rather than pleasure. For reasons which are not too difficult to discern, the buttocks have constituted a preferred locus for spanking the child. This region is closely related to

*For the most striking case on record see A. Montagu, *The Elephant Man* (New York: Dutton Books, 1979). See also D. Beres and S. J. Obers, "The Effects of Extreme Deprivation in Infancy on Psychic Structure in Adolescence: A Study in Ego Development," *The Psychoanalytic Study of the Child*, vol. 5 (New York: International Universities Press, 1950), pp. 212–235; A. M. Clarke and A. D. B. Clarke, *Early Experience: Myth and Evidence* (New York: Free Press, 1976).

the sexual organs, and supplied by sensory nerves which form part of the nervous plexus associated with the sexual functions. Hence spanking on the buttocks may produce distinctively erotic sensations in children, including sexual orgasm. Children have been known to misbehave deliberately in order to receive such desired "punishment," pretending to be distressed while experiencing it.

Rousseau relates that when he was eight (he was actually ten) he learned to know sexual pleasure from the spankings administered by his governess, who used to lay him over her knees in order to attend to him *a posteriori*. Far from being distressed by these assaults upon his integrity, he tells how he welcomed them, and how finally his bed was removed from his governess's room when she became aware of the effects her punishments were having upon her charge.

Whether or not some element of perverted sadism is present in the personality of a particular discipliner, the early conditioning of the association between pain and sexual pleasure produced by spanking may result in a permanent pathology,* the disorder known as *algolagnia*. Algolagnia is a condition in which pain and cruelty provoke voluptuous sexual pleasure. It may be either active or passive. Masochistic algolagnia renders the experience of pain, disgust, or humiliation one which produces sexual excitement. Sadistic algolagnia is the opposite, making the infliction of pain, discomfort, fear, or humiliation upon others the source of sexual pleasure in oneself.

Spanking and slapping with the open hand in order to punish children is still too often indulged. Inflicting pain upon them in this manner deprives children of the comfort the skin usually communicates to them; as a result, they may come to associate their own skin and that of others with fear of contact and pain, and thus may avoid skin contacts in later life.

Quite often biting, pinching, scratching, and gripping

---

*For a good discussion of the pathological effects of spanking see J. F. Oliver, *Sexual Hygiene and Pathology* (Philadelphia: Lippincott, 1965), pp. 63–67.

caresses, even to the point of pain, are intermixed with normal sexuality and are enjoyed by one or both partners. In pathological sexuality such behavior is often intensified, and the skin becomes a dominant factor in the experience of sexual pleasure. Flagellation, generally on the buttocks and thighs, has been a most frequent form of sexual perversion, with every kind of whip imaginable used for this purpose. Establishments have long existed on the continent of Europe especially, and doubtless have existed or continue to exist in North and South America, in which the clients—for a consideration—are all but flayed alive in the search for sexual satisfaction.

The pinching of women's bottoms by "dirty old men" constitutes an example of a sexual perversion which society has clearly understood and found not unamusing. Interestingly enough there are some women who similarly exhibit their interest in males by pinching them with such passion that they leave them black and blue. In sexual arousal the whole sensory character of the skin is heightened. Sensations that under ordinary circumstances would be painful often become intensely pleasurable. Some women in the midst of orgasm will cry out to be hurt and will enjoy the pain inflicted upon them—a pain always directed at and experienced through the skin. Others will indulge in "love-bites." As Van de Velde says, "Women are conspicuously more addicted to love-bites than are men. It is not at all unusual for a woman of passionate nature to leave a memento of sexual union on the man's shoulder in the shape of a little slanting oval outline of tooth-marks. The bite occurs almost without exception *during coitus* or immediately afterwards, while the generally gentler, slighter, or at least less noticeable love-bites given by the man to his partner, are part of the erotic play before, or the final stage after, coitus." In the case of the male, "many blue marks or bruises on women's arms are witnesses of the man's *tourbillon.*" Van de Velde believes that the feminine inclination to bite during the sexual act arises mainly from the wish to give a kiss more intense than is humanly possible. It is a wish, as it were, to make a permanent integumentary impression, the intensification of the tactile sensation. "Indeed," writes Van de Velde, "both the active and passive partner feel a peculiarly keen, erotic pleasure in the tiny, delicate, gentle or sharp but never really painful nips man and woman exchange as the love-play quickens, especially when such caresses are applied in rapid succession and in adjacent places" (p.155). The line between the normal and the abnormal is a thin one here, a subject which has been admirably discussed by Havelock Ellis and others.

The extraordinary frequency with which individuals with abnormalities of sexuality suffer from pathologies of the skin suggests not merely a centrifugal psychosomatic effect, but a centripetally originating one. This is evidenced by the frequency with which such individuals strive to solve their sexual conflicts by securing a close, dependable, and passive relationship to the mother or a mother surrogate. It may be postulated that failure of adequate mothering, and especially adequate communication through the skin, almost certainly occurred in the early lives of such individuals.

Scopophilia, to which reference has already been made, the pleasure in looking, may become a perversion, which is then known as *voyeurism.* The voyeurism may be restricted exclusively to the genitals, or be connected with the overriding of disgust, as in looking on excretory functions. Or instead of being preparatory to the sexual aim, it may supplant it, as in exhibitionism.

During the first year of life the association between looking at objects, touching them, and taking them into the mouth is a closely linked one. The association between looking and touching is especially closely connected. The experiences of urination and defecation are pleasantly relieving ones and warming. If, however, the oral needs are unsatisfactorily satisfied, and come to be characterized by greed, hunger, insatiety, with fears of the ensuing hostile aspects of these processes, the visual functions may come to have a similar compulsive, devouring quality, and later tend to be defended by complex inhibitory systems of various sorts. Instead of libidinal oral, anal, tactile, and visual functions being harmoniously integrated, these functions become anarchically and dysfunctionally associated. Thus, looking comes to replace normal sexual outlets as in scopophilia, as does touching, often in abnormal ways such as pinching, scratching, or biting, with or without the accompanying desire to inflict pain, or the various forms of exhibitionism. Women do not usually expose the genital region in exhibitionism, but they will expose breasts or buttocks. This, of course, they have done, with the vagaries of fashion, quite normally for millennia. Exposure of the breasts in ancient Crete was customary, and at various periods in the Western world, devices drawing attention to the breasts as well as to the buttocks have been the vogue. But what appears to be the boldest attempt of all, the attempt to draw attention to the external genitalia, namely, the miniskirt, is a development of the 1960s. Topless dresses have not become the fashion, and see-through blouses have gained a limited popularity.

These phenomena, however, are not in any sense pathological evidences of sexual disturbance. What they are evidence of is the expression of the need for love; and since love and sex have come to be identified in the Western world, sexual attractiveness becomes a means of achieving "love." In this manner love establishes itself as "skin-deep." The more skin she exposes, the more lovable the female becomes. This kind of scopophilia has become normal for most males in the Western world who, upon the perception of a female possessing the proper distribution of curvilinear properties, will phototropically migrate in her direction. Hence the emphasis upon nudity. In such cases it is not so much skin as sex that is involved. The true exhibitionist, however, may be an extreme prude insofar as nudity is concerned, and may never allow either himself or his wife to see the other in the nude. Puritanical attitudes of this kind are well known to be characteristic of the families of exhibitionists. In such families, cutaneous as well as related deprivations are common throughout childhood.

The motivations of strippers appear to confirm our views. Skipper and McCaghy studied thirty-five strippers, and found that some 60 percent came from broken or unstable homes in which the father was in some way inadequate. Lacking the strong response from a father, these girls had to settle for substitutes. In baring their bodies, strippers may be merely asking for the attention and affection denied them by their fathers. The girls in this study estimated that between 50 and 75 percent of strippers are lesbians. This fact further tends to confirm the view that the stripper still nurses the feeling of paternal rejection she suffered in childhood.

Anatole Broyard captures something of the poignancy of the tragedy in a review of a book on *Fathering* when he writes: "It would be pleasant to imagine father back in place and the situation amended: In a sleazy theater or nightclub, as the band plays a heavily accented version of *I've Got You Under My Skin* and a young woman stands naked with an impassive face, a middle-aged man runs up on to the stage and helps her put her clothes back on."

GOOD AND BAD TOUCH. In 1984 the National Center for Child Abuse in Washington reported that over a million children had been abused in the previous year. It is believed that at least 30 percent of girls and 10 percent of boys are sexually molested before they are eighteen. The almost daily reports of sexual abuse of children in the media has spread fear among many parents that they may be doing the wrong thing in fondling their children, that perhaps they shouldn't hug and kiss them or otherwise touch them.

Such alarm is understandable in a society that has so confounded love, sex, affection, and touch. But genuinely loving parents have nothing to fear from their demonstrative acts of affection for their children or anyone else. Erogenous zones, however, should be avoided; these include the lips, nipples, external genitalia, and buttocks—the lips because, in addition to their erotogenicity, they are frequently transmitters of infection by kissing. During bathing time there should be no hesitation in washing these areas, but they should not become a focus of attention.

In preindustrial societies, the so-called "primitive societies," such advice would properly be regarded as nonsensical and ridiculous, for these peoples were not as confused about these matters as the so-called "civilized" peoples of the world. Everyone in the Western world understands that touching is socially permissible as long as it avoids any implication of sex. If parents and others will bear that in mind, they have nothing to fear. There can be nothing whatever wrong with parents sleeping together with their children or bathing with them. The rightness or wrongness of any behavior depends upon the parents' motives and what the child comes to believe about them.

SEX DIFFERENCES IN TACTUALITY. Sex differences in tactile sensibility become apparent very soon after birth, girls having lower touch and pain thresholds than boys, a difference which remains throughout life. At all ages the female is very much more responsive to tactile stimuli than the male, and more dependent upon touch for erotic arousal than the male, who depends more upon visual stimuli. The difference seems to be, at least in part, genetic, but cultural differences undoubtedly also play a role in the development of tactual responsiveness as between the sexes.

Boys respond less to talking and to touch than girls, so parents may find it more rewarding to talk to and touch girls than boys; and within a few months girls show more interest in faces than boys. Beverly Fagot at the University of Oregon studied sex differences in toddlers' play and related these to parental behavior. She found that parents both join in play more with boys than with girls, but paradoxically they also leave boys to play alone more often. Boys being left alone more often may as a result become more independent than girls.

Tactile stimulation is much more meaningful to females than it is to males. As Fritz Kahn says, bodily contact is to a woman an act of great intimacy and a far-reaching concession. Hence, a woman who refuses intimate connection with a man is roused to indignation if he touches her against her will and repulses him with the withering words, "How dare you touch me!"

The unique quality of female tactuality has long been recognized in such a demotically meaningful phrase as "the feminine touch."

Another of the differences between the sexes of tactual interest lies in the greater frequency with which the paraphilias—obsessive responses to unacceptable stimuli in order to achieve orgasm—occur in males as compared with females. Examples are necrophilia (attraction to corpses), exhibitionism (genital exposure), coprophilia (arousal by feces), masochism (pleasure in pain), urophilia or uridinism (arousal by being urinated upon), narratophilia (need to be told erotic stories), pictophilia (arousal through pictures), scatophilia (dirty talk), zoophilia (arousal by animals), voyeurism (Peeping Tomism), sadism (arousal by infliction of pain or discipline), and frottage (the act of rubbing against another person in order to achieve orgasm, usually in crowded places). Such paraphilias are largely masculine abnormalities. Paraphilias are not only infrequent in women, but are almost exclusively limited to touch, the feel and touch of another woman in homosexuality or the feeling and touch of a pet in zoophilia. Stealing love or pregnancy substitutes as in kleptomania may serve as a sexually arousing stimulus in women. While feel and contact are essential to a woman's arousal, the male is erotically attracted from a distance.

SEX DIFFERENCES IN TACTILE EXPERIENCES. With the exception of the United States, there is little information available relating to the differences between civilized societies in the tactile experience to which each of the sexes is exposed. Margaret Mead has drawn attention to the fact that American mothers tend to be closer to their daughters than to their sons, an observation that has been many times confirmed. Goldberg and Lewis, for example, found that at one year of age girls show more attachment behavior towards their mothers than do boys. Moreover, they found that for both sexes the amount of touching the mother provides is correlated with the amount of attachment at this age. By attachment behavior Goldberg and

Lewis mean desire for proximity of the mother, touching her, and response to the mother's departure.

Erikson draws a picture, based on his clinical experience, of the American mother as one who in her son's "early childhood . . . deliberately understimulated him sexually and emotionally," with "a certain determined lack of maternalism." Sears and Maccoby, in their retrospective study of childrearing patterns in the United States, found that baby girls received more demonstrations of affection than boys, and that mothers seemed to be happier about having girl babies than they were about having boy babies. It was also found, as in the Fischers' study of a New England town, that girls were weaned later than boys, suggesting that the later weaning indicated a more indulgent attitude towards girls. Clay, in her study of American mother-infant tactile interactions, also found that female children received more tactile stimulation than male children. Reva Rubin, associate professor of nursing at the University of Pittsburgh, states that it is her impression that "boys are handled less, caressed less often, and held for shorter periods than girls." Baby girls are more responsive to being touched, whether gently or roughly, and within a few minutes show more interest in faces than boys of the same age.

Perhaps this difference in tactile experience, at least in part, accounts for the American female being so much less uptight about tactuality than the American male.

There is evidence that extroverts are more arousable in the tactual system and that they show stronger sexual arousal.

TWINS AND TOUCHING. It is of interest that twins appear to receive less touching than singletons. Lytton, Conway and Sauvé, in a study of forty-six sets of male twins, seventeen of which were identical and twenty-nine fraternal, compared with forty-four non-twin boys, from age twenty-five to thirty-five months, found that the parents of single children showed more affection toward their children, with relatively more "positive actions" such as hugging or approving; they also spoke significantly more to their children than the parents of twins did to theirs. Following from this, they also used more "control behavior," involving more commands and prohibitions, with more reasoning and suggestion. The twins spoke much less than the single children, and their vocabulary was less mature. The double burden of twins seems to allow for less time and energy to be devoted to each child, with resulting significant effects upon twins. Furthermore, it is known that the close spacing of siblings has a greater adverse effect on the intellectual development of the younger child than wider spacing. Twinship, representing as it does the ultimate in close spacing, affects both children.

7 Growth
   and Development

Man is a growing animal, and his birthright
is development.
                                    —Anon.

Growth is increase in dimension. Development is increase in
complexity. What role, if any, does tactile experience play in
the growth and development of the organism? The evidence,
both for animals in general and humans in particular, is unequivocally clear: Tactile experience plays a fundamentally important role in the growth and development of all mammals
thus far studied, and probably also in nonmammals.

   Lawrence Casler has drawn attention to the fact that the ill
effects of maternal deprivation so ably discussed by Bowlby
and others are probably the result of perceptual deprivations,
principally tactile, visual, and probably vestibular. The vesti-
bule is the central part of the inner ear connecting in front with
the cochlea, the essential organ of hearing, and above and behind with the semicircular canals, which give us our sense of
balance. Perceptual deprivations are undoubtedly involved,
but this is only another way of speaking of social deprivation—and the elements comprising that are complex. When we
have learned appreciably more than we know at present concerning the components of maternal love, we shall undoubtedly be able to describe it as a function of biochemical,
physiological, kinesic, tactile, visual, auditory, olfactory, and
other factors. From observations made on nonhuman animals
we may gain some insight into the manner in which tactile experience, with which we are here mainly concerned, may affect
the growth and development of humans. So we will begin with
a discussion of the findings on nonhuman animals, and then

proceed to the evidence for the effects of tactile experience upon our own species.

THE EVIDENCE FROM NONHUMAN ANIMALS. In a series of experiments carried out by Dr. John D. Benjamin of the University of Colorado Medical School, Denver, Colorado, one group of twenty laboratory rats, supplied with exactly the same kinds and amounts of food and living conditions, were caressed and cuddled by the investigator, while the other group was treated coldly. "It sounds silly," one investigator is reported to have remarked, "but the petted rats learned faster and grew faster."

Far from sounding silly, this is exactly what we would expect. The living organism depends to a very large extent upon the stimulation of the external world for its growth and development. Those stimuli must for the most part be pleasurable ones, just as they must be in learning. Hence, as we would expect, animals that have been handled in infancy later tend to be less emotional in open-field tests, defecating and urinating less, and showing more willingness to explore a strange environment, than those animals who have not been handled in the pre-weaning period. Also they are better able to learn a conditioned avoidance response. Handling before weaning also results in a heavier weight of the brain, and in greater development of the cortex and subcortex. More cholesterol and the enzyme cholinesterase have been found in the brains of gentled rats than ungentled ones, thus indicating a more advanced stage of neural development, especially in the formation of fatty sheaths that surround nerve fibers, the myelin sheaths.

Gentled rats show greater liveliness, curiosity, and problem-solving ability than ungentled rats. They also tend to be more dominant than ungentled rats.

Skeletal and body growth are more advanced in gentled than in ungentled control rats, food is better utilized, and evidence has been cited earlier showing that gentled experimental animals show less emotionality in stressful situations. (See pp. 31–32.) Attention has also already been drawn to the fact that gentled animals show, as adults, a more efficiently developed immunological system than rats that have been ungentled in infancy. This is a really quite remarkable finding. How precisely this works is at present unclear, but it has been suggested that environmentally responsive hormones may affect the development of thymic function, which plays a significant role in the establishment of immunologic competency. The hypothalamus, which is known to play a role in the regulation of immunity, may also play a role here. (See pp. 198–203.)

Gentling leads to more rapid maturation of the pituitary-adrenal axis—that is to say, the alarm-reaction system of the body. Rats so gentled in infancy recover from electroconvulsive shock to a degree that is highly significant compared to ungentled rats.

We would expect that early tactile stimulation would in most respects be more important than later tactile stimulation in the development of the organism, and this, indeed, is experimentally found to be the case. Thus, Levine found that handled rats exhibited greater emotional stability, as measured by excretory activity, general activity, and so forth, than nonhandled rats. Furthermore, extra-handled rats, those receiving more than ordinary handling, are better at learning and retention than ordinarily handled or unhandled rats.

Larsson found that repeated handling of male maturing rats made them sexually more responsive to the female. In this way, the onset of puberty was seemingly advanced by several days. Rats that were handled twice a minute for a few seconds and then dropped to the female showed shorter intercopulatory intervals and increased ejaculations, from 3.7 to 5.3 per hour. Thus, sexual activity was greatly increased as a result of handling.

While there can be little doubt that genetic factors enter into the structure of the behavior with which animals respond to handling or gentling, the evidence is unequivocally clear that all animals respond favorably to handling or gentling, and respond more effectively to whatever tests or trials they are put to than animals which have not undergone such tactile experience. Urie Bronfenbrenner has summed up the findings very well.

> First, the effects are generally salutary for the organism both physiologically and psychologically. Thus, handling has been shown to enhance the organism's later capacity to withstand stress, its general activity level, and its learning ability. Second, the presence or absence of handling has its maximal impact during the first ten days of life, although significant effects have been reported for animals handled as late as fifty days of age.

On the organismic level, growth and development are controlled by endocrine and neural factors. It is well known that emotional factors are capable of influencing the growth and development of the organism, principally through the differential action of hormones. Animals that have enjoyed adequate tactile experiences will respond very differently from those who have been failed in such experiences. The differences will be measurable, emotionally, in neural, glandular, biochemical, muscular, and cutaneous changes. Such differences have been measured in handled and nonhandled animals, and the findings have been in the expected direction, namely that in all these respects the handled animals are more advanced than the nonhandled animals.

The inadequately gentled animal, we may, I believe, safely assume, is an emotionally unsatisfied creature. The satisfaction of tactile needs has not hitherto been considered a basic need, a basic need being defined as one which must be satisfied if the organism is to survive. But the fact is that the need for tactuality *is* a basic need, since it must be satisfied if the organism is to survive. With complete cessation of skin stimulation, the organism would die. An organism deprived of its skin cannot live. What we are, of course, generally concerned with is quality, quantity, frequency, and sensitive periods when the organism must receive certain amounts and qualities of tactile stimulation, rather than with all-or-none considerations. And what the evidence abundantly indicates is that there are sensitive periods in the development of every organism possessing a skin during which that outer integument must receive sufficient stimulation if the organism is to develop in a healthy manner.

The preweaning period, whenever that may occur, is critically important here, for the new complexities of existence introduced into the life of the newborn and neonate confront it with the kind of insecurities that the beetle placed on its back experiences when its feet lose contact with the earth. The infant wants tangible evidence of security, the experience of reassuring contacts with another body.

THE EVIDENCE IN INFANTS. The early development of the nervous system of the infant is to a major extent dependent upon the kind of cutaneous stimulation it receives. There can be no doubt that tactile stimulation is necessary for its healthy development. As Clay says:

> The need for peripheral skin stimulation and contact exists throughout life, but it appears to be most intense and crucial in the early phase of reflex attachment. Ribble goes so far as to say that the nervous system of the infant requires some sort of stimulus feeding at this early period. Certainly the young child needs an optimum period for the gratification of his sensual needs, which are both oral and tactile. This is why the preverbal years are considered a critical period for tactile learning. From this time on the needs for tactile contact decline, but tactile stimulation must still be age-graded according to the developmental needs of the human organism.

The evidence indicates clearly that the skin is the primary sense organ of the human infant, and that during its reflex attachment period it is tactile experience that is critical for continued growth and development. This may be seen in a variety of ways, but most particularly in the growth and development of tactile sensitivity in the infant receiving an adequate amount of tactile stimulation as compared with the infant who has received an inadequate amount.

There is every reason to believe that, just as the salamander's brain and nervous system develop more fully in response to peripheral stimulation, so do the brain and nervous system of the human being.

Yarrow, in an investigation of the effects of early maternal care on babies, states that perhaps the most striking finding was the extent to which developmental progress during the first six months appeared to be influenced by maternal stimulation. The amount of stimulation and the quality of stimulation were highly correlated with maternal IQ. "These data suggest," writes Yarrow, "that mothers who give much and intense stimulation and encouragement to practice developmental skills tend to be successful in producing infants who make rapid developmental progress." The conclusion is reinforced, suggests Yarrow, that in institutions it is stimulus deprivation in early infancy that is a causative factor in developmental retardation.

Yarrow also reports on several children who, as a consequence of contact failures in infancy, reacted with disturbances in tactility to any difficulty in the mother-child relationship.

Provence and Lipton, comparing seventy-five institutionalized infants with seventy-five infants reared in families, found that institutionalized infants reacted peculiarly to being held, engaged in much rocking behavior, and were usually quiet and slept excessively. "They did not adapt their bodies well to the arms of the adults, they were not cuddly, and one noted a lack in pliability.... They felt something like sawdust dolls; they moved, they bent easily at the proper joints, but they felt stiff or wooden." By the age of five to six months rocking appeared in most infants and by eight months was present in all of them. Provence and Lipton distinguish four types of rocking: (1) a transient rocking as a normal reaction to frustration; (2) rocking as an autoerotic activity in children who have suffered some degree of maternal deprivation; (3) rocking as withdrawal of attention and extreme preoccupation in children suffering from infantile psychoses; and (4) rocking which serves the purpose of discharge or self-stimulation.

Shevrin and Toussieng of the Menninger Clinic, observing

the disturbed tactile behavior of their juvenile patients, postulated the existence of a need for optimum tactile stimulation in early infancy, which had somehow been denied them. "Such major disturbances were found," they write, "in the history of all the children we have studied thus far." When infants receive too little or too much tactile stimulation, according to these investigators, conflicts are generated which interfere seriously with psychic development. The course of these conflicts can be traced in the thoughts and actions of severely disturbed children of all ages. The main way these children cope with tactile conflicts is not by repression or other psychic defenses. It is either by a defensive raising of thresholds for all stimuli emanating from the environment or from inside the body, or through protective fluctuations in the physical distance between themselves and other people. The fantasy productions of these children yield strong evidence of the conflict, which usually assumes the form of an elaborate denial of the need for closeness. But in spite of this the need for tactile stimulation persists. Shevrin and Toussieng hypothesize that certain rhythmic behavior, such as rocking, is used to prevent a total loss of tactile stimulation resulting from excessive raising of thresholds.

The infant's need for body contact is compelling. If that need is not adequately satisfied, even though all other needs are adequately met, he will suffer. Because the consequences of the lack of satisfaction of such basic needs as hunger, thirst, rest, sleep, bowel and bladder elimination, and avoidance of dangerous and painful stimuli are fairly obvious, we are conscious of the importance of satisfying them. In the case of the tactile needs, the consequences of failing to satisfy them are far from obvious, and so these needs have been mostly overlooked. It is important that we begin to understand how necessary it is for the healthy growth and development of the child that tactile needs be adequately satisfied.

Until recently we did not have much evidence of a direct kind that tactile stimulation or its absence affects the growth and development, physical or psychological, of the human infant. Such direct evidence was largely lacking for the simple reason that it had not been sought in humans. Today, as we have seen, we not only have plenty of direct evidence of this sort for nonhuman animals, but also a great deal of direct evidence for human infants which thoroughly supports the view that tactile stimulation is at least as important in the physical and psychological growth of the human infant as it is in the nonhuman infant.

The failure to satisfy tactile needs in the human infant shows how damaging such deprivations can be, and how important such early satisfactions are.

The maternal deprivation syndrome, consisting of the effects of a minimum amount of mothering, unquestionably involves substantial tactile deprivations, among others. It is an interesting fact that almost invariably the skin of such children, instead of exhibiting the roseate firm character of the healthy infant, shows instead a deep pallor and loss of tone, as well as various other disorders.

Patton and Gardner have published detailed records of children who had been maternally deprived and shown how severely their physical as well as their mental growth had been disturbed, a three-year-old child's bone growth in such a maternally deprived situation being just half that of the bone growth of a normal child. Emotionally deprived children everywhere suffer serious retardations in growth, both physical and behavioral. The literature on this subject is now extensive.

As we have already seen (pp. 202–203) it has been demonstrated that children who are emotionally disturbed as a result of an unfavorable home environment tend to suffer from hypopituitarism, with deficiencies in ACTH and growth hormone the commonest defects, associated with short stature and mental retardation. When such children are removed to favorable environments they show a spectacular increase in growth and the development of normal growth hormone secretion.

The physiological mechanisms involved in tactile deprivation appear to be clearly related to those involved in maternal deprivation and emotional disturbances, in whatever way induced. All these mechanisms add up to the one complex series of processes expressed in the word *shock*.

The process of birth represents a prolonged series of shocks which every infant experiences, and nothing exists more powerfully calculated to assuage the effect of those shocks than the fondling and nursing the mother is designed to give the child virtually immediately after its birth. When afforded such reassurance through the skin, the effects of the shock of birth are gradually mitigated. But if the infant is not afforded such an alleviation of his shock, the effects of that experience will continue, and will more or less affect his subsequent growth and development.

Today we know a great deal more about the nature of shock and its effects than was the case only a few years ago. Indeed, we are today in a position to discuss the nature of shock at a cellular level.

Essentially shock is a molecular disorder producing metabolic derangements revolving around aerobic glucose metabolism, resulting in increased amounts of lactic acid which greatly contribute to anxiety, and the production of amino acids, fatty acids, and phosphoric acids. The deficient metabolism of acids produces disruption in the membranes of the sacs of digestive and lytic enzymes known as lysosomes, with resulting death of the cell. The energy upon which the cell is dependent, ATP (adenosine triphosphate) is decreased, with a consequent derangement of protein synthesis and cell membrane pump function. The derangement in protein synthesis interferes with growth and the ability to withstand shock, and the derangement in cell pump function results in swelling. The circulation tends to slow down, blood pressure falls, red blood cells tend to agglutinate, oxygen supply to the tissues of the body is reduced, there is a general wasting away, until the heart stops and the brain is no longer excited. This is, of course, the extreme end effect of unrelieved shock; it is, however, very likely that all these processes occur to some extent in varying degrees in infants receiving inadequate cutaneous stimulation. And, just as in shock, the process is usually reversible by the use of blood volume, antacids, oxygen, corticosteroids, vasodilators, and energy production solutions like glucose, potassium, and insulin, so the consequences of inadequate cutaneous stimulation in the infant can be reversed by giving him all the tender, loving care he needs, principally in the form of what he best and most immediately understands: warm, fondling, embracing tactuality. The effects upon the infant of such satisfactions of his tactile needs are remarkable.

Temerlin and co-workers, in a study of thirty-two nonverbal retarded males of a median age of nine years, found that the children who received active mothering and maximum skin contact made significantly higher weight gains during the period of the experiment than the subjects in the control groups.

WHAT THE INFANT FEELS.   In full-term infants, pain and touch are not well differentiated. McGraw remarks,

> When only a few hours or days old some infants exhibit no overt response to cutaneous irritation such as pinprick. It is impossible to know whether such absence of response should be attributed to an undeveloped sensory mechanism or to lack of connection between sensory and somatic centers, or between receptor centers and those mechanisms governing crying. Such infants usually do respond to deep pressure stimulation. In any event, this period of hypaesthesia is brief; by the end of the first week or ten days most infants respond to cutaneous irritation.

The relative insensibility of the newborn to cutaneous stimulation has been noted by many investigators.

With growth the number of sensory receptors increase in the skin over a wider area and in close proximity. Part of the newborn's reduced sensibility may be due, as Greenacre suggests, to sensory birth fatigue.

At first the infant's tactile sense is very generalized; it acts as a mass effect rather than as a sharply discriminating critical point effect. Touch and pain are not well differentiated, and the development of critical discrimination of tactile stimuli follows much the same course as the development of returning sensation after a nerve has been cut. The physiology of this Henry Head, the distinguished English neurologist, described in some detail. As sensation begins to return, it is experienced in a very generalized way; this Head termed *protopathic* sensation. The touch which at first is only distinguishable for the area in general, in time becomes more localized, more critical, so that one can locate it exactly; this Head termed *epicritic*. At first the newborn's tactile sense is largely protopathic; only gradually does it develop the epicritic ability which enables it to localize the point of the stimulus precisely.

It is approximately between seven and nine months of age that specific localization really begins to develop, and becomes well established by between twelve and sixteen months.

Infants probably differ in skin sensitivity. As Escalona has said, "There can be no doubt that something like skin awareness, or sensations of the kind generated by the skin, are sharp and frequent throughout the day for some babies and less intense for others." And she goes on to point out that just such skin-sensitive babies will receive an inordinate amount of attention and handling. Such babies tend to receive a considerable amount of tactile stimulation for the greater part of their waking and half-waking hours. In the Western world it is perhaps a great advantage for an infant to have a sensitive skin or diaper rashes or some other dermatological disorder, for then, at least, it can be assured of receiving something resembling an adequate amount of cutaneous stimulation. Ribble believes that diapering, at least in America, is "invariably overdone." She considers that the desire to keep the baby dry in the first months is misplaced, "except for the comfort of the adults handling the child." And she adds that the frequent diaper-changing may focus the child's attention on this area, "and thus foster later emotional reactions which become deeply involved with the function of elimination." In many cases this may well be so. Escalona points out that there are extraordinary differences in the amount and kind of tactile stimulation to which babies are exposed, and that "the baby's life is largely a succession of sharply felt touches, sounds, sights, movements, temperatures, and the like"(p. 19).

Escalona's reference to "sharply felt touches" almost certainly does not accurately describe what the newborn and young infant feels. The evidence, on the other hand, indicates that the baby tends to feel rather more protopathically than epicritically, and only gradually learns to discriminate discrete point sensations. It would seem to be an admirably adaptive provision that the baby should not at first feel "sharply," but for the most part only in a generalized way, for it is such a general rather than a "sharp" or specific sensing of assurance that he requires in his early days. Not that the infant is incapable of discriminating and localizing discrete point sensations. This he is undoubtedly able to do, but almost certainly in most cases not "sharply." It is on the foundation of his generalized tactile experience that he subsequently learns and refines the sharply felt touches, sounds, sights, movements, temperatures, and the like, into specific, recognizably distinctive and meaningful modalities.

Some babies are born with tactile hypersensitivity, experiencing being touched as painful. This apparently provides a hazard to being comfortable with closeness and to seeing oneself as part of another person. Lourie points out that if such a baby remains unrelated, this can result in a long-lasting expectation that dependency involves pain, and in this way masochism may develop, pain in some of these individuals becoming not only a need but also a pleasure. Usually such a developmental abnormality is overcome by the end of the first year, but if it is not, a fear of being touched together with a mistrust of any dependency may result.

More than three hundred years ago Thomas Hobbes wrote, "For there is no conception in man's mind, which hath not first been begotten upon the organs of Sense." The shape and form and space of the outer world of reality, its figures and the background from which they emerge, are gradually built by the infant out of the building blocks of its experience, entering through all its senses, always contingent, correlated, measured, and evaluated by the criterion of touch. If this object that holds me so pleasurably does so long and consistently enough, I come to identify her face and eventually all its tangibly visible parts with pleasure. It is, however, my skin which primarily tells me that this face is pleasure-giving, since, as a baby, it is principally through the skin that I can make that judgment. And so it is with all the other sensations I experience.

How does this sensation, whatever it is, "feel"? Since the various senses are really skin receptors of different sorts, the eyes and ears and nose and certainly the tongue, at first "feel" rather than see, hear, smell, and taste. As soon as he is able, the baby will put to the test whatever he can, by putting it into his mouth, and what he there feels with hand and mouth will tell him what he desires to know. Gradually he will come to increase the distance between what he tactually feels and what he experiences through the other senses, until he is eventually able to recognize each experience or object as separate and distinct from others, and by its own attributes rather than by reference to the verdict of the skin.

As Sylvester has stated: "The mother's sensitivity and selectivity of response facilitates the transition from prevalent orientation by close receptors to orientation by distance receptors. In the earliest stages, the infant's security is a matter of skin contact and kinesthetic sensations of being held and supported. Later, security is derived also from orientation by sight and sound and from the infant's ability to maintain contact with his mother through these perceptive modalities." Sometimes, Sylvester goes on to say, the infant continues to depend upon skin contact, and fails to develop the ability to use sight and sound for orientation and communication. This can occur because of "primary maternal attitudes," or as the result of conditions leading to increased skin sensitization (such as infantile eczema, or the loss or absence of other sensory organs). Often, according to Sylvester, the beginnings of "habitual defects in orientation or body image" can be traced to such early difficulties.

The mother mutually adapted to her child will respond in

rhythm to her child's needs. Her flexibility will reflect itself in the child's perceptual development. The mother, as the main source of the infant's ebb and flow of incoming stimuli, is thereby also the main source of his comfort and the performer of the tasks that will later be assumed by his ego. According to Sylvester, "if a mother prevents her child from regulating approach and retreat autonomously, he may react to threats by drawing closer to or by taking flight from inanimate objects. It is possible that such enforced substitution of gadgets for people is one of the roots of human mechanization."

During the earliest postnatal days the baby spends recovering from the shock of birth, and in the months that follow, he is occupied with the organization of perceptions—tactile, visual, auditory, taste, and so on. From a base in such experiences, the infant begins to differentiate himself from the world which is not self. Objects which at first appeared to have no permanence now become the first conceptual invariants in his mental furniture. The differentiation of self from the world of objects is a major achievement, and it is one in which touch plays a dominant role. The three principal developments that emerge from this differentiation are the *self* (the agent of action), *objects* (the objects of action), and the *action relation* between them. With the growing differentiation of the self from other persons, the need for communication increases, a need which, as Sinclair has pointed out, is made even more pressing as the increasing mobility of the child reduces direct physical contact with others. The earliest forms of vocalization are designed to communicate the emotional and need states of the infant. From such vocalizations, later language abilities will develop.

"From his first day onward," writes Escalona, "the baby is reacted to and himself reacts to other persons. The nature of these contacts, more frequent, varied, and complex the older he gets, is perhaps the single most important determinant of how he shall experience his world and of the kind of human relationships which he will be able to have as he grows up" (p. 33).

The infant will develop a sense of trust or mistrust depending upon his sensory impressions, received mainly through the skin, whether gratifying or not. The infant's sense of space, time, and reality are all of a piece, being experienced first as whatever is durably gratifying, then as what is perceptually meaningful, and later as events which can be anticipated. Chronologic time remains meaningless until much later in the infant's development. The earliest steps in the development of mastery of time and space have been imagined by Escalona to be something like this:

> At first, the world is a succession of different sensations and feeling states. What varies is the quality and distribution and intensity of sensations. Except for the difference in the nature of the sensations involved, hunger, which we say originates from within, and a sharp sound or cold breeze, which we cannot imagine except as something that reaches us from outside, are indistinguishable. There is no awareness of such things as approach, withdrawal, or direction of any sort. Even if the baby turns his head toward the nipple and grasps it, his sensation is that the nipple comes or is; no other state with which to contrast this exists. Light and darkness; harshness and softness; cold and warmth; sleep and waking; the contours of mother's face as seen from below, vis-à-vis, or even from above; being grasped and released; being moved and moving; the sight of moving people, curtains, blankets, toys; all these recede and approach and comprise the totality of experience in whatever constellation they occur at each split second in time. With recurrence, there develop islands of consistency. For instance, a certain way of being grasped, certain kinesthetic sensations, and the change in visual environment afforded by the vertical position combine into an awareness of being lifted, being moved, as an entity.

The importance of recurring experiences of the same kind is the essence of this developmental process, and Escalona believes that such "islands of consistency," with a definite rhythm and sameness to them, in respect to such important experiences as feeding and bathing, may enable infants to acquire a sense of themselves as entities to whom things happen and who can make things happen. "The one who is not held, moved about, and rocked is less likely to become aware of himself through the sensation of passive motion and less likely to recognize his mother's characteristic touch and tempo" (p. 26).

The infant is at first not only lacking in psychic structure, but also in psychic and somatic boundaries. He is unable to distinguish between inside and outside, between "I" and "not-I"; in brief, he is in a state of psychic nondifferentiation. In this stage the primary identifications he makes are with his need gratifications as part of his own body. And, as Spitz points out, primary identification is made difficult by mothers who withhold from their children the need gratification inherent in being touched:

> They extensively restrict the occasions for primary identification through withholding tactile experiences. Yet, if the infant is to differentiate himself from his mother, these primary identifications, tactile and otherwise, have to be dealt with, severed and overcome. Action-directed motility first, and locomotion later, are the child's devices for dealing with primary identification and achieving differentiation. When differentiation from the mother has been accomplished, the infant can form those secondary identifications which pave the way to autonomy and independence.

Tennyson, in his magnificent elegiac poem, *In Memoriam,* refers to the process of individuation, which he clearly fully understood. Though published in 1850, many parts of the poem were written much earlier.

> *The baby new to earth and sky,*
> *What time his tender palm is prest*
> *Against the circle of the breast,*
> *Has never thought that 'this is I':*
>
> *But as he grows he gathers much,*
> *And learns the use of 'I' and 'me,'*
> *And finds 'I am not what I see,*
> *And other than the things I touch.'*

So rounds he to a separate mind
From whence clear memory may begin,
As thro' the frame that binds him in
His isolation grows defined.

This use may lie in blood and breath,
Which else were fruitless of their due,
Had man to learn himself anew
Beyond the second birth of Death. (*XLV*)

The process of what Mahler has called individuation-separation leads to individuation through secondary identifications. By taking over the mother's techniques of caring for him through identification with them, the infant makes the first steps towards ego formation, the stage of secondary identification, beginning in the second half of the first year. In this stage the infant acquires the techniques and devices by means of which he achieves independence from his mother. In these first six months tactile experiences are fundamental in the development of the stage of primary identification and the mechanism of secondary identification.

Erasmus Darwin, in his *Zoonomia,* published in 1794, had arrived at much the same conclusion. He wrote:

The first ideas we become acquainted with, are those of the sense of touch; for the foetus must experience some varieties of agitation, and exert some muscular action, in the womb; and may with great probability be supposed thus to gain some ideas of its own figure, of that of the uterus, and of the tenacity of the fluid, that surrounds it. . . .

Many of the organs of sense are confined to a small part of the body, as the nostrils, ear, or eye, whilst the sense of touch is diffused over the whole skin, but exists with a more exquisite degree of delicacy at the extremities of the fingers and thumbs, and in the lips. The sense of touch is thus very commodiously disposed for the purpose of encompassing smaller bodies, and for adapting itself to the inequalities of larger ones. The figure of small bodies seem to be learnt by children by their lips as much as by their fingers; on which account they put every new object to their mouths, when they are satiated with food, as well as when they are hungry. And puppies seem to learn their ideas of figure principally by the lips in their mode of play.

We acquire our tangible ideas of objects either by the simple pressure of this organ of touch against a solid body, or by moving our organ of touch along the surface of it. In the former case we learn the length and breadth of the objects by the continuance of this pressure on our moving organ of touch.

It is hence, that we are very slow in acquiring our tangible ideas, and very slow in recollecting them; for if I now think of the tangible idea of a cube, that is, if I think of its figure, and the solidity of every part of that figure, I must conceive myself as passing my fingers over it, and seem in some measure to feel the idea, as I formerly did the impression at the ends of them, and thus am very slow in distinctly recollecting.

The modalities of space, time, and reality, shape, form, depth, quality, texture, the three-dimensionality of our vision, and the like, are almost certainly developed in large part on the basis of the infant's tactile experiences. As Escalona has put it,

Awareness of the body in space, and of space surrounding the self must come about in a thousand ways. As the baby's legs kick and stretch, the pressure of the diaper increases, his feet contact the blanket, gown, or end of the crib. As he flails his arms, he encounters the side of the crib, nothing, the surface on which he lies, or portions of his own body. As he is lifted, he temporarily feels the absence of contact with anything firm except the part of the body where his mother is grasping him. Simultaneously, kinesthetic sensations are quite different from before, the contours and range of his visual field change strangely as he is brought to the vertical position. It is at about the time when visual coordination and focusing occur more easily that purposive body movement begins to emerge.

As we shall see in the next chapter, the varieties of cutaneous experiences to which children are exposed, within one culture and cross-culturally, make very significant differences in the rates at which they mature and the ways in which they relate to their fellows.

Landauer and Whiting have produced some interesting evidence suggesting that the handling which results in increase in size in rodents, as a consequence, they assume, of stress effects, is similarly operative in the human species. In order to throw some light on this matter they studied cross-culturally the relation between apparently stressful infant care practices and the stature of adult males in some eighty different societies for which appropriate information was available. The stresses they studied were:

1. *Piercing:* Nose, lips, circumcision, infibulation, etc.
2. *Molding:* Stretching arms, legs, shaping head, etc.
3. *External:* Heat, hot baths, fire, intense sunlight, etc.
4. *Extreme cold:* Baths, exposure to snow, cold, etc.
5. *Internal stressors:* Emotions, irritants, enemas
6. *Abrasions:* Rubbing with sand, etc.
7. *Intense sensory stimulation*
8. *Binding:* Swaddling.

Upon analysis, it was found that "In societies in which the heads or limbs of infants were repeatedly molded or stretched, or where their ears, noses, or lips were pierced, where they were circumcised, vaccinated, innoculated, or had tribal marks cut or burned in their skin, the mean adult male stature was over two inches greater than in societies where these customs were not practiced."

Here the question may well be raised as to the difference between "handling" and "gentling." Many investigators have interpreted "handling" to signify the equivalent of a stressful experience, while "gentling" has been regarded as a comforting, reassuring experience for the animal exposed to it. The practices used as criteria by Landauer and Whiting were undoubtedly largely stressful. There remains, however, the very real question whether they were not in part also pleasurable. The practices which these investigators found most significantly correlated with increased growth are for the most part associated with elevations in status, the passage from one grade into another, greater attractiveness, and therefore greater self-esteem. Thus, whether as a direct or an indirect result of the stressful tactile experience, the subsequent pleasurable rewards of these operations are very considerable. In numberless societies the decoration of the skin by incision, puncture, the rubbing of dirt in the wounds, tattooing, and the like, though painful, has nevertheless been voluntarily sought for its rewarding end effects. Even in rodents who have been handled, reward is not missing, for the release unharmed from the handling to the freedom of the cage must be considered to constitute a reward. In human beings the combination of the stressful cutaneous experience with the highly rewarding experiences which follow probably constitutes a factor in the observed increase in growth.

Physiologically, the involvement of the sympathetico-adrenal axis, with added secretion of pituitary growth hormone, in the colligation of conditions described, would be sufficient to explain the results observed.

Developmental abnormalities which are thought to be the direct result of lack of adequate contacts with the maternal figure often express themselves in reactive skin disorders. As Flanders Dunbar put it, in summarizing the evidence: "It may well be said that the skin, like other sense organs, is likely to become sick when contact of the sufferer with his parents and with the outside world has been disturbed at an early age, and it appears that many skin disorders are relieved when emotional contact with the outer world is improved." Many skin sufferers have experienced early prohibitions of tactile expression and experience. D. W. Winnicott says: "The smallest skin lesion, if it concerns the feelings, concerns the whole body. Prohibitions relative to tactile experience are those in the area of: 'No, no; don't touch!' and, by way of corollary, 'Don't let yourself be touched.'" *Noli me tangere.* Because the skin is the organ of embrace and contact, many skin disorders can be understood as the expression of ambivalence relating to such intimate tactual experience.

Since tactile communication is essentially an interactional process, from the first contact with the hands of the person who has touched the baby to the contact with the mother's body, any significant failure in the experience of such contacts may lead to a profound failure or disorder in later interactional relationships, which may sometimes express itself in autism, schizophrenia, as well as in a variety of other behavioral disorders, not to mention such respiratory disorders as asthma and the like.

AUTISM AND TOUCHING. Bruno Bettelheim, as in so much else, has provided one of the best accounts of the autistic child extant, a brief résumé of which follows, because it is both typical and illuminating, and also lays the groundwork for an understanding of the role of touch in the treatment of such children.

Joey was the offspring of an Army post marriage in which neither genitor was prepared for parenthood. At birth the mother thought of Joey "as a thing rather than a person." Even before that he made little impression; she never knew she was pregnant, she said, meaning that pregnancy did not in any way alter her life. Joey's birth "made no difference." He was kept on a rigid four-hour schedule, and not touched unless necessary, nor cuddled nor played with. Joey soon became a headbanger, a crier "most of the time," and a body swinger. His crying was dealt with punitively by his father.

It is of interest that while Joey at first named his foods correctly, "butter," "sugar," "water," and so on, he later abandoned this in favor of terms characterized "by the way they feel to the touch." In this way sugar became "sand," butter "grease," water "liquid," and so on.

Bettelheim thinks that this replacement of names for foods by tactile terms was due to the fact that Joey wanted his words to match how *he* experienced things—and things only, not people. Physical quality replaced nutritive quality because he was fed only physical substances and not emotions. So he deprived food of taste and smell and replaced these qualities by the way they felt to him. In thus translating the evidence of the minimal involvement shown him by his mother into tactile terms, he created "a language to fit his emotional experience of the world," by framing it in a form as near as possible to the tactile experience of which he had been deprived.

At first, when he came to the Orthogenic School at the University of Chicago for therapy at the age of four, Joey was afraid of being touched and of touching other people. He related that shortly after coming to the school, he experienced the desire to touch one of the members of the staff because he was fat, and that reminded him of his mother when pregnant with his younger sister. As he later explained, by touching Mitchell, the staff member, he was really wanting to express the fact that at that time he wished his mother were pregnant again with him, to be reborn so that he could start life anew.

More or less, that is much the same history of most autistic children. The condition is characterized by a failure to relate in the ordinary way to people and situations by repetitive activities, developmental language disorders, and marked inability to adjust socially. It is sometimes called childhood schizophrenia. The approach to the treatment of autism has, in the past, been mainly a study in psychological anarchy and ineffectuality, and this in spite of the fact that striking leads such as Gertrude Schwing's success with autistic children by cuddling and embracing them, published in 1953, have for the most part not been followed up. What appears to be something of a breakthrough came in 1983 with the publication of the Tinbergens' book *Autistic Children: New Hope for a Cure.*

Professor Niko Tinbergen is the Nobel prizewinning ethologist at Oxford University. His wife and he have traveled widely in the investigation of the causes and treatment of autism, and in their fascinating book, the first scientific book of its kind, they inquire into the whole subject of autism—causes, treatment, varieties of both autism and treatment—and following the most detailed and exhaustive study conclude that the *autistic condition* is an anxiety-dominated emotional imbalance, which leads to social withdrawal, and in its wake failure to learn from social interaction and from exploratory behavior.

The Tinbergens postulate a number of autismogenic factors which modern life styles contribute to the vulnerability of infants. Among the most important of these factors, they find, is often the mother's relation to her child. The frequency with which this relationship crops up is highly significant.

Dr. Martha Welch, child psychiatrist and president of The Mothering Center at Cos Cob, Connecticut, whose fascinating article on the retrieval from autism is presented in the Tinbergens' book, reports great success with "forced" holding of the child. This may frequently be a very trying experience for both mother and child. The child may do his best to resist being held, screaming and kicking, wrestling and crying, but the mother must not give up. She must hold the child closely and try to establish eye contact. During the ensuing battle the mother must hold on until the child relaxes, "molds to her body, clings, gazes into her eyes, explores her face lovingly and gently, and eventually talks." A soft couch or mat protects the pair from physical injury.

> The mother is asked to hold the child on her lap, face to face. The father is asked to sit beside and put his arm around the mother. The child sits astraddle the mother with knees bent, one on each side of the mother. The mother places the child's arms around her and secures them under her arms. She then is free to hold the child's head with her hands in order to make eye contact. This position is not necessarily comfortable for either person.

> The therapist remains near enough to closely observe and interpret the mother's and child's actions and reactions. Sessions of holding the child for an hour at least each day, and whenever the child signals distress, must be adhered to. The father's holding should supplement, not substitute for, the mother's holding. The therapist must not do the holding. Dr. Welch makes it quite clear that child-holding therapy is an exhausting undertaking and involves the intensive treatment of the whole family, but the results are very much worth the effort. In addition to Dr. Welch's own case histories, which she

gives in her article, I have seen reports from abroad on the successful use of her therapy in the treatment of autistic children, as well as children with other behavioral disturbances, including stuttering.

The important thing to note here is that whatever other factors enter into the "forced" holding technique in achieving cures of autism, it is the holding, the tactile experience, which is primary, and is beneficial to the mother as well as the child.

Autistic children act as if they have been severely deprived of maternal love; whether they have or have not, the most effective therapy for autistic children is to treat them as if they have been maternally deprived. Dr. Temple Grandin, herself once an autistic child, has much to say most impressively on this subject.

Though claims have been made for genetic determinants in the causation of autism, it is unlikely that any are involved, for we have quite a number of records of identical twins, one of whom was autistic and the other not. There undoubtedly exist different degrees of vulnerability to environmental pressures of various sorts in children, some becoming autistic while others do not. The most prominent of these pressures appears to be maternal deprivation of more or less severity.

In England, Dr. Gerald O'Gorman had the brilliant idea of calling upon certain institutionalized mentally defective girls, under the supervision of nurses, to fondle, cuddle, and sleep with autistic children. There was an immediate and dramatic response in the autistic children. They developed coordinated motor behavior and speech. The foster mothers were also happy in their role.

In his excellent book, *Touching Is Healing,* Dr. Jules Older reports the unpublished work with autistic children by child-care worker Meredith Leavitt-Teare in Vermont. In the class she was teaching, composed of Down's syndrome children and autistic ones, she encouraged the Down's children to hug the autistic ones and to reinforce their responsive behavior. "The autistic children," writes Older, "who would not tolerate the touch of an adult, apparently felt less threatened by these same-size huggers, and they quickly grew quite tolerant of their touch."

Dr. Michele Zappella of the Ospedale Regionale of Siena has also observed that normal children interact unusually well with autistic ones, developing a kind of dialogue with them, and eliciting many more responses and general interest than is seen in the hospital setting. In Dr. Zappella's approach to the autistic child, touching and holding play an important role, in this aspect of his work having been much influenced by the methods of Dr. Welch.

It seems to be clear that in the treatment of autistic children various approaches through touching are destined to play an important role.

SCHIZOPHRENIA AND TOUCHING. Alexander Lowen has written an excellent account of the failure of early tactile experience and its relationship to schizophrenia in his book *The Betrayal of the Body*. Based on the clinical study of many schizophrenics, Lowen shows that the feeling of identity arises from a feeling of contact with the body. To know who one is, the person must be aware of what he feels. This is precisely what is wanting in the schizophrenic. There is a complete loss of body contact to such an extent that, broadly speaking, the schizophrenic doesn't know who he is. He is out of touch with reality. He is aware that he has a body, and is therefore oriented in time and space. "But since his ego is not identified with his body and does not perceive it in an alive way, he feels unrelated to the world and to people. Similarly, his conscious sense of identity is unrelated to the way he feels about himself." There is a dissociation between image and reality in the schizoid state. The healthy person has an image of himself which agrees with the way he feels and looks, for normally images derive their reality from association with feeling and sensation. Loss of touch with the body results in loss of touch with reality. Personal identity has substance and structure only insofar as it is based on the reality of bodily feeling.

The fundamental trauma of the schizoid personality,

Lowen states, is the absence of pleasurable physical intimacy between mother and child. "The lack of erotic body contact is experienced by the child as abandonment. If the child's demands for this contact are not met with a warm response, it will grow up with the feeling that no one cares" (pp. 105–106). In order to cut off unpleasant feelings and sensations, the child will hold his breath, suck in his belly, and immobilize his diaphragm. He will lie very still to avoid being afraid. In short, he will "deaden" his body in order not to feel pain, and by these means abandon reality. By such dissociation, especially when fear of the body becomes unendurably terrifying, the ego dissociates from the body, completely splitting the personality into two contradictory identities. One of these identities is based on the body, the other is based on the ego image.

As Otto Fenichel has pointed out, "A lack of emotions which is due not to mere repression but to real loss of contact with the objective world gives the observer a specific impression of 'queerness.' " Sometimes these individuals "seem normal because they have succeeded in substituting 'pseudo contacts' of manifold kinds for a real feeling contact with other people; they behave 'as if' they had feeling relations with people." And as Lowen adds, pseudo contacts often take the form of words, which serve as substitutes for touch. Such people are among the innumerable casualties who find it difficult to be closer to others than words. Another form of pseudo contact is role playing, which serves as a stand-in for emotional involvement. The main complaint of the schizoid personality is that, as Herbert Weiner puts it, he is unable to feel any emotions; he is estranged from others, withdrawn, and detached.

Involvement and identity become established by involvement and identification between mother and infant, and this mainly through touch. Tactile failure in infancy results only too often in estrangement, uninvolvement, lack of identity, detachment, emotional shallowness, and indifference—all marks of the schizoid or schizophrenic personality. (See pages 133–139.)

The body-feeling image we have of ourselves as sensitive

or insensitive, sensuous or unfeeling, relaxed or tense, warm or cold, is largely based on our tactual experiences in infancy, and subsequently reenforced by our experiences in childhood. The skin of those who have been tactually deprived is "turned off" to those experiences which the tactually satisfied enjoy. The turned-off individual may be so cutaneously uptight that he actually recoils from the slightest touch. It is interesting to learn that George Washington was such a person. He hated to be touched. T. E. Lawrence, the English writer and adventurer, had a "morbid horror" of being touched, apparently having received very little tactile stimulation when he was young. In such persons, there is a feeling of tenseness about their skin, as if they were wearing an ill-fitting garment or were encased in a suit of armor from which, even if they wished, they were unable to extricate themselves. The "armored" feeling often gives such individuals a sense of invulnerability to the attempted incursions of the external world upon their ego. Such unreachableness begins at the skin, but it is not really an unreachableness that cannot be breached. It does, however, present an appearance to the world that often takes the form of a complete indifference to its overtures of love or warmth. The "cold fish" really feels like a cold fish. In some cases he really would like to "feel more alive," if he only knew how. Indeed, in every failed individual there is a *potentially* warm, loving creature struggling to get out. The trick is so to interact with the individual who has been tactually failed as to release that potentiality for something resembling the kind of humanizing experiences he should have enjoyed in infancy and childhood.

Body awareness is produced through stimulation of the body, chiefly through the skin, and this commences at birth, if not before.

Persons who are callously unresponsive to human need, who have become so "hardened" that they are no longer in touch with the human condition, are not merely metaphorically so, but clearly physiologically so. The evidence suggests that those who have been inadequately touched during their early years have simply not experienced as full a development of the neurotactile elements in the skin as those who have been adequately touched. These neurotactile elements grow and develop throughout the growing period of the individual, up to about twenty-five years or more. The greater plasticity of the nervous system of children enables them to make far better recoveries, for example, from nerve section than adults. Furthermore, children have to learn tactual-kinesthetic localization, and until they have done so they are relatively poor at localizing stimuli. From the eighth to the twelfth year, tactual-kinesthetic localization is superior to visual localization. The dominance of vision as a source of information leading to tactile localization does not appear until after the age of twelve.

EYE CONTACT. The newborn baby can see quite clearly and is sometimes so evidently interested in what is going on around him it is a wonder to behold. In any event, all babies will establish "eye contact" with their mothers very quickly. This is important for the bonding which will take place between them. For this reason, silver nitrate should not be introduced into the baby's eyes immediately after it is born, because this will interfere with vision and with the bonding with his mother that would otherwise take place. Similar eye contact between father and baby will be prevented, and bonding between them delayed. Half an hour after the baby has "visited" with its parents following birth, an antibiotic ointment, preferably tetracycline rather than silver nitrate, which often causes swelling, redness, and discharge from the eyes, should be applied.

There is something about eye contact between parents and newborn which is almost palpable—a contact which survives into adult life, and is often experienced as such. That eyes have a language of their own has long been understood, as in the twenties song, "Your lips tell me 'No, no' but there's 'Yes, yes' in your eyes."

The kind of tactuality experienced during infancy and childhood not only produces the appropriate changes in the brain, but also affects the growth and development of the end organs in the skin. The tactually deprived individual will suffer from a feedback deficiency between skin and brain that may seriously affect his development as a human being.

Bodily connectedness is the basis of that interconnectedness with others that we call *sociality,* and this is brought about by the closeness of mother and child in infancy. Such a close bodily relationship is the basis of good feelings about oneself, and the feeling of bodily connectedness leads to a feeling of self-esteem. Fundamentally the source of self-esteem is love. The infant uses its body to express its love, its emotions.

In a study of the relationship between self-esteem and tactuality, Drs. Alan F. Silverman, Mark E. Pressman, and Helmut W. Bartel, utilizing eighty male and female students, found that the higher the subject's self-esteem, the more intimate he or she was in communicating through touch, especially when communicating with a female.

Lack of touch is experienced as a separation anxiety—lack of contact, of connection. "Only connect," as E. M. Forster enjoined his characters in his novel *Howard's End.* Something of the nature of this anxiety becomes evident in adults who have been deprived of physical contact and who are able to put into words what it feels like. Dr. Jimmie Holland and her colleagues then at the University of Buffalo School of Medicine have reported on leukemic patients who as part of their treatment were isolated in "germ-free" rooms, which consisted of a large transparent bubble with two-way visibility and verbal communication facilities, serving to prevent all skin contact between the patient and others. It was found that the chief drawback of the unit was human touch deprivation. Three-fourths of the patients experienced an acute sense of isolation, chiefly related to the inability to touch or be touched directly. The loss of human physical contact generated feelings of loneliness, frustration, a sense of coldness, and a lack of emotional warmth. The staff, too, were sometimes troubled by their inability to touch and comfort the patient. One woman patient put it very graphically:

About a week ago, it started to get on my nerves . . . not being able to feel other people and hoping I could soon come out. I felt like everything was closing in on me and I couldn't stand it anymore. I just had to *feel* other people, I wanted to feel somebody, touch another human being. If I could have done this, I could have stuck it out longer. . . . But since I couldn't there was no way I could touch anyone or in any way express my feelings toward somebody just by touching their hand or squeezing it. This is very difficult to explain—It leaves you at a loss for words. You just feel you are all alone in the world and everything is cold. There is no warmth. The warmth is all gone and you just feel like there isn't anything.

In her book *Lonely in America,* Suzanne Gordon defines loneliness "as a feeling of deprivation caused by the lack of certain kinds of human contact." Loneliness is very much in the same class and of much the same kind as the separation anxiety that infants and children experience when they are deprived for any length of time from contact with their mothers. It is a separation anxiety which causes us, as adolescents and adults, to become restless when alone for any durable period of time, and at any cost to seek out the company of others. It is this deprivation of contact with others that makes solitary confinement among the most cruel of punishments . . . even when it is in the confines of the home.

Loneliness is a state of being unconnected, to be out of touch with others, of wanting to be with somebody who isn't there, of having nobody to turn to who can affirm one's essential humanity.

In a review of Simon Gray's play *Otherwise Engaged,* Clive Barnes described it as "A savage indictment of a contemporary morality that is uncaring in its detached permissiveness, of people who do not wish to be touched, of a world of art and letters that cannot be penetrated by life itself."

In such a world people pursue parallel lives without touching, substituting proximity for relationship, a world in which, as Rollo May has said, touching is at best a sightless fumbling, in which we move our fingers over the body of another trying to recognize him or her, but unable, in our self-enclosing darkness to do so.

Studies on the communication of affection between cancer patients and their spouses, carried out at the Roswell Memorial Institute at the University of Buffalo Medical School and Hospital by Dr. Lillian Leiber and her colleagues, showed that while the desire for sexual intercourse decreased among these patients, the desire for physical closeness increased.

It is sad to reflect that in the Western world the only time that many married couples will exhibit nonsexual physical closeness or genuine intimacy is when a serious illness befalls the one or the other. Women are usually far more ready to display such affection than men, but men often have an inhibiting effect upon their wives by actively discouraging any display of physical affection. Such men literally act as if they feared to be touched, and become quite anxious, often confused, and not infrequently hostile, when they are touched. Their love is unexpressed and often unexpressible. The care they lavish on things becomes a quite straightforward token for the affection they have no confidence in placing elsewhere.

> *How scared he is of human contact,*
> *The clumsy touch of other men.*

So writes the Russian poet Yevgeny Vinokurov. How cut off we are from each other by outmoded traditional conditionings. This is underscored by the results of an experiment conducted by Kenneth and Mary Gergen and William H. Barton of the department of psychology at Swarthmore College, who found that when persons, mostly students, between the ages of eighteen and twenty-five were introduced into a pitch-black room in which there were half a dozen strangers, persons they knew they would never meet again, more than 90 percent touched each other on purpose, while almost none of the subjects in a similar lighted room did. Almost 50 percent of the dark-room participants hugged each other. Almost 80 percent of the dark-room subjects said they felt sexual excitement, while only 30 percent of the light-room subjects said they did.

The experimenters were struck by the desire for intimate alliance among their dark-room subjects, that with the simple subtraction of light a group of perfect strangers moved within about thirty minutes to a stage of intimacy seldom attained in years of normal acquaintanceship. The experimenters concluded that people share strong yearnings to be close to each other, but that our social norms make it too costly to express these feelings and tend rather to keep us at a distance. Perhaps, they add, these traditional norms have outlived their usefulness.

It is, however, questionable whether these norms ever had any usefulness. As one boy wrote, "Felt joy over the possibility of not having to look at people in clichéd ways. Enjoyed feeling of self-awareness surrounded by a rich environment. . . . Enjoyed the wantonness of just crawling around and over other people to get from one place to another."

Similar observations were made by D.A., a student, relating to a group of Psychology I students who were individually blindfolded and led downstairs to a pitch-black room, in which strange sounds were emanating from a record player. Then they heard a woman sobbing, who then burst into hysterical laughter. While the students listened, unblindfolded individuals went around to massage the back of each blindfolded student, and smeared a sweet-smelling cream over their hands and faces. They were then led to the middle of the room where there was a huge pile of plastic bags. The students played in this pile. They used their sense of touch to feel their way around and "see" things. They held hands, touched each others' faces. Some of them even began kissing each other. Small groups sat in circles in the plastic and held hands. Soon the students rose and began to dance. Groups of four or five blindfolded and unblindfolded students were all huddled together dancing. Almost all of the students felt happy and free. In the middle of the music, the blindfolds were removed. Most of the psychology students were embarrassed by their behavior. They used only their sense of touch to "see" around them. Now that they were "caught" hugging and dancing with strangers without their blindfolds, they were embarrassed. "What a strange turn of events," remarks D.A., "in a group of people who were so happy just moments before."

These observations throw a much needed light on the value systems, as it were, of vision as compared with touch. Vision, in its social aspect, is the censor of the senses. It is, of course, the brain that does the actual censoring, but vision is the medium through which what is seen is conveyed to the brain, where it is judged. But, then, so is what is touched, with this difference: that touch has no censorship qualities. Touch is free and open. Vision acts, as it were, as an arbiter of behavior, an inhibitor or stimulus thereto; touch is free of censorship, censoriousness, or inhibition. Vision is the medium of perceptual prejudice, and as Dr. August F. Coppola has said, it is so much taken for granted that few realize the extent to which most of our prejudices are bound up with the way we view things. "It almost seems blasphemous to mention it, but the culprit here is sight, which dictates most of our values and dominates practically every aspect of our society. Skin color, conspicuous display of wealth, classification of people by dress and appearance, are all based on distinctions made available to us through vision. To be accepted we must fit into the sighted world, even if we are blind." As Dr. Coppola goes on to say, the importance of sight is beyond question, nevertheless it can be overestimated in the sense that it can blind us to those things that are not meant to be seen but to be felt. Blindness and deafness, handicapping as they are, are not incompatible with an adequate adjustment to the situation. With a loss of touch or bodily feeling there would, however, be little sense of life. And for the feeling of being alive and the potentials of interpersonal relations, touch has a fundamental value and significance not included in the world of sight.

We will happily relate to strangers by touch when we cannot see them, but the moment we do see them we become "appropriately" distant. The student who wrote that he felt joy over the possibility of not having to look at people in clichéd ways in the dark put it in a nutshell. The clichés and stereotypes in which he had been conditioned visually by his culture, when rendered nonfunctional, allowed the enjoyment of tactile experiences and the complete overriding of the "Don't touch" taboo, without inhibition or conventional restraint. This was clearly understood by that extraordinary spirit, William Blake, when in his poem *The Everlasting Gospel* he wrote,

> *This life's five windows of the soul*
> *Distorts the Heavens from pole to pole,*
> *And leads you to believe a lie*
> *When you see with, not thro', the eye.*

Cheek patting, hair patting, and chucking under the chin are, in the Western world, forms of behavior indicating affection, and all are tactile.

The "laying on of hands" is an ancient practice extending into remote antiquity. Since the hand is the most active organ of the body, performing every kind of act, whether ordinary, magical, or religious, it is understandable that it should have come to stand as a symbol for power. As such, in many cultures, it came to be regarded as an important means of transmitting the powers inherent in a person who touches another, just as the mere lifting up of the hand over another causes a rapport even without actual contact. From *The New Testament* we learn that when Jesus came down from the mountain, "great multitudes followed him. And behold, there came a leper, and worshipped him, saying, Lord, if thou wilt, thou canst make me clean. And Jesus put forth his hand and touched him, saying, I will; be thou clean. And immediately his leprosy was cleaned" *Matthew* 8:1–3. "And they brought young children to him, that he should touch them . . . and he took them up in his arms, put his hands upon them, and blessed them" *Mark* 10:13.

The "laying on of hands," "the King's touch," for the cure of specific diseases like scrofula, known as "the King's evil," was at one time widely practiced, and often said to be effective. Healing rites have everywhere involved a "laying on of hands." The royal touch dates back to the Capetians in France and the

Normans in England. The sacred and miraculous character of kings was considered to give them divine powers of healing, especially in such a disease as scrofula—that is, tuberculosis of the lymphatic glands. During the Middle Ages almost all the kings of France and England exercised the royal touch, and the practice continued into modern times. In England in the eighteenth century, with the advent of the House of Hanover, the custom was discontinued. In France the practice is recorded as late as 31 May 1825, when Charles X touched between 120 and 130 persons. . . . The Sisters at the Hospice Corbeny-St-Marcoul, where the rite took place, fourteen weeks after the ceremony were able to find only five persons cured. As Marc Bloch remarks in his splendid book *The Royal Touch,* "During the ages of real faith, it was a very wise rule to exercise patience in this matter."

From the frequent association of the laying on of the royal hands with scrofula it came to be known as "the King's evil." Samuel Johnson, who had contracted scrofula from his wet-nurse, was taken by his mother to London at the age of two and a half on 30 March 1712, where he was among the 200 persons touched by Queen Anne, alas, at least in his case, without effecting a cure. The healing gesture was performed for the last time in England by the queen some three years later on 27 April 1714, three months before her death. But even though royalty ceased to practice the rite, the belief lingered on into the twentieth century in the form of medallions bearing the royal image to which the power of the royal touch had been transferred.

In children affected by any skin disease or disorder the touch of the human hand is especially important; hence some dermatologists recommend that when a mother applies medication it should be done with the hand, so that the child feels the caress rather than the impersonal application of a cotton swab or tongue depressor. Since very few skin diseases or disorders are infectious, the mother need usually have no fear of contracting the condition.

The belief in the curative power of the laying on of hands

is still widespread throughout the "civilized" world. For example, in Ireland it is believed that the seventh son of a seventh son invariably has the "gif." Finbarr Nolan is said to be such a one. By 1974, at the age of twenty-one, he was said to have already earned half a million pounds in "contributions" from those who have sought his healing touch. In February 1974 he extended his activities to England, with great success as measured by the more than six thousand contributions he received within a few days in London.

At least 40 percent of skin disorders have an emotional component, which if not treated will lead to the skin condition becoming chronic.

The need to share one's life with others, in that healthy tissue of human contacts which is so characteristic a basic need of our species, is reflected in that mirror, our skin. A most notable contrast in its health is seen in the maternally deprived child and in the skin of the abandoned adult. The malaise in the skin is often the expression of deep emotional problems.

In the matter of allergic disorders, Dr. Maurice J. Rosenthal made a direct test of the thesis "that eczema arises in certain predisposed infants because they fail to obtain from their mother or mother-substitute adequate physical soothing contact (caressing and cuddling)." Towards this end he investigated twenty-five mothers with children under two years of age suffering from eczema, and found that, indeed, the hypothesis he set out to test was abundantly confirmed. The majority of these infants had mothers who had failed to give them an adequate amount of cutaneous contact.

In discussing a case of infantile eczema, Spitz raises an interesting question. "We might ask ourselves," he writes, "whether this cutaneous reaction represents an adaptive effort, or alternatively, a defense. The child's reaction could be in the nature of a demand addressed to the mother to incite her to touch him more frequently. It could also be a form of narcissistic withdrawal, in the sense that through the eczema the child would be giving himself the stimuli in the somatic sphere which his mother denies him. We do not know."

It has, however, been pointed out that the demands the eczematous child makes upon its mother, the constant daily skin care, the inhibition of scratching, the exhausting attention to medical details, can play havoc with the mother-child relationships.

A review of the evidence leads Lipton, Steinschneider, and Richmond to conclude that in eczema itching may in some instances be primary and not secondary to the diseased skin. Through the autonomic nervous system, which has some control over the structures and functions of the skin, it is possible that a significant influence may be exerted by psychosocial and cultural factors on disordered skin function.

Over the years, Dr. Herman Musaph has hundreds of times observed that drivers who are forced to stop at a traffic light begin to scratch. In most cases it is the head that is scratched. He has called this "the red light phenomenon." It seems to him justifiable to assume that in many cases the emotion which is transferred into a motor discharge—that is, scratching—is pent-up anger, an anger which cannot be expressed verbally. Boring lectures, dull reading, being kept waiting, being awakened against one's will are some examples. The experience of itching and the motor discharge in scratching cause the underlying emotion to disappear.

The use of the skin as a tension reliever assumes many forms, perhaps the most familiar in Western cultures being head scratching in men. Women do not usually behave in this manner; indeed, the sexual differences in the use of the skin are marked. In states of perplexity men will rub their chins with their hand, or tug at the lobes of their ears, or rub their forehead or cheeks or back of the neck. Women have very different gestures in such states. They will either put a finger on their lower front teeth with the mouth slightly open or pose a finger under the chin. Other masculine gestures in states of perplexity are: rubbing one's nose, placing the flexed fingers over the mouth, rubbing the side of the neck, rubbing the infraorbital part of the face, rubbing the closed eyes, and picking the nose. These are all masculine gestures; so is rubbing the back of the hand or the front of the thigh, and pursing of the lips.

These all appear to be self-comforting gestures, designed to relieve or reduce tension. Similarly, in states of alarm or grief the wringing of hands, the holding on to oneself by clasping or grasping one's hands is comforting. In ancient Greece it was customary, and is still so in much of Asia, to carry a smooth-surfaced stone, or amber, or jade, sometimes called a "fingering-piece." Such a "worrybead," as it is also named, by its pleasant feel, serves to produce a calming effect. The telling of beads by religious Catholics seems to produce a similar result. "Worrybeads" in the United States have, in recent years, enjoyed increasing sales. Quite recently "executive tranquilizers" have been introduced in the form of small pieces of polished wood called "Feelies." Apropros of "worrybeads," it is of more than passing interest to note here that during World War II Dr. Jenny Rudinesco, who provided sanctuary for orphaned schizoid children, observed that many of them rolled a small pellet of paper between thumb and index finger. And J. C. Moloney, in his interpretation of these rolled pellets of paper as "stand-ins" for the absent mothers, points out that "they are 'mothers' that can be controlled by the emotionally disturbed child because they are 'mothers' created by the child."

Rubbing of thumb and index finger together is often observed in persons under tension. This may also be extended to rubbing all the fingers simultaneously against the palm of the same hand.

In the matter of skin disorders, Dr. S. Hammerman of the department of psychiatry of Temple University Medical School, Philadelphia, has reported to me the case of a girl who suffered very badly from acne, and who was cured by treatment involving tactile stimulation in a beauty parlor to which she was sent by a perceptive physician when every other form of orthodox medical treatment had failed. As Dr. J. A. M. Meerloo has stated, many skin disorders unconsciously express the need for continual skin contact and skin protection, as well as the need for attention and affection. Acne may sometimes represent the expression of repressed sexual feelings. Other dermatoses are sometimes an expression of defense against incestuous skin contact. During World War I, after suffering numerous episodes of bombardment, many soldiers developed dark skins or fear melanosis. In World War II, during the bombing of Rotterdam, many people reacted with paleness of the skin and various skin eruptions, as if to assume a camouflage.

For those who have not been lovingly and securely held in infancy, the fear of falling is a not unexpected development in later life. Lowen points out that the fear of falling, whether from high places or falling asleep, is related to the fear of falling in love. Indeed, the patient who presents any one of these anxieties is usually found to be susceptible to the others, the common factor in all three being an anxiety about the loss of full control of the body and its sensations. Such patients experience these fears as a "sinking" sensation, and they can be terrifying and utterly immobilizing. Such sensations "are the delight of little children, who seek these sensations on their swings, slides, and similar amusements. The healthy child loves to be thrown into the air and to be caught by the waiting arms of a parent."

In the matter of distance, it is of interest that in the theater certain directors tell their actors not to touch each other when playing comedy, but certainly not to refrain from doing so when playing tragedy. It is like the difference between extraversion and introversion. In comedy distance is required, noninvolvement, hence one refrains from touching. In tragedy it is the very reverse, involvement is what must be communicated, hence touching is encouraged. Again, gestures may be vertical in comedy, but they should be horizontal in tragedy. In comedy such vertical gestures are or tend to be manic, in tragedy horizontal gestures tend to suggest sympathy, embrace. Thus, Helen Hayes has said, "In comedy I have found that I must keep myself up, arms must be held higher, gestures must be of an upward nature. In tragedy just the reverse."

Sexual differences in cutaneous behavior are very marked

in probably all cultures. Females are very much more apt to indulge in every sort of delicate tactile behavior than males. Also females appear to be much more sensitive to the tactile properties of objects, as for example, when they pass their hands over a fabric in order to appreciate its texture or quality, something males seldom do. Fondling and caressing are largely feminine activities, as is gentleness of approach on every level. Backslapping and handshake crushing are specifically masculine forms of behavior. Cultural differences in these respects are also marked. As Hall points out, the Japanese are very conscious of the significance of texture. "A bowl that is smooth and pleasing to the touch communicates not only that the artisan cared about the bowl and the person who was going to use it but about himself as well." Hall goes on to add that the rubbed finishes of his works in wood reflected the medieval craftsman's feeling he had about the importance of touch. "Touch," he writes, "is the most personally experienced of all sensations. For many people, life's most intimate moments are associated with the changing textures of the skin. The hardened, armorlike resistance to the unwanted touch, or the exciting, ever-changing textures of the skin during love-making, and the velvet quality of satisfaction afterward are messages of one body to another that have universal meanings."

Bowlby has postulated certain responses in the infant that function to tie mother and child reciprocally to one another. These responses are sucking, clinging, following, crying, and smiling. The baby initiates the first three responses: the second two are signals to the mother to respond to him. Bowlby found that in his experience the mother's acceptance of clinging and following is consistent with favorable development, even in the absence of breastfeeding, while rejection of clinging and following by the mother, even in the presence of breastfeeding, is apt to lead to emotional distance. Furthermore, it was Bowlby's impression that fully as many psychological disturbances, including the most severe, could be initiated in the second year when clinging and following are at their peak, as in the early months when they are rudimentary.

The psychoanalyst Michael Balint has found that in his patients the need to cling represents a reaction to a trauma, "an expression of, and a defense against, the fear of being dropped or abandoned ... its aim being the restoration of proximity and touch of the original subject-object identity." This identity, expressed by identity of wishes and interests between subject and object, Balint calls primary object relation or primary love.

Balint divides these patients into two types, the *philobatic,* that is, those who enjoy swings, thrills, trapezes, and the like, and the *oncophilic,* those who cannot stand swings, high places, and similar "perils." The philobatic tends to be a loner, relying on his own resources, while the oncophilic constantly struggles with the fear that the object might fall.

The suggestion is that the child who has enjoyed a satisfying primary object relationship—that is, the child who has been satisfyingly tactually stimulated—will not need to cling, and will enjoy high places, thrills, and being swung about. By contrast, the child who has been failed in his clinging needs, especially during his preverbal reflex period of development, will react to this traumatic experience with an excessive need to hold on, to cling, with fear of the unsteady and of the support that may fail.

Two different perceptual worlds are involved here; one is *sight-oriented,* the other is *touch-oriented.* The touch-oriented world is more immediate and friendly than the sight-oriented world. In the sight-oriented world space may be friendly, but also often horribly empty or filled with dangerous and unpredictable, unsteadying objects. Georges Braque, the French painter, has remarked that tactile space separates the viewer from objects, while visual space separates objects from each other.

As Drs. Arthur Burton and Robert E. Kantor have pointed out, humans are creatures of the earth, bound in continuous tactual contact to *terra firma.* When, by flying or diving, we surrender that contact, anxiety is created because we lose "touch" with that upon which we depend.

The extraordinary frequency with which one comes upon

accounts of breakthroughs brought about by body contact in reaching schizophrenics who had for years been inaccessible to other therapeutic approaches is striking. In May 1955 the successes with catatonic schizophrenics of Paul Roland, a physical therapist at Veterans Administration Mental Hospital, Chillicothe, Ohio, were reported in the press. Roland began by sitting with the patient and then after a time touching his arm. Before long Roland was able to give the patient a rubdown. Once that occurred, rehabilitation proceeded rapidly. Gertrude Schwing has reported how she was able to break through to schizophrenic children by embracing them. Waal has given an excellent description of massage therapy with an apparently autistic boy, in which "the therapist gives the patient a general soft and maternal massage, with the stimuli of rhythmical petting and very gentle tickling and touching." The solar plexus, the neck, and the whole length of the spine, are massaged while the chest, chin, hands, and palms are tickled very sensitively and cautiously. After this the therapist proceeds to the eyes, and to a second stage in which there is a provocative massage of jaws, chest, shoulders, and eyes again. In this second stage the pressure of the therapist's hands is no longer soft. The patient reacts by screaming and crying and kicking, and is told that these are the reactions of a disappointed baby, and that they are all right. After these outbursts the patient receives soothing and mothering in an uninvolved, objective manner from the therapist. The effect of the therapy, according to Waal, seems to be a bodily maturation and a break in autistic withdrawal, and it seems to have a quicker effect than any other technique thus far attempted.

TOUCH IN PSYCHOTHERAPY. There has long been a taboo on touching the client or patient in psychotherapy. Of American psychoanalysts, as Dr. Karl Menninger unequivocally phrased it, "transgressions of the rule against physical contact constitute . . . evidence of the incompetence or criminal ruthlessness of the analyst."

The psychoanalytic taboo against touching originated with

Freud. It was his view that the therapist should not intervene between himself and the patient but remain completely objective, neither stimulating nor adding anything of himself to the patient. The therapist was to remain invisible to the patient, hence he was enjoined to sit behind the patient's couch. Many psychoanalysts still observe these practices. But as Dr. Bertram R. Forer has put it, "Verbal contact alone leaves one in a limbo of isolation from one's own body and from other persons." As a psychotherapist who believes that the inescapable need for skin contact is psychologically more crucial than hunger for food, Forer strongly urges the use of touching, in informed and skillful hands, in the psychotherapeutic situation. Forer points out that personal integrity represents a continual search for and intake of social nourishment through close relationships, including tactual experience and its reverberations throughout the body. "Most clients and many therapists," he writes, "are struggling with internalized parents in the form of an oppressive conscience which they needed originally to give them psychological structure. One potential function of the therapist is to become more appetizing or precious to the client than the internal parents have been."

The appropriate contact tells the client a good deal more about the therapist's emotional relationship to him, and what he may expect, than purely verbal comments. The therapist's touching is reassuring and at the same time serves to produce a dissolution of the client's fears and unhappy expectations, and thus demonstrates the client's own resistance to human relationships.

His emotional response may surprise him into a recognition of deep longings. He can then be helped to recognize that his oppressive conscience and the roles that he has played to get along with it have limited his freedom to give and obtain from others. Thus, taking the therapist inside is an antidote to the destructive residuals of early relationships and opens the closed system of the person to new interpersonal experiences.

The primitive reaction to being touched gently at critical periods is a feeling of body relaxation and reassurance that one is not alone, that old feelings of unworthiness are not justified. If he is still caught in an unresolved fusion with a destructive parent, contact may at first be rebuffed as a threat of annihilation to the self. Such persons may be literally out of contact and have an enormous need for contact.

"Touching," Dr. Forer concludes, "makes for mutuality and is part of the process of testing whether one dares to become or will be permitted to become an equal." The touching involved is that in which the patient or client touches the therapist, as well as the therapist's touching of the person who has sought his help. Nevertheless, to this day psychoanalysts in the English-speaking world at least desist from so much as shaking hands at the beginning and end of each hour. The reason given for this prohibition is that it would be introducing into the analytic situation an unnecessary and hence unwelcome psychic stimulus, a stimulus which might be disadvantageous to the course of the analysis. The analyst's interests must be in the determinants of the patient's thoughts and behavior. Whatever the analyst says or does, it is held, should be subordinated to that attitude.

Why touching between patient and therapist should constitute a barrier to an understanding of the patient's thoughts and behavior it is difficult to understand. Freud felt that such behavior might easily lead to eroticism of some sort and in this way to complete collapse of the analytic therapy. There have been some abuses of this kind, but the responsible therapist will remain responsible. Both client and therapist are presented with problems throughout the therapeutic experience. One of the most important of these is the experience of soothing reassurance which is integrative, passing into an excited erotic or sensual experience which may at first appear to be disintegrative. Shame and guilt resolved by self-alienation and turning off of body acceptance probably followed developmentally upon this transition from reassurance to sensual or erotic feelings. Forer puts its significance for both therapist and client very well:

This erotic psychosomatic arousal and the fantasies associated with it are crucial therapeutic raw material, but they are a major source of the disrepute into which contact has fallen. Such feelings have fostered ethical controls lest the therapist lose his perspective about his responsibilities. Some therapists themselves may experience erotic feelings and become upset out of their own unresolved shame and guilt. If they need to defend themselves against such awareness, they are likely to be rejecting and confirm their patients' own convictions that words are good and touch is always erotic or destructive and bad. Both therapist and client need to learn tolerance for their own excitement and realize that fantasies need not lead to action. Thus the therapist's nonerotic touch may break through the client's defenses and help him to separate and tolerate the two kinds of experiences.

Drs. Arthur Burton and A. G. Heller, while agreeing with the general psychoanalytic viewpoint that with rare exceptions the patient need not be touched, also conclude that it is a probably valid generalization that most psychotherapists at the unconscious level dislike their own bodies. This, together with legalistic definitions of touching behavior, they feel, make it extremely difficult to be free and spontaneous in this area of treatment.

The answer to such a view may perhaps be that such psychotherapists are not the proper people to treat those who are psychologically troubled, that nonswimmers should not act as lifeguards.

Bartenieff and Lewis note that the quality of the therapist's touch can be critical to the patient-therapist relationship. Touch, they point out, can vary in shape and effort such as the elements from a fleeting light poke or a sudden poke, to a constricting two-dimensional grip, to a supportive, reassuring, and sustained, slightly bound hold or to an indirect enveloping hold. Touch should be a form of three-dimensional shaping, they suggest, which is supportive rather than a form of more linear impositions such as poking. Some children (and adults) may never have been held in a three-dimensional way that is initiated from the body center and may also be transmitted through peripheral speech. No touching by the therapist, they hold, should be made without this awareness.

While we are on this subject, it should be added that in every branch of the practice of medicine, touching should be considered an indispensable part of the doctor's art. As a member of a family, the doctor should know what the human touch is capable of achieving in soothing ruffled feelings, in assuaging pain, in relieving distress, in giving reassurance, in making, in short, all the difference in the world. The world of humanity is the family writ large, and on a smaller scale the relationship seen in the family holds true between patient and doctor.

What the patient expects from the doctor is a human touch and healing effect. Touch always enhances the doctor's therapeutic abilities and the patient's recuperative capabilities. The laying on of hands has for centuries been well understood in religious communion. It would be well if it were similarly understood within the healing community.

Interestingly enough, the one branch of the healing community which has recognized the importance of touch is the nursing profession. In the nursing periodicals many valuable articles have appeared on the therapeutic benefits of touch. First, as women, and second, being so much closer to the patient than the doctor, nurses have been in a far better position to appreciate the importance of touching in the care of the patient, in understanding that the care of the patient begins with caring for the patient. Caring is not optional, it is something that is natural and obligatory, to be caring (for which loving is another word) is to be involved, intimate.

TOUCH AND ASTHMA. In 1953 I reported the case of Mrs. C———, a thirty-year-old Englishwoman, of upper-class background, divorced and childless, height 5 feet 4 inches, weight 90 pounds, seen in July 1948, in London. Mrs. C——— was one of identical twins. Both had suffered approximately fortnightly episodes of asthma since they could remember. For the six years prior to 1948 Mrs. C———had been in and out of sanitaria for treatment. Her doctor had then informed her that if she suffered another attack it might be her last. It was this shocking prognosis that brought me into the case. In calling upon her at her home in London, Mrs. C——, a pretty young woman, seemed rather tense but otherwise appeared quite healthy. She greeted her caller with a cold limp hand, and then folded her forearms over her chest. She then sat down on a davenport against the back of which she soon, in a quiet and unobtrusive manner, began rubbing her back. To the question whether her mother had died early, she replied that her mother had died at her birth, and in some astonishment inquired why I had asked that particular question. I explained that the possibility had occurred to me on the basis of the following observations: (1) the way she had limply shaken hands; (2) her folding of her forearms across her chest; and (3) her rubbing herself against the back of the davenport. All this had suggested that she might have failed to receive adequate cutaneous stimulation as an infant; and since this frequently came about as a result of the early death of the mother, I had thought of this as one possibility.

The theory of the relationship between tactile stimulation and the development of the respiratory system was explained, particular pains being taken to emphasize the fact that this was merely a theory, and that there was nothing about it that had yet been proved, but that there existed a certain amount of evidence which suggested such a relationship, and that if she desired she might try testing it. It was suggested that she might attend a physiotherapy clinic in London where, according to instructions, she would be expertly massaged. To this she readily agreed, and several days later, following her first massage, she was overflowing with enthusiasm. She was then told that the probabilities were high that if she continued with the massage for some time, she would never experience another asthmatic attack unless, possibly, she underwent some serious emotional disturbance. She continued with the treatment for several months, and during the many years which have since elapsed she has not suffered a single serious asthmatic episode.

Mrs. C———'s sister had experienced identical attacks of asthma until she married a famous author, whereupon her attacks declined in frequency, although they did not altogether cease. Subsequently there was a divorce, soon after which she died during an asthmatic seizure. In the case of Mrs. C——— her attacks were greatly alleviated. She subsequently remarried and has lived happily ever after.

There may, of course, be little or no relation in this case between the amelioration of the asthma and the cutaneous stimulation Mrs. C——— received. On the other hand, the relation may be a very direct one. In my original paper I wrote:

> This case has been cited for its suggestive value. It is to be hoped that those having the adequate opportunities may carry out the observations necessary to show whether or not persons suffering from asthma and other disorders that may be related to inadequate cutaneous stimulation in infancy may be relieved by a course of cutaneous stimulation given them on the theory outlined in this paper.

While that paper aroused a considerable amount of interest, it does not appear to have stimulated much research on the relation of tactile stimulation to asthma.

In connection with asthma, it has been noted on an earlier page that putting one's arm around the shoulders of the sufferer during an asthmatic attack is likely to alleviate or bring the attack to a halt.

Sir William Osler once remarked that "Taking a lady's hand gives her confidence in her physician." And, indeed, taking almost anyone's hand under conditions of stress is likely to exert a soothing effect, and by reducing anxiety give both the receiver and the giver a feeling of greater security.

How is it, we may ask, that tactile stimulation, in the form of caressing, fondling, cuddling, embracing, stroking, and the like, is capable of working such remarkable effects upon emotionally disturbed individuals?

The explanation is quite simple: Tactile stimulation appears to be a fundamentally necessary experience for the healthy behavioral development of the individual. Failure to receive tactile stimulation in infancy results in a critical failure to establish contact relations with others. Supplying that need, even in adults, may serve to give them the reassurance they need, the conviction that they are wanted and valued, and thus involved and included in a connected network of values with others. The individual who is awkward in his contact relations with others, is clumsy in his body relations with them, in shaking hands, in embracing, in kissing, in any, and often all, of his tactile demonstrations of affection, is so principally because he has been failed in his interactive body-contact relations with his mother. His mother has failed him in *motherliness,* which Garner and Wenar define as maternal gratification of the infant's needs for body care and pleasurable stimulation in ways that also provide the mother herself with satisfaction. Not only does the motherly woman provide her child with gratifications, but she also derives gratification from doing so, as she provides her infant with the close physical contact and protection he needs for growth and development. These investigators show that psychosomatic disorder tends to develop in individuals who have lacked the experience of motherliness—a hypothesis that has been many times confirmed. A basic ingredient of motherliness is close physical contact, the hugging, cuddling, caressing, embracing, rocking, kissing, and other tactile stimulations that a motherly mother gives her child.

Restriction or deprivation of the opportunity for tactile and manipulative experience early in life of the infant is likely to derange its later tactile and affective behavior. In a rather horrible experiment, Professor Henry W. Nissen and his colleagues at the Yerkes Laboratory at Yale University encased the limbs of a male infant chimpanzee, from the age of four months to thirty-one months, in cardboard cylinders. When freed, no defects in the perception of size, form, and depth were found, but what was found was that this young chimp, unlike others of its age, did not cling to the attendant, nor did it groom; furthermore "the lip movements and sounds which are part of this presumably instinctive pattern were completely absent." Such extreme treatment is never meted out to human infants; nevertheless, the findings on this deprived chimpanzee are consonant with the general finding that any prolonged deprivation of tactile experience in infancy is likely to produce inadequacies in the child's later tactile and affective behavior.

Body contact is a basic mammalian need which must be satisfied if the individual is to develop those movements, gestures, and body relatednesses which will be normally developed during the growth of one's experience in relation to one's mother's body. Deprivation of this experience has been experimentally shown to produce the most atypical movements and postures. On an earlier page we saw how this affects sexual behavior, contributing to the awkwardness of the socially deprived male in copulatory behavior. As Mason and others have shown, in such socially deprived individuals, deficiencies in social communication are the rule. While the need is there, one learns to nuzzle, root, cuddle, embrace, kiss, and tenderly and lovingly care for others as a consequence of experiencing such behavior from one's mother. In the absence of such maternal behaviors the need remains, but the performance of the behaviors associated with it is left more or less crudely unrealized. Indeed, to a very significant extent, a measure of the individual's development as a healthy human being is the extent to which he or she is freely able to embrace another and enjoy the embraces of others . . . to get, in a very real sense, into touch with others.

The tactually failed child grows into an individual who is not only physically awkward in his relations with others, but also psychologically, behaviorally, awkward with them. Such persons are likely to be wanting in that tact which the *Oxford English Dictionary* defines as the "Ready and delicate sense of what is fitting and proper in dealing with others, so as to avoid giving offence, or win good will; skill or judgement in dealing with men or negotiating difficult or delicate situations; the faculty of saying or doing the right thing at the right time."

In 1793 we find Dugald Stewart, the Scottish philosopher, writing in his *Outlines of Moral Philosophy* of "The use made in the French tongue of the word *Tact,* to denote that delicate sense of propriety which enables a man to feel his way in the difficult intercourse of polished society." Here the word "feel," feeling one's way, nicely reflects the initial tactile explorations with which we begin our first communications with another human being. On that ground we either develop as tactful beings or, if we have been failed in the experience of tactuality, we do not, becoming instead awkward and insensitive to the needs of others. It is no accident that the awkward and the insensitive are usually those who have been failed in the need for love, the earliest and most basic component of which is touch.

There appears to be a very distinct carryover from tactile experience in infancy to tactful behavior in later life. It is interesting that the word "tact," derived from the Latin *tactus* meaning "touch," was not infrequently used in England in place of the word "touch" down to the middle of the nineteenth century. *Tact,* in its modern sense, was adopted from the French early in the nineteenth century. What the word really means is clearly "to delicately touch" the other. Both the etymological and the psychological relationship of *tact,* in its contemporary meaning, "to touch," have not altogether escaped attention, for we will say of a tactless man that he has a "heavy touch." What is so interestingly inherent in the use of the word "tact" in its modern sense is the uncannily clear understanding of the importance of early tactile experience in the development of that delicate sense of fitting and proper behavior implied by the word. "Tact" in its original meaning remains very much alive in the synonym for "touch"—namely, "contact," the act of touching or meeting (Latin, *com-*, together, and *tangere,* to touch).

FEELING AND TOUCH. Both truth and communication begin with a simple gesture: touch, the authentic voice of feeling. The loving touch, like music, often utters the things that cannot be spoken—nothing need be said, for everything is understood. Feelings often have a tangible quality, and this is often expressed in our language, as when we say, "I felt the words were like a caress," "This material feels good," "It was a severe blow to his esteem," and so on. Indeed, common synonyms for "touch" are "feel" and "contact." *Emotion, feeling, affect,* and *touch* are scarcely separable from one another. Emotions, even when not induced by touch, frequently have a tactile quality about them. As commonly understood, feeling refers to the sensations arising spontaneously within the organism as a whole. One *feels* well or not. The state is an affective one. The larger part of what we call *feeling* appears to be made up of perceptions of complex blends of tactile components drawn mainly from the skin, but also from joint, muscle, and visceral senses.

What is clearly necessary for the development of human feeling is the satisfaction of the sensory needs, the proprioceptive-vestibular functions, and the visual senses.

Situated in the brainstem immediately above the spinal cord and extending upward is the reticular formation, which is largely involved in changes in level of consciousness, and is therefore often called the reticular activating or arousal system. It is extremely complex and little understood, but what is known is, that among other things, it is particularly sensitive to tactile stimuli. When we are unexpectedly touched, for example, there is a perceptible increase in the level of alertness, we are activated, aroused. Tactile stimulation plays an important role in influencing emotional tone and attention span.

Activity levels, the brain's ability to conceive, organize, and carry out unfamiliar actions and action sequences, is heavily dependent on tactile input. Through touch we are able to discriminate the internalized images of our body parts. A simple example will illustrate this. Bring your palms together and interlace your fingers, then bend your forearms to bring your hands almost under your chin. Ask someone to point to, not touch, one of the six middle fingers. Try to move that particular finger. Notice how hard you have to think in order to move the correct finger. Now have the person touch one of the fingers and see how easily you can move the correct one. Tactile information gives you an immediate answer. Without touch you have greater difficulty, from the unusual view of your hand, determining which move to plan and execute.*

TOUCH SENSATIONS FROM THE FINGERS AND HANDS. Until recently it was believed that most sensory pathways in the nervous system are "fixed" or "hard wired" by the maturation of anatomic connections, either just before or soon after birth. Dr. Michael Merzenich and his collaborators at the University of California in San Francisco and Vanderbilt University have shown that in the squirrel and owl monkey's brain pathways for registering touch sensations are not hard wired, but remain fluid in adulthood.

Each animal, it was found, organizes its touch information into a topographically unique area in the cortex, varying somewhat idiosyncratically for each animal. When a finger is removed, sensory inputs from the remaining adjacent fingers gradually move, in the course of several weeks, into the missing finger's exclusive brain area, resulting in a finer-grained representation of the adjacent fingers than they possessed before. A similar sort of shift, but with some loss of acuity, occurs following injury to a somatosensory region of the brain. Sensory maps in the brain appear to be self-organizing. It looks as if temporal correlations among neural inputs are the underlying force of this self-organizing property. The activity of a single neuron is trivial. What is crucial is a nerve's role in a "network" where it becomes part of a vast repertoire of inputs garnered from experience. What a single neuron does is temporary, its role in the network depending on its history in that network. A vast array of signals are probably measured and eventually evaluated across such networks. It is in the study of the dynamic properties of neural networks, rather than in the study of static neural structures, that the greatest promise lies.

*I owe this example to Ms. Susan Merrill.

The great importance of these recent studies lies in the light, among other things, they throw upon cognitive function, and for understanding how the different forms of touching, or the lack of them, may affect the development of the person.

ADAPTIVITY AND REACTIVITY OF THE SKIN. Among the remarkable capacities of the skin is its ability to develop increased acuity and to compensate for deficiencies in other sensory systems. Thus, Zubek, Flye, and Aftenas found that in sixteen hooded students confined to a room in complete darkness for one week, there was a marked increase in cutaneous sensitivity as well as in sensitivity to pain. In the blind there is considerable variability in the development of cutaneous sensitivity, some individuals showing increases, other showing decreases. It is a matter worthy of further investigation.

Not only will the skin react to every kind of stimulus with the most appropriate physical changes, but it will also do so behaviorally, for the skin is capable of behaving in very perceptible ways. The reference here is to stimuli originating at the skin surface. The skin is not merely a complex cellular structure, it is an equally complex chemical one; moreover, the substances present on its surface play an important role in the defense system of the body. For example, contact of human plasma or whole blood with the skin accelerates clotting time. If the skin is washed with alcohol, the clotting time is prolonged.

Reactivity of the skin to stimuli originating at the skin surface can only occur after mediation of the originating sensory stimuli through the nervous system. It begins to appear that whatever changes are capable of being produced in the skin by stimuli originating in the mind are also capable of being produced in the skin by changes originating at the level of the skin. Such, for example, are the skin disorders resulting from inadequate tactile stimulation. Clearly, sensory stimuli at the skin level have to be interpreted at the cortical level and the appropriate motor reactions initiated. The skin itself does not think, but its sensitivity is so great, combined with its ability to pick up and transmit so extraordinarily wide a variety of signals, and make so wide a range of responses, exceeding that of all other sense organs, that for versatility it must be ranked second only to the brain itself. This should not be surprising, for as we have seen, the skin in fact represents the external nervous system of the organism. The sensitivity of the skin can, however, be considerably impaired by the failure to receive the tactile stimuli necessary for its proper development. In this respect, such influences as family, class, and culture play a fundamental role.

8 Culture and Contact

Each culture fosters or specifically trains its young as children and as adolescents to develop different kinds of thresholds to tactile contacts and stimulation so that their organic, constitutional, temperamental characteristics are accentuated or reduced.

—Lawrence K. Frank,
"Tactile Communication,"
Genetic Psychology Monographs,
56 (1957), p. 241.

The existence of a wide range of class and cultural differences in attitudes and practices relating to tactile behavior affords a fertile field for the investigation of the relation of such social differences in tactile experience to the development of personality, and to some extent to cultural and national traits. In general, while the culture prescribes the customary socializing experiences to which the infant and child shall be exposed, idiosyncratic differences within particular families may substantially depart from the prescribed modes of behavior, with more or less significant consequences for the individuals involved.

There are families in which a great deal of tactile contact occurs, not only between mother and child, but also between all the members of the family. There are other families, within the same culture, in which there is a minimal amount of tactile contact between mother and child and all the other members of the family. There are whole cultures that are characterized by a *"Noli me tangere,"* a "Do not touch me," way of life. There are other cultures in which tactility is so much a way of life, in which there is so much embracing and fondling and kissing it appears strange and embarrassing to the nontactile peoples.

And there are cultures that play every possible variation upon the theme of tactility. In this chapter the attempt will be made to inquire into cultural and individual (familial) differences in attitudes towards tactile contact, the practices to which these attitudes lead and the manner in which they express themselves both in the individual and in his culture.

EXTEROGESTATION AND TACTILITY. Exterogestation constitutes the continuation of the uterogestative process in the environment outside the womb. The exterogestative process is designed to continue the feedback relationships between infant and mother, to continue the development of both, but especially of the infant for its increasingly complicated postnatal functioning in an atmospheric world bounded and unbounded by all sorts of experiences of space. The latter is an important aspect of the organism's experience which has received insufficient recognition.

Within the womb the fetus is enclosed and intimately bounded by the supporting embracing walls of the uterus. This is a comforting and reassuring experience. But with birth the infant experiences a more or less open-ended environment; he must learn to grow accustomed to the very least variations of his new and challenging environment. To the last day of his postnatal life, the most fearful and emotionally most disturbing experience that can befall the individual is the sudden withdrawal of support. The only instinct-like reaction remaining in humans, other than the reaction to a sudden loud noise, is the reaction to a sudden withdrawal of support. The uterogestate fetus, embraced, supported, and rocked within his amniotic environment, as an exterogestate requires the continued support of his mother, to be held and rocked in her arms, and in close contact with her body, swallowing colostrum and milk in place of amniotic fluid. He needs to be enclosed in his mother's arms, embraced, in contact with her warm skin, for among other things the newborn is most sensitive to temperature changes, and one of the dangers to which he is often exposed in hospitals is a chilling ambient room temperature, especially in air-conditioned delivery rooms. The professional mode of dealing with this is to place the baby either in a heated bassinet—a most inadequate substitute for the warm ambience of the mother's embracing, supportive body—or to place a heater above the baby, which may damage his eyes and skin.

The boundaries of the uterogestate's world are the walls of the uterus. It is necessary to understand that the neonate is most comfortable when the conditions within the womb are reproduced as closely as possible in the exterogestational state, that is, when the baby is enfolded in his mother's arms at her bosom. The infant needs to learn, on the firm foundation of closeness, what closeness, proximity, distance, and openness mean. In short, he has to learn the meaning, and the manner, of accommodating himself to a great variety and complexity of spatial relationships—all of which are closely bound up with his experiences of tactility, principally in relation to his mother's body.

To remove the newborn baby from its mother and place it on its back or its front on a flat surface, often uncovered, is to fail to understand the newborn's great need for enfoldment, to be supported, rocked, and covered from all sides, and that the infant may only gradually be introduced to the world of more open spaces. From the supporting, continuous, tangible presence of his mother the infant will gradually come to move some distance toward the outside world. One sees this particularly vividly in older infant mammals, and especially in juvenile monkeys and apes, who from tentative proximate separation from the mother gradually increase the distance until they can achieve an independence more or less complete physically, and to some extent emotionally.

TRAUMAS AT SKIN LEVEL. We must ask ourselves here whether, in removing the newborn from his mother, as is customary in hospitals, and placing him in the open space of a bassinet or crib, we are not visiting a seriously disturbing trauma upon the baby, a trauma from which, perhaps, he never completely recovers? A trauma, moreover, which in the civilized world of the

West, and those cultures that have been affected by the West's childbirth practices, is repeatedly inflicted upon the infant during the early years of his life. It may be that fear of open spaces (agoraphobia) or of heights (acrophobia), or of sudden drops, may have some connection with such early experiences. It may also be that a preference for having one's bedclothes about one's body rather than tucked in at the foot and sides of the bed reflects a desire to re-create the conditions enjoyed in the womb, in reaction to the lack of body support experienced in infancy. There are those who like to sleep with their bedroom doors closed; there are others who cannot abide a closed bedroom door. As one might expect, those who like their bedclothes snugly embracing them also tend to prefer their bedroom doors closed, whereas the more loosely tucked-in-around-the-edges-of-the-bed types prefer their bedroom doors open. What the range of variability is in these matters I do not know. There is a suggestion here for some interesting inquiries in which a good many other variables, such as breastfeeding, maternal affection, deprivations of various sorts, hospital deliveries or home births, and the like are considered.

It is during the exterogestative period that the infant is first and continuously exposed to the culturalizing effects of his society. And from the moment of birth every society has evolved its own unique ways of dealing with the child. It is on the basis of repeated sensory experiences of the culturally prescribed stimulations that the child learns how to behave according to the requirements of his culture. And it is because of the differences in the kinds and modalities of the individual's tactile experiences within the family, especially in relation to his or her mother, as determined for the most part by particular cultures or segments thereof, that individuals and peoples will differ behaviorally in many fundamental ways from one another.

It should be evident why, during the exterogestative period, the kind of tactile experience the infant undergoes will exert so fundamental an effect upon his development. The explanation is very simple: It is because a fundamental part of his learning is done during this period through his experiences at the level of the skin. The exterogestative period constitutes a developmental period during which the quality of communication experienced through the skin is critical. It is critical because upon the quality of the tactile communication experienced during that period will depend the kind of psychomotor, the sort of emotional response, the infant learns to make to others. This sort of emotional response will become a fixed and permanent part of his personality, upon which he will subsequently build many learned secondary responses. In view of the fact that the exterogestative tactile learning period has not been adequately recognized as a critical period in the development of every organism, and especially in the human species, we shall have to consider giving children more tactile attention than they have hitherto received.

CULTURE AND TACTILITY. The differences in the quality, frequency, and timing of the tactile experience that the newborn, infant, child, adolescent, and adult undergoes in different cultures run the whole gamut of possible variations. We have already touched upon such differences in several cultures in Chapter Four. Here we shall discuss cultural differences in early tactile experience and their relation to personality and to behavior. We can commence with the evidence from nonliterate societies, and then proceed to a discussion of the technologically more advanced societies.

THE NETSILIK ESKIMO. The Netsilik Eskimo live on the Boothia Peninsula in the Canadian Arctic of the Northwest Territories. There they have been studied with particular insight by Richard James de Boer, who lived in a snowhouse among them during the winter of 1966–1967. Maternal-infant caretaking relationships were the focus of de Boer's interest. The Netsilik mother, even though she lives under the most difficult of conditions, is an unruffled personality who bestows warmth and loving care upon her children. She never chides her infant or interferes with it in any way, except to respond to its need. De Boer writes:

At parturition and the onset of exterogestation, the Netsilik infant is placed in the back of its mother's attiggi (fur parka) in such a position that its ventral torso is pressed firmly against its mother's back just below the shoulder blades. The infant assumes a sitting posture with its tiny legs around its mother's waist or slightly above and with its head flexed right or left which usually elicits the tonic neck reflex that facilitates the straddling placement of the legs as extensor tonus decreases in either of these limbs. When the infant is in the proper position, the mother ties a sash around the attiggi exterior, across her chest above the breasts and down under the axillae, and where it passes across her back it forms a sling that supports her infant under its buttocks and prevents it from slipping down and out of the garment. The infant wears tiny diapers fashioned from caribou skins, but otherwise it snuggles naked against its mother's skin. Most of the infant's ventral anatomy is in a close tactile and cutaneous contact with its mother and its dorsal body is completely encased in fur, protecting it from the fierce Arctic cold. From outward appearances, the Netsilik mother bearing her infant in this traditional manner presents the appearance of a congenital hunchback, but her awkward appearance is more apparent than real, since her infant's weight is distributed in close proximity to her intrinsic center of gravity. The Netsilik infant is carried about in this fashion until it achieves locomotor ability and thence intermittently until it acquires what the Netsilik Eskimo calls "ihuma" or cognitive sense.

Netsilik mother and child communicate with each other through their skins. When hungry the Netsilik infant roots and sucks on the skin of its mother's back, alerting her to its need. Then it is brought round to the breast and suckled. Activity needs are satisfied by the various motions to which the infant is subjected in the postural and locomotory and other movements of the mother as she pursues her daily tasks. The rocking movements and contact with the mother's skin promote the sleep the infant so much enjoys. Bowel and bladder elimination occur on the mother's back. The mother's removal of these eliminations serves to prevent any continuing discomfort to the infant. Since the mother anticipates most of the infant's needs with all those sustaining nurturance responses designed to meet his needs, the Netsilik infant seldom cries. The infant's needs are anticipated by the mother tactually.

The Netsilik mother's care of her infant beautifully meets the requirements of its phylogenetically programed needs; the infant's responses are invariably pleasant. This invariability of pleasurable response, de Boer suggests, is the key to the Netsilik Eskimo's stress-coping ability.

> The Netsilik Eskimo [writes de Boer] is seldom if ever assaulted by aversive and stress-producing interpersonal stimuli, but he is constantly threatened with the uncertainties of his eco-system. Ecologically stressful situations never upset his emotional homeostasis and he confronts a raging polar bear with the same coolness and equanimity that he exhibits when faced with the threat of food deprivation. The invariability of the homeostatic emotional response does not imply that these responses are stereotypic; on the contrary, homeostasis implies a dynamic life force, but a force that functions below the threshold of disorganization. Evolutionarily, this homeostatic equilibrium has offered the greatest selective advantages to the individual and his group in the struggle for survival.

By the time he or she is three years of age the Netsilik child has acquired "the only two motivational characteristics necessary to his functioning as a self-regulated human being," namely, pleasant or altruistic responses to interpersonal relationships, and the power of symbolic manipulative ability. Because dominance-subservience relationships are absent in parental and especially maternal-infant relations a harmonic balance is achieved between the Netsilik individual and his society, with the individual in this manner gratifying his needs for mutually altruistic interpersonal relationships.

It is, of course, not possible to say with certainty that the altruistic behavior of the Netsilik individual is largely the product of his experiences in infancy, and especially of those he undergoes in relation to his mother's body; these experiences are later reinforced by the behavior of almost everyone else in his small world. The evidence, however, is strongly suggestive that it is the early experiences that are the most influential.

The Netsilik infant may defecate and urinate upon his mother's back without causing any disturbance other than the mother's cleaning of both the infant and herself. Such relaxed behavior undoubtedly exerts significantly relaxing effects upon the child's responses to its excretory activities. Such a child would never become an anal-erotic who hoards his feces or grow to become a niggardly adult. The openness and generosity of the Eskimo character is, no doubt, in part at least, due to the unuptightness of his early toilet experiences.

It is, however, unusual for an Eskimo baby to urinate or defecate while in the pouch or *amauti* of her parka. When Dr. Otto Schaeffer asked an Eskimo mother how she knew when her baby needed to urinate and always got the message in time, she was astonished by the implication of his question that any mother could be so "dumb" as not to know. She assured him that any capable mother knew when her child needed to void by movements of his legs and always attended to him immediately.

In answer to his question, Dr. Schaeffer writes, the mother he questioned "indicated by movements that an infant normally rests in the *amauti* with his legs abducted on the mother's back, but makes spasmodic movements, abduction with the thighs, when the bladder is full and before the sphincter is opened. The interaction and understanding between baby and mother is so intense and complete that every urge of the infant is attended to immediately, ensuring optimal physical and emotional satisfaction and preventing a buildup of feelings of frustration."

The motions of his mother during her daily activities give the Eskimo child a view of the world from virtually every possible angle, a view from which its spatial skills will grow and be reinforced by its subsequent experiences. The extraordinary

spatial faculties of the Eskimo, and probably also their remarkable mechanical abilities, may be closely related to these
early experiences upon the mother's back. Edmund Carpenter
has provided a fascinating account of the remarkable spatial
and mechanical abilities of the Aivilik Eskimo of Southampton
Island in the northwest boundary of Hudson Bay.

"Aivilik men are first-class mechanics," writes Carpenter.
"They delight in stripping down and reassembling engines,
watches, all machinery. I have watched them repair instruments which American mechanics, flown into the Arctic for
this purpose, have abandoned in despair. Working with the
simplest tools, often handmade, they make replacements of
metal and ivory. Towtoongie [an Eskimo friend] made a hinge
for me. I had to hold it directly before my eyes to see how it
worked." And so on.

Sheila Burford, in her book *One Woman's Arctic*, describes
the Arctic Eskimos she came to know and admire as "superb
natural mechanics and improvisers," and literally stood in awe
of their "incredible accuracy and coordination." Among the
Eskimos of Northwest Baffin Island, "Little boys of three or
four would play with a miniature dogwhip, the lash nevertheless being about fifteen feet, curling it back then flicking the
target of a stone or a stick."

Carpenter thinks that the explanation for the phenomenal
ability of the Aivilik lies in the overall picture of Aivilik time-
space orientation, in that the Aivilik do not conceptually separate space and time, but see a situation as a dynamic process;
furthermore, they are acutely observant of details. Moreover,
they view space not as a static enclosure, but as a direction in
operation. For example, when handed a copy of an illustrated
magazine they will not turn it right side up, indeed they are
highly amused when the white man does so, but will look at the
pictures whether they are upside down or horizontal, and see
them as if they were right side up!

Whether or not these abilities are related to the tactile,
spatial-visual experiences on the maternal back, must, again of
course, remain a matter for further research specifically aimed

in that direction. It would seem not unlikely. The infant's eye-view from all positions as the mother moves about would suggest the development of a rather special kind of spatial ability. As Carpenter puts it, "Space fluctuates in continuous activity. . . . The visual experience becomes a dynamic experience. Thus Aivilik artists do not confine themselves to the reproduction of what can actually be seen in a given moment from a single vantage point, but they twist and tilt the various possible visual aspects until they fully explain the object they wish to represent." The twisting and tilting may very well reflect something of the twistings and turnings the infant experienced while being carried on the mother's back.

"In most myths," writes Carpenter, "there is an alternative shrinking and growing of men and spirits in their mutual relations. Nothing has a static, invariable shape or size. Men, spirits, animals, have unstable, ever-changing dimensions." Again, a view of the world very reminiscent of the kinds of visual experiences the infant undergoes from his dorsal elevated viewpoint, experiences of adults whom he can see face to face, as well as children, animals, and other things that, from his high perch in his parka, are small and difficult to see, but suddenly change in size when mother bends, or kneels, or assumes a horizontal position.

From his early orientations to the spatial dimensions of the world the child relies virtually entirely upon his sense of touch, and by this most primitive of all sensory agencies, by thigmotropism (from the Greek *thigma,* "touch," and *trope,* "turn," that is, by responding to contact or touch), learns to find his way about in the world of the environment his mother provides. The child's first space is tactile. Initially it is passively tactile, experiencing tactile sensations that are gradually converted into perceptions, that is, sensations endowed with meanings. With these meanings the child then actively begins to scan the world for itself. James Gibson, who has made these distinctions between passive and active touch, in an experiment designed to judge the accuracy of the information received by each form of touch, found that active touch enabled subjects to reproduce abstract objects that were screened from view with 95 percent accuracy. Only a 49 percent accuracy was achieved with passive touch.

Active touch is stereognostic; that is, it enables one to understand the form and nature of objects. This ability is gradually developed in relation to the mother's body, the taking of the breast into the mouth, and the pressure of the lips and jaws on the areola, the hand resting on the breast, the infant's own lips, nose, eyes, genitals, hands, feet, and other parts of its body. Each of these has its own special characteristics and gradually comes to be recognized through active touch. In its mother's parka the Eskimo child, in addition to receiving communications from her body and body motions, will at first receive also a great many signals from her of an auditory nature, and it will come to associate these with each other. Hence vocal sounds will come to have a soothing tactile quality about them, a repetitive lulling character. One perceives this reflected very clearly in much of the poetry of the Eskimo. Consider such a poem as the following: a dance song, typical of those composed by Eskimos generally, but in this case the creation of a Copper Eskimo of Victoria Island, south of the North Magnetic Pole.

DANCE SONG
I am quite unable
To capture seals as they do, I am quite unable.
Animals with blubber since I do not know how to capture,
To capture seals as they do I am quite unable.
I am quite unable;
To shoot as they do, I am quite unable.
I am quite unable,
A fine kayak such as they have I am quite unable to obtain.
Animals that have fawns since I cannot obtain them,
A fine kayak such as they have I am quite unable to obtain.
I am quite unable
To capture fish as they do, I am quite unable.
I am quite unable
To dance as they do, I am quite unable.

Dance songs since I do not know them at all,
To dance as they do I am quite unable.
I am quite unable to be swift-footed as they are,
I am quite unable . . .

This song in its rhythm and metre, as well as its phrasing, repeats something similar to what a child would experience while being carried in a sling on its mother's back. It remains a fascinating and unexplained fact that in many parts of the world children who were probably never carried in this way compose chants or songs in similar metres and rhythms and phrases. Nevertheless, as we have seen in relation to music, it is a speculation worthy of further inquiry whether there may be a connection between the rhythms and metres of the Eskimos' songs and poetry and their experiences of motion on their mothers' backs.

Song making is highly valued among all Eskimos, and it is the custom to improvise songs for almost every occasion. What can be more humanly beautiful than this song, improvised by Takomaq, an old Iglulik Eskimo woman living on the Melville Peninsula, east of the Netsilik Eskimo? The old lady was about to serve a meal she had prepared for Knud Rasmussen and his companion, when Rasmussen presented her with some tea. This touched her so deeply that she at once joyfully improvised the following song:

Ajaja—aja—jaja.
The lands around my dwelling
Are more beautiful
From the day
When it is given me to see
Faces I have never seen before.
All is more beautiful,
All is more beautiful,
And life is thankfulness.
These guests of mine
Make my house grand,
Ajaja—aja—jaja.

These likable people show their friendliness towards those they have never seen before—not strangers, but visitors or guests—by touching and stroking them. From their very first encounter with whites Eskimos seem to have taken the view that there are no strangers, only friends whom one had not yet met. Stefansson tells how he and his party were welcomed by the Copper Eskimo in 1913. "Our welcome was as warm and friendly as it could possibly be, and nearly that noisy. Little children jumped up so as to be able to touch our shoulders and men and women stroked and handled us in a very friendly way."

In their snowhouses, where the temperature is often in the vicinity of 100 degrees, and only slightly less at night, Eskimos usually sleep in the nude in close body contact with one another. A man will customarily lend his wife for the night, as an act of courtesy, to the male visitor. The mixture of body odors, burning blubber oil, and other odors, which white men sometimes find unendurable, is far from unappealing to the Eskimo, whose acute sense of smell has been remarked upon by more than one observer. This trait, too, is perhaps not unrelated to the experiences of the infant in his mother's parka.

Following and in relation to tactility, the sense which is next elaborated is not vision but hearing. The mother hums and sings to the child, while she pats and hugs him, and holds him close to her body in her parka, and in time he learns to identify and respond to her voice as a surrogate for her touch. It is a reflexive form of conditioning, in which the sign of the original stimulus, the voice, replaces the touch, but the voice always retains its tactile quality, soothing, caressing, reassuring. It stands for the presence of the loving mother, whose love the infant initially knows primarily through the warmth and support, and yieldingness, and softness of her skin, and who attends to the infant's needs by actively as well as passively stimulating its skin, in carrying, cleaning, and washing it.

Eskimos are not given overmuch to washing, since water is scarce and ice is melted into water only at the great expense of burning the difficult-to-come-by blubber. Urine will sometimes be used as a substitute. Among the far northern Ingalik, who are a Northern Athapaskan group who speak both Ingalik and Eskimo, following the initial bath which a baby receives soon after birth, the mother licks the face and hands of the baby with her tongue every morning to clean them, until the baby is old enough to sit upon the bench. Though I have found no reference to this practice among Eskimos proper, it is possible that it occurs.

Visual perception almost certainly follows upon the development of auditory perception among the Eskimo. Carpenter confirms this in observing of the Aivilik Eskimo that

> They define space more by sound than by sight. Where we might say, "Let's see what we can hear," they would say, "Let's hear what we can see." . . . To them, the ocularly visible apparition is not nearly as important as the purely auditory one. The essential feature of sound is not its location, but that it *be,* that it fill space. We say "the night shall be filled with music," just as the air is filled with fragrance; locality is irrelevant. The concert-goer closes his eyes.
>
> I know of no example of an Aivilik describing space primarily in visual terms. They don't regard space as static, and therefore measurable; hence they have no formal units of spatial measurement, just as they have no uniform divisions of time. The carver is indifferent to the demands of the optical eye; he lets each piece fill its own space, create its own world, without reference to background or anything external to it. Each carving lives in spatial independence. Size and shape, proportions and selection, these are set by the object itself, not forced from without. Like sound, each carving creates its own space, its own identity; it imposes its own assumptions.

It is perhaps not unreasonable to suppose that this auditory view of reality is related to the Aivilik child's much earlier and longer continued conditioning in vocal than in visual experience. This conditioning is, of course, perpetuated through its oral traditional training.

THE KAINGANG OF BRAZIL. The Kaingang tribe of the highlands of Brazil are a splendidly tactile people. Jules Henry, who has written the classical account of them, speaks of the children who "lie like cats absorbing the delicious stroking of adults." Children receive an enormous amount of attention from adults, and can always depend upon someone to caress and cuddle them. When the children grow up, young men love to sleep together, not as homosexuals, but simply for the sheer pleasure of tactile contact. "Married and unmarried young men lie cheek by jowl, arms around one another, legs slung across bodies, for all the world like lovers in our own society. Sometimes they lie caressing that way in little knots of three and four. Women never do these things." Never do the men make an overt sexual gesture at one another. "The basis," writes Henry, "for man's loyalty to man has roots in the many warm bodily contacts between them.... The relationships built on these hours of lying together with anyone at all bear fruit in the softening of conflicts that are so characteristic of the Kaingang." Violent conflict occurs only between men who have never shared such caresses.

Little boys and girls play together in rough and tumble. Brothers and sisters, brothers- and sisters-in-law, and cousins, sleep side by side, cross legs, or embrace. The corollaries to this are that marriages and love affairs may take place among all classes of relatives, with the exception of parents and full brothers and sisters. There is also a complete lack of emphasis on temperamental differences between the sexes, with consequent lack of inhibition on the part of women.

THE TASADAY OF MINDANAO. In July 1971 the world was startled by the announcement of the discovery of a people so primitive, that up to their encounter with a member of another tribe who taught them to trap, they were exclusively foodgatherers. This people, consisting of fourteen children and thirteen adults, are the Tasaday of southern Mindanao in the Philippines. Everyone who meets them is immediately impressed by their sensitivity, gentleness, and loving nature. Peggy Durdin, who spent some days with them, writes of them with enthusiasm: "Babies are in constant bodily contact with their parents." And she adds,

> Among the most quickly discernible and attractive Tasaday traits are their capacity for affection (and relaxed expression of it) and their sense of humor. Adults and children do not seem afraid of being openly loving. Twelve or 15 onlookers did not prevent Balayem from hugging Sindi (his wife) close to him. Lobo, a strikingly beautiful and intelligent boy of 10 or 12, and Balayem, whose extrovert manner contrasts with a mobile, sensitive face, unaffectedly throw their arms around Manda [anthropologist Manuel Elizalde], nuzzle up to him, rub their cheeks against his and sit very quietly next to him for extended periods with an arm around his shoulders.... The Tasaday live this partly communal life in very close quarters year after year, as their ancestors told them to do, with remarkable harmony. I found no one who had heard them exchange harsh words or even speak sharply to the young. In the face of something displeasing, they seem to use the tactic of evasion: They simply walk away.

John Nance, in his book on the Tasaday, abundantly confirms these observations.

In some societies, as among the Mundurucu Indians of Brazil, men and women do not touch except as a tentative invitation to sex.

Tactile qualities are frequently recognized in traits or modalities not directly associated with touch. The tactile quality of sound of certain kinds, for example, is described as "silky," "smooth," "soft," "abrasive," "coarse," and the like. Some writers pride themselves on an almost tactile knowledge of their craft, as if they were more artisans than writers—Flaubert and Kipling were such. Painting is a medium in which tactility has almost constituted an essential part of the artist's communication. One thinks especially of the works of Van Gogh, Segonzac, the Impressionists generally, and many others.

TOUCH AND SOUND. It has sometimes been remarked, perhaps more as a metaphor than anything else, that sound has a tactile quality. There exists, however, a far deeper relationship between touch and sound than most of us are aware. The versatility of the skin is such that it is capable of responding to sound waves just as it is to those of pressure. A. S. Mirkin, of the Pavlov Institute of Physiology at Leningrad, has shown that the sensory receptors for pressure (deep touch), which are present around muscles, joints, ligaments, and tendons, the Pacinian corpuscles, possess very definite resonance properties. Mirkin subjected Pacinian corpuscles, in mesenteric tissue adjacent to the intestines, to acoustic stimulation in a uniform acoustic field, and found that these receptors possess resonance properties, and that a conditioned connection is obtainable between an optimal frequency of stimulation and periods of bioelectric activity, thus strongly suggesting a biomechanical resonance in Pacinian corpuscles. This is of great interest because touch and pressure receptors in the skin tell the brain what they pick up about body position.

Madsen and Mears, using deaf subjects, found that sound vibrations have a significant effect upon the tactile threshold, that a 50 cycles per second tone at both high and low pressure desensitizes the skin and raises the threshold, while a 5,000 cycles per second tone at both high and low pressure levels sensitizes the skin.

Gescheider has shown that the skin is able to localize sound waves of different intensities with remarkable accuracy.

Which suggests all sorts of possibilities.

TOUCH AND PAINTING. In the 1890s Bernard Berenson, improving upon a notion of Goethe's that a work of art must be "life-enhancing," suggested that one way of achieving this is by the artist making us imagine that we are enjoying genuine physical feelings when we look at a painting or sculpture. Such feelings Berenson called *ideated sensations*. Ideated sensations exist only in the imagination and are produced by the work of art by making us realize its being and live its life. The most important of the ideated sensations Berenson called tactile values. The work of genuine art stimulates our ideated sensations of touch, and such stimulation is life-enhancing. Form, not to be confused with shape, represents that radiance from within when it realizes itself completely. Form is the life-enhancing aspect of visible things, and form is but another word for tactile values. "Through all the ages," writes Berenson, "and in every place, whenever a visual representation is recognized as a work of art and not as a mere artifact, no matter how elaborate, smart, and startling, it has tactile values. It may have much besides, which is of more or less importance or none at all, but to be accepted as a work of art these other attractions must rest on a basis of tactile values, or be in close connection with them."

The artist, in creating a work of art—unconsciously for the most part, sometimes consciously—imagines all the sensations felt or which he supposes to be felt by whatever he is attempting to organize and harmonize into an equivalent of what he feels it to be intrinsically, and what at the same time it says and means to us. I can think of no better illustration and corroboration of Berenson's view than Van Gogh's painting of a straw-seated kitchen chair. The tactile values of that painting make that chair so real that the chair itself would look almost unreal by comparison. The writer, as Berenson points out, will do the same thing with words, as will the artist in virtually every other medium. "The painter," he writes, "can accomplish his task only by giving tactile values to retinal impressions."

In some painters tactility is so prominent it almost reaches out and touches one. John Constable is an outstanding example of such a painter. As Robert Hughes has written of him, "His childhood was substance rather than fantasy: tactile memories of mold, mud, woodgrain and brick became some of the most 'painterly' painting in the history of art. The foreground of *The Leaping Horse* is all matter, and the things in it—squidgy earth, tangled weeds and wild flowers, prickle of light on the dark skin of water sliding over a hidden ledge—are troweled and spattered on with ecstatic gusto. This is the landscape of touch." This is, of course, true of many impressionist and modern painters. The ideated sensation of texture is also seen in many of Rubens' paintings.

Marshall McLuhan speaks of TV as essentially tactile, and he and Parker very cogently remark that "the social, the political and the artistic implications of tactility could only have been lost to human awareness in a visual or civilized culture which is now dissolving under the impact of electric circuitry." These notions have a very real foundation, well understood by the eminent anthropologist Alfred Kroeber. In a letter to Meyer Schapiro, the art critic, Kroeber wrote with reference to Berenson's "tactile values" in painting:

> These can appeal only through the eye, and never actually to the sense of touch, nevertheless they refer to something that underlies the vision which is at the center of visual art: namely, that feeling by touching precedes sight, phylogenetically and ontogenetically in every human baby. We all touch first, learn to see later, and in learning erect a nearby visual world on a tactile base, giving a double quality to all perceptions of objects, first within immediate reach, and later within ultimate or potential reach. All children, and many adults, want to handle a new sight. The two senses of course are disparate: they operate through different sense receptors. But what is seen and touched is always made part of ourselves more intensely and more meaningfully than what is only seen. And so in art representation the representative picture we *only* see but cannot, in imagination, touch, does not carry the same attraction and concentration of interest as the one we can, imaginatively, handle and touch as well as see clearly.

To this Kroeber added orally, "that perhaps abstractionism of whatever era has a more intellectual, a lesser appeal, the subconscious tactile aspects having been withdrawn and abandoned."

Jacob Epstein, the distinguished American-English sculptor, was the most tactile of artists, the major portraitist in bronze of the great men of the twentieth century, who executed his works in an almost painterly concern for light, shade, and texture.

Another modern tactile sculptor is Henry Moore, the notable English versatilist. "For me," he has said, "everything in the world of form is understood through our own bodies. From our mother's breast, from our bones, from bumping into things, we learn what is rough and what is smooth."

The tactile qualities of some human voices has already received comment. Some music, we have already noted, also possesses tactile qualities; lullabies, for example, have a soothing, caressing effect. Some music is almost physically assaultive, while other music is gentling and affectionate.

It becomes clear, as we think about it, that touch is in a sense a new dimension, a new discovery, an unexplored territory, holding much promise of secrets yet to be revealed.

When the visual experience, we feel, is inadequate, touch adds the missing dimension and completes the experience. In some individuals touch is regularly linked with particular images from other sensory modes. This is known as *cross-modal transfer.* For example, people will speak of the "feel" of the sound of someone's voice, its "velvety" or "caressing" quality, and will actually experience it as a tactile sensation. Or we are "touched" or "moved," not merely in a metaphoric sense, by an affecting experience. Margaret Mead possessed this capacity for synesthesia or cross-sensing. She could perceive the same sensation in more than one sense, she could "touch" an aroma, "hear" color, and "see" sound. She once described a woman friend's voice as a "brush," somewhere between a pig's bristles and a silk brush—but definitely not nylon.

As Ernest Schachtel has pointed out, the distance senses, sight and hearing, both phylogenetically and ontogenetically attain their full development later than the proximity senses, touch, taste, and smell. And, as he rightly states, the proximity senses are neglected and to a considerable extent even tabooed by Western civilization. He adds, "Both pleasure and disgust are more intimately linked with the proximity senses than with the distance senses. The pleasure which a perfume, a taste, or a texture can give is much more of a bodily, physical one, hence more akin to sexual pleasure, than is the more sublime pleasure aroused by sound and the least bodily of all pleasures, the beautiful."

In the daily lives of animals the proximity senses play an important role. In man, if they are not repressed in sexual relations, then they are otherwise tabooed in interpersonal relations, "the more a culture or a group tends to isolate people, to put distance between them, and to prevent spontaneous relationships and the 'natural' animal-like expressions of such relations."

Marcuse remarks that civilization demands the repression of the pleasures to be derived from the proximity senses in order to ensure the desexualization "of the organism required by its social utilization as an instrument of labor." Nevertheless, we want to be close to those we cherish—distant from those we dislike. "I was very close to him." "He keeps a proper place."

Perhaps it would be more accurate to say that the taboos on interpersonal tactuality grew out of a fear closely associated with the Christian tradition in its various denominations, the fear of bodily pleasures. Two of the great negative achievements of Christianity have been to make a sin of tactual pleasures, and by its repression to make of sex an obsession.

The tactile quality of vision is apparent in the touching of another with the eyes. Hence one avoids looking or staring at strangers, except in certain conventionally accepted situations. It is of great interest to observe here that under natural conditions gorillas and chimpanzees avoid looking directly at a stranger, and especially regard a direct look, until friendly relations have been established, with suspicion. This is also true of baboons, and of many other monkeys.

We recognize something of the tactile quality of looking or gazing when we speak of "eye contact" between people. Eye contact is avoided with strangers, just as much as tactile contact is avoided with them, and for much the same reason: One does not establish physical contact with anyone until a certain intimacy has been achieved.

It is of interest that in some cultures eye contact is regarded as a form of touch. This belief is probably quite ancient. In India, in Vedic times, between 1500 and 500 B.C., part of a person's essence, it was believed, could be made to pass from his eyes and touch or affect others.

FEELING, WRITING, AND TOUCH. In every culture, whether literate or nonliterate, the author or storyteller, the fabulist or lyricist, "grapples" with the words that will best express what he wants to say. Inchoate ideas must be given not only form and meaning, but an enduring life of their own. Léon-Paul Lafargue has put it well:

> *The idea is that which exists, but has no form,*
> *It is art not yet realized.*
> *The idea is a point of departure,*
> *The lifting of a veil's edge,*
> *a faint stirring,*
> *or like the leap of a violin*
> *in a moment of despairing gloom.*

For the writer, finding the right word is often a physical struggle with the stubbornness of language. That, presumably, is one of the reasons why so many writers take to drink. There is a prehensile compulsion to wring out the right word from the vocabulary, and through one's hands and fingers give it that leap of the violin. As Osip Mandelstam, the great Russian poet, said, in art we want to describe the indescribable: nature's instantaneous text. We can, however, never wholly succeed, though genius sometimes in a radiant moment brings us close to the truth. In art we achieve so lucid a communication, even through an idea, that it speaks to our fingertips, or to our memory, of what our fingertips, or we, felt.

It is feeling that bridges the spatial gap that separates us from others, and puts us in touch with them. That is the function of language, whether it be through speech, writing, or other communication. Feelings often have a tactile quality. Writers "speak" to us, "stir" us, through their writing. Hence, the importance, when listening to each other, of hearing the feelings as well as the words. Touch is a language of its own with a very large vocabulary. Through touch we communicate what cannot be spoken, for touch is the true voice of feeling, for even the best words lack the honesty of touch. This is not to say that the feelings we convey through words may not equal those we communicate through touch. It is remarkable how often we interchangeably use the words "feeling" and "touch." It is mostly through thought and imagination that we attempt to make ourselves "felt," in the many ways in which we choose to express ourselves. The notable level and range of which our thought and imagination are capable have been achieved through tactile and visual experiences interwoven with language. It is the function of thought and imagination to develop the experiences and wisdom gained through touch and vision. However, there are occasions when we are so busy thinking what we should say, we forget the feelings that tell us what we ought to do.

The intelligibility of language is nothing more nor less than the unintelligibility of nature made artificially clear. But the language of touch is nature, and requires no artifice. It is characteristic of the best writing that it has an immediacy, a kind of tangibility which renders the scenes the author depicts, the characters he creates, as real as if we were palpably experiencing them. They remain with us, these creations of the author's imagination, as the living presences who by their humanity, their magnanimity or wisdom, have affected us, and become a part of ourselves. As Christopher Ricks has said, "We who are alive can touch each other through language only because we are touched by those who are no longer alive."

ORDER OF SENSORY DEVELOPMENT. The senses of *Homo sapiens* develop in a definite sequence, as (1) tactile, (2) auditory, and (3) visual. As the child approaches adolescence the order of precedence becomes reversed, as (1) visual, (2) auditory, and (3) tactile. It is much more important to experience tactile and auditory stimulations in the early developing years than it is to experience visual ones. As soon, however, as one has developed through one's tactile and auditory senses the knowhow of being human, vision assumes a special importance. Yet a vision can only become meaningful on the basis of what it has felt and what it has heard.

It has long been believed that touch educates vision, that as Bishop Berkeley suggested in the eighteenth century, the infant discovers size, shape, location, and distinctiveness, by touching. Experiments conducted in recent years require some modification of this view. It has been found, for example, that children have far more difficulty discriminating objects they have touched but not seen, than they do objects that they have seen but not touched. It is now quite clear that vision is well developed at birth, and that the human infant has good depth perception before he has had any opportunity to learn it in any way.

Bower, by an ingenious series of experiments, has shown that by the end of the second week of life an infant expects a seen object to have tactile properties. He concludes from his experiments that in humans there is a primitive unity of the senses, with visual experience specifying tactile qualities, and that this primitive unity is built into the structure of the human nervous system.

As one would expect, younger infants protest tactual separation from the mother more than do older infants. The older infant tends to make more frequent contact and to manipulate more objects than the younger. It is this tactual-manipulative character of his perceptual exploration that sets the more actively adept older child apart from the younger infant.

Older children inspect objects manually more thoroughly than do younger ones. The three- or four-year-old explores an object with fixed static movements, in contrast to the older child's active exploration of the object and its contour. By touch adult humans can recognize an object after seeing it once, whereas a chimpanzee requires five hundred trials before he can do so. By the time the human child reaches adult years he has become strikingly efficient at recognizing objects by touch.

Zaporozhets, in a study of preschool children, had one group of children manipulate several irregular geometric forms by inserting them into a formboard. Children in a second group inspected the forms visually but never touched them, while those in a third group only manipulated them tactually. When the children were required to discriminate geometric from a group of unfamiliar forms, it was found that those who had both visually and tactually manipulated the original forms made less than half the errors made by the two other groups. The children in the first group, as they grew older, appeared not to need to manipulate the forms to do well on the task, whereas the children who only touched the forms continued to do poorly; the children, however, who only saw the forms became progressively more accurate with age. For older children, it would seem, physical contact with an object is unnecessary for making a perceptual discrimination; seeing it is sufficient.

Dr. Irvin Rock and Charles S. Harris found, in adult subjects, that when the sense of touch conveyed information that disagreed with what they were seeing, the visual sense predominated and determined the meaning they gave to their sensations.

How dependent our knowledge of the external world is upon the sense of touch is dramatically illustrated by the case of the young Englishwoman Sheila Hocken. Sheila lived nearly thirty years from birth as a blind person. After she recovered her sight, she had to learn what everything was. As she explained, "The eye picks up a visual picture, but translates it and sends impulses to the brain. And I am afraid that my brain did not know what to do with them. So everything I saw I had to touch." Information about things that could not be obtained by touch she would either smell or taste. Individuals who have become blind after having led a sighted life also become, as is well known, dependent upon touch for the recognition of objects in the external world.

THE GANDA OF EAST AFRICA. Dr. Mary Ainsworth has made a detailed study of rearing practices in infancy among the Ganda of East Africa. Her field study was carried out in a single village some fifteen miles from Kampala. The effects of white contact have long been operative upon the Ganda, but nevertheless the majority of mothers still carried their infants on their backs and enjoyably breastfed them for a year or more. Ganda babies spent most of their waking hours being held by someone. While holding the baby, the mother gently patted or stroked him. The total care of this kind given by the mother was very considerable. From her comparative observations, Dr. Ainsworth concludes: "It is better for a baby to be held a lot, to be picked up when he cries, to be given what he wants when he wants it, and to be given much opportunity and freedom to interact than it is for a baby to be kept for long periods in his crib apart from other people, where his signals cannot be perceived and consequently where he cannot experience a sense of predictable consequence and control." The rate of sensorimotor development was accelerated in most babies. They sat, stood, crawled, and walked much earlier than the average baby in Western societies. Ainsworth attributes this to the kind of infant care the Ganda give, "with much physical contact, much interaction between the infant and his mother, much social stimulation, prompt gratification of creature-comfort needs, lack of confinement, and freedom to explore the world."

Unfortunately, Ainsworth's study deals only with the first fifteen months of the Ganda child's development, and tells us nothing at all of the later personality traits of the Ganda adult. The anthropological literature on the Ganda is not much more helpful in this connection, and such other information as is available on this score is largely anecdotal. Audrey Richards emphasizes the fact that there was a remarkable unanimity in the early European visitors' accounts of the Ganda, emphasizing their good manners, politeness, and charm, their cleanliness, neatness, modesty, orderliness, dignity, and intelligence. But it was also observed that they were touchy, competitive, legalistic, capable of cruel behavior, reticent, and difficult to know well. There seem to be many contradictions here, but they may not really be so. It may well be that the congenial qualities of Ganda adults owe much to the motherliness they received during their first year or so, and that their less desirable qualities were engendered by later conditionings.

This would appear so from the findings of Dr. Marcelle Géber, who studied 308 children in Kampala. Here, also, the newborns and infants up to two years showed remarkable advances both in physical and intellectual development, as well as in personal-social relations, than European children of comparable age, and what is even more significant, over Ganda children brought up in European style. Children examined before and after weaning showed marked differences in their behavior. The attitudes of the mothers toward the children seemed to be largely responsible for the differences. Before the child is weaned the mother's whole interest is centered on him. She never leaves him, carries him on her back—often in skin-to-skin contact—wherever she goes, sleeps with him, feeds him on demand at all hours of the day and night, forbids him nothing, and never chides him. He lives in complete satisfaction and security, always under her protection. The child is, moreover, continually being stimulated by seeing her at her various occupations and hearing her interminable conversations, and because he is always with her, his world is relatively extensive. He is also the center of interest for neighbors, and visitors, to whom he is offered, as a matter of course, as soon as the usual greetings have been exchanged. If, however, he shows the slightest sign of displeasure, he is at once taken back by his mother. While the Gesell tests were being administered to the children, the loving and warm behavior of the mothers, always ready to help if help were needed, showed very clearly how the children were surrounded by affection. The mothers' interest in the tests and the detailed answers they gave to the questioning were further evidence of this solicitude.

Dr. Géber's follow-up studies showed that there were some other aspects to childrearing in this society that did not encourage and accelerate the growth of the children. For when the child reaches eighteen months to two years of age, it is taken away from its mother and given to another woman in another village to be disciplined and "socialized." The natural mother had been required to love her child, fondle and feed it, and generally stimulate its development, but not to "train" it. This was the task of the foster mother. Dr. Géber found that these children underwent a remarkable deceleration in their developmental progress, some children showing even less ability than before, presumably because they had lost skills acquired earlier.

BUSHMEN OF THE KALAHARI. Dr. Patricia Draper, who lived among the !Kung Bushmen, on the edges of the Kalahari Desert in Botswana, Southwest Africa, found that they lived in bands of thirty people, and that they very much liked being close together and touching. In camp, resting, talking, doing chores, they prefer to gather in knots or clumps, leaning against each other, their arms brushing, their crossed legs overlapping, physical contact reaching its highest expression in children, with girls showing more physical contact than boys.

Lorna Marshall, who has spent much time living among the !Kung over a period extending from 1950 to 1961, observed that they are extremely dependent emotionally on the sense of belonging and companionship, a sense which is constantly being reinforced by their frequent touching. She writes:

> !Kung babies are carried most of the time by their mothers, tied in soft leather slings against their mother's side, where they can easily reach their mother's breast. They nurse at will. !Kung women have excellent lactation. All the babies are plump. The babies wear no clothes and are in skin-to-skin contact with their mothers. They sleep in their mother's arms at night. When they are not in their mother's arms or tied to

their sides, they are in someone else's arms, or if they are set down to play they clamber over their elders as they lie chatting and resting, or play within arm's reach. The babies are constantly in the presence of people who are gentle and affectionate with them and who are watchful. The babies have no special toys, but are allowed to play with any of the adults' possessions that come to their hands and mouths, except knives and hunting equipment. These items are hung carefully in the bushes, out of reach of children.

The !Kung never seem to tire of their babies. They dandle them, kiss them, dance with them, and sing to them. The older children make playthings of the babies. The girls carry them around, not as a task set them by their parents (though they might carry babies around for that reason also), but because they play "mother." The boys also carry babies around, give them rides, and drag them on karosses (a favorite game). If the babies utter a whimper they are carried back to their mothers to nurse. Altogether the babies appear to be as serene and contented as well-fed young puppies.

When people are sitting at leisure, they spend time teaching the babies. They help them to stand or to take their first steps between outstretched arms of the adults and they play little games with them.

Dr. M. J. Konner was much impressed by the amount and quality of tactile stimulation that !Kung children received from their mothers. Compared to these Bushmen, he remarks, the American child can be considered to be "deprived" of physical stimulation. He notes that the experiences of children in each culture are, of course, related to the nature of the culture. The Bushman infant grows up in a world in which survival arises from mutual economic dependence, and is dependent upon cooperation, whereas the world of the American infant favors competition and mobility.

From the first weeks the Bushman infant is carried on the hip or side in a sling contoured to support the back, buttocks, and thighs. In connection with this posture Konner quotes the remark of Gesell and Amatruda concerning the six-month-old sitting up, "His eyes widen, pulse strengthens, breathing quickens and he smiles when he is translated from the supine horizontal to the seated perpendicular. This . . . is more than a postural triumph. It is a widening of horizon, a new social orientation."

> From their position on the mother's hip [these children have] available to them her entire social world, the world of objects (particularly work in the mother's hands) and the breast, and the mother has immediate easy access to the infant. When the mother is standing, the infant's face is just at the eye level of desperately maternal 10- to 12-year-old girls, who frequently approach and initiate brief, intense, face-to-face interactions, including mutual smiling and vocalization. When not in the sling they are passed hand to hand around a fire for similar interactions with one adult or child after another. They are kissed on their faces, bellies, genitals, sung to, bounced, entertained, encouraged, even addressed at length in conversational tones long before they can understand words. Throughout the first year there is rarely any dearth of such attention and love.

> Breastfeeding may continue as long as six or eight years, the child feeding on demand. Such early experiences in interaction with the mother's body and her nurturing support undoubtedly exert a powerful influence upon the Bushman personality, a personality which has charmed so many different writers. One of the outstanding traits, almost certainly related to this regimen, Dr. Konner remarks, is the continual giving and receiving of food among adults.

> Throughout a great part of Black Africa similar variations are played on much the same theme.

NEW GUINEA. From New Guinea we have some excellent accounts of the relationship of early childhood experience to the development of adult personality, in which tactile experience clearly played a significant role. These accounts, by Margaret Mead, are principally of the Arapesh and Mundugumor societies.

Among the Arapesh, children are always being held by someone. The infant is carried by the mother in a small net bag suspended from her forehead. A child's crying is a thing to be avoided, the breast being immediately given to comfort it. Breastfeeding is continued for three or four years. The children usually sleep in close contact with the mother's body, either hung in a thick net bag against her back, crooked in her arm, or curled on her lap as she sits cooking or plaiting. The child thus enjoys a continuous warm sense of security. Later, when the mother is away for a whole day working in the garden, she will compensatorily make up for her absence by a full day of nursing, when the infant, held in her lap, may suckle at will, play about, suckle again, play with her breasts, and gradually regain any sense of security he may have lost. This is an experience the mother enjoys as much as the child. The mother takes an active part in the suckling process. She holds the breast in her hand and gently vibrates the nipple inside the child's lips. She blows into its ear, or tickles its ears, or playfully slaps its genitals, or tickles its toes. The child in turn plays little tattoos on its mother's or its own body, plays with one breast while suckling the other, teases the breast with its hands, plays with its own genitals, laughs and coos, and makes a long pleasant game of suckling. "Thus," Mead remarks, "the whole matter of nourishment is made into an occasion of high affectivity and becomes a means by which the child develops and maintains a sensitivity to caresses in every part of its body." Interestingly enough, no Arapesh child sucks its thumb or a finger, but there is a great deal of playing with one's lips during the increasingly prolonged absences of the mother. The lip playing is continued for some time after weaning and much later. Boys are encouraged to stop lip playing after initiation and permitted to chew betel nut, while girls may continue till they have borne children.

Half an hour's cuddling, and the child will follow anyone

anywhere. The response to demonstrative affection is immediate. As a result of such demonstrations of affection from everyone on every possible occasion, the Arapesh child grows up with a complete sense of emotional security in the care of others. The result is an easy, gentle, receptive, unaggressive adult personality, and a society in which competitive or aggressive games are unknown, and in which warfare, in the sense of organized expeditions to plunder, conquer, kill or attain glory, is absent.

The Mundugumor, a river people living to the south of the Arapesh, by contrast with the latter, are an aggressive, hostile people who live among themselves in a state of mutual distrust and uncomfortableness. Even before a child is born there is much discussion as to whether it shall be saved or not, depending on its sex, mothers preferring boys, fathers girls. In Mundugumor society the child lives an unloved life. From birth on the infant is carried in a rough-plaited basket, semicircular in profile, suspended from the mother's forehead. The basket is harsh, stiff, and opaque. No warmth from the mother's body can penetrate it, and the infant lies cramped within it, seeing nothing but narrow slits of light at both ends. At home the infant in its basket is hung up. When it cries, without touching its body, the mother or other female scratches the outside of the basket with her fingernail, making a harsh grating sound. Children generally respond to this sound. If, however, the crying does not stop the infant is suckled—the mother standing up while doing so. There is no playful fondling between mother and child. The moment suckling stops, the child is returned to his prison. Children therefore develop a strong fighting attitude, holding on to the nipple as firmly as possible, frequently choking from swallowing too rapidly. The choking angers the mother and infuriates the child, thus further turning the suckling experience into one of anger and frustration, struggle and hostility, rather than one of affection, reassurance, and contentment.

Children of one or two years are carried on the mother's back. A crying, crawling child will be picked up firmly and placed on the mother's neck, holding on to its mother by her hair. The breast is given only when it is thought the child is in need of food, never to comfort it in fright or pain. From the time he begins walking his mother's hostility toward suckling is made very evident to the child, who is pushed away, and as often as not slapped. Thus, weaning is accomplished with hostility. A few Mundugumor children suck the back of the hand or a pair of fingers, with an unmistakable peevish, fretful, anxious look on their faces.

It is hardly surprising that with such a socializing experience in childhood the Mundugumor child becomes the kind of unattractive, aggressive, cannibalistic creature he is.*

Dr. James Ritchie of the University of Wakaito, New Zealand, tells of a delightful experience he enjoyed on a field trip to New Guinea where he met a psychiatric nurse who had been given a manual of sensitivity training. As a result of reading it she had begun letting her Melanesian patients, with whom she had no language contact, touch each other, and letting herself touch them. "It took nerve to do it," writes Dr. Ritchie, "to meet her own reactions and more still to meet their response. They returned her touch; they stroked her hair, greeted her with the gentlest of finger caresses, held her hand for hours at a time. She now moves through her ward, previously filled with agitated and mute humanity with a new sense of fulfilling her mission—to heal."

THE ATIMELANG. Among the Atimelang of the Netherlands East Indies island of Alor, when an individual is dying it is the custom for one of the grown children or some kinsman to hold the dying person in his lap, much as parents hold children. Dr. Cora DuBois, who observed this, suggests that such behavior constitutes a reversion to infantile nurturing patterns in the search for which she suspects many men have spent their lives.

---

*This is how the Mundugumor were in 1930; since then they have undergone considerable change.

THE DUSUN OF NORTH BORNEO. Williams has made the only anthropological study known to me of tactuality in a nonliterate culture. He studied the Dusun of the mountain highlands of North Borneo, an agricultural-hunting people whose principal crop is rice. Williams has emphasized the need for studies devoted to the various ways in which, in different cultures, individuals are required or expected to relinquish particular tactile experiences or practices and develop compensatory symbolic substitutes at different periods in life. "The transformation," he writes, "of tactile experience into abstract conceptualizations would seem crucial to understanding the way some cultural conceptions are acquired by the individual in the course of cultural learning and transmission."

Concern with and recognition of tactile experience in Dusun life is complex, but can be observed in both overt behavior and in a variety of linguistic, gesture, and body posture surrogates for touch used in many social situations. Contacts such as "living touch" are distinguished from a "non-living touch" while "touchy," and "touchable," and "touched," each are differentiated from the "act of touching," "tickling," and "touching together." Linguistic uses for specific tactile contacts, including terms denoting limits and acceptability of such experience, comprise a special lexicon. Other surrogates for tactile experience commonly used in Dusun life are in the form of culturally structured gestures meant to be suggestive of particular touch actions; some 40 gestures are used to note emotion, while at least 12 have openly sexual meanings denoting acts of intercourse.* Body posture surrogates for tactile experiences often involve a complex set of actions, including inclinations of the head, facial expression, and hand, arm, and trunk movements. The behavior repertoire of the coquettish Dusun woman includes a variety of such complex body posture surrogates for tactile experience. Such body actions are

*"Thus, the thumb inserted between the first and second fingers of the same hand is a symbol of intercourse, while the waving of hands alongside the ears, with fingers up and palms forward denotes fright and derision."

used generally to indicate approval, or dislike, of displays of body arts, grooming, and decoration as invitations to direct touch experience.

In greeting another no tactile contact is involved in Dusun society, while strict boundaries of permitted tactile contacts exist for various social action situations. It is of interest that the Dusun newborn is isolated for some eight to ten days from all tactile contacts, except those of the mother. Among the phrases used in the several rituals to which the child is exposed during his first year of life is one saying that "no stranger will be allowed to touch you to bring you harm."

The way in which the members of a culture learn to deal with the sense of touch is culturally defined, and this is made explicitly clear in Williams' excellent study. Williams' plea for further investigation of this important, but most neglected aspect of human behavior, can only be echoed here.

OTHER NONLITERATE CULTURES. James Prescott of the National Institute of Child Health and Development, Bethesda, Maryland, and Douglas Wallace of the University of California Medical School, San Francisco, in an interesting cross-cultural study of the relationship between tactile (somatosensory) experience and the origins of aggressive behavior covering forty-nine nonliterate cultures, found that there existed a highly significant correlation between the two in all but one of these cultures. The Jivaro of Brazil were the one exception. In general it was found that in those cultures in which tactile experience was high, adult aggression was low, while in those cultures in which such experience was low, adult aggression was high. In thirteen cultures which seemed to be exceptions to the rule it was found that five of the six that were characterized by high infant affection and high adult violence were repressive of premarital sexual behavior, while six of the seven cultures that exhibited low physical affection toward infants and had low adult violence were characterized by permissive sexual behaviors. The somatosensory pleasure hypothesis was thus confirmed for both the prepubertal and postpubertal stages of development.

THE TACTILE EXPERIENCE OF THE AMERICAN CHILD. Passing from nonliterate cultures such as the Dusun, the Ganda, the Eskimos, or the Bushman to the highly sophisticated culture of the United States, we find that the differences in tactile experience of infants and young children in each culture are very revealing. For the United States there is available an excellent study of the tactile experience of children from infancy to four and a half years of age in working-class, middle-class, and upper-class families. This is an unpublished doctoral dissertation by Vidal Starr Clay entitled "The Effect of Culture on Mother-Child Tactile Communication." Forty-five mother-child pairs were the subjects of this study, with twenty boys and twenty-five girls. The observations were made on public, country-club, and private beaches. In Table 3 the findings are set out for the average tactile contacts by age and class for one hour of observation of children in groups designated A, B, C, and D, according to the age of the children. From this table it will be seen that tactile contact becomes a diminishing factor in the mother-child affectional system with the increasing age of the child. When, however, tactile frequency and duration scores are compared by age and social class, a surprising exception occurs in the youngest or infant group, where the highest degree of tactile contact would be expected.

In all three classes [writes Clay], the tactile frequency scores were less for the youngest children, the neonates and non-walking ones, than they were for the walking children. The duration scores were lower also for the working class and upper class infants than they were for the children just above them in age. Only the middle class duration score shows the pattern we would expect to find: the highest score for the youngest age group. The middle class mother's duration score was much higher than the duration score for the mothers of the other classes: nearly forty minutes in contact for each child

Table 3. CONTACTS AND PATTERNS OF PLAY BY AGE
AND SOCIAL CLASS
For one hour of observation at the beach.
Number of children = 45

	MEAN NUMBER CONTACTS				MEAN TIME IN CONTACT			
GROUP	W*	M*	U*	GROUP AVERAGE	W	M	U	GROUP AVERAGE
A	4.5	4.2	4.0	4.2	0.0	8.0	9.7	7.5
B	3.1	5.5	15.3	6.3	3.0	8.0	22.3	8.2
C	2.6	3.3	6.0	3.7	1.4	1.3	3.4	1.8
D	—	5.3	4.8	5.0	—	8.3	2.8	4.9
Average for total	3.1	4.4	7.0	4.9	2.2	5.8	8.2	5.6

	MEAN TIME NEAR				MEAN TIME AWAY			
GROUP	W	M	U	GROUP AVERAGE	W	M	U	GROUP AVERAGE
A	4.0	3.0	31.0	27.2	13.0	20.0	20.0	17.7
B	30.5	13.5	19.0	22.9	19.6	30.0	15.7	20.5
C	22.4	22.0	28.7	23.8	23.0	24.0	20.0	22.6
D	—	15.0	25.2	21.1	—	31.3	29.2	30.0
Average for total	27.4	16.2	25.8	23.3	20.5	27.4	23.2	23.7

*W = working class; M = middle class; U = upper class.
SOURCE: Vidal S. Clay, "The Effect of Culture on Mother-Child Tactile Communication" (Ph.D. dissertation, Teachers College, Columbia University, 1966), Table IV, p.
284. By permission.

in the hour observed. It was this figure that skewed the duration score average and made it appear that the youngest children in the field study sample received the most time in tactile
contact. Therefore the conclusion about tactile contact and
age must be rephrased to say that overall tactile contact does
decline with age but in this culture, as it was observed in the
field study, it is the just walking child who receives the most
frequent tactile contact and the contact of longest duration,
not the infant and non-walking child. From a high at this
time, just walking to two years of age, the amount of contact
declines regularly as the child grows older.

It is a general assumption that the neonate and infant receive most tactile stimulation, but the truth seems to be that with the advent of hospital deliveries, bottlefeeding, clothes which form a barrier between the caretaker and the infant's skin, the A group child, in the group from two months to fourteen months of age, the nonwalkers, receives less tactile experience than the B group child, the just-walkers from fourteen months to two years. The C group included twelve children between two and three years, and the D group included ten three- and four-year-olds. In view of the actual needs of the infant, this is a very striking and significant finding.

Reva Rubin, who has had many years of experience in obstetrical nursing, has remarked how struck she has been by the very small number of American mothers who, even at the end of the first year, are sufficiently comfortable to hold their babies up close to their chests in pure enjoyment and pleasure of contact. Those who are most likely to do so, she found, were the mothers who really enjoyed breastfeeding, and, of course, she adds, grandmothers and aunts.

Harlow and his co-workers found that in the rhesus mother-infant affectional system three phases were clearly evident: (1) attachment and protection, (2) ambivalence, and (3) separation. The stage of attachment and protection is characterized by virtually total positive conduct, cuddling, cradling, nursing, grooming, restraining, and retrieving. The stage of ambivalence includes both positive and negative responses, such as mouthing or biting, cuffing or slapping, clasp-pulling the fur, and rejecting attempts to maintain physical contact. The stage of separation results in the termination of contact between mother and infant. There is no doubt that similar stages or phases occur in the maternal affectional development of the human mother, and that the behaviors associated with them are of great consequence for the development of the infant. This is especially most significant in the phase of attachment and protection. It is precisely in this most important of these phases that the American mother seems to fail most. In the rhesus monkey the mother normally exhibits a high degree of interest in her infant for the first thirty days, and then begins to display ambivalent responses. In the human mother the period of attachment is normally of much greater duration. But, as Clay says:

> Unlike the primate mother, and mothers of many other societies, the American mother largely omits the phase of close bodily attachment. In this culture, the separation of the bodies of the mother and child at birth is the end for the most part of the mother-child physical symbiosis. Instead of a relationship where the mother's need for intimate physical contact exceeds that of the infant, there is a relationship where the mother shows maternal attachment behavior only in response to the child's gross vocal and kinesthetic demands. This difference in the American maternal pattern in the infant's first four months of life is of course due to the fact that close mother-infant tactile contact is not the norm for this culture. The fact that American mothers did not themselves experience close physical contact with their own mothers no doubt reinforces this behavior. The lack of physical proximity between mother and young child, whereby the mother stimulates the infant and in turn picks up and responds to the cues that the infant gives back to her, also reinforces the cultural pattern of separation.

In America both mother and infant are clothed even during breastfeeding, so that the baby, as he is fed, often experiences little more of her skin than the breast, and perhaps an occasional handstroking. In the bottlefeeding situation, which is fortunately declining in America, the infant experiences the very minimum of reciprocal tactile stimulation. The deprivation of tactile stimulation experienced in this way by both infant and mother explains the institutionalization in American culture of the nonexpression of affection, especially between mother and baby, through close physical contact. Tactile contact between the American mother and child expresses caretaking and nurturance, rather than love and affection. This is clearly evident from the fact that mothers in this culture touch their walking children more frequently than they do when their children are nonwalking.

In keeping with the findings of other investigators, Clay found that girl babies received more demonstrative acts of affection than boy babies. Mothers seem to be happier about having girl babies than boy babies, and girl babies tend to be weaned later than boys. Moss, Robson, and Pedersen, in a detailed study of maternal stimulation of infants, in Washington, D.C., found that mothers talked, kissed, and rocked in a rocking chair their male infants, at the examining age of one month, more than they did their female infants at the same age. These investigators suggest that the difference probably reflects a social-affectionate orientation towards the males, involving behaviors that tend to soothe and modulate rather than excite or activate the infant. The mothers significantly more often resorted to the distance receptors of vision and hearing in dealing with their female children than with their male infants at one month of age. Moss and his collaborators suggest that since female infants develop earlier than male infants, the more expressive mothers may have adjusted the type of stimulation they provided for their infants in consonance with the developmental requirements or status of the child. Thus male infants would have received more talking to, more kissing, and more rocking, whereas female infants with their more advanced developmental status would tend to be stimulated through their active attention and the processing of stimuli (auditory and visual) ordinarily associated with higher cortical (cognitive) functioning.

Interestingly enough, the animation of the mother's voice was found to be highly reliably predictive of the amount and type of stimulation she provided her infant at one month and three months of age. The animated mothers were found to give their children more stimulation than the soft-spoken mothers. Less educated mothers tended to provide more physical stimulation than more educated mothers. The better educated mother tended to spend more time talking to her male infant. Fear of strangers and gaze-averting behavior at eight to nine and a half months of age was definitely found to be related to the type of stimulation the infant received from his mother in earlier infancy. The more stimulation, particularly of the distance receptors, the infant received, the more comfortable the infant appeared to be with a stranger at age eight to nine and a half months. These investigators suggest that children who are accustomed to experiencing novel visual and auditory stimulation may have a better mental organization for coping with and assimilating "strangeness." Since strange stimuli are less novel for such children they tend to evoke less of a sense of subjective uncertainty in them. That is to say, the children who receive more stimulation through the distance receptors become more complex cognitively and therefore have more resources for dealing with unfamiliar auditory or visual stimuli.

It is of interest to note that, according to Kathleen Auerbach, in countries in Europe and Asia where males are highly valued, they are breastfed for a longer time than female infants. In the United States, however, the reverse is true. The sexual implications of breastfeeding are such that male infants are less likely to be nursed as long as their sisters are. Clay's work confirms this.

Tactile demonstrations of affection between mother and daughter are not as inhibited as they are between mother and son. The very thought of any such demonstration of affection between father and son is something that still makes many American fathers squirm. A boy putting his arm around the shoulders of another boy is cause for real alarm. It is simply not done. Even women are reluctant to indulge in such open displays of affection toward members of their own sex. One touches others largely in a sexual context. To touch another out of such context is open to grave misinterpretation, since touching is to a large extent restricted to and associated with sex. When intercourse is completed, the male ceases to touch his partner and usually retires to his twin bed to spend the rest of the time in pleasurable lack of contact with himself.

The replacement of the double bed in which husband and wife sleep together by twin beds in which husband and wife sleep apart may well be significantly correlated with the decline in both breastfeeding and the reduction in maternal-infant tactile stimulation that prevailed in earlier times. I have earlier suggested that parents who sleep together in the same bed are likely to develop a quite different relationship to one another and toward their children than parents who habitually sleep in separate beds, and that "same-bed" families tend to be more cohesive. "Keeping in contact" in the same bed comprises a very different experience from the contactless separateness of twin-bed sleeping arrangements. In her novel *Strange Fruit,* Lillian Smith makes Alma, the wife of Dr. Tracy or "Tut," reflect as follows:

> Sometimes all she could remember of her's and Tut's nights together was the lifting of his leg off her body. There was something almost *dissipated* about the way Tut slept, letting himself go, so, so uncontrolled, you might say. Alma had thought of twin beds but had never done anything about it, for she doubted in her heart that husbands and wives should sleep separately. It was all a little vague to her, but sleeping together, cold weather or hot, seemed a necessary thread in the fabric of marriage, which, once broken, might cause the whole thing to unravel.
>
> Just how she was not certain. She was convinced, however, that her own mother's custom of sleeping in a room separate from father's had caused their family life to be not as successful as it should have been.

Alma was quite right. Such husbands and wives tend to grow "out of touch" with one another. The subject has been investigated by two American anthropologists working in Japan. William Caudill and David W. Plath studied the co-sleeping patterns of parents and children in Japanese families in Tokyo and Kyoto. They found that in urban Japan an individual can expect to co-sleep in a two-generation group, first as a child and then as a parent, over approximately half his life. Commencing at birth, this goes on till puberty, and then commences again with the birth of the first child, continuing till about the time of the menopause in the mother, and recurring for a few years in old age. In the intervening years the individual generally sleeps in a one-generation group with a sibling after puberty, with a spouse for a few years after marriage, and again with a spouse in late middle age. Sleeping alone is a reluctant alternative most commonly occurring in the years between puberty and marriage. Caudill and Plath offer the broad generalization that "sleeping arrangements in Japanese families tend to blur the distinctions between generations and between the sexes, to emphasize the interdependence more than the separateness of individuals, and to underplay (or largely ignore) the potentiality for the growth of conjugal intimacy between husband and wife in sexual and other matters in favor of a more general familial cohesion."

The speculation the authors offer

> concerns the coincidence of those age periods when sleeping alone is most likely to occur, with the age periods when suicide is most likely to occur in Japan. The rates for both types of behavior are highest in adolescence and young adulthood, and again in old age. It might be that sleeping alone in these two periods contributes to a sense of isolation and alienation for an individual who, throughout the rest of his life cycle, seems to derive a significant part of his sense of being a meaningful person from his sleeping physically close by other family members.

Under the conditions of co-sleeping in Japanese families described by Caudill and Plath, the kind of relationships they have postulated may well exist. But under other conditions the opposite effects may be produced. For example, among the working classes of Europe and elsewhere children are often forced to occupy the same bed with strangers taken in by the parents as lodgers. The revulsion caused by such experiences may have enduring effects, resulting in avoidance of any kind of physical contact with strangers, as well as in other forms of rejection and withdrawal.

The Japanese psychiatrist Takeo Doi believes that the passive dependence of the Japanese child upon the ever-present mother represents a critical motivating factor in Japanese adult life. The sense of *amae* or longing for dependency, the sense of oneness with the mother, is fostered by long indulgence and close contact. Eventually, Doi states, this longing develops into a denial of the fact of separation from the mother and leads the adult to attempt a reestablishment of this sort of intimate relationship with his or her superiors. The result is the sort of vertically structured, group-oriented society that is found in Japan today.

John Douglas has pointed out that while the American mother stimulates her child, who becomes more active and vocal, the Japanese mother tends to soothe and pacify her child, who emerges more passive and quiet. Thus, at an early age children are being well trained to fit into their respective societies. Douglas adds:

> So constant is the physical contact of Japanese children with their parents that the relationship between them is sometimes called "skinship." And so complete is the sustained dependence of the child upon the mother that it results in a lifelong search for belonging, a primary identification as a member of a group rather than as an independent person.

Hall points out that the Japanese are pulled in two directions. One is a deeply involved enveloping intimacy that begins in the home in childhood and extends far beyond. "There is a deep need to be close, and it is only when they are close that they are comfortable." The other pole is to keep one's distance. In public, and in the ceremonial occasions of everyday life, the emphasis is on distance, self-control, and the concealment of feelings. Until very recently there was no public display of intimacy or touching in Japan. And yet from his interpretation of the evidence Hall believes that deep down the Japanese feel quite uncomfortable about the ceremonial, institutionalized side of life. Their principal drive is to move from the "stand on ceremony" side towards the homey, comfortable, warm, intimate, friendly side. "Their drive to be close and get to know other people is very strong."

PURITANISM, CLASS DIFFERENCES, AND TACTUALITY. In New England, one would expect that the effect of Puritanism would tend to be characterized by childrearing practices that reduce reciprocal tactile stimulation between mother and child to a minimum, and this is indeed the case. The Fischers in their study of Orchard Town childrearing practices found that most babies spent a good part of each day alone in a crib, playpen, or in the yard. "Such contact as a baby has with other human beings is not marked by close bodily contact as in many societies."

New Englanders, in what remains of their Puritanism, closely resemble the English from whom they originated, and, in common with the English, they suffer from the effects of residual primness. The upper-class Englishman—and especially the upper-class Englishwoman—has notoriously been characterized by an inability to exhibit emotion, and a certain striking lack of warmth.* Not all members of the upper classes are characterized by these traits, and certainly many members of the middle and working classes exhibit them. But such traits are generally due to a lack of parental love, a failure experienced in early infancy and throughout childhood which expresses itself in an inability to relate warmly and affectionately towards others.

The custom among the English upper and middle classes of sending their children away to boarding schools at an early age, of institutionalizing them, as it were, outside the warm ambience of the family, deprives these children of the love and affection so necessary for the development of a healthy personality. Having learned the boundaries of courtesy, which, among other things, included respect for the other's personal

*Derek Monsey speaks of "the frigid voluptuousness of the dedicatedly unsatisfied English gentlewoman" in his novel, *Its Ugly Head* (New York: Simon & Schuster, 1960), p. 38.

space, the distancing was further reinforced in the schools. The privation of parental love, and especially love in the form of tactile stimulation, during infancy, probably constitutes one of the principal causes of the apparent coldness, the seemingly unemotional character, of the upper-class, and often the middle-class, Englishman. On this aspect of the Englishman's character, E. M. Forster has some illuminating comments:

> People talk of the mysterious East, but the West also is mysterious. It has depths that do not reveal themselves at the first glance. We know what the sea looks like from a distance; it is of one color, and level, and obviously cannot contain such creatures as fish. But if we look into the open sea over the edge of a boat, we see a dozen colors, and, depth below depth, the fish swimming in them. That sea is the English character— apparently imperturbable and even. The depth and the colors are the English romanticism and the English sensitiveness— we do not expect to find such things, but they exist. And—to continue my metaphor—the fish are the English emotions, which are always trying to get up to the surface, but don't quite know how. For the most part we see them moving far below, distorted and obscure. Now and then they succeed and we exclaim, "Why, the Englishman has emotions! He actually can feel!" And occasionally we see that beautiful creature, the flying fish, which rises out of the water altogether into the air and sunlight. English literature is a flying fish. It is a sample of the life that goes on day after day beneath the surface; it is a proof that beauty and emotion exist in the salt, inhospitable sea.

Douglas Sutherland, in his book *The English Gentleman,* states the situation more plainly. A gentleman, he writes, looks on his wife with kindly patronage, and on his children with qualified affection. "A gentleman's deepest affection is, however, reserved for his dogs." And, as he correctly states, it is a feeling that cuts across all classes.

Frances Partridge, the English author, writes of the "scrupulously suppressed signs of parental love," and of her mother's rigorously undemonstrative behavior, although she believed her mother to be a warm and emotional character, who gave her as a child delightful hugs and snugglings, and suddenly stopped them as Frances grew older, with not even a peck on the cheek as greeting on her return from boarding school.

Jane Austen, in 1816 in her novel *Emma,* had already commented on the seeming indifference of the middle-class Englishman towards those for whom he actually cared, when she relates the meeting of the Knightley brothers after an absence of a year: "How d'ye do, George?" and "John, how are you?" The author comments, they "succeeded in the true English style, burying under a calmness that seemed all but indifference the real attachment which would have led either of them, if requisite, to do everything for the good of the other."

Somerset Maugham, the English novelist, whose mother died when he was eight and his father two years later, and was then sent to live with an aging clerical uncle and aunt, was a typical example of untouchable childhood experience. He grew up to be an egotistical homosexual who hated to be touched and who would greet his guests, "coming forward with arms outstretched in welcome, then dropping them to his sides to avoid contact." The outstretched arms, we may be sure, were an evidence of his desire to love, and their dropping to his sides the tragic testimony of his inability to do so.

A few other interesting examples of the upper-class and middle-class types of English cold fish are represented by Winston Churchill, Sir William Eden, the father of Anthony Eden, and by the English novelist Hugh Walpole, and many others, such as "Shropshire Lad" A. E. Housman and T. E. Lawrence "of Arabia." An American counterpart for unredeemed coldfishedness is William Randolph Hearst, whose life was tellingly portrayed in Orson Welles' film, *Citizen Kane.* Yet another casebook history of the unloved child is provided by the victim himself, the English newspaperman Cecil King. All these individuals, representative of untold thousands like them, were alike in having suffered a lacklove childhood and an inability to behave with affection. This is interesting in the light of the fact that in her study of a group of American mothers Clay found that upper-class mothers gave their infants somewhat more tactile affection—tactile affection being defined as behavior through touch designed to convey love—than both working-class and middle-class mothers.

Upper-class English attitudes toward continental European tactile interchanges are reflected in English working-class attitudes. For example, in the predominantly male immigrant community of Pakistanis living in all-male communes in London, English workers find their affectionate ways repellent. "They're not natural," was the comment of a dockworker. "A lot of queers if you ask me, look at the way they hold hands."

In the bathing of babies in America, a situation in which one would expect to find increased magnitudes of tactile stimulation for the infant, this is not necessarily the case. Margaret Mead has pointed out how the attention of the American baby is directed away from the personal relationship to his mother by toys which are introduced into his tub. Hence his attention is focused on things rather than on persons. As Mead says, "The average American woman may never hold a little baby until she nurses her own, and even then she often behaves as though she were still afraid that the infant might break in her hands. In New Guinea and Bali, on the contrary, they know all about babies. Small infants are looked after by child nurses as young as 4 years old, and this familiarity is shown in all their movements."

With the passing of the extended family, in which grandparents, aunts and uncles, cousins and other relatives often gave children large amounts of tactile stimulation of various sorts, that kind of experience is now limited to a rather undemonstrative mother. Clay remarks that she observed a grandmother sitting under a tree next to her grandchild strapped in a plastic carrier. "The grandmother," reports Clay, "told me with a degree of sadness that she wanted to pick up the baby, he wanted it, but his mother had told her he had to learn to be by himself."

Class differences in touching are revealing. The general law seems to be, the higher the class the less the frequency of touching, the lower the class the greater the frequency of touching. As between classes the rule is that while members of the superior class may touch members of the inferior class, members of the inferior class may not touch members of the superior class. The same rule holds true for caste and status differences. One recalls the Untouchables of India. In the matter of status, although one may be a member of the same class as another who is of superior status, say in occupational hierarchy, rank or assigned role, the status difference is usually sufficient to inhibit touching of the individual of higher status by the individual of lower status. As Nancy Henley has remarked, touch may be regarded as the nonverbal equivalent of calling another by first name. Just as members of higher class or status may call members of inferior class or status by their first names, so they may also touch them, while confidently expecting that members of inferior rank will not do so. Indeed, it is considered a breach of etiquette of the most serious kind when, occasionally, some forward individual ventures to break either one or the other rule.

Touching, like being called by first name, is considered an act of intimacy, a privilege usually granted only to those of one's own class or status whom one has allowed to pass across those social barriers which serve to exclude the unprivileged. Among members of one's own class or status, being called by first name or a touch may be used to establish an immediate friendly relationship. The acceptance or rejection of such an advance will be quickly indicated by the response made to it.

Touch, however, very much more than first-name-calling, reduces social distance and often constitutes a declaration of intimacy: It is for this reason that it is usually regarded as an incursion upon one's privacy by those who resent such intrusions. By extension, any accidental or unnecessary touching, even from an intimate, may be found annoying or unacceptable.

It is evident, then, that in social encounters touch is regarded as a token of power exercised nonreciprocally at the discretion of one's betters or reciprocally between equals. Since in the power structure of Western societies females are regarded as inferior in status to males, and are treated as if they belonged to an inferior class or caste, females from their earliest days receive a good deal more touching than males. In infancy daughters are touched by both parents more frequently than sons, and daughters, according to a familial study by Jourard, touch both parents more than sons do. In another study by Jourard and Rubin it was found that mothers touch their sons more than fathers do, and fathers touch their daughters more than they do their sons; daughters touch their fathers more than sons do, and sons touch their mothers more than their fathers. Touching between males is, then, less frequent than it is between females and males within the family. It was also found that both mothers and fathers touch daughters in more regions of the body than they do sons, and that daughters do more of this kind of touching of both parents than do sons. These observers also found that males touch their female best friends in more regions than females report touching their male friends.

Jourard and Rubin are of the opinion that touching is equated with sexual intent, either consciously or at a less conscious level. As a general rule but not as a universal one, this is probably a sound statement. Nancy Henley reports a piece of research by a male assistant of hers in which it was found that under ordinary conditions males touch females more frequently than females touch males. However, when females enjoy greater status advantages than males they are more likely to initiate touching. Henley concludes that between the sexes it is status rather than sex that determines the frequency of touching, and that touching by males is used as one of the means of keeping women in their places, "another reminder that women's bodies are free property for everyone to use." Henley feels that women should refuse to accept such male tactual assertion, and "remove their hands from the grasp of men who hold them too long," to reject unsolicited and unwanted touch, and when the situation is appropriate to begin touching men.

If in the politics of sex and touch men are still for the most part Tories, women are enjoined to look deeper, to get to the root of things, and to become more radical.

TACTILE STIMULATION AND SLEEP. Anna Freud has pointed out that "it is a primitive need of the child to have close and warm contact with another person's body while falling asleep, but this runs counter to all the rules of hygiene which demand that children sleep by themselves and not share the parental bed." She goes on to say, "The infant's biological need for the care-taking adult's constant *presence* is disregarded in our Western culture, and children are exposed to long hours of solitude owing to the misconception that it is healthy for the young to sleep, rest, and later play alone. Such neglect of natural needs creates the first breaks in the smooth functioning of the processes of need and drive fulfillment. As a result, mothers seek advice for infants who have difficulty in falling asleep or do not sleep through the night, in spite of being tired."

In Western cultures one constantly encounters the phenomenon of children begging their mothers to lie by their side or at least to stay with them until they fall asleep, a supplication which the mother tends to discourage. The endless calls from the child's bed, the demand for the presence of the mother, for an open door, a drink of water, a light, a story, to be tucked in, and so on, are all expressions of the child's need for that primary object, his mother, to whom he can securely relate. A cuddly toy, a pet one can take to bed, soft materials, a security blanket, some object to which the child is particularly attached, and autoerotic activities such as thumb-sucking, rocking, masturbation, are the child's means of facilitating the transition from wakefulness to sleep. When these objects are given up, a new wave of difficulties in falling asleep may develop.

As Judith Jobin has eloquently said:

For thousands of American kids, every night is the loneliest night in the week come 9 P.M., when their happy, loving families abruptly turn into untouchables. Junior is sent up to his lonely bed, freshly made up with Donald Duck sheets. After a brief kiss and a warning look ('Don't give me a hard time') his parents avert their eyes, for there are few sights sadder than the thin back of a child as he goes off to face the night alone. His tiny bones quiver with betrayal, and there is the awful moment at the foot of the stairs when he turns to fix Mommy and Daddy with one last imploring look.

Donald Duck sheets are no substitute for the warm comfort of one's parents' bodies, and the nightly deprivation the child suffers, as every one of us who has experienced it knows, is felt as an abandonment, an incomprehensible betrayal, which equally incomprehensibly appears to be part of the order of things.

Among many peoples of the world co-family sleeping, in which children and parents sleep together, is a regular occurrence. It is a practice which has many advantages for everyone involved. Children may sleep either in the same bed with their parents or with their siblings. It would be a matter for each family to work out according to its needs. Tine Thevenin has written a book on the subject, *The Family Bed,* in which she makes a strong case for co-family sleeping.

Children who have spent their first years in the family bed are more intimately bound to the closely bonded family, they wake up more cheerfully, are more cuddly, and sleep better; and are more responsive. When siblings sleep together rivalry and bickering diminish. "If you talk with family sleepers," writes Tobin, "their body language is more expressive than any written sentiment: they make baby faces, raise their voices an octave or two, and give themselves friendly little hugs." And that, if it doesn't say all, tells us how much body contact means to family sleepers.

It is in his second year that the child experiences the need for the close contact that will enable him to fall asleep. It should be given him. A mother or father who is involved in the welfare of the child should not find it insuperably difficult, even in the modern world, to lie at bedtime by its side. This will usually be necessary only during the second year. One need stay only until the child falls asleep. It is quite possible that with further discoveries in this area the time that should be devoted to this will be reduced or even eliminated. One possibility has been pioneered by the members of the New Zealand Christchurch Parents Centre. These women became interested in the idea that babies might benefit from lying on the soft, springy fleece of lambskins and derive the same sort of comfort that adult patients obtain from invalid-care sheepskins. The lambskins are specially tanned.

Lambskin infants seem easier to put down after breast-feeding, they remain drier, and when wet they are still warm. Such infants are less demanding and will lie contentedly awake for an hour without requiring attention. The rug encourages "tummy" sleepers to nuzzle into it, and explore it with their face and hands. Suffocation is almost entirely removed as a possibility, since the circulation through the wool is quite thorough.

Several studies have shown that not only infants, but also prematures do much better on lambskins. The lambskin prematures make remarkable gains in weight, they also lose less body heat, consume less oxygen, and are less restless. It has also been noted that the lambskin protects the premature's delicate skin from the abrasion that often results from lying on linen, and there is less pressure on the head.* Mothers of handicapped, and especially cerebral palsied children, report enthusiastically the extra comfort their babies seem to gain from lying on lambskin rugs. It is quite possible that when babies are started off on such a lambskin sleeping rug they may have less difficulty in achieving sleep later on. It is an experiment worth trying.

*It is important not to use artificial sheepskin for prematures or infants. The fibers of such sheepskins tend to come loose and may be swallowed by the infant, resulting in respiratory difficulties.

A further report on lambskins indicates that not all skins are suitable. The best skins must be of large area, with a fine, dense fleece such as is grown by Corriedale or Merino breeds or the Southdown Romney cross-lamb. Preliminary tests with the latter type of lambskins indicated that babies were more content and slept longer on them than on conventional sheets and mattresses. When deprived of the skins, the babies invariably became restless.

Following a lecture I delivered at the University of Ottawa in January 1976 a psychiatrist informed me that she had had considerable success in the treatment of patients by getting them to sleep on lambskin rugs.

Reference to security blankets draws attention once again to the attachment qualities of cutaneously comforting materials. The general belief that the blanket provides the child with a feeling of security, and serves as a mother substitute, is borne out by experiment and observation. Drs. Richard Passman and Paul Weisberg found that nondistress, play, and exploration were facilitated significantly by giving attached children their security blanket, as compared to giving other preschoolers their favorite hard toy or no familiar object. When the mother was in the room with the child, her presence had similar facilitative properties to the blanket. For children who had no attachment to blankets, the blanket's presence was no more functional than the control condition in which no familiar object was present. Similar results were found with regard to learning.

In a third study Dr. Passman found that there is a limit to the functional properties of the blanket. In cases of heightened arousal, the mother is significantly more effective than the blanket in increasing play and exploration and in decreasing distress. The relative potency of the maternal attachment bond is far superior to that attaching to the blanket. Dr. William Mason's theory that stimuli more suitable for clinging provide more arousal reduction is supported. That is to say, hard toys offer fewer opportunities for clinging than blankets, and blankets fewer than mothers.

Since almost half of all middle-class children become attached to inanimate objects, mostly security blankets, often also to pets that they can take to bed with them and carry around, it is highly desirable to recognize the importance of such needs to children. Among the functions of the security blanket is its service as a defense against anxiety, and as a helpful means in making the transition from the world of inner to the world of outer reality. As is said in one of the most famous of all stories bearing on this subject:

> ... *so wherever I am, there's always Pooh,*
> *There's always Pooh and Me.*
> *"What would I do?" I said to Pooh,*
> *"If it wasn't for you," and Pooh said, "True,*
> *It isn't much fun for One but Two*
> *Can stick together," says Pooh, says he,*
> *"That's how it is," says Pooh ...*
>
> —A. A. Milne, *Now We Are Six*

As is well known, many individuals hang on to their loved objects well into adult life. Today there is much evidence that many who do not would be better off if they did.

The security blanket, whatever form it may take, is clearly a means or vehicle of solace, a transitional object which substitutes for the soothing presence of the mother when she is temporarily absent. Dr. Paul Horton has made a compelling case for the necessity of such vehicles of solace, and that, indeed, they increase in importance throughout a healthy life; their forms may change with maturity; music, a religious idea, a sailboat, even a psychiatrist will take the place of a stuffed toy. The adult, Horton argues, who cannot relate to some such transitional object will have, among other things, no outlet for hostile drives.

In connection with pets, it is of interest to note that many persons who, for one reason or another, experience difficulty in touching others, often satisfy their tactile, and through them related, needs with pets. The very word itself, "pet," and the verb "to pet" in one of its meanings is "to stroke or pat gently;

fondle; caress," and colloquially, "to kiss, embrace, fondle intimately, etc., in making love."

Recognizing the importance of relatedness to animals, Dr. Boris M. Levinson has developed a pet-oriented child psychotherapy, in which he uses animals, chiefly dogs, in the diagnosis and treatment of psychologically disturbed children. The thesis of his book on the subject is that "contact with the inanimate and particularly the animate world via the pet is most important to a wholesome emotional development."

There can be little doubt that in many an emotionally refrigerated home, the mental health of a child has been saved by the presence of a pet with whom it could communicate, in the physical presence of human beings who could not. In this connection Drs. Samuel and Elizabeth Corson and their colleagues in the department of psychiatry at Ohio State University have conducted some interesting experiments in custodial institutions with patients ranging from adolescents to the old and infirm. The experimenters selected patients who had failed to respond to the traditional forms of therapy and brought in dogs of various breeds who were offered as pets to the patients. The responses were dramatic. Only three of the fifty patients refused to accept the dogs as pets, but the other forty-seven adopted them with enthusiasm, and from the outset showed a striking improvement. One man who had not spoken for twenty-six years began to speak.

As S. A. Corson and his collaborators state, the attachment humans develop for pet dogs is probably related to the ability of these animals to offer love and tactile reassurance without criticism, "and their maintenance of a sort of perpetual infantile innocent dependence which may stimulate our natural tendency to offer support and protection." As they say, the success of pet-facilitated psychotherapy is based on the assumption that many patients will accept the love of a dog before they are able to accept love from or give love to a human being.

Tactual interchange between dog and human is important as "an ice-breaker," but it is not the only important exchange involved in the resocialization of the withdrawn patient. The sense of responsibility that the patient develops for the welfare of the dog, his care for it, the sense of reciprocal commitment he experiences, all minister to the opening up of a view of the world in which he can find others to whom he can relate, and interrelate.

Interestingly enough, child-battering and abusing parents, who were themselves neglected and abused as children, rarely report having had a childhood pet.

Companion animals, as pets are coming to be called among students of the subject, confer many benefits upon humans, among them a socially acceptable outlet for touching. Hand contact in the form of patting, stroking, rubbing, and scratching provide an opportunity that American men, especially, are reluctant to engage in.

In a number of institutions great success has also been achieved with the aged by voluntary periodic visits of small children. The children readily accept the caresses of the old and return them with interest. Withdrawn and unhappy people undergo a transformation which brings them out of their introversion and in every way improves their feelings about themselves.

THE TACTILE EXPERIENCE OF THE INDIAN CHILD.   Throughout the greater part of India children receive much tactile attention from their earliest days. Babies from about one month to six months are regularly bathed and massaged with such mixtures as turmeric paste and castor oil. As children they run around naked until six or seven; from their earliest days they are hugged and kissed by everyone.

Frederick Leboyer has published a detailed photographic account of this traditional Indian art of baby massage. This is most illuminating, for there is not a nook or cranny of the baby's body that is not lovingly massaged by the mother's hands.

THE TACTILE EXPERIENCE OF THE JAPANESE CHILD.   Dr. William Caudill and Mrs. Helen Weinstein have made a valuable comparative study of childrearing methods in Japan as compared with those in the United States. They studied a selected matched sample of thirty Japanese and thirty American infants, three to four months old, equally divided by sex, all firstborn, and all from intact middle-class families in urban settings. On the basis of previous studies, these investigators predicted they would find Japanese mothers spending more time with their infants, and that they would emphasize physical contact over verbal interaction, and would have as a goal a passive and contented baby. The American mothers, they predicted, would spend less time with their infants, would emphasize verbal interaction rather than physical contact, and would have as a goal an active and self-assertive baby. These hypotheses were generally confirmed by the investigators, and indeed they agree fully with those of other students of Japanese and American culture. Caudill and Weinstein found that "largely because of different patterns of interaction with their mothers in the two countries, infants have learned to behave in different and culturally appropriate ways by three to four months of age. Moreover, these differences in infant behavior are in line with preferred patterns of social interaction at later ages as the child grows to be an adult in Japan and America."

It is generally agreed that Japanese are more "group" oriented and interdependent in their relations with others, while Americans are more "individual" oriented and independent. Associated with this is the tendency of Japanese to be more self-effacing and passive as contrasted with Americans, who tend to be more self-assertive and aggressive.

> In matters requiring a decision, Japanese are more likely to rely on emotional feeling and intuition, whereas Americans will go to some pains to emphasize what they believe are the rational reasons for their action. . . . Japanese are more sensitive to, and make conscious use of, many forms of nonverbal communication in human relations through the medium of gestures and physical proximity, in comparison with Americans, who predominantly use verbal communication within a context of physical separateness.

We have already touched upon the co-sleeping family habits of the Japanese in contrast to the separate sleeping habits of Americans, from the earliest age, and the resulting differences in tactile experience in the two cultures. In keeping with these sleeping habits, at least as significant, are the bathing practices of Japanese and Americans. In Japan, from the earliest possible age, approximately at the beginning of the infant's second month, the whole family bathes collectively. The mother or another adult holds the infant in her arms while they bathe together in the deep bathtub (*furo*) at home or in the neighborhood public bath (*sento*). This pattern of shared bathing continues for the Japanese child until he or she is about ten years old, and even later. In contrast with this, the American mother rarely bathes with an infant, but rather gives him a bath from outside the tub, and communicates with him verbally and by positioning his body. Breastfeeding is still more widespread in Japan than is bottlefeeding, and while babies are started on semi-solid food at the end of the first month in America, this is not the case until the end of the fourth month for Japanese babies. Quite clearly the Japanese infant receives a great deal more reassuring tactile stimulation than does the American infant, and of a kind which by the early age of three to four months has already made a distinctively perceptible behavioral difference in the infants of these two cultures. Caudill and Weinstein summarize their findings as follows:

American infants are more happily vocal, more active, and more exploratory of their bodies and their physical environment, than are Japanese infants. Directly related to these findings, the American mother is in greater vocal interaction with her infant, and stimulates him to greater physical activity and exploration. The Japanese mother, in contrast, is in greater bodily contact with her infant, and soothes him toward physical quiescence, and passivity with regard to his environment. Moreover, these patterns of behavior are in line with the differing expectations for later behavior in the two cultures as the child grows to be an adult.

Caudill and Weinstein predicted that when they were ready to report their findings on two-year-olds and six-year-olds from each culture, they would probably find that these early patterns of behavior will jell and persist.

As Douglas Haring says,

> One outstanding fact not stressed in the literature but amply verified involves the almost uninterrupted bodily contact of Japanese infants with mother or nursemaid. Practically never is a baby left to lie alone quietly. Always he rides on someone's back or sleeps close to someone. When he is restless his bearer sways or jiggles from one foot to the other. Some writers deem this jiggling a fearsome experience for the infant. . . . My own unsystematic observations indicate that most Japanese think it soothes the child. At any rate the infant almost constantly feels the reassuring touch of human skin. When he cries he is given the breast, and in lower-class families his sexual organs are manipulated until he falls asleep. Many better-educated Japanese repudiate the latter practice, but they employ nursemaids versed in the folkways rather than in the niceties of genteel refinement.

Then when the child reaches walking age he is quite drastically left on his own a great deal of the time, and must learn to conform to the implicit taboo on touching other people.

As Haring points out, the sudden break in the infant's habitual basic dependence on contact with other persons involves frustration, and frustration will result in emotional behavior designed to compel attention to the need that has been frustrated. In the Japanese boy this takes the form of temper tantrums, the expression of which, either in verbal or physical abuse, is permitted upon the body of the mother, but not upon the father. The expression of temper in girls is strictly forbidden. In the rigidly defined situation of Japanese life no adequate outlets are provided for the effects of frustration, except in childhood abuse of animals and of the mother for boys, and also perhaps through alcoholic intoxication. Girls must repress their expressions of frustration.

Long postponed revenge for childhood frustration—a motivation of which the individual is unconscious—may be accomplished either in suicide or in the sadistic outbursts of war and torture of the helpless. In males these latter outbursts receive social approval. Females apparently live with their repressions, unless the common neurotic malady called *hisuteri* (derived from the English hysteria—usually nymphomania) may be regarded as a consequence.

Undoubtedly related to the sudden cessation of tactility, and especially the relaxing manipulation of the external genitalia of the small child, is the reactive behavior of adolescent and adult males towards their own bodies and those of others. All the visceral functions that received such lavish attention in infancy, in the older Japanese male come to symbolize frustration. Sexual functions, even though they may provide occasion for boasting, are repudiated in disgust: "The unconscious conflict within the growing boy finds in sex a symbol of frustrated aggression and longing for dominance. Behavior related to sex is tinged with sadistic violence; the fierce obscenity of Japanese schoolboys, homosexuality, contempt for wives, and sexual mutilation of helpless enemies all stem perhaps from these unresolved conflicts."

While these socialization processes and the behavioral responses to them characterize pre-World War II Japan, to varying degrees they remain true of large segments of Japanese society today.*

Quite clearly the differences in tactile stimulation under-

* For pre-World War II Japan see Alice Bacon, *Japanese Girls and Women* (Boston: Houghton Mifflin, 1902); Lafcadio Hearn, *Japan: An Attempt at Interpretation* (New York: Macmillan, 1904); R. F. Benedict, *The Chrysanthemum and the Sword* (Boston: Houghton Mifflin, 1946); B. S. Silberman (ed.), *Japanese Character and Culture* (Tucson: University of Arizona Press, 1962); G. DeVos and H. Wagatsuma, *Japan's Invisible Race: Caste and Culture in Personality* (Berkeley: University of California Press, 1966); R. J. Smith and R. K. Beardsley, *Japanese Culture: Its Development and Characteristics* (New York: Viking Fund Publications in Anthropology, vol. 34, 1962); E. O. Reischauer, *The Japanese* (Cambridge, Mass.: Harvard University Press, 1977).

gone by Japanese and American infants play a considerable role in the development of their behavioral differences. What these behavioral differences are has already been suggested in the studies we have cited.

NATIONAL, CULTURAL, AND CLASS DIFFERENCES IN TACTILITY. National and cultural differences in tactility run the full gamut from absolute nontouchability, as among upper- and middle-class Englishmen, to what amounts to almost full expression among peoples speaking Latin-derived languages, Russians, and many nonliterate peoples. Those who speak Anglo-Saxon-derived languages stand at the opposite pole in the continuum of tactility to the Latin peoples. In this continuum Scandinavians appear to occupy an intermediate position. I do not propose here a calculus of tactile variations among the peoples of the world. The necessary information for such a discussion is simply not available. Clay's study on a small sample of the population of one local region in North America is the only one of its kind. However, from general observation of the marked differences in tactility observable among different peoples today, it is possible to draw certain obvious conclusions.

There exist not only cultural and national differences in tactile behavior, but also class differences. As I have earlier already remarked, in general it seems possible to say that the higher the class, the less there is of tactility, and the lower the class, the more there is. As we have seen, this was not found to be the case by Clay in her American sample, in which the upper-class mothers seemed to be more at ease with tactility than the lower-class mothers. It is possible that this finding could be generalized for the American population as a whole, with exceptions represented by blacks and other "minority" groups. Whereas in Europe, for example, and especially in England, the upper classes are likely to be hereditary and long entrenched in their ways, in America social mobility is so great that one can move from lower- to upper-class status in a single generation. Parents of the second generation move very much more freely than their own parents did, not only in the class achieved for them by earlier generations, but in their ideas on such important matters as childrearing practices. Hence, in America, new members of the upper classes will often give their children more rationalized attention than the members of other classes. Whatever the explanation may be for Clay's sample, there does seem to exist a highly significant correlation between class membership and tactility, and this appears to be largely due to early conditioning.

Among the upper classes of England relationships between parents and children were, and continue to be, distant from birth till death. At birth the child was usually given over to a nurse, who either wet-nursed it for a brief period or bottlefed it. Children were generally brought up by governesses and then at an early age sent away to school. They received a minimum amount of tactile experience. It is, therefore, not difficult to understand how, under such conditions, nontouchability could easily become institutionalized as part of the way of life. A well-bred person never touched another without his consent. The slightest accidental brushing against another required an apology, even though the other might be a parent or a sibling. Too often a lacklove childhood combined with a minimum of tactile stimulation, compounded by the experience of a public school (which in England is so called because the public is not admitted to it), produced a rather emotionally arid human being who was quite incapable of warm human relationships. Such individuals made poor husbands, disastrous fathers, and efficient governors of the British Empire, since they were seldom capable of understanding genuine human need.

I do not know of a single book by a member of the upper classes that reveals the slightest insight into the nature of these conditions; the few writings produced on the subject were all by members of the middle classes.* It is not that the members

---

* One of the best of these is George Orwell's *Such, Such Were the Joys* (New York: Harcourt, Brace, 1953). A near approach by a member of the upper classes is Timothy Eden's (Anthony's brother) *The Baronet and the Butterfly* (London: Macmillan, 1933).

of the middle classes necessarily required more tactile affection than members of the upper classes, but that they were simply, in some cases, more articulate about the losses and the indignities they had suffered.

The English public schools, as is well known, were breeding grounds for homosexuality, for these were all-boy schools in which all the teachers were males, and usually the only love a boy ever received was from another boy or a master.* The parental inadequacies from which many of these boys suffered produced a high rate of homosexuality. Among writers such famous figures as Algernon Swinburne, J. A. Symonds, Oscar Wilde, Lord Alfred Douglas, A. E. Housman, E. M. Forster, T. E. Lawrence, W. H. Auden, and numerous others, were all products of such parents, and such schools. It is not to be wondered at that parentally abandoned children sought to find some human relationship in sexual friendship with others in the same predicament as themselves.

The conditioning in nontactility received by so many Englishmen of the upper classes seems to have produced a virtual negative sanction on tactility in English culture. This was so much the case that the sense of touch and the act of touching have both been culturally defined as vulgar. The public demonstration of affection is vulgar, touching is vulgar, and only men who are quite outside the pale, like Latin types, Italians, and the like, would ever dream of putting their arms around one another, not to mention committing such effeminacies as kissing one another on the cheek!

The essentially human is dismissed as "effeminate."

It is of more than passing interest to note that in England the National Guidance Marriage Council, in one of its publications, suggested that the rising divorce rate is largely due to a lack of physical contact in the English family, even to the extent of admonishing small boys not to embrace their mothers

---

* For a brilliant account of these "nurseries of vice" see John Chandos, *Boys Together* (New Haven, Conn.: Yale University Press, 1984).

during some little crisis, but to retain their manhood by maintaining a "stiff upper lip." The council advised that the English "need to touch, stroke, and comfort one another more often."

Even more far gone in nontactility, if such a thing can be imagined, than the English, are the Germans. The emphasis upon the warrior virtues, the supremacy of the hardheaded martinet father, and the complete subordination of the mother in the German family made for a rigidified, unbending character which renders the average German, among other things, a not very tactile creature.

Austrian males, however, unlike Germans, are tactually more demonstrative, and will embrace close friends. In Germany this rarely occurred, except among men of Jewish extraction—but that is quite another thing, for among Jews tactility is highly developed.

The Jews, as a tribe, culture, or people, are characterized by a high degree of tactility. "The Jewish mother" has become a byword, for her deep and consuming care for her children. This meant that until recent times the children were breastfed on demand, that there was a great deal of fondling of children by mother, father, and siblings. Hence, Jews tend to be tactually very demonstrative and it is considered perfectly normal for an adult male to continue to greet his father with a kiss and an embrace and to do so also on parting. In fifty years of close observation I have only once seen an adult American male (in this case in his middle twenties) publicly greet his father with a kiss. Of what cultural origins this American male may have been I do not know.

Americans of Anglo-Saxon origin are not quite as untactual as the English or the Germans, but they do not lag far behind. American boys neither kiss nor embrace their fathers after they have "grown up"—"grown up" in this sense is generally taken to be about ten years of age. Nor do American males embrace their friends as Latin Americans do.

There are occasions, however, when American males will spontaneously drop their inhibitions and joyfully embrace each other, even kiss each other with complete abandon. This is most likely to occur when they win an important match or series. The hugging on such occasions is something to behold, and it is all the more impressive because of its utter spontaneity.

There are clearly contact peoples and noncontact peoples, the Anglo-Saxon peoples being among the latter. Curious ways in which noncontactuality expresses itself are to be seen in the behavior of members of the noncontact cultures in various situations. It has, for example, been observed that the way an Anglo-Saxon shakes hands constitutes a signal to the other to keep his proper distance. In crowds this is also observable. For example, in a crowded vehicle like a subway, the Anglo-Saxon will remain stiff and rigid, with a blank expression on his face which seems to deny the existence of other passengers. As Germaine Greer has remarked, "Crushed against his brother in the Tube the average Englishman pretends desperately that he is alone." The contrast on the French Metro, for example, is striking. Here the passengers will lean and press against others, if not with complete abandon, at least without feeling the necessity either to ignore or apologize to the person against whom they may be leaning or pressing. Often the leaning and lurching will give rise to good-natured laughter and joking, and there will be no attempt to avoid looking at the other passengers. A protesting Englishman on such occasions is regarded as a rather pathetic figure of fun.

While waiting for a bus, Americans will space themselves like sparrows on a telephone wire, in contrast to Mediterranean peoples, who will push the crowd together.

Sydney Smith, "The Smith of Smiths," the great English wit, writing in 1820, amusingly described the varieties of the handshake. "Have you noticed," he wrote,

> how people shake your hand? There is the *high-official*—the body erect, and a rapid, short shake, near the chin. There is the *mortmain*—the flat hand introduced into your palm, and hardly conscious of its contiguity. The *digital*—one finger held out, much used by the higher clergy. There is the *shakus rusticus,* where your hand is seized in an iron grasp, betokening

rude health, warm heart, and distance from the Metropolis; but producing a strong sense of relief on your part when you find your hand released and your fingers unbroken. The next to this is the *retentive shake*—one which, beginning with vigour, pauses as it were to take breath, but without relinquishing its prey, and before you are aware begins again, till you feel anxious as to the result, and have no shake left in you. Worse, there is the *pisces*—the damp palm like a dead fish, equally silent, equally clammy, and leaving its odour in your hand.

Sydney Smith did not quite exhaust the varieties of handshaking. Two forms of the handshake observable at the present day are the following: Shaking hands and at the same time grasping the elbow or forearm of the shaken arm. Or to grasp the shakee's hand with both hands. I know a young woman who does this. When I commented on the fact, she surprised me by saying that she was quite unaware that she shook hands in this manner.

It is of interest to note that free-living chimpanzees will stretch out the hand to let it be touched by another as a gesture of friendliness. So will the gorilla. It also constitutes a measure of one's opposite number's intentions. Contact greetings of this sort take a variety of forms among chimpanzees. For example, they will place a hand on the thigh, or place the hand on the other's body in gentle reassurance.

The reference to the handshake brings us to the matter of tactile salutations in general. These represent a form of tactile behavior that has received very little attention. The handshake is clearly an evidence of friendliness. Ortega y Gasset has elaborated an anthropologically quite unsound theory of the origin of the handshake. In this he sees the submission of the vanquished or of the slave to his master. The theory is not by any means novel, but, as Westermarck points out, handshaking in many cases seems to have the same origin as other ceremonies consisting in bodily contact. Salutatory gestures may express not only absence of evil intentions but positive friendliness. Whatever its origins, the handshake is quite obviously a tactile communication. So is the placing together of the palms of the hands, placing the hand on the heart, nose rubbing, embracing, kissing, and even the backslapping, cheek-tweaking, and hair-mussing in which some people indulge. Westermarck long ago recognized that these various forms of salutation by contact "are obviously direct expressions of affection." He goes on to add that

> we can hardly doubt that the joining of hands serves a similar object when we find it combined with other tokens of good will. Among some of the Australian natives, friends, on meeting after an absence, "will kiss, shake hands, and sometimes cry over one another."* In Morocco equals salute each other by joining their hands with a quick motion, separating them immediately, and kissing each his own hand. The Soolimas, again, place the palms of the right hands together, carry them to the forehead, and from thence to the left side of the chest. [p. 151]

Among the Andaman Islanders of the eastern Bay of Bengal Radcliffe-Brown observed that

> When two friends or relatives meet who have been separated from one another for a few weeks or longer, they greet each other by sitting down on the lap of the other, with their arms around each other's necks, and weeping and wailing for two or three minutes until they are tired. Two brothers greet each other in this way, and so do father and son, mother and son, mother and daughter, and husband and wife. When husband and wife meet, it is the man who sits on the lap of the woman. When two friends part from one another, one of them lifts up the hand of the other towards his mouth and gently blows on it.

Dr. Sandor S. Feldman points out that in handshaking we cling to the other person. In his view, the gesture means that we

---

* For an account of weeping as a form of salutation, see W. G. Sumner, A. G. Keller, and M. R. Davie, *The Science of Society* (4 vols., New Haven, Conn.: Yale University Press, 1927), vol. 4, pp. 568–570.

should trust each other, as a baby has perfect and complete trust in his mother. There is a right way and a wrong way of handshaking. In the right way the hands of the two persons are fused, and both feel a certain pressure. Each expects the same pressure of the other. When one feels an uneven exchange of pressure, he feels let down.

The showoffs crush the hand they grasp. The handshake of the meek and mild is vapid. Feldman thinks that those who merely extend a finger, do so usually out of a fear of contact, a social anxiety.

To the sensitive observer the handshake will often reveal the mask behind the persona. Harold Lyon, Jr., revealingly tells how "In 1969, several years before Frederick Perls, who is noted for his work in Gestalt therapy, died, I met him at Esalen Institute. The brief exchange involved an introduction during which Perls and I shook hands, with me giving my habitual firm 'military' handshake. Fritz Perls winced and withdrew his hand immediately, shouting, 'Not so hard!' Somewhat shocked, I replied defensively, 'Well, a good firm handshake, you know, is—' 'Is a sign of weakness,' interrupted Perls. 'It's a cover-up for a lack of warmth and sensitivity, which can be expressed in a gentle handclasp,' which he proceeded to share with me in a most moving way. In the enlightening days that followed for me at Esalen, I was to learn a great deal more about my cover-ups, masks, and macho-ness, and my mistaken beliefs that toughness was strength."

Dr. August Coppola has very rightly drawn attention to the fact that in the handshake something immediate and direct is told us about the other person, that however much people may attempt to "put on" with their handshake, the tactile image is directly related to the effort involved, the way in which one person attempts to know the other. As Coppola says, "There are no poses, no lies, nothing static, for even a hand that is still, limp, effortless, would be read as withdrawn in relation to the other, and would in turn provoke a response.... Since our only way of knowing each other is to sense the slightest movements, it seems impossible for people to mask their reactions, for the very attempt would be sensed as a hesitation or restraint within the touch relation." In the world of touch, personality constitutes the very process of engagement.

It is no accident that in being introduced to another we say such things as, "Delighted to meet you," "How do you do?" "I'm glad to know you," and the like, for as Coppola says, in the handshake the tactile awareness is underscored of the "very sensitive reciprocity of two persons attempting to know each other, opening a series of responses that go beyond the abyss at the edge of the touch world." Coppola very appropriately quotes from Rilke's poem, "Palm of the Hand," which shows Rilke's grasp of this idea when he says, "It enters into other hands, it turns its own kind into landscape: journeys and ends its journey in them, filling them with arrival."

So remember, when you next shake hands you may be—whether you are aware of it or not—embarking upon a journey of discovery.

Cheek patting, head patting, chin chucking are all, in the Western world, forms of behavior indicating affection, and all are tactile. Such tactile salutations, as evidence of friendliness or affection, are probably founded on the earliest experiences of touch received from the mother (and others) as a child.

Social exclusion can be a very powerful communication by denial of the hand extended or the embrace rebuffed.

A form of greeting as of 1982–83 made its appearance in New York, apparently popular among the successful executive class. At parties, soirees, and the like, when those present find themselves holding a drink in one hand and a canapé or whatever in the other, they will rub their shoulder against that of the new arrival, who either accepts the rub with a smile or enthusiastically rubs back. No cold shoulders, we trust, at such celebrations. To "rub shoulders" with the best has long been the desire of the upwardly mobile.

Sexual differences in salutations are of interest here. For example, in the Western world it is customary for men to shake hands, but not for women to do so. Women kiss or embrace when they are friends, and shake hands only when meeting for the first time or as casual acquaintances. Men do not shake hands with women, but bow, unless the woman extends her hand, when in the English-speaking world it will be shaken, and in the Latin-speaking world kissed. In recent years, in their growing affection for women, after some acquaintance men have taken to kissing them where formerly they would merely have bowed or shaken hands. Different times, different mores. In Elizabethan England kissing as a greeting was extended to all members of the same class, whether friends or strangers. Erasmus (1466?–1536), in a letter to his friend Faustus Andrelinus written in the summer of 1499, comments on this delightful custom among the English:

> There is a fashion which cannot be commended enough. Wherever you go you are received on all hands with kisses; when you leave you are dismissed with kisses; if you go back your salutes are returned to you. When a visit is paid, these sweets are served; and when guests depart kisses are shared again; whenever a meeting takes place there is kissing in abundance; in fact, whatever way you turn you are never without it. Oh Faustus, if you had once tasted how soft and fragrant those kisses are, you would wish to be a traveler, not for ten years, like Solon, but for your whole life, in England.

It would not be too bold an inference from this that perhaps the English, as children, received a great deal more tender loving care in Elizabethan days than they did in a period like that of Victoria and her son Edward, a period, as Rupert Brooke said of Victorian Sundays, full of impalpable restraints.

It is of great interest that in the middle 1960s something of the importance of the skin should have been rediscovered by so-called encounter, marathon, and sensitivity training groups. These groups usually consist of adults or older adolescents. A principal emphasis in such groups is on touching. All diffidence is dropped and one is encouraged to embrace others, caress them, hold hands with them, bathe in the nude with them, and even be massaged by them.

In a most thoroughgoing investigation of encounter and sensitivity training groups Dr. Kurt W. Back concludes:

> The encounter group is based on little coherent theory, mainly on the touch-and-go kind of technique, and even the practitioners do not claim to know particularly what they are doing. ... In fact, most people leading encounter groups would not claim any lasting beneficial effects on the patients or participants, and thus the question of the danger involved becomes important. The question of breakdowns in encounter groups is controversial and we have to rest here on a few well-established facts: there have been some breakdowns, suicides, and psychotic episodes in members of encounter groups.

Of sensitivity training, Dr. Back concludes that it may be more a symptom of what ails society than a cure for its ills.

Rather more favorable judgments concerning such groups have been expressed by Dr. J. R. Gibb, who examined 106 research studies on such human relations groups, and concluded that they were of distinct therapeutic value. Carl Rogers, after a broad survey of the evidence, concludes that encounter groups do bring about much in the way of constructive change.

Everyone enjoys having his back scratched, and to be massaged constitutes one of the supreme pleasures. But these are physical gratifications. These various groups are concerned with much more than physical pleasures. What they seek to achieve is a greater behavioral aliveness to their own and others' presence, relatedness to the environment; they seek to put people who have become dissociated back into touch with their fellow humans and with the world in which they are living.

The idea is a good one even though it comes late in the day for many of the participants. It runs counter to the Freudian notion that touching should comprise no part of therapy. Freud himself was a bit of a cold fish, and one cannot avoid the suspicion that he was insufficiently fondled when he was an infant. However that may be, the rediscovery of the skin as an organ which, in its own way, requires just as much attention as the mind, is long overdue. Allowing for all the failures, the therapeutic benefits resulting from the experiences in these various groups in which tactility plays a significant role have been reported to be appreciable.

Canadians of Anglo-Saxon origins perhaps even outdo the English in their nontactuality. On the other hand, French Canadians are as tactually demonstrative as their counterparts are in their land of origin.

The manner in which Frenchmen will embrace and kiss their male friends, and the embracing and kissing that takes place on ceremonial occasions, as when a general conferring a decoration upon another officer will embrace and kiss him ceremonially on both cheeks, embarrasses Anglo-Saxons into deprecatory giggles, whereas the nontactuality of Anglo-Saxons signifies to most tactual peoples that they are unemotional and cold.

Constrained and intimidated by custom, class, and education, the landowning and middle classes of pre-Communist Russia presented a fascinating contrast of much tactile experience in childhood and adolescence, combined with an adult distance between persons who, like the characters in a Chekhov play, could come together, touch, embrace in half-abstracted caresses, and spin apart again, to bemoan their tragic fate in the diminutives of their delicately tactile and sonorous language.

The swaddling which most Russians customarily underwent as infants ensured them a great deal of tactile stimulation, for they were usually unswaddled in order to be breastfed, otherwise fed, bathed, cleaned, and in other ways attended, a fact which seems to have been overlooked by the proponents of the "swaddling hypothesis" who claimed that many of the national traits of Great Russians (central and northeastern Russians) could be explained by the restraints such children suffered as infants as a consequence of swaddling. The child was kept isolated from its parents, with only siblings and maids for human contact, and was only brought out of the nursery or children's quarters in order to perform in some manner such as the recitation of poetry, the playing of a musical instrument, or singing. During infancy, according to the swaddling hypothesis, the swaddling inhibits muscular activity, while the release from swaddling in order to be fed and otherwise cared for becomes associated with an "all or none" feeling toward pleasure which the Russian adult displays in his emotional life, an emotional life in which gratification is experienced as orgiastic.

There has been much misunderstanding concerning the nature of swaddling. It takes skill to do it. As Peter Wolff has written:

> *Swaddling* is a very effective method to quiet a fussy baby, provided it is done by someone who knows how, and who sees to it that the baby is immobilized. When the swaddling is done unskillfully so that the clothing simply restricts the range of movement without inhibiting it totally, the procedure has a marked arousal effect and may provoke the "mad cry." The critical difference is probably that "poor" swaddling generates a constant background of *variable* proprioceptive feed-back, whereas "good" swaddling generates a constant background of tactile stimulation.

Swaddling constitutes a massive comforting embrace. Since increased tactile stimulation is known to reduce stress, it should not be surprising that many different peoples have discovered the beneficial effects of swaddling in soothing the infant.

It has been stated that swaddling late premature babies to the maternal breast has proven beneficial to them, but I know of no clear evidence for this.

The swaddling hypothesis has been severely criticized and found wanting on virtually every ground. Under the Soviet system, swaddling has been largely abandoned.

In *The Study of Culture at a Distance,* edited by Mead and Métraux, there is a valuable account of the sense of touch among the Russians, written by a sensitive woman informant in the Research on Contemporary Cultures project. It is well worth reproducing here in its entirety.

The Dictionary of the Russian Language defines the sense of touch as follows: "In reality all five senses can be reduced to one—the sense of touch. The tongue and palate sense the food; the ear, sound waves; the nose, emanations; the eyes, rays of light." That is why in all textbooks the sense of touch is always mentioned first. It means to ascertain, to perceive, by body, hand, or fingers.

There are two words to express the idea "to feel." If one feels with some outer part of the body, it is *ossyazat;* but to feel without touching, without direct contact, is *oschuschat* physically, morally, or spiritually: "I feel (*oschuschat*) too cold or cold," and "I feel (*oschuschat*) happiness." But when I feel something with my fingers, I *ossyazat*—I don't really feel, I finger, grope.

Though there exists an adverb *ossyasatelny* (tangible), Russians avoid using it. I have never heard anybody using it, nor have I come across it in literature. Tangible evidence in Russian will be "material proof." Touch is not considered the right way of exploration. One does not have to finger a thing when one can see it with one's eyes. One of my [Russian] college professors complained that his students were "savages." When he showed them a bone, drawing their attention to a cavity, the majority of the students poked their fingers into it. Children were taught not to touch things. They learned very quickly, and when you handed a child something you wanted him to feel—like a piece of velvet or a kitten—the child picked it up and put it against his cheek.

The standard joke among lower-class people was for a man to ask a woman, "Nice calico you are wearing. How much did you pay a yard?" And under the pretext of feeling the material, he would pinch the woman.

Russians in general touch each other much less than Americans do. There is hardly any horseplay, slapping on the back, patting, fondling of children. The exception is when somebody is very happy or drunk. Then he hugs somebody. But that is not touching. He opens his arms wide as if to embrace the whole world, and then presses you against his breast. The breast is the dwelling place of the soul, and this gesture means that he has taken you to his heart.

These are interesting observations, though not entirely internally consistent. For example, if Russians are nontactile, why is it that the students poked their fingers into the cavity of the bone? In spite of the fact that this informant states that hugging is not touching, the fact is that it is very much so. Soviet officials when they meet embrace and often kiss each other, and may behave in this manner towards nationals of other countries, if one may depend upon what one sees in TV news reports and photographs.

Several students have reported the emphasis they believe Russians place on visual experience. Thus Leites writes of their "desire to translate all the abstractions visually." Haimson believes that in contrast with the "objective" thinking that characterizes Western society, and which he believes is largely founded on motor activity and tactile manipulation of external objects, the visual thinking of Great Russians is singularly lacking in specificity, especially when evaluated by the measure of manipulation. The suggestion is that tactual manipulation is important in the development of abstract and conceptual thought. These students suggest that an element is lacking in Russian abstract thought, present in the concrete situation, and which may be approached through tactual or physical manipulation. Combined with the supposed effects of swaddling upon the kinesthetic movements of the child, the lack of the tactual/manipulative approach to experience is somehow seen to affect the Russian's ability to grasp the essentials of a given whole, to break up a given whole in parts, to isolate and synthesize them. The "whole," on the contrary, is likely to be seen as consisting of overlapping and contradictory items, all of which being lumped together, constitute one diffused whole, to which one responds with "emotion and intensity." Russian thinking is declared to be deficient in logical simplicity, consistency, and completeness.

Interesting as these observations are, it would be of value to have them explored further, and to have the comments of informed students of the childhood and development of "Great Russians."

THE CRADLEBOARD. The cradleboard is used among many peoples in managing the child. Among the Navaho Indians of the Southwest, the newborn was placed in a temporary cradle, and then after three or four weeks transferred to a permanent tightly laced cradle. Before being placed in the cradle the infant was tightly wrapped in clothes in such a way, sometimes, that its legs were separated and firmly encased. The cradle itself would be lined with some soft material, formerly the soft bark of the cliff rose. A canopy would be placed at the top and a footrest at the bottom of the board. The infant, fully wrapped, would then be strapped to the cradle by a lacing cord, which in zigzag fashion between cloth or buckskin loops was attached to the sides of the board and was finally fastened through a loop on the footboard. From the canopy a cloth could be lowered to cover the whole cradle to keep out light, flies, and cold. Babies were taken out of the cradle only to be breastfed, cleaned, and bathed. Babies of two months averaged two hours a day out of the cradle; those of nine months averaged nearly six. In addition to these times of full release from the cradle, the child's arms might be freed for varying intervals two or three or four times a day.

An infant's movements are sharply restricted for most of the day and all of the night by its binding to the cradleboard. Its position is varied from the vertical to the horizontal, but the infant cannot move of its own volition. This would suggest a severe limitation on its tactile experience. There is also a restriction upon its response to internal stimuli, such as anger, hunger, or pain. It cannot kick or wriggle; it can only cry or refuse to suck or swallow. Leighton and Kluckhohn suggest that the desire for bodily movement may be lost after repeated frustration. I believe another more physiological explanation is possible. The snugness of the cradleboard continues the snugness of the womb, and far from feeling frustrated by the restriction of movement the baby may feel a great deal more secure than he would be were he abandoned to the insecurity of the open space of a crib. The mother carries the cradleboarded baby wherever she goes, on her back, and placed upright when she is spinning or similarly engaged, so that the child may always see her. In the cradle he receives a great deal of tactile stimulation from his mother and everyone else, for his face is continually being patted and caressed, and the cradled baby joggled by relatives and others. Furthermore, the cradle permits the baby to be comfortably in an upright position so that he is able to keep in touch with what is going on around much more effectively than the baby who is lying down. The fact of interest is that far from being restricted in the cradle, the Indian infant greatly enjoys its comforts, and will often cry to be returned to it.

When one observes the spasmodic movements of babies during the first two or three weeks, and especially soon after they have been born, one cannot help being struck by their resemblance to the movements of a person falling through space. May it not be that with the removal from the snug comfort and support of the womb to the open space of a crib the baby experiences something of a similar feeling of insecurity—something the cradleboard and swaddling serve to prevent? May it not be that the complete lack of fear of great heights exhibited by American Indians, which makes them such popular and successful construction workers on skyscrapers, is related to their early cradleboard experience? Leighton and Kluckhohn comment upon the missionaries, teachers, and others who urge the Navaho mothers "to give up those savage cradles and use cribs like civilized folks," that it should never be forgotten that every people's way of life represents their particular set of solutions to the conditions of life with which they have been confronted. With the cradleboard they appear to have come a great deal nearer to providing the baby with a far superior environment than the modern crib.

The experience on the cradleboard in no way retards the motor development of the child. Hopi infants who have been kept on the cradleboard walk no later than those who have not experienced it at all, and show no differences whatever in motor skills. Indeed, the pediatrician Margaret Fries suggests that the practice of propping the cradled child in an upright position before he can even crawl may facilitate his motor development. Balance and vision are then in the same plane as when the child is walking. His legs are kept constantly extended, with the feet flexed against the footboard in the position for standing.

A white mother, a teacher living in Arizona, has written of the great advantages of the cradleboard on which she raised her own infants. Mrs. Louise Calley points out that the child feels snug and secure on the cradleboard, as if someone were holding him tightly and continuously. The child is more comfortable on the board for any prolonged period than he can possibly be in someone's arms. In the evening her son would be rocked and sung to sleep in his own cradle made to fit his growing size, instead of being plunked into a big cagelike bed. He was always sleeping in a familiar bed no matter where his parents might be. Mrs. Calley states that one of her sons would not go to sleep unless strapped on the cradleboard for the first eight months of his life. He always gratefully acquiesced in going back to the board after his abundant romps, and would voluntarily put his arms to his sides ready to be strapped in. "Surely," Mrs. Calley remarks, "the Indians have been ahead of their white brothers in the art of childrearing."

Far, then, from tight binding and swaddling exerting any unfavorable effects upon the development of the child, the very opposite seems to be true. These practices would seem to have real psychological advantages, in no way interfering with the motor development of the child and, if anything, affording him more tactile satisfactions than many children receive in non-cradleboard cultures.

BABY CARRIERS AND INFANT DEVELOPMENT. Among the primates, babies are carried in their mothers' arms, and very quickly the babies begin clinging to the mother's fur, riding on the mother's back or clinging to the front, forms of transport they are free to claim whenever they wish. Human infants do not enjoy such an advantage, and to be carried they are completely dependent upon the mother's support. Different peoples have devised all sorts of baby carriers. Among the Australian aborigines, babies were often carried in a wooden receptacle, which at other times would be used for domestic purposes or as a dish. In many parts of Africa, the young are carried in a net facing the mother, the net often hanging from her head or neck. Among the Eskimo, the infant is carried in the *amauti* on the mother's back, a position that seems to be favored by most peoples.

In a study of ten gatherer-hunter societies, Lozoff and Brittenham found that infants are carried or held more than half the day until they begin to crawl. The sling or flexible pouch in which they are carried allows them to mold their body to that of the mother. Contact is as continuous as it can be by day and by night. Breastfeeding, on demand, lasts for several years. When not at the breast the infant, unless swaddled, enjoys complete freedom to move about. Care is uniformly affectionate, with immediate nurturant response to a cry or discomfort. "The close responsive relationships," the authors write, "and extensive body contact, do not seem to create overly dependent children. Autonomy and independence are generally early and gradual, so that by two to four years of age children spent more than half the day away from the mother in company of peers. Usually the father is frequently involved with the child."

Drs. Nicholas Cunningham and Elizabeth Ainsfield have been interested in determining how a mother's carrying of her infant in a soft baby carrier during the first months of life affects the mother-infant relationship as well as the infant's development. Preliminary results reveal significant differences between a control group and an experimental group of fifteen babies each. Soft-carrier mothers and infants, it was found, are more responsive and more coordinated with one another than the controls in hard-seat carriers. Significantly fewer soft-seat infants averted their faces from their mothers, and they look more into their mothers' faces. Mother and infant vocalize more often in the soft-carrier group. In many instances in the hard-seat infants the mothers talked a lot, but the babies did not respond. Mothers who are responsive to their infants at an early age often have infants who at one and one and a half years are more advanced in their cognitive and linguistic development than their peers. Cunningham suggests that in order to forestall the possibility of child neglect and abuse, soft baby carriers could be introduced as an intervention in clinic populations with the aim of fostering better relations between mother and infant, and reducing the chances of child abuse and neglect.

MOTHER, FATHER, CHILD, AND SKIN. In the symbiotic relationship in which the infant is programmed to continue with his mother, skin contact, as we have seen, plays a fundamental role. It is a communication which the father is also designed to make through the skin, if not in quite as massive and continuous a manner as the mother. But in civilized societies men are even more enveloped by clothes than women, and so this important cutaneous means of early communication between father and child tends to be nullified by this artificial barrier. A basic factor in the development of the ability to love is the growing reciprocal involvement in the source from which the pleasure-giving sensory stimulations are received. Between mother and child there is normally an exchange of pleasure-giving experiences. The father, in civilized societies, is to a large extent deprived of the possibility of such direct reciprocal pleasure-giving exchanges. It is, therefore, not surprising that children in these societies should develop such close identifications with the mother.

The male in all societies is at greater risk in this, as in all other connections. As Ritchie has pointed out, "The female, as she grows and develops, has before her in more or less continuous direct relationship, the model of her mother. The man, as he goes through life, begins his life also in primary relationship to a maternal object but he has to give it up, he has to leave off identification with the mother, he has to take on the full male role. Males have to switch identification during development, and all sorts of things can go wrong in this."And, unfortunately, they frequently do. The male has a much harder time than the female does, in growing up and separating himself from the loving mother, and in identifying himself with a father with whom he is nowhere nearly as deeply involved as he remains with the mother; this often puts some strain upon him. The switch in identification he is called upon to make results in something of a conflict. This he usually seeks to resolve by, in part, rejecting the mother and relegating her to a status inferior to that into which he has, so to speak, been thrust. Masculine antifeminism can be regarded as a reaction-formation designed to oppose the strong unconscious trend toward mother-worship. When the male's defenses are down, when he is *in extremis,* when he is dying, his last, like his first word, is likely to be *mother,* in a resurgence of his feeling for the mother he has never really repudiated, but from whom, at the overt level, he has been forced to disengage himself.

If in our culture we could learn to understand the importance of fathers as well as mothers giving their infants adequate tactile satisfactions, we would be taking a considerable step toward the improvement of human relations. There is nothing to prevent a father from bathing his infant child, from drying it, fondling it, caressing it, cuddling it, changing its diapers and cleaning it, from holding it, rocking it, carrying it, playing with it, and continuing to give it a good deal of affectionate tactile stimulation. The only thing that stands in the way of such behavior on the part of males is the ancient and outmoded tradition that such conduct is feminine and therefore unbecoming a male. Fortunately, this is a tradition which is rapidly breaking down; increasingly one sees young fathers involved with their children very much more deeply and in all sorts of "feminine" ways which only a generation or so ago were considered beneath the dignity of a "real" male. Dignity, as Laurence Sterne observed, is usually a mysterious carriage of the body calculated to conceal the infirmities of the mind.

There is good evidence that a strong bond of attachment is capable of being formed between father and child within the first few days of its life, and also of being reinforced by his subsequent attentions to the infant. Not only this, Dr. Ross D. Parke of Madison, Wisconsin, in an investigation of the interaction between middle-class fathers with their two- to four-day-old infants found that in the triadic situation—mother, father, and infant together in the mother's hospital room—the father tends to hold the baby nearly twice as much as the mother, vocalizes more, touches the baby slightly more, and smiles at the baby significantly less than the mother. The father's presence significantly influenced the mother's emotional state. In the presence of the father, mothers smiled more at their infant and explored more.

Dr. Parke tentatively concluded that the father is much more involved in his infant and responsive to it than our culture has acknowledged; that the practice of excluding the father from early interaction with his infant merely reflects and reinforces a cultural stereotype. A critical issue for Dr. Parke is that the care of infants be acknowledged as natural and appropriate male behavior.

Winnicott has observed that the physical holding of the child is a form of loving; that it is, in fact, perhaps the principal way in which a mother can show the infant her love for it. This is equally true for the father or, for that matter, for anyone else. And as Winnicott says, "There are those who can love an infant and there are those who cannot; the latter quickly produce in the infant a sense of insecurity, and distressed crying."

TACTILE STIMULATION AND THE EXPRESSION OF HOSTILITY. During the nineteenth century, and probably also in earlier centuries, males in the Western world often indulged in the peculiar custom of greeting children with noxious manipulations of their skin. Such practices lasted well into the twentieth century. The victims of these assaults must have been sorely puzzled by such behavior and in some cases probably developed strange ideas concerning the relationships between skin, pain, and the putative demonstration of affection. It is of interest to note that males exclusively were guilty of such sadistic practices, and then usually only toward male children, although girls with braids did not entirely escape their attentions. A favorite trick was to grasp the child's cheek between thumb and forefinger and give it a thorough tweak, or the ear might be so treated or pulled or given an even more painful flick with a finger. Graham Greene in his autobiography, *A Sort of Life,* tells how, when he was eight years old, his schoolmaster at Berkhamsted "indulged his jovial ogrish habit of screwing a fist in one's cheek till it hurt." Hair-mussing, pinching, a spank on the bottom or a push were among the other engaging indignities to which children, all in the guise of affection, were subjected. A hearty slap on the back was usually reserved for older adolescent boys and males up to middle age. Such demonstrations of affection by painful attacks on the skin could only have been performed by individuals who had themselves been the victims of similar abnormal treatment.

Just as those who have been inadequately loved, or have been frustrated in their need for love as infants, will exhibit a great deal of hostility in their verbal activities, so too those who have been failed in the experience of tactile affection will often be awkward and crude in their attempts at demonstrations of such affection. There are men who almost crush the hand they shake when introduced to another male, who with their familiars punch them in the chest or abdomen, as a mark of affection. The same males tend to be rough, awkward, and crude with "the gentler sex." Since a lacklove infancy and the privation of tactile affection generally go together, it is not surprising to find that the unloved child grows up to be not only awkward in his demonstrations of love, but also awkward in his body relationships toward others. Such persons rub others the wrong way because they have been failed in the experience of being stroked the right way.

There has been a great change in the earlier forms of hostile demonstration of "affection" towards boys, but what remains is the expression of anger towards the child in the form of aggressive tactilisms, such as slapping, spanking, or shoving. "Corporal punishment" is still widely practiced throughout the Western world, and the skin not only made a target and a vehicle for the experience of pain, but an organ which is directly associated with anger, punishment, sin, aggression, naughtiness, and evil. As Lawrence Frank has remarked,

> Spanking and slapping are often used to punish a child, utilizing this tactual sensitivity as the chief mode of making him suffer, thus depriving him of his usual comforting, and giving instead painful contacts.
>
> This infantile tactuality, like his other organic needs, is gradually transformed as the child learns to accept mother's voice as a surrogate, her reassuring tones of voice giving him an equivalent for his close physical contacts, her angry scolding voice serving as a punishment and making him cry as if hit.

An unkind remark "hurts" just as if it were a slap or a painful blow to the body. A cutting remark causes its target to "bleed" just as if his skin were slashed. Words may also "sting to the quick."

Class differences in the use of angry words containing the threat of tactile punishment were very marked in Clay's study. The working-class mothers used words harshly, the middle class used them sparingly, while the upper class "used them most often in a kind of affectionate play and, more than the other classes, they combined touch and words."

Some parents, particularly fathers, make it a point to tell their children before they strap them why they are being punished. One can thus learn to dissociate the infliction of bodily pain from the display of any emotion at all. The Nazis were particularly adept at this, and there can be little doubt, as we have seen, that their affectless inhumanity was in no little part due to their early conditioning, with tactile experience largely neglected or else restricted to a punishing kind.* This would seem to be an especially undesirable form of conditioning.

The canings, usually administered by senior prefects, customary in English public schools, during which any display of emotion on the part of either the caner or his victim was strictly tabooed, undoubtedly served to produce a dissociation between pain and emotion. Hence, one could not only remain uninvolved with the pain of others, but inflict it upon them without in any way feeling that one was being anything but just. Hence, the great pleasure educated Englishmen have often taken in wit that was cruel, accompanied by a complete indifference to the consequences of their conduct.†

TATTOOING. One wonders whether those dermatological graffiti known as tattoos may not be related to an exhibitionistic desire to reward oneself and one's skin through a regressively painful experience resulting in a permanent embellishment or disfiguration of the abused organ. The tattoo has been seen as a defense practiced by those who expect to be attacked and who arm themselves this way by emphasizing appearances. This explanation would appear to fit the elaborate tattooing to which the Japanese *yakuza* or gangsters submit themselves, and who in the feudal period grew to be a symbol of resistance to despotism. Florence Rome, who made a special study of the *yakuza,* says that "Because it was such a test of strength to endure the pain of tattooing, it began to take on other aspects—manliness, courage, health, vitality and so on—and the *yakuza* in adhering to this custom feel themselves to be the possessors of such attributes."

Similar motivations appear to be at work among young

* For an illuminating discussion of these matters see Alice Miller's *For Your Own Good* (New York: Farrar, Straus & Giroux, 1983).

† This was strikingly exhibited in the English film *If,* widely seen in the United States in 1969.

gang members and delinquents in the Occident as well as in the Orient. Dr. J. H. Burma, in a study of tattooing among male delinquents in one school, found 67 percent to have tattoos. In a similar school for girls, 33 percent were found to be tattooed. There was an average of five to ten different kinds of tattoos over their bodies, and most were in clearly visible places, a greater proportion being visible in boys than in girls. The words and phrases associated with the tattoos frequently revealed identification with a gang or a significant friend. The delinquents themselves were not unaware of the fact that their tattoos advertised their affiliation with power sources. It is a way of declaring: "I am such and such a kind of a person and you can expect me to behave in certain brave, strong, forceful ways."

In the United States about 10 percent of the population is tattooed. Males are much more commonly tattooed than females. It is said that tattooing increases in frequency during periods of crisis.

The motivations for tattooing are probably many. In Egypt, tattooing is believed to confer sexual potency on both male and female, and, indeed, is considered sexually attractive by each sex. In Iraq, tattooing was used to induce and also to maintain pregnancy. Since the custom has been virtually worldwide and practiced for every conceivable reason, it would be folly to attempt to attribute it to a single cause. However, whatever the cause—initiation, religious, sexual, ostentation, prestige—the element of self-gratification can be seen to run like a red thread through all the ostensible motivations. This is clearly evident in the tattoos with which so many sailors and soldiers, long deprived of the society of women, choose to decorate their bodies—usually their arms. The sexual motif is often quite explicit, and its presence obviously gratifying. The tattoo legitimizes a continuous erotic involvement.

THE DECORATED BODY. The skin has provided the canvas for virtually every society which has engaged in treating the human body as art. Through such artificial means as tattooing, scarification, and body painting, naked skin becomes a living ornament. The human body is a living mirror held out to the world. Nude, masked, painted, or adorned, it has the power to attract, charm, captivate, frighten, or seduce. Each society has found its own ways of decorating, and thus celebrating, the human form. In those societies that have maintained direct and permanent contact with nature, "the combination" as André Virél has put it, "of naked skin and adornment accompanies, commemorates, or simply suggests birth, love, and death. Newborn babies, men and women toiling day after day, engaged couples, circumcised boys, excised girls, dancers—we always see their naked bodies as *celebrating* bodies."

In every society the individual, through the canvas of his body, makes statements to the world, whether idiosyncratic, customary, ritual, decorative, or mere embellishment. It is always, more or less, an act of communication.

CORPORAL PUNISHMENT. It is astonishing to find how widely the barbarism of spanking children is still defended—principally among members of the working classes. A group of such women whom I met in June 1976, and still another on a TV talk show in the winter of 1982, maintained that spanking was good for children. Two of the most articulate proponents of this view mentioned that they had divorced their husbands because they were wife-beaters. When I asked them whether they did not think it possible that parent-beaten boys might later become wife-beaters, they considered the suggestion absurd.

It is becoming increasingly evident that parents who become child batterers and abusers were in most cases themselves neglected and abused as children. In the dozen or more studies thus far reported, it was found that 25 percent and more of batterers had themselves suffered separation from the mother.

Dr. Henry Kempe of the University of Colorado Medical School has stated that the most important indicator of whether a child will be abused is the mother's attitude at the time of the baby's birth. If she does not smile, does not want to see and hold the baby, and if the father behaves in the same way, they will need help in raising the child. Since some several thousand children die of abuse annually in the United States, the follow-up of such families is imperative.

Dr. Ray Helfer in a study of about one hundred adolescent males brought into juvenile court found that more than 85 percent had abusive parents and suffered very negative experiences as children. Abusive parents cannot identify one friend who would help them in time of trouble, and a significant number tend to have phones with unlisted numbers. The prematurity rate of abused children is twice that of the general population, and the cesarean section rate is many times more than that.

Professor Selma Fraiberg, in discussing Dr. Helfer's paper, stated that although all the battering parents she had studied remembered the actual abuse they had suffered in childhood in stunning and chilling detail, they did not remember the effect of the experience—that is, being abused and injured. When her group could help such parents reach the point of saying, "Oh, God, how I hated him when he would get that strap and lay me out and begin to beat me. Oh, how I hated him," only then could some progress be made. When her group helped the parents to remember the anxiety and the sense of terror that had come over them with the abuse of a powerful parent, they could demonstrate that the parents' behavior toward their own children changed. Thus, it was with the actual reexperiencing of the terrifying feelings involved that changes occurred.

In immediate anticipation of a spanking and during the assault the child is often terrified, exhibiting all the accompaniments of extreme fear, pallor, muscle rigidity, accelerated heartbeat, and weeping. In later years, under conditions of emotional upset persons who have undergone such childhood experiences will frequently exhibit similar reactions. Or in an effort to defend themselves against the autonomic discharge of feeling, they will "bite their lips," grow rigid, or clasp one hand with the other in a firm grip. This is a way, like keeping "a stiff upper lip," of preventing one's emotions from expressing themselves, of holding back the tears, of bracing oneself for the blow by employing muscle tension. Muscle tension as a method of keeping emotionally disturbing feelings under control has been remarked by many observers. Or one can dig one's nails into the palms of one's hands until they bleed, in an effort to counteract the expression of emotion, or use the skin ambivalently as a means of both drawing attention to one's needs and at the same time rejecting the other. As Clemens Benda has put it, "Skin diseases vividly demonstrate the difficulties of maintaining contact—a sore skin, a running nose, an infected mouth—each area of external or internal contact is a possible spot for an interference with the even flow of human exchange."

It is here being suggested that behavior of this kind is significantly related to the tactile experiences of the individual during infancy and childhood.

The weeping which is usually associated with physical punishment in childhood may, in later years, express itself in weeping through the skin. Kepecs and his co-workers in a series of ingenious experiments have shown that in emotional weeping the visible expression "is not limited in its effects to the lacrimal glands, but also finds expression in other parts of the body, including the skin." Having, under hypnosis, induced an artificial cantharides blister in the skin of their experimental subjects, the investigators then induced various emotional states in them and measured the amount of fluid exudation into the blister site. Emotional states were associated with a rise in the exudation rate, especially in weeping; the heavier the weeping, the higher the exudation rate. Interestingly enough, as would be expected, inhibition of weeping was associated first with a fall and then with a great rise in exudation rate. Thus, the male of the English-speaking world who is everywhere taught that "a little man" doesn't cry, having repeatedly been caused to repress his desire to weep until he has become incapable of weeping from his lacrimal glands, often begins, in later life, to weep through his skin or his gastrointestinal tract.

It is now well established that in a large proportion of cases of atopic dermatitis, there is associated a strong but inhibited desire to weep.

INFANT-DIRECTED TACTILE BEHAVIOR TOWARD THE MOTHER. Harlow has made it clear, in his studies of rhesus monkeys, that the most important of the young animal's experiences, for its subsequent development, is bodily contact with its mother, and so it is with the young of *Homo sapiens*.

The four phases of the child-mother affectional system, in both human infants and infant monkeys, are: (1) a reflex stage in which the infant reacts automatically to the stimuli presented by the mother; (2) a stage of affectionate attachment; (3) a security stage; and (4) a stage of independence. The reflex stage lasts only a few weeks in rhesus monkeys and a few months in human infants. The phase of affectionate attachment begins in the human infant within the first thirty minutes after birth, but it is not until between two and three months of age that this becomes very evident in the infant's behavior. By smiling, cuddling, gurgling, and the like the baby begins to show active voluntary affection for its mother. The primary tie to the mother appears to operate, in the rhesus monkey, through the two systems of nursing and contacting; these are primarily operative during the first year. Clinging and following—that is, visual and auditory responsiveness to the mother—are at their peak in the second year.

The third stage, the security stage, follows shortly after the commencement of the attachment phase. The so-called six-months anxiety is thought to mark the beginning of this phase, which is considered to be the period at which the infant begins to experience visually induced fear reactions. However, in the human infant visually induced fear reactions may occur as early as the end of the second week. Fear of heights seems to develop only after the infant has had some experience of locomotion. Among the maternal responses to the infant at this stage are acts of comfort, protection, and reassurance in all situations in which the infant feels fearful and insecure. Under such conditions little monkeys run to their mother and attach to her. "Within minutes or even seconds after attaching, the subject's hands and body relax and the monkey (or child) will visually explore the frightening stimulus with little or no sign of anxiety." In time, the security responses of the infant, derived from the security-giving satisfactions his mother has afforded him, enable the young monkey to leave the mother and explore the world tentatively at first, and later, more securely, for himself.

As Clay puts it, "The mother can be thought of as the center or pivot of the small child's security. As the child becomes able to move about he no longer wants to remain physically in contact with the mother; visual contact is sufficient. The concept of behavior distance can be used to explain the distance from the mother that the mobile child is able to experience comfortably." As a child grows older in the socialization process, behavior distance is increased.

In her study Clay found that it was the nonwalking toddlers who spent most time in contact with their mothers. It was at this period that the children's affectionate attachment to their mothers was at its height. As soon as the child is able to walk, his independent forays away from the mother in the "exhilaration of his new mobility and excitement of learning about the world around him" grow more frequent. His independence, however, is tentative, for he must maintain visual contact with his mother or know where she is in order to feel safe.

The child, Clay found, who had not experienced satisfactory tactile contact with his mother did not make any tactile approaches to her. There were two examples of this behavior, both of them in children in the crawling stage, who stayed away from their mothers during the period when affectionate attachment is usually at its height. However, it appeared that children who had experienced a highly satisfactory tactile relationship with the mother did not come to the mother for more. Finally, overanxious children tended to have very high tactile needs, a condition which showed itself in the physical use of the mother as a haven of security. One of these children had suffered from inadequate maternal responsiveness, while two others appeared to be reacting to marital difficulties between their parents. "Like the infant monkeys, all three children clung to their mothers and were unable, except for relatively short sallies, to go out, explore and play in the environment."

In Clay's group middle-class children expressed more tactual affection towards their mothers than did the children of the other two classes. Clay suggests that this may have been due to the greater duration of tactile contact they received in the neonate and just-walking stages of development.

The Harlows remark that "all the mother-infant interactions relating to nursing, bodily contact, and following-imitation contribute to security, although there is evidence that sheer bodily contact-comfort is the dominant variable in the rhesus monkey." This appears also to be the case in the human infant.

MATERNAL-DIRECTED BEHAVIOR TOWARD THE INFANT. Drs. Anna Kulka, Carol Fry, and Fred Goldstein have observed that while one of the most important pleasures a mother derives is from contact with her baby, they have seen babies who have received too little cuddling, resulting in an accumulation of muscular tension in the infant.* Such babies become very difficult for the mother to hold. The baby seems to want to squirm out of her arms, and the mother is likely to report that the baby "doesn't want to be held." This seeming rejection of the mother by the baby is distressing to the mother, making her feel inadequate or angry at the baby and thereby perpetuating a vicious circle between the two.

In many instances, Dr. Kulka was able to convince the mother that with the proper persistence and the proper sort of

---

* Dr. Carol Fry measured the tension in such infants, and also under other conditions, by careful myoelectric studies, which unfortunately were cut short by her premature death. She had shown me her detailed records, which were very impressive. There were remarkable differences in muscle tension in infants who were being happily breastfed contrasted with those who were being breastfed by less involved mothers.

handling and holding, the baby would respond by completely relaxing.

CONTACT AND PLAY. The importance of play in learning is now recognized by almost everyone, and, as Harlow has pointed out, all forms of play behavior reduce to expressions of the fundamental motive of exploration and manipulation. "Social play is preceded by exploration of the physical environment and play with inanimate objects, and apparently social exploration and play take precedence over environmental exploration and play because of the greater regard and feedback given by animate rather than inanimate objects."

Among the monkeys observed by the Harlows, object exploration preceded social exploration, and each involved three identifiable components: (1) a visual exploration, in which the monkey orients closely to, and peers intently at, the object or other animal; (2) an oral exploration, a gentle mouthing response; and (3) a tactual exploration, limited to a transient clasp, either of a physical object or of another animal. Here, once more, we perceive that the tactile sense remains the dominant one, and it is important to note that these components are not separate but interrelated, so that when one speaks of visual exploration, this is not to be construed as a behavior unrelated to the tactual-oral explorations, but coordinated with them.

In the rhesus monkey close physical ties between infant and mother must cease before play can develop with agemates and peers. Here, too, three stages may be identified: (1) a reflex stage; (2) a manipulation stage; and (3) a stage of interactive play. In the reflex stage during the early weeks of life, infants will fixate each other visually and make approach attempts. If they contact each other, they cling to one another reflexly as they do to their mothers. When two infants are involved, they cling in a ventral-to-ventral manner; if more than two are involved, they will cling in a typical "choo-choo" pattern. In the manipulation stage, beginning at the end of the first month, the infants explore each other as they would objects, with eyes, hands, mouth, and body, alternating manipulation of agemates with manipulation of the physical environment. Like the preceding stage, this is a presocial period in peer relationships, the exploratory activity characterizing it persisting into the stage of interactive play. As they come to learn more from their experiences of each other, they gradually begin to respond to one another as social rather than as physical objects, and social play emerges from the matrix of manipulatory play. The third stage, interactive play, marks the development of genuine social interactions between peers. This occurs at about three months of age, and overlaps with manipulatory play and sequence of exploration of the physical environment. Interactive play develops in the human infant during the second year of life.

Clay observed a pattern of development of play behavior in her subjects consisting of alternating periods of mother-child interaction, followed by periods of play at a distance from the mother, with a subsequent return to her for further communication.

As the child grows older and extends his behavior distance, the time actually in contact with the mother, or next to her, decreases and the time spent away from her increases. The kinds of contact and the kinds of feedback that the child requires from the mother for his emotional well-being change also. Where at first the small child or toddler might want to sit upon the mother's lap for several minutes, the actively mobile child may just run up to his mother and say, "Hi!" This kind of psychological tagging in at the source of security is a pattern that was observed for almost all the children. It was especially noticeable among the older children whose mothers allowed them a larger circle of play.

The "tagging in" is especially important in making certain that contact is still maintained, especially when one is beginning to explore other parts of the world for oneself. As Clay found, with time the child comes to depend less and less upon his mother for physical contact, and devotes more and more time to play away from her. At the younger ages he is still not ready to play independently at any remove from her for more than short periods of time. He still needs the reassurance of contact with her, to keep in touch both physically and visually.

As Clay emphasizes, the young of all mammals must learn to play. The development of the ability to play in relation to the mother will depend on whether or not the infant's tentatively playful approaches are rewarded. Working-class mothers apparently do not encourage their young to play with them as much as middle-class and upper-class mothers do—the upper-class children, in Clay's study, make more tactile play approaches to their mothers than do middle-class children.

Interestingly, Clay found that mothers who did not give their youngsters much tactile stimulation nevertheless encouraged their children to play with them. It was almost as though the direct physical contact and the feelings it arouses were considered uncomfortable, but that physical contact, through games, mediated often through objects like a ball, a picnic spoon, or a popsicle stick, were acceptable substitutes.

Clay refers to Williams' study of tactility among the Dusun of Borneo, in which he called attention to the need to study " . . . ways in which individuals are required, or expected, to relinquish particular tactile experiences and develop compensatory symbolic substitutes at different periods in enculturation." This kind of learning of symbolic substitutes for tactility is seen in the behavior of the children who approached their mothers with various play objects. And it is important to understand that a great many other forms of symbolic learning of a similar kind constitute but an extension of the learning based on the mind of the skin.

Tsumori has shown how important the prolonged experience of exploratory play activities is in the development and discovery of new adaptive behaviors in Japanese macaques, and Hall makes it quite clear that much of the later behavior of the nonhuman primate is learned in social situations and practiced in play.

These observations hold true with even greater force in the human species.*

The separation or detachment from the mother in all mammals plays an important role in the initiation and extension of the infant's contacts with the rest of the world. As Rheingold and Eckerman point out, even when the infant is carried about, his contacts with the world are necessarily circumscribed. Only when he leaves his mother's side by himself can many new kinds of learning occur.

> The infant comes in contact with an increasing number and variety of objects. Through touching them he learns their shapes, dimensions, slopes, edges, and textures. He also fingers, grasps, pushes, and pulls, and thus learns the material variables of heaviness, mass, and rigidity, as well as the changes in visual and auditory stimuli that some objects provide. He moves from place to place within a room, and from one room to another. From the consequent changes in visual experience, coupled with his own kinesthetic sensations, he learns the position of objects relative to other objects. He also learns the invariant nature of many sources of stimulation. In a word, he learns the properties of the physical world, including the principles of object constancy and the conservation of matter.

It is a striking characteristic of monkeys and apes that they are strongly moved to touch any object that interests them. This is true of humans even more markedly, unless they have

* For several other valuable books on play, see J. Huizinga, *Homo Ludens* (New York: Roy Publishers, 1950); H. C. Lehman and P. A. Witty, *The Psychology of Play Activities* (New York: A. S. Barnes, 1927); P. A. Jewell and C. Loizos (eds.), *Play, Exploration and Territory* (New York: Academic Press, 1966); S. Miller, *The Psychology of Play* (Baltimore: Penguin Books, 1968); J. S. Bruner, A. Jolly, and K. Sylva (eds.), *Play: Its Role in Development and Evolution* (New York: Basic Books, 1976); J. N. Lieberman, *Playfulness: Its Relationship to Imagination and Creativity* (New York: Academic Press, 1977); Marie W. Piers (ed.), *Play and Development* (New York: Norton, 1972); Catherine Garvey, *Play* (Cambridge: Harvard University Press, 1977); Robert Fagen, *Animal Play Behavior* (New York: Oxford University Press, 1981); Roger Callois, *Man, Play and Games* (New York: Free Press, 1961).

been conditioned to believe that to touch is ill-bred. To touch means to communicate, to become part of, to possess. Whatever I touch becomes part of me, I possess. When I am touched by another, that other transfers part of himself to me. When I touch another I transfer part of myself to them. When I touch a relic, the person to whom it once belonged is, as it were, touched by me, and has in turn touched me. An autograph letter by a famous person delights us because it is the touch of his hand that we vicariously experience. There is an immortality, a continuity, which we feel when we touch things that others have touched who are no longer with us, through such things we feel their lives touching ours. Even in our ordinary correspondence we expect the typewritten letter to be subscribed by hand.

TICKLING. The sensation of tickling is produced by light stroking of the skin, especially in certain sensitive areas, such as the armpits, the sides of the body, between the toes, and the soles of the feet. Fused with the light pressure sensation is considerable feeling tone and impulses to laughter and spasmodic withdrawal movements—which may be uncontrollable. Despite the tendency to withdrawal, tickling may be pleasant, children especially seeking it. The sensation is particularly strong when least expected. Many years ago, I knew a young chimpanzee, Meshie, a female, who particularly delighted in being tickled.

Tickling is particularly interesting because it is not possible to tickle oneself—that is, to respond with laughter to the tickling. Infants begin to laugh between the fourth and the eighth month, and respond most easily with laughter between the fourth and the sixth months.

It has been observed that children laugh more frequently in social settings than when they are alone. The laughter evoked by tickling appears to depend entirely upon the social situation. For example, it is difficult, if not impossible, to be tickled into laughter under unfavorable conditions or by persons one dislikes. As Darwin remarked, in what is still the best discussion of tickling, "The imagination is sometimes said to be tickled by a ludicrous idea; and this so-called tickling of the mind is curiously analogous with that of the body."

In a study of sixty preschool-age boys and girls representing three different ethnic groups, all American-born, white American, Afro-American, and Cape Verdean, Dr. Nancy Blackman of the University of Rhode Island found that tickling was experienced as the most intense of sensations. She points out that tickling is more overtly calculated to be an act of tactile stimulation, and that this is the unique character of tickling. All three groups of children indicated that the abdomen and armpits were their favorite tickling places. The Afro-American children preferred the abdomen to be tickled. The minority children pinpointed more specific areas where they are tickled by their fathers. The white parents were found to be the least ticklers of the group.

Why the armpits, the abdomen and the sides of the trunk, the sides of the knees, and the soles of the feet, should be so susceptible to tickling remains unexplained. The three anthropoid apes, orangutan, chimpanzee, and gorilla, are all fond of tickling, especially when young, so the trait is probably an ancient hominoid one. As humans grow older the capacity for being tickled appears to decline.

CONTACT, INDIVIDUATION, AND AFFECTION. Awareness of self is largely a matter of tactile experience. Whether we are walking, standing, sitting, lying, running, or jumping, whatever the other messages we receive from muscle, joint, and other tissue, the first and most extensive of these messages are received from the skin. Long before body temperature either falls or rises from external causes, it is the skin that will register the change and communicate to the cortex the necessary messages designed to initiate those behaviors which will lead to the appropriate response.

In separating himself from the mother, the exploratory activities in which the infant engages, though based on what he sees, fundamentally constitute an extension of learning through tactile experience. Vision endows the tactile experience with a formal meaning, but it is the tactile meanings which largely endow the objects seen with form and dimension.

In summarizing the results of her study, Clay concludes: "The question that we have been pursuing in this project, whether the amount and kind of tactile stimulation and contact that American mothers give their babies and young children is adequate to their physiological and emotional needs, must therefore be answered negatively." The mothers observed at the beach were not so much concerned with holding, cradling, cuddling, caressing, or expressing love to their babies and young children, as with controlling their behavior and attending to their nurturance needs. "Comforting, playing and giving tactile affection were maternal behaviors of much less importance and frequency." Repeatedly Clay observed that tactile contact between mothers and preverbal children most often expressed caretaking and nurturance, rather than love and affection.

The impersonal childrearing practices that have long been the mode in the United States, with the early severance of the mother-child tie, and the separation of mothers and children by the interposition of bottles, blankets, clothes, carriages, cribs, and other physical objects, will produce individuals who are able to lead lonely, isolated lives in the crowded urban world, with its materialistic values and its addiction to things. Clay properly feels that perhaps a higher degree of closeness within the family, commencing with the primary mother-child tactile tie, would help Americans to feel somewhat more anchored in the family, while an acceptance of the importance of emotional tactile needs beyond childhood might help them to withstand the impersonal pressures of our times and the inevitable vicissitudes of life.

This is, perhaps, expecting too much of touch relationships within the family, but the common adoption of such tactile practices is certainly a consummation devoutly to be wished. The contemporary American family constitutes only too often an institution for the systematic production of mental illness in each of its members, as a consequence of its concentration on making each of them a "success." Which, in practice, means that the individual is gradually converted into a device with a built-in design for achievement in accordance with the prevailing requirements, entailing the suppression of emotion, the denial of love and friendship, the ability to trade with whatever serves one for a conscience, while conveying an unvarying appearance of rectitude. Toward this end, parents feel that they must not give their children "too much" affection, even in the reflex and affectionate stages when children, so much in need of it, literally cannot receive too much affection. All sorts of reasons and rationalizations are produced: the child will be spoiled, he will become too dependent upon others, he will develop abnormal interests in his mother, or in other boys or even girls, he will become feminine, and so on. The cultural goal is to make "a he-man" of the male, and a successful manipulator of her world of the female. Given the emphasis on such goals, whether consciously or unconsciously followed, the success-oriented American would still constitute the problem he presents, no matter how adequate the tactile experience of the young might be. The importance of tactility in the socialization process, therefore, is not likely to be overemphasized, nor should it be, as it has been, underemphasized.

The importance of tactile experience, especially in the preverbal stages of human development, cannot, in fact, be overemphasized, and it is the burden of this book to convey that message.

9 Touch and Age

The wiser mind
Mourns less for what age takes away
Than what it leaves behind.

—Wordsworth,
The Fountain.

Everyone wants to live long, but no one wants to grow old, for old age, as someone has aptly put it, is a dirty trick. The answer to that, of course, is to die young—as late as possible. But that is mainly a matter of the spirit. In most cases the body wears out long before we are ready to vacate the premises. Diseases and disorders may increase, and increase in severity; strength, energy, and mobility may be reduced.

Aging often brings limitations due to health problems or disability, but this does not have to bring an end to the quality of life, for while the premises inhabited may break down the spirit will flourish—if it is encouraged to. Aging is not a terminal illness, but a timeless estate, a rich inheritance. In our society the elderly are regarded as biodegradable and superfluous, instead of what they really represent: a biological elite who, with weathered wisdom, have much to offer the world. Almost universally the old have been regarded as the repositories of tradition and wisdom and the conservators of the mores. This has given them a prestige and a reverence that has seldom been ignored. But in a society in which the cult of youth has become a multibillion-dollar industry, age grading and age stratification add to the problem of the disengagement and stratification that has taken place, separating the young, the middle-aged, and the elderly from each other. These social categories constitute dividing lines which set people apart from one another, with social and political consequences of the most destructive kinds.

The young see the old as superannuated, and, with privileged disrespect, as the vernacular has it, "on the way out," and the old are inclined to accept the verdict. But the truth is that age is a special privilege which, with its accumulated wisdom and experience, is far superior to the state of unresolvedness from which it will take years for the young to emerge. By the time they emerge—if they do—they will be elderly and in safe harbor.

Aging is a poor word for growing. We must find new definitions for old words which have lost their meaning. The way to grow is to retain and develop that youthfulness of spirit which results in the wisdom and genuine youthfulness of the elderly. As the song says:

> You have a headstart
> If you are among the very young at heart.

In short, it is better to live in style, to wear out rather than to rust out. In the course of time the skin changes in character, but the spirit within us, like good wine, is capable of improving with time.

The skin presents the most visible of the evidences of aging: wrinkling, spotting, pigmentary changes, dryness, loss of elasticity, and so wearisomely on. With aging, the various tactile nerve endings undergo significant changes. The structure of nerve endings within the organized corpuscles of the skin undergoes neurofibril breakdown. Tactile or Meissner's corpuscles decrease, exhibiting marked changes in size, shape, and relationship to the epidermis. Throughout the nervous system and its appendages there is evidence of change, mostly in the form of cell and fiber loss. This is reflected in decreased acuity in the sense of touch, in the ability to sharply localize stimuli, speed of reaction to tactile stimuli, and speed of reaction to pain stimuli. One of the striking changes with age is, in many cases, the apparent loss of the great sensitivity of the palmar surfaces of the hands. The fingers and palms, in which the greatest number of neurotactile elements are located, seem as it were to have become indurated, as if the "callused" skin has undergone a loss of its ability to transmit and receive its former communications.

However, tactile needs do not seem to change with aging—if anything, they seem to increase. Yet in the Anglo-Saxon world we are taught that the tactual behavior of childhood is inappropriate in adolescents and adults. The taboo upon such behavior is almost complete for the male, for females much less so. Males as adolescents and adults may embrace their mothers, but not their fathers; a favored aunt or grandmother may also be embraced, but not their male counterparts. Males may embrace girls on certain private occasions, but may not do so publicly unless a generally accepted mutual understanding exists between them. Compared to the female, the male is culturally encouraged, in the Western world, to remain all the days of his life a virtually nontactile creature—hungering for tactual experience, and seeking it, mainly, through sexual contacts. When, in old age, the male's sexual capacities are diminished or completely reduced, the tactual hunger is more powerful than ever, for it is the only sensuous experience that remains to him. It is at this time, when he has again become so much dependent upon others for human support, that he is in need of embraces, of an arm around his shoulder, of being taken by the hand, caressed, and given the opportunity to respond. Women need such communications even more than men. Yet this is where we fail the aging quite miserably—as we do in so much else. The aged desire neither to be patronized nor tolerated, but to be understood, respected, and worthy of the love they have bestowed on others. Because we are unwilling to face the fact of aging, we behave as if it isn't there. It is this massive evasion that is the principal reason for our failure to understand the needs of the aging.

The most important and neglected of these needs is the need for tactile stimulation. One has only to observe the responses of older people to a caress, an embrace, a handpat or clasp, to appreciate how vitally necessary such experiences are for their well-being. On the basis of the kind of evidence cited in this book, it may be conjectured that the course and outcome of many an illness in the aged has been greatly influenced by the quality of tactile support the individual has received before and during the illness. Furthermore, in a substantial number of cases one may suspect that it was the individual's history of tactile experience prior to his or her illness, and particularly during it, as well as expectations of its continuation, that made the difference between life and death.

In the aged especially, the need for tactile stimulation is a hunger which has so often remained unsatisfied that, in their disappointment, its victims tend to become uncommunicative concerning their need for it. A perfunctory peck on the cheek is no substitute for a warm embrace, nor is a conventional handshake capable of replacing a caressing hand, "the only touch of love."

As Nurse Cathleen Fanslow has pointed out, the elderly often have impaired hearing, visual acuity, mobility, and vitality, problems that can make them feel helpless and vulnerable, and as she says, it is through the emotional involvement of touch that one can reach through the isolation and communicate love, trust, affection, and warmth.

It is especially in the aging that we see touching at its best as an act of spiritual grace and a continuing human sacrament.

Nothing in the whole range of English literature expresses so eloquently and poignantly the older person's need for "the touch of love" than Donna Swanson's moving poem, *Minnie Remembers*.

> *God,*
> *My hands are old.*
> *I've never said that out loud before*
> *but they are.*
> *I was so proud of them once.*
> *They were soft*

*like the velvet smoothness of a firm, ripe
peach.
Now the softness is more like worn-out sheets
or withered leaves.
When did these slender, graceful hands
become gnarled, shrunken claws?
When, God?
They lie here in my lap,
naked reminders of this worn-out
body that has served me too well!*

*How long has it been since someone touched me
Twenty years?
Twenty years I've been a widow.
Respected.
Smiled at.
But never touched.
Never held so close that loneliness
was blotted out.*

*I remember how my mother used to hold me,
God.
When I was hurt in spirit or flesh,
she would gather me close,
stroke my silky hair
and caress my back with her warm hands.
O God, I'm so lonely!*

*I remember the first boy who ever kissed me.
We were both so new at that!
The taste of young lips and popcorn,
the feeling inside of mysteries to come.*

*I remember Hank and the babies.
How else can I remember them but together?
Out of the fumbling, awkward attempts of new
lovers came the babies.
And as they grew, so did our love.
And, God, Hank didn't seem to mind
if my body thickened and faded a little.
He still loved it. And touched it.*

And we didn't mind if we were no longer beautiful.
And the children hugged me a lot.
O God, I'm lonely!

God, why didn't we raise the kids to be silly
and affectionate as well as
dignified and proper?
You see, they do their duty.
They drive up in their fine cars;
they come to my room to pay their respects.
They chatter brightly, and reminisce.
But they don't touch me.
They call me "Mom" or "Mother"
or "Grandma."

Never Minnie.
My mother called me Minnie.
So did my friends.
Hank called me Minnie, too.
But they're gone.
And so is Minnie.
Only Grandma is here.
And God! She's lonely!

Donna Swanson*

It is well known in professional circles that young nursing students tend to avoid touching elderly patients, and especially the acutely ill. Reference has already been made to this on an earlier page. Drs. Ruth McCorkle and Margaret Hollenbach, practicing nurses, have pointed out that touching as a therapeutic event is not as simple as a mechanical procedure or a drug, because it is, above all, an act of communication. From their own observations as practicing nurses, they suggest: "The use of touch and physical closeness may be the most important way to communicate to acutely ill persons that they are important as human beings and that their recovery is related to their

* From *Images, Women in Transition*, compiled by Janice Grana (Winona, Minnesota: St. Mary's College Press, 1977).

desire to improve." "Yet," they write, "patients in critical care units are seldom touched in nontechnical ways," and they conclude: "Some important questions need to be answered. Under what conditions do patients' needs for human contact take precedence over their needs for mechanical care and their own personal space? Should specific structured interventions be developed for patients in critical care environments? If so, what effects would such interventions have on recovery?"

The authors provide an example of such a structured program in the care of patients who are present for bone-marrow transplants, and who undergo multiple procedures that are particularly painful and exhausting. Such patients often feel alone, confused, and isolated. They have a 50 percent chance of survival. "They want human contact but retreat when someone touches them because their memories are filled with only the pain and not the pleasure associated with touching."

McCorkle and Hollenbach found that structured experiences in which the nurse very gradually establishes a relationship with the patient may enhance the patient's quality of living during the transplant process. The structured procedures they follow extend over five days, as follows:

Days 1 and 2: Nurse remains about five feet from patient during interaction.
Day 3: Nurse moves within three feet to interact.
Day 4: Nurse moves within one foot of patient.
Day 5: Nurse interacts with patient in some systematic non-procedural way (such as hand-holding).

Such steps have been found to be especially valuable in establishing a relationship with children and in helping them tolerate the invasive procedures. "The outcomes observed have been improved self-concept, less depression, and a shorter overall hospital stay." "Research," they recommend, "is needed if touching acutely ill patients in noninvasive ways over time will affect their sense of who they are and eventually their recovery."

And here is an address to nurses by a ninety-year-old woman, found in her locker in an English nursing home, after her death. It was called "A Crabbéd Old Woman":

> *The body it crumbles. Grace and vigor depart.*
> *There is now a stone where I once had a heart.*
> *But inside this old carcass, a young girl still dwells,*
> *And now and again my battered heart swells.*
> *I remember the pain, and I remember the joys,*
> *And I'm living and loving all over again.*
> *And I think of the years, all too few, gone too fast,*
> *And accept the stark fact that nothing will last.*
> *So open your eyes, nurse, open and see*
> *Not a crabbéd old woman.*
> *Look closer. See me.*

The expression of such feelings tells us something of the loneliness, the failure of acceptance, and the abandonment that so many of the elderly experience, who are too frequently regarded as redundant relics who have outstayed their welcome. These cruelly insensitive attitudes towards the elderly constitute a serious indictment of the values of our society—values which need to be reexamined and replaced by a view which sees age as a special privilege and the most promising of challenges, for the best of our growing still lies ahead of us.

ENVOI

Camerado, this is no book,
Who touches this touches a man.
          —Walt Whitman,
                So Long!

In the preceding pages we have seen that the human significance of touching is considerably more profound than has hitherto been understood. The skin as the sensory receptor organ which responds to contact with the sensation of touch, a sensation to which basic human meanings become attached almost from the moment of birth, is fundamental in the development of human behavior. The raw sensation of touch as stimulus is vitally necessary for the physical survival of the organism. In that since it may be postulated that the need for tactile stimulation must be added to the repertoire of basic physical needs in all vertebrates, if not in all invertebrates as well.

Basic physical needs, defined as tensions which must be satisfied if the organism is to survive, are the needs for oxygen, liquid, food, rest, activity, sleep, bowel and bladder elimination, escape from danger, and the avoidance of pain. It should be noted that sex is not a basic physical need, since the survival of the organism is not dependent upon its satisfaction. Only a certain number of organisms need satisfy sexual tensions if the species is to survive.* However that may be, the evidence points unequivocally to the fact that no organism can survive very long without externally originating cutaneous stimulation.

Cutaneous stimulation may take innumerable forms, such as those of temperature or radiation, liquid or atmospheric stimulation, pressure, and the like. Such cutaneous stimulation is clearly necessary for the physical survival of the organism. Yet even this elementary fact does not seem to have been adequately recognized. Important as such cutaneous stimulation is, the form with which we have been principally concerned in this book is tactile stimulation—that is, touching. By touching is meant the satisfying contact or feeling of another's or one's own skin. Touching may take the form of caressing, cuddling, holding, stroking or patting with the fingers or whole hand, or vary from simple body contact to the massive tactile stimulation involved in sexual intercourse.

As we have seen, in our brief survey, different cultures vary in both the manner in which they express the need for tactile stimulation and the manner in which they satisfy it. But the need is universal and is everywhere the same, though the form of its satisfaction may vary according to time and place.

The evidence presented in these pages suggests that adequate tactile satisfaction during infancy and childhood is of fundamental importance for the subsequent healthy behavioral development of the individual. The experimental and other research findings on other animals, as well as those on humans, show that tactile deprivation in infancy usually results in behavioral inadequacies in later life. Significant as these findings are, it is their practical value that is of principal interest to us. In short, how may these findings be utilized in the raising of healthy human beings?

It should be evident that in the development of the person, tactile stimulation should begin with the newborn baby. The

* For a discussion of the basic physical needs see Ashley Montagu, *The Direction of Human Development* (revised edition, New York: Hawthorn Books, 1970); for the basic behavioral needs, see Ashley Montagu, *Growing Young* (New York: McGraw-Hill, 1981).

newborn should, whenever possible, be placed in his mother's arms, and allowed to remain by her side as long as she may desire. The newborn should be put to nurse at his mother's breast as soon as possible. The newborn should not be removed to a "nursery" nor placed in a crib. The cradle should be restored to universal usage as the best auxiliary and substitute for cradling in the mother's arms ever invented. Fondling of the infant can scarcely be overdone—a reasonably sensible human being is not likely to overstimulate an infant—hence, if one is to err in any direction, it were better in the direction of too much rather than too little fondling. Instead of baby carriages, infants should be carried on their mothers' fronts or backs, and also on their fathers' fronts or backs, in the equivalent of the Chinese *madai* or Eskimo parka.

Any abrupt cessation of fondling should be avoided, and it is recommended that in cultures of the Western world, and in the United States particularly, parents express their affection for each other and for their children more demonstratively than they have in the past. It is not words so much as acts communicating affection and involvement that children, and indeed adults, require. Tactile sensations become tactile perceptions according to the meanings with which they have been invested by experience. Inadequate tactile experience will result in a lack of such associations and a consequent inability to relate to others in many fundamental human ways. When affection and involvement are conveyed through touch, it is those meanings, as well as the security-giving satisfactions, with which touch will become associated. Hence, the human significance of touching.

APPENDIX 1
Therapeutic Touch

In recent years there has developed from the practice of "laying on of hands" what has come to be called "therapeutic touch." Based on the views and practice of Dora Kunz, therapeutic touch has been developed by her student Dolores Krieger, professor of nursing at New York University. In her book *The Therapeutic Touch* (1982), Krieger tells how she learned and subsequently taught therapeutic touch, and presents the reader with the theory, and the facts—so far as they are known—upon which therapeutic touch is based. To the question of what led her to therapeutic touch, Krieger says that it came to her by way of the neurophysiology she knew, and for many years taught, as well as from what she learned in reading of the health practices of Yoga, Aruvedic, Tibetan, and Chinese medicine, as well as from *prana,* the Sanskrit name for the system of energies which refers to "the organizing factors that underlie what we call the life process," and is responsible, among other things, for such phenomena as regeneration and wound healing.

In her book, Krieger prints the accounts of many practitioners of therapeutic touch who have successfully treated conditions ranging from the quieting of crying in babies to the healing of injuries and functional disorders of various sorts. She also gives a number of case histories of self-healing by therapeutic touch. Krieger postulates that the functions of the human body occur by means of electrical conduction, and that each individual has a personal field, within and surrounding the body, which carries the charge. In therapeutic touch, the healer redirects the healee's (the ill person's) field by moving the hands on or close to the body in a more or less sweeping gesture with strong intent to heal the healee. The healer focuses herself on healing the healee. This is called "centering," the concentration of energy upon helping the healee. Centering is described as a state of altered consciousness, a form of deep relaxation and intense concentration in which extraneous thoughts are suppressed; simply wanting to heal is not enough.

With the hands four to six inches from the healee's body, the passage of the healer's hands over the healee's body picks up areas of "excess energy" indicating accumulated tension or illness, which by therapeutic touch the healer is able to redirect or redistribute; this is called "unruffling the field," so that the healee's field is assisted to mobilize its own resources for self-healing, a process in which the healer, using the hands, also directs energy to the affected parts of the body of the healee.

The healer, then, is an individual whose health gives her access to an overabundance of *prana,* and whose strong sense of commitment and intention to help ill people gives her a certain control over the projection of this vital energy. The act of healing, then, writes Krieger, "would entail the channeling of this energy flow by the healer for the well-being of the sick individual . . . although the healer projects this energy, *prana,* for the use of another person, the healer herself is not depleted or deprived of energy unless she identifies herself too closely with the process."

Among the few controlled experiments to test the soundness of therapeutic touch, Dr. Krieger reasoned that since *prana* involves respiration, hemoglobin values should be higher in therapeutic touch healees as compared with a control group of untreated persons. And this was, indeed, found to be the case at the .01 level of significance. This finding has been confirmed in two other studies.

Dr. Janet Quinn of the College of Nursing of the University of South Carolina, a student of Krieger, in a study of patients hospitalized with cardiovascular disease, found a highly significant decrease in acute anxiety following noncontact therapeutic touch, when treated for only five minutes by nurses with several years of experience with the method. In the control group of nurses with no knowledge of therapeutic touch who mimicked the motions of noncontact therapeutic touch, but without knowledge of energy exchange between nurse and patient or centering or intent to heal the patient, there was no change in the patients' anxiety.

In order to discover what EEG changes may occur in the healer as well as the healee during sessions of therapeutic touch, Drs. Erik Peper of the Center for Interdisciplinary Science of San Francisco State University, and Sonia Ancoli of Langley Porter Neuropsychiatric Institute of the University of California at San Francisco, found that there was a preponderance of fast beta EEG in Dr. Krieger, whereas in the three patients no major changes were seen in electroencephalogram (EEG), electromyogram (EMG), or electrocardiogram (EKG). The three patients were a sixty-year-old male with a five-year history of severe neck, back, and head pain; a thirty-year-old female with a history of fibroid cysts in her breasts; and R. G., a twenty-three-year-old female with a three-year history of severe chronic migraine, as well as one grand mal seizure. All three patients reported that the therapeutic touch was relaxing and that they would volunteer again. The experience was important to the patients. One of them, R. G., remarked: "This was the first time that I felt that somebody (D. K.) really cared. It is so rare that somebody cares in a medical group. In addition, I had tried to do something for myself. This made me feel better."

"The improvement," the authors write, "may not be related to the therapeutic touch experience and no claims can be made.... Possibly therapeutic touch could be a technique to investigate placebo dynamics."

Reported successes with therapeutic touch may, of course, amount to nothing more than a statement of the placebo effect.

It has therefore been argued that until its claims have been put to the proper test, it must remain *sub judice*.

In a sympathetic account of therapeutic touch, Nurse Marie-Thérèse Connell has observed that in a scientific sense, therapeutic touch has made "little headway in describing its nature or in predicting its effects, and only a small amount of confidence can be placed in existing findings." Indeed, much of the evidence cited for therapeutic touch is anecdotal and has not been carried out in a scientific manner. Insufficient care has been taken to test for the role other factors may have played in producing the reported effects. What is needed are more scientifically controlled experiments of therapeutic touch. Meanwhile, good accounts of the theoretical, scientific, and philosophical foundations of therapeutic touch have been written by Patricia Heidt in the book of readings edited by her and Marianne Borelli entitled *Therapeutic Touch,* in which many other articles of interest will be found.

Therapeutic touch and midwifery have been ably discussed by the practicing nurse-midwife Iris S. Wolfson, but here, once more, further independent systematic studies are needed.

Dr. Judith Smith of the University of Pennsylvania School of Nursing has written a criticism of the claims that have been made for therapeutic touch which should be read by everyone interested in the subject. As Dr. Smith points out, in referring to Jerome Frank's fine book of 1961, *Persuasion and Healing,* what he had said well she says even better: "The significance for healing is what the healer communicates. The effective medium of transaction for the sick person is love, caring, the deep desire to help. The healer is actively communicating feelings of concern, care, and the patient responds with a confident hope. Presumably in this view, the gestures and manipulations of the healer in therapeutic touch function as a way of communicating the healer's attitude."

NEUROLOGY AND THERAPEUTIC TOUCH. It is somewhat surprising that none of the writers on therapeutic touch venture to discuss the neurophysiological mechanisms by means of which their therapy may, at least in part, achieve their claimed results. Were they to do so, they would be able to make out a far better theoretical case for their claims than they have thus far done. In addition to social interaction, what is involved physiologically in every form of touch are changes in electrochemical impulses. When touched, the neurons receiving the stimulus activate generators of weak electrical currents which lie on the surface membrane of nerve cell bodies, as well as along the sensory dendrites and motor axons.

The fundamental structure of the nervous system is the neuron which transmits the signals to the tissues and parts of the body to which it is related. Reduced to its simplest form, a *neuron* consists of a cell body from which extend two main fiber systems, the sensory dendrites and the motor axons. The dendrites are usually short and arranged in a complicated branching to form a bushy tree around the cell body. It is the dendrites that receive incoming signals. Axons are usually longer, often give off branches called collaterals, and end in a much smaller terminal knob. Excitation starts with the end brush of the dendrite and is transmitted to the ends of the axon. The latter may act directly on muscle or gland or transmit the excitation to the dendrite or another axon. The area at which the axon of one neuron establishes contiguity—*not* continuity—with a dendrite of another neuron is the *synapse*. A synapse consists of two parts: the knoblike tip of an axon terminal and the receptor region of another neuron. Some kinds of synaptic junctions are established between axon and axon, and between dendrite and dendrite. A neuron may have as many as 10,000 synapses.

At the synaptic junction, the axonic knob, which is the information-delivering part of the synapse, and contains many vesicles holding thousands of molecules of chemical transmitters, releases those molecules into the synaptic cleft (the area separating axons from dendrites), as shown diagrammatically in Figure 5. The release is triggered by arriving electrical impulses propagated by the axon membrane. The nerve impulse

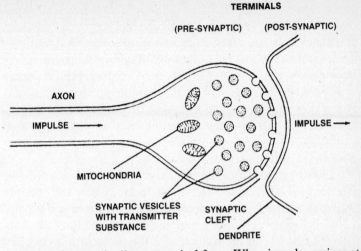

FIGURE 5. Synapse in diagrammatical form. When impulse arrives at pre-synaptic terminal, transmitter is released into cleft, and impulse is reactivated in post-synaptic terminal, on dendrite of second cell. (From L. M. Stevens, *Explorers of the Brain.* New York: Knopf, 1971, p. 181. By permission.)

or action potential is a self-propagated wave of electrical negativity, and as Robert Miller has suggested, it is possible that temporary changes in impulse frequency carry meaning. While Miller refers to neuronal changes in the brain, his suggestion probably also holds true for changes in the neurons of the peripheral nervous system. The passage of an action potential along a neuron or nerve fiber is almost a simultaneous event.

The sensory receptors of the skin, of which there are probably more than half a dozen varieties, are electrically activated when stimulated. The electrical voltages or generator potentials vary from 10 to 100 millivolts,* a voltage almost as high as that of an action potential. In the varieties of touch, pressure, and vibration, much electrical activity occurs, varying with age, physical, and other idiosyncratic conditions. Such electrical activity can not only be measured directly from the neurons in-

* A millivolt is a thousandth of a volt.

volved, but also from feedback to the skin by skin conductance tests similar to those that have become familiar to the public in so-called lie-detector tests. In that connection, it should be stated in the strongest terms that "lie-detector" tests are utterly valueless, for they cannot possibly measure so complex a series of physiological changes as are involved in whether a person is telling the truth or not. As a psychogalvanometer or Wheatstone bridge, the instrument has its uses in measuring skin conductance in response to a simple stimulus, but claims beyond that are not justified.

Tactile signals from the skin pass into the spinal cord and then into the somesthetic area of the brain, where they mainly stimulate neurons of the postcentral gyrus where it dips into the central gyrus (Figure 6), here to establish relations not only with the neurons in the six layers of the postcentral gyrus, but especially with the somesthetic area posterior to the postcentral

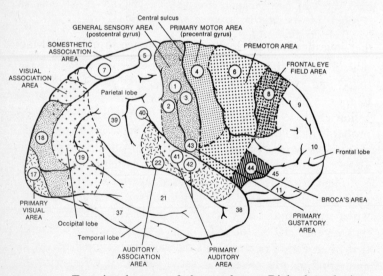

FIGURE 6. Functional areas of the cerebrum. Right lateral view. Broca's area is usually in the left hemisphere. (From Tortora and Anagnostakos, *Principles of Anatomy and Physiology,* 3rd ed. New York: Harper & Row, 1981, Fig. 14-7, p. 341. By permission.)

gyrus, where a great deal of integrative activity occurs in the interpretation not alone of tactile sensations, but of many others from within and outside the body. The electrical and chemical changes involved should serve to suggest how touch, in all its forms, may affect the living organism.

ELECTRONOGRAPHIC STUDIES. Studies of the electroluminescent image thrown by the skin on a photosensitive film have been described by Dr. C. Guja of the anthropological laboratory of the Institut "V. Babe" of Bucharest. In the latest of his reported studies on over a thousand individuals, Dr. Guja found that while each person had his or her own individual bioelectric pattern of imaging, it was possible to classify these variant forms under three headings: (1) fundamental, (2) elementary, and (3) polarizing. As a result of his experiments, Guja suggests the possibility of a bioelectric typology of humans and the possible anthropological differentiation of individuals.

Bioelectronography appears to be a promising field for further investigation, especially with reference to individual tactility, and possibly therapeutic touch. The psychophysical and psychoneuroimmunological bases of touching remain wide open and promising fields for future research.

APPENDIX 2

The Effects upon the Mother of Removal of the Infant Immediately after Birth

To the solid ground
Of Nature, trusts the mind which builds for aye.
—Wordsworth

A CANINE DEMONSTRATION.* About four weeks ago our be-loved collie, Jeanie, produced eight pups. The experience proved so interesting (in its implications) I thought you might like to hear about it. Theoretically she belongs to the three children, and since some of Jeanie's pups were whelped in the daytime hours before the children's bedtime, they were able to be on hand to watch, utterly fascinated, of course.

She began having them so fast and was also so fatigued trying to catch up with the cleaning and decording of each puppy before the next was on the way that I removed them one by one to a nearby box lined with soft flannel as soon as she had occupied that part of her maternal duties, thinking to help her and give her a rest, as well as to prevent her possible rolling on an earlier pup when she gave birth to a later one. She's such a trusting soul where we are concerned that she permitted this human interference without too much anxiety, and continued with her whelping until all eight had arrived. When it seemed that no more pups would be forthcoming, I returned them to her for a few seconds for reassurance purposes, and then re-moved them all again, this time for an hour or so, to give her a

* Reprinted by permission of the author, Betsy Marvin McKinney, and *Child-Family Digest,* vol. 10, 1954, pp. 63–65.

"real rest." She was very tired, and had been working hard for some hours.

Last year, as soon as the fourth and last pup of her first litter was born, she was eager to leave her whelping box for an airing and needed no urging, but this time she wouldn't budge. She would *not* get out and seemed, moreover, to be getting more and more anxious about her squirming little pups. So I put them back beside her, whereupon they began to root around and nuzzle and in very short order, to nurse. I suddenly realized that this was the first real opportunity I'd given her puppies to nurse her despite the fact that several hours had elapsed since the first birth.

I stayed with her a few hours more in case any more pups might still arrive (went to bed around dawn that day!) and when at the end of that time and despite all the wiles I knew I *still* couldn't get that listless dog out of her whelping box for the relief I knew she must need by then, the full impact of what I had done began to dawn.

Finally, by means of really stern scolding, I forced her to go outdoors for a few necessary seconds, after which she returned to her box to stay there, nursing those pups, *for over 24 hours!*

It was a shock to realize with shame and abashment that I had performed on Jeanie the same type of cultural deprivation and damage that is performed on many human mothers when their babies are taken away from them at birth without permitting the immediate nursing that is an instinctive urge of the newborn.

As for Jeanie, that poor animal was in bad internal shape, and I am afraid it was all due to me. She *had* to stay there hours longer than she'd otherwise have needed to, to be nursed back into reasonable internal health by her puppies. She was in a bad way, hemorrhaged during the night, and I could have kicked myself for being so stupid. As it was, it took our Jeanie a pretty long time to come back to normal—and in all probability because I'd deprived her of the immediate therapeutic suckling which would have pulled her together when she needed it most—directly following the birth and clean-up of each puppy!

You know I wonder sometimes if this same situation occurs without anyone realizing it, in the case of human mothers; if there is any tie-in between slow recoveries from childbirth and the removal, sometimes for long periods, of the new mother's baby? I wonder if the standard injection of pituitrin routinely used to contract the uterus following delivery could, despite its possible need in many cases, have the long-term effect that immediate and continued nursing has, wherein the baby and mother answer each other's needs at exactly the tempo and to the exact extent that both require, over an extended period of time? It is almost symbiotic, that early relationship, the mother giving her baby security along with the stimulus to nourishment while the baby serves her as a therapeutic agent speeding her recovery from her own recent tiring labors in bringing her baby forth.

At any rate, Jeanie certainly demonstrated this principle in an unmistakable way and I felt very badly at my own share in her discomfort.

REFERENCES

CHAPTER ONE. THE MIND OF THE SKIN

Page and Line

3:11–12   R. REGISTER, "In Touch with Feeling," *Human Behavior,* vol. 4 (1975), pp. 16–23.

4:3–4   G. GOTTLIEB, "Ontogenesis of Sensory Function in Birds and Mammals," in E. Tobach, L. R. Aronson, and E. Shaw (eds.), *The Biopsychology of Development* (New York: Academic Press, 1971), pp. 67–128.

:7–11   D. HOOKER, *The Prenatal Origin of Behavior* (Lawrence, Kansas: University of Kansas Press, 1952), p. 63.

:14–20   A. MACFARLANE, *The Psychology of Childbirth* (Cambridge, Mass.: Harvard University Press, 1977), pp. 10, 88.

5:14–18   F. WOOD JONES, *The Principles of Anatomy as Seen in the Hand* (2nd ed., Baltimore: Williams & Wilkins, 1942), pp. 324 et seq.

:28–36   A. VIRÉL, *Decorated Man: The Human Body as Art* (New York: Abrams, 1980), p. 12.

:19–21   C. M. JACKSON, "Some Aspects of Form and Growth," in W. J. ROBBINS (ed.), *Growth* (New Haven: Yale University Press, 1928), pp. 125–127; G. R. De Beer, *Growth* (London: Arnold, 1924), pp. 10, 34.

:26–30   L. CARMICHAEL, "The Onset and Early Development of Behavior," in L. Carmichael (ed.), *Manual of Child Psychology* (2nd ed., New York: Wiley, 1954), pp. 97–98; E. T. Raney and L. Carmichael, "Localizing Responses to Tactual Stimuli in the Fetal Rat in Relation to the Psychological Problem of Space Perception," *Journal of Genetic Psychology,* 43 (1934), pp. 3–21; A. W. Angulo y Gonzalez, "The Prenatal Development of Behavior

Page and Line

in the Albino Rat," *Journal of Comparative Neurology,* 55 (1932), pp. 395–442; E. A. Swenson, "The Development of Movement of the Albino Rat Before Birth" (Ph.D. diss., University of Kansas, 1926); W. Preyer, *Specielle Physiologie des Embryo* (Leipzig: Grieben, 1885); A. Peiper, *Cerebral Function in Infancy and Childhood* (New York: Consultants Bureau, 1963), pp. 34–40.

7:11–20   S. ROTHMAN (ed.), *The Human Integument* (Washington, D.C.: American Association for the Advancement of Science, 1959); D. R. Kenshalo (ed.), *The Skin Senses* (Springfield, Ill.: Charles C Thomas, 1968); R. I. C. SPEARMAN, *The Integument* (New York: Cambridge University Press, 1973).

:22–25   H. STRUGHOLD, "Ueber die Dichte und Schwellen der Schmerzpunkte der Epidermis in den verschiedenen Körperregionen," *Zeitschrift der Biologie,* vol. 80 (1924), p. 367; C. INGBERT, "On the Density of the Cutaneous Innervation in Man," *Journal of Comparative Neurology,* 13 (1903), pp. 209–222.

:26–34   E. F. DuBOIS, *Basal Metabolism in Health and Disease* (Philadelphia: Lea & Febiger, 1936), pp. 125–144.

8:1–4   S. ROTHMAN, *Physiology and Biochemistry of the Skin* (Chicago: University of Chicago Press, 1954), pp. 493–514.

:5–8   H. YOSHIMURA, "Organ Systems in Adaptation: The Skin," in D. B. Dill et al. (eds.), *Adaptation to Environment* (Washington, D.C.: American Physiological Society, 1964), p. 109.

:14–19   R. F. RUSHMER et al., "The Skin," *Science,* 154 (1966), pp. 343–348.

:21–26   ROTHMAN, *Physiology and Biochemistry of the Skin;* W. Montagna, *Structure and Function of Skin* (New York: Academic Press, 1956); D. Sinclair, *Cutaneous Sensation* (New York: Oxford University Press, 1967); H. Piéron, *The Sensations* (London: Miller, 1956); Rothman, *The Human Integument.*

9:37 to   J. HORDER, "Hugging Humans," *The Listener* (London),
10:1–9   April 12, 1979.

12:28–33   VIRÉL, *Decorated Man,* p. 12.

:37 to   P. BLUM, *La Peau* (Paris: Presses Universitaires de France,
13:6   1960).

:7–12   B. RUSSELL, *The ABC of Relativity* (New York: Harper & Bros., 1925).

Page and Line

14:4–14   G. H. BISHOP, "Neural Mechanisms of Cutaneous Sense," *Physiological Reviews,* 26 (1946), pp. 77–102.

:22–27   W. PENFIELD and T. RASMUSSEN, *The Cerebral Cortex of Man* (New York: Macmillan, 1950), p. 214.

:28–35   KENT C. BLOOMER and CHARLES W. MOORE, *Body, Memory, and Architecture* (New Haven: Yale University Press, 1977).

:36 to   Cf. J. J. GIBSON, *The Perception of the Visual World* (Boston: Houghton Mifflin, 1950), pp. 97, 98.
17:5

:5–9   B. B. GREENBIE, *Spaces: Dimensions of the Human Landscape* (New Haven: Yale University Press, 1981), p. 9.

:14–15   A. R. LURIA, "The Functional Organization of the Brain," *Scientific American,* 222 (1970), pp. 66–78.

:22–32   E. SÉGUIN, *Jacob-Rodriguez Pereire. Notice Sur Sa Vie et Ses Travaux et Analyse Raisonnée de Sa Methode* (Paris: Ballière, Guyot & Scribe, 1847). For a brief good account of Pereire and his method, see Harlan Lane, *The Wild Boy of Aveyron* (Cambridge, Mass.: Harvard University Press, 1976), pp. 150–152; Harlan Lane, *When The Mind Hears* (New York: Random House, 1984).

18:24–27   A. MONTAGU, "The Sensory Influences of the Skin," *Texas Reports on Biology and Medicine,* 2 (1953), pp. 291–301.

19:13–14   W. J. O'DONOVAN, *Dermatological Neuroses* (London: Kegan Paul, 1927).

:15–17   M. E. OBERMAYER, *Psychocutaneous Medicine* (Springfield, Ill.: Charles C Thomas, 1955). See also J. A. Aita, *Neurocutaneous Diseases* (Springfield, Ill.: Charles C Thomas, 1966); H. C. Bethune and C. B. Kidd, "Psychophysiological Mechanisms in Skin Diseases," *The Lancet,* 2 (1961), pp. 1419–1422.

20:11–36   F. S. HAMMETT, "Studies in the Thyroid Apparatus: I," *American Journal of Physiology,* 56 (1921), pp. 196–204, p. 199.

21:30 to   F. S. HAMMETT, "Studies of the Thyroid Apparatus: V," *Endocrinology,* 6 (1922), pp. 221–229; J. Older, *Touching Is Healing* (New York: Stein & Day, 1982); C. C. Brown (ed.), *The Many Facets of Touch* (Skillman, New Jersey: Johnson & Johnson Baby Products, 1984).
22:27

22:5–7   M. J. GREENMAN and F. L. DUHRING, *Breeding and Care of the Albino Rat for Research Purposes* (2nd ed., Philadelphia: Wistar Institute, 1931).

23:23 to   J. A. REYNIERS, "Germ-Free Life Studies," *Lobund Re-*

Page and Line

24:2   *ports,* University of Notre Dame, No. 1 (1946); No. 2 (1949).

:5–19   Personal communication, November 10, 1950.

:20–26   R. A. McCance and M. Otley, "Course of the Blood Urea in Newborn Rats, Pigs and Kittens," *Journal of Physiology,* 113 (1951), pp. 18–22.

:27 to
25:5   L. Rhine, "One Little Kitten and How It Grew," *McCall's Magazine,* July 10, 1953, pp. 4–6.

:6–13   R. W. Schaeffer and D. Premack, "Licking Rates in Infant Albino Rats," *Science,* 134 (1962), pp. 1980–1981.

:14 to
26:3   J. S. Rosenblatt and D. S. Lehrman, "Maternal Behavior of the Laboratory Rat," in H. L. Rheingold (ed.), *Maternal Behavior in Mammals* (New York: Wiley, 1963), p. 14; T. C. Schneirla, J. S. Rosenblatt, and E. Tobach, "Maternal Behavior in the Cat," ibid., in Rheingold, p. 123; H. L. Rheingold, "Maternal Behavior in the Dog," ibid., pp. 179–181; P. Jay, "Mother-Infant Relations in Langurs," ibid., p. 286; I. DeVore, "Mother-Infant Relations in Free-Ranging Baboons," ibid., pp. 310–311.

:4–6   H. Fox, "The Birth of Two Anthropoid Apes," *Journal of Mammalogy,* 10 (1929), pp. 37–51; R. D. Nadler, "Three Gorillas Born at Yerkes in One Month," *Yerkes Newsletter* (Emory University), 13, 2 (1976), pp. 15–19.

:27 to
27:1–2   L. L. Roth and J. S. Rosenblatt, "Mammary Glands of Pregnant Rats: Development Stimulated by Licking," *Science,* 151 (1965), pp. 1403–1404.

:3–18   H. G. Birch, "Source of Order in the Maternal Behavior of Animals," *American Journal of Orthopsychiatry,* 26 (1956), pp. 279–284; T. C. Schneirla, "A Consideration of Some Problems in the Ontogeny of Family Life and Social Adjustments in Various Infrahuman Animals," in M. J. E. Senn (ed.), *Problems of Infancy and Childhood* (New York: Josiah Macy, Jr., Foundation, 1951), p. 96.

:33 to
28:4   G. F. Solomon S. Levine, and J. K. Kraft, "Early Experiences and Immunity," *Nature,* 220 (1968), pp. 821–823.

:6–11   G. F. Solomon and R. H. Moos, "Emotions, Immunity, and Disease," *Archives of General Psychiatry,* 2 (1964), pp. 657–674.

:17–22   O. Weininger, "Mortality of Rats under Stress as a Function of Early Handling," *Canadian Journal of Psychol-*

ogy, 7 (1953), pp. 111–114; O. Weininger, W. J. McClelland, and R. K. Arima, "Gentling and Weight Gain in
the Albino Rat," *Canadian Journal of Psychology,* 8
(1954), pp. 147–151; L. Bernstein and H. Elrick, "The
Handling of Experimental Animals as a Control Factor
in Animal Research—A Review," *Metabolism,* 6 (1957),
pp. 479–482; S. Levine, "Stimulation in Infancy," *Scientific American,* 202 (1960), pp. 81–86; W. R. Ruegamer,
L. Bernstein, and J. D. Benjamin, "Growth, Food Utilization, and Thyroid Activity in the Albino Rat as a
Function of Extra Handling," *Science,* 120 (1954), pp.
184–185.

:23–36   G. ALEXANDER and D. WILLIAMS, "Maternal Facilitation
of Sucking Drive in Newborn Lambs," *Science,* 146
(1964), pp. 665–666.

29:3–7   H. BLAUVELT, "Neonate-Mother Relationship in Goat and
Man," in B. Schaffner (ed.), *Group Processes* (New
York: Josiah Macy, Jr., Foundation, 1956), pp. 94–140;
p. 116; ibid., p. 116, H. S. Liddell.

:8–16   R. A. MAIER, *Maternal Behavior in the Domestic Hen; III:
The Role of Physical Contact,* Loyola Behavior Laboratory Series, vol. 3, 3 (1962–1963), pp. 1–12.

:17–23   W. H. BURROWS and T. C. BYERLY, "The Effects of Certain
Groups of Environmental Factors upon the Expression
of Broodiness," *Poultry Science,* 17 (1938), pp. 324–330;
Y. Saeki and Y. Tanabe, "Changes in Prolactin Content
of Fowl Pituitary during Broody Periods and Some Experiments on the Induction of Broodiness," *Poultry Science,* 34 (1955), pp. 909–919; D. S. LEHRMAN,
"Hormonal Regulation of Parental Behavior in Birds
and Infrahuman Mammals," in W. C. Young (ed.), *Sex
and the Internal Secretions* (2 vols., Baltimore: Williams
& Wilkins, 1961), vol. 2, pp. 1268–1382; A. T. Cowie and
S. J. Folley, "The Mammary Gland and Lactation,"
ibid., pp. 590–642.

:24–33   N. E. COLLIAS, "The Analysis of Socialization in Sheep and
Goats," *Ecology,* 37 (1956), pp. 228–239.

:36 to   L. HERSHER, A. U. MOORE, and J. B. RICHMOND, "Effect of
30:10   Postpartum Separation of Mother and Kid on Maternal
Care in the Domestic Goat," *Science,* 128 (1958), pp.
1342–1343.

:11–16   L. HERSHER, J. B. RICHMOND, and A. U. MOORE, "Modi-
fiability of the Critical Period for the Development of

Page and Line

Maternal Behavior in Sheep and Goats," *Behaviour,* 20 (1963), pp. 311–320.

:17–26   B. M. McKINNEY, "The Effects upon the Mother of Removal of the Infant Immediately after Birth," *Child-Family Digest,* 10 (1954), pp. 63–65.

:25–26   M. H. KLAUS and J. H. KENNELL, *Maternal-Infant Bonding* (St. Louis, Mo.: C. V. Mosby, 1976); Sheila Kitzinger, *Some Mothers' Experiences of Induced Labour* (London: The National Childbirth Trust, 1975); D. Haire, "The Cultural Warping of Childbirth," Milwaukee, Wisconsin: International Childbirth Education Association, *I.C.E.A.: News,* 11 (1972), pp. 27–28.

:27 to 31:9   H. F. HARLOW, M. K. HARLOW, and E. W. HANSEN, "The Maternal Affectional System of Rhesus Monkeys," in Rheingold (ed.), *Maternal Behavior in Mammals* (New York: Wiley, 1963), p. 268.

:13–18   V. H. DENENBERG and A. E. WHIMBEY, "Behavior of Adult Rats Is Modified by the Experience Their Mothers Had as Infants," *Science,* 142 (1963), pp. 1192–1193.

:19–23   R. ADER and P. M. CONKLIN, "Handling of Pregnant Rats: Effects on Emotionality of Their Offspring," *Science,* 142 (1963), pp. 412–413.

:24–29   J. WERBOFF, A. ANDERSON, and B. N. HAGGETT, "Handling of Pregnant Mice: Gestational and Postnatal Behavioral Effects," *Physiology and Behavior,* 3 (1968), pp. 35–39.

:29 to 32:4   A. SAYLER and M. SALMON, "Communal Nursing in Mice: Influence of Multiple Mothers on the Growth of the Young," *Science,* 164 (1969), pp. 1309–1310.

:7–23   O. WEININGER, "Physiological Damage under Emotional Stress as a Function of Early Experience," *Science,* 119 (1954), pp. 285–286; Weininger, ibid.

:24–31   H. SELYE, *The Physiology and Pathology of Exposure to Stress* (Montreal: Acta, 1950); C. Newman (ed.), *The Nature of Stress Disorder* (Springfield, Ill.: Charles C Thomas, 1959); H. G. Wolff, *Stress and Disease* (2nd ed., Springfield, Ill.: Charles C Thomas, 1968); R. B. CAIRNS, "Fighting and Punishment from a Developmental Perspective," in *Nebraska Symposium on Motivation* (Lincoln, Nebraska: University of Nebraska Press, 1972), pp. 59–124.

:31 to 33:7   O. WEININGER, "Physiological Damage under Emotional

Page and Line

Stress as a Function of Early Experience," *Science,* 119 (1954), pp. 285–286.

:21–24   J. L. FULLER, "Experiential Deprivation and Later Behavior," *Science,* 158 (1967), pp. 1645–1652.

:25–31   L. HERSHER, J. B. RICHMOND, and U. MOORE, "Maternal Behavior in Sheep and Goats," in Rheingold, *Maternal Behavior in Mammals,* p. 209.

:31–33   D. H. BARRON, "Mother-Newborn Relationship in Goats," in Schaffner, *Group Processes,* pp. 225–226.

:36 to   G. G. KARAS, "The Effect of Time and Amount of Infantile
34:2   Experience upon Later Avoidance Learning" (M.A. thesis, Purdue University, 1957).

:2–8   S. LEVINE and G. W. LEWIS, "Critical Period for the Effects of Infantile Experience on Maturation of Stress Response," *Science,* 129 (1959), p. 42.

:8–12   R. W. BELL, G. REISNER, and T. LINN, "Recovery From Electroconvulsive Shock as a Function of Infantile Stimulation," *Science,* 133 (1961), p. 1428.

:12–15   V. H. DENENBERG and G. G. KARAS, "Effects of Differential Handling upon Weight Gain and Mortality in the Rat and Mouse," *Science,* 130 (1959), pp. 629–630; V. H. Denenberg and G. G. Karas, "Interactive Effects of Age and Duration of Infantile Experience on Adult Learning," *Psychological Reports,* 7 (1960), pp. 313–322; V. H. Denenberg and G. G. Karas, "Interactive Effects of Infant and Adult Experience upon Weight Gain and Mortality in the Rat," *Journal of Comparative and Physiological Psychology,* 54 (1961), pp. 658–689.

:16–21   R. NOREM and FRED CORNHILL, "The TLC Factor and Heart Disease," *Science News,* 116 (1979), p. 188.

:34 to   G. HENDRIX, J. D. VAN VALCK, and W. E. MITCHELL,
35:8   "Early Handling by Humans Is Found to Benefit Horses," *New York Times,* December 27, 1968.

:9 to   E. KARSH, "If You Want a Friendly Cat," *Science News,* 24
36:3   July 30, 1983.

:22–23   A. F. MCBRIDE and H. KRITZLER, "Observations on Pregnancy, Parturition, and Post-Natal Behavior in the Bottlenose Dolphin," *Journal of Mammalogy,* 32 (1951), pp. 251–266.

:34 to   R. A. GILMORE, "The Friendly Whales of Laguna San Ig-
37:9   nacio, *Terra,* 15 (1976), pp. 24–28.

Page and Line

:10–34   A. GUNNER, "A London Hedgehog," *The Listener* (London), February 16, 1956, p. 255.

38:9–12   H. F. HARLOW, "The Nature of Love," *The American Psychologist,* 13 (1958), pp. 673–685.

38:13–33 Ibid., p. 676.

:34 to   HARLOW, HARLOW, and HANSEN, "The Maternal Affec-
41:6   tional System," p. 260.

42:12 to Ibid., p. 279.
43:4

:8   L. L. ROTH, "Effects of Young and of Social Isolation on Maternal Behavior in the Virgin Rat," *American Zoologist,* 7 (1967), p. 800.

:11–34   J. TERKEL and J. S. ROSENBLATT, quoted in J. S. Rosenblatt, "Onset and Maintenance of Maternal Behavior in the Rat," in Lester R. Aronson et al. (eds.), *Development and Evolution of Behavior* (San Francisco: Freeman, 1970), pp. 502–503.

:35 to   HARLOW HARLOW, and HANSEN, "The Maternal Affec-
44:4   tional System," pp. 260–261.

:5–10   P. JAY, "Mother-Infant Relations in Langurs," in Rheingold, *Maternal Behavior in Mammals,* p. 286.

:11–16   H. F. HARLOW, *Learning to Love* (New York: Ballantine Books, 1971).

:16–26   M. SHIRLEY, *The First Two Years: A Study of Twenty-Five Babies* (3 vols., Minneapolis: University of Minnesota Press, 1931/33).

:35 to   P. MARLER, "Communication in Monkeys and Apes," in I.
45:2   DeVore (ed.), *Primate Behavior* (New York: Holt, Rinehart & Winston, 1965), p. 551.

:6–7   H. HEDIGER, *Wild Animals in Captivity* (London: Butterworth, 1950).

:15–16   A. JOLLY, *The Evolution of Primate Behavior* (New York: Macmillan, 1972).

:16–23   T. R. ANTHONEY, "The Ontogeny of Greeting, Grooming, and Sexual Motor Patterns in Captive Baboons (Superspecies *Papio cynocephalus*)," *Behaviour,* 31 (1968), pp. 358–372; J. Sparks, "Allogrooming in Primates: A Review," in Desmond Morris, ed., *Primate Ethology* (Chicago: Aldine, 1967), pp. 148–175; J. VAN LAWICK-GOODALL, "Mother-Offspring Relationships in Free-hanging Chimpanzees," ibid., pp. 287–346.

:33–35   JOLLY, *Primate Behavior.*

:35–36   ANTHONEY, "Patterns in Captive Baboons," pp. 358–372.

CHAPTER TWO. THE WOMB OF TIME

Page and Line

47:4–14   M. SARTON, "An Informal Portrait of George Sarton," *Texas Quarterly,* Autumn 1962, p. 105.

52:13–17   R. W. JONDORF, R. P. MAICHEL, and B. B. BRODIE, "Inability of Newborn Mice and Guinea Pigs to Metabolize Drugs," *Biochemical Pharmacology,* 1 (1958), pp. 352–354.

:17–20   I. D. ROSS and I. F. DEFORGES, "Further Evidence of Deficient Enzyme Activity in the Newborn Period," *Pediatrics,* 23 (1959), pp. 718–725.

:20–28   C. SMITH, *The Physiology of the Newborn Infant* (3rd ed., Springfield, Ill.: Charles C Thomas, 1960); E. H. Watson and G. H. Lowrey, *Growth and Development of Children* (5th ed., Chicago: Yearbook Medical Publishers, 1967), pp. 203–204; C. A. Villee, "Enzymes in the Development of Homeostatic Mechanisms," in G. W. Wolstenholme and M. O'Connor (eds.), *Somatic Stability in the Newly Born* (Boston: Little, Brown, 1961), pp. 246–278; H. F. R. Prechtl, "Problems of Behavioral Studies in the Newborn Infant," in D. S. Lehrman, R. A. Hinde, and E. Shaw (eds.), *Advances in the Study of Behavior* (2 vols., New York: Academic Press, 1965), vol. 1, p. 79.

53:21–31   A. MONTAGU, *The Human Revolution* (New York: Bantam Books, 1967), pp. 126–138; A. Montagu, "Time, Morphology and Neoteny in the Evolution of Man," *American Anthropologist,* 57 (1955), pp. 13–27; A. Montagu, "Neoteny and the Evolution of the Human Mind," *Explorations,* No. 6 (Toronto, 1956), pp. 85–90; G. DeBeer, *Embryos and Ancestors* (3rd ed., New York: Oxford University Press, 1958); F. Kovács, "Biological Interpretation of the Nine Months Duration of Human Pregnancy," *Acta Biologica Magyar,* 10 (1960), pp. 331–361; A. Portmann, *Biologische Fragmente* (Basel: Benno Schwalbe & Co., 1944); A. Montagu, "The Origin and Significance of Neonatal Immaturity in Man," *Journal of the American Medical Association,* 178 (1961), pp. 156–157; S. J. Gould, *Ontogeny and Phylogeny* (Cambridge: Harvard University Press, 1977); A. Montagu, *Growing Young* (New York: McGraw-Hill, 1981).

54:2–5   J. BOSTOCK, "Exterior Gestation, Primitive Sleep, Enuresis

Page and Line

and Asthma: A Study in Aetiology," *Medical Journal of Australia,* 2 (1958), pp. 149–153; 185–188.

:10–20   D. B. and E. F. P. JELLIFFE, "Human Milk, Nutrition, and the World Resource Crisis," *Science,* 188 (1975), pp. 557–561; D. B. and E. F. P. Jelliffe, *Human Milk in the Modern World* (New York: Oxford University Press, 1978).

56:14–27   A. MONTAGU, *Prenatal Influences* (Springfield, Ill.: Charles C Thomas, 1962), pp. 413–414; P. Gruenwald, "The Fetus in Prolonged Pregnancy," *American Journal of Obstetrics and Gynecology,* 89 (1964), pp. 503–505; P. B. Mead, "Prolonged Pregnancy," *American Journal of Obstetrics and Gynecology,* 89 (1964), pp. 495–502; W. E. Lucas, "The Problems of Postterm Pregnancy," *American Journal of Obstetrics and Gynecology,* 91 (1965), pp. 241–250; M. Zwerdling, "Complications of Prolonged Pregnancies," *Journal of the American Medical Association,* 195 (1966), pp. 39–40; R. L. Naeye, "Infants of Prolonged Gestation," *Archives of Pathology,* 84 (1967), pp. 37–41.

57:9–22   A. MONTAGU, *Prenatal Influences;* A. Montagu, *Life Before Birth* (New York: New American Library, 1964); N. J. Berrill, *The Person in the Womb* (New York: Dodd, Mead), 1968; A. J. FERREIRA, *Prenatal Environment* (Springfield, Ill.: Charles C Thomas, 1969); H. C. Mack (ed.), *Prenatal Life* (Detroit: Wayne State University Press, 1970; T. Verney with J. Kelly, *The Secret Life of the Unborn Child* (New York: Summit Books, 1981).

61:24–29   C. M. DRILLIEN, "Physical and Mental Handicap in the Prematurely Born," *Journal of Obstetrics and Gynaecology of the British Empire,* 66 (1959), pp. 721–728; see also B. Corner, *Prematures* (Springfield, Ill.: Charles C Thomas, 1960).

:30 to 62:20   M. SHIRLEY, "A Behavior Syndrome Characterizing Prematurely-Born Children," *Child Development,* 10 (1939), pp. 115–128.

:25–33   A. J. SCHAFFER, *Diseases of the Newborn* (Philadelphia: Saunders, 1965), pp. 45–46.

:34 to 63:5   A. P. KIMBALL and R. J. OLIVER, "Extra-Amniotic Caesarean Section in the Prevention of Fatal Hyaline Membrane Disease," *American Journal of Obstetrics and Gynecology,* 90 (1964), pp. 919–924.

:6–9   R. J. MCKAY, JR., and C. A. SMITH, in W. E. NELSON (ed.),

Page and Line

Textbook of Pediatrics (7th ed., Philadelphia: Saunders, 1959), p. 286.

:9–21   G. W. MEIER, "Behavior of Infant Monkeys: Differences Attributable to Mode of Birth," *Science,* 143 (1964), pp. 968–970.

:27–32   S. SEGAL and J. CHU, in T. K. OLIVER, JR. (ed.), *Neonatal Respiratory Adaptation* (Bethesda, Md.: U. S. Dept. of Health, Education, and Welfare, National Institutes of Health, 1966), pp. 183–188.

:33–36   T. K. OLIVER, JR, A. DEMIS, and G. D. BATES, "Serial Blood-Gas Tensions and Acid-Base Balance during the First Hour of Life in Human Infants," *Acta Paediatrica,* 50 (Stockholm, 1961), pp. 346–360.

:37 to   M. CORNBLATH et al., "Studies of Carbohydrate Metabo-
64:10   lism in the Newborn Infant," *Pediatrics,* 27 (1961), pp. 378–389.

:11–14   L. J. GROTA, V. H. DENENBERG, and M. X. ZARROW, "Neonatal Versus Caesarean Delivery: Effects upon Survival Probability, Weaning Weight, and Open-Field Activity," *Journal of Comparative and Physiological Psychology,* 61 (1966), pp. 159–160.

:34 to   W. J. PIEPER, E. E. LESSING, and H. A. GREENBERG, "Per-
65:16   sonality Traits in Cesarean-Normally Delivered Children," *Archives of General Psychiatry,* 2 (1964), pp. 466–471.

:28–30   M. STRAKER, "Comparative Studies of Effects of Normal and Caesarean Delivery upon Later Manifestations of Anxiety," *Comprehensive Psychiatry,* 3 (1962), pp. 113–124.

:30–33   W. T. LIBERSON and W. H. FRAZIER, "Evaluation of EEG Patterns of Newborn Babies," *American Journal of Psychiatry,* 118 (1962), pp. 1125–1131.

66:3–29   D. H. BARRON, "Mother-Newborn Relationships in Goats," in B. Schaffner (ed.), *Group Processes* (New York: Josiah Macy, Jr., Foundation, 1955), p. 225–226.

:30–33   MEIER, "Behavior of Infant Monkeys . . . ," *Science,* 143 (1964), pp. 968–970.

:33 to   R. A. MCCANCE and M. OTLEY, "Course of the Blood Urea
67:2   in Newborn Rats, Pigs and Kittens," *Journal of Physiology,* 113 (1951), pp. 18–22.

:8–9   H. B. PACK, "Mother-Newborn Relationship in Goats," in Schaffner, *Group Processes,* p. 228.

:10–14   Editorial, "The Gut and the Skin," *Journal of the American*

Page and Line

> *Medical Association,* 196 (1966), pp. 1151–1152; M. E. OBERMAYER, *Psychocutaneous Medicine* (Springfield, Ill.: Charles C Thomas, 1955), pp. 376–377; L. Fry, S. Shuster, and R. M. H. McMinn, "The Small Intestine in Skin Disease," *Archives of Dermatology,* 93 (1966), pp. 647–653; M. L. Johnson and H. T. H. Wilson, "Skin Lesions in Ulcerative Colitis," *Gut,* 10 (1969), pp. 255–263.

:15–27   F. REITZENSTEIN, "Aberglauben," in M. Marcuse (ed.), *Handwörterbuch der Sexualwissenschaft* (2nd ed., Bonn: Marcus & Weber, 1926), p. 5.

CHAPTER THREE. BREASTFEEDING

Page and Line

69:1–3   O. RANK, *The Trauma of Birth* (London: Allen & Unwin, 1929).

71:10–16   A. KULKA, C. FRY, and F. J. GOLDSTEIN, "Kinesthetic Needs In Infancy," *American Journal of Orthopsychiatry,* 33 (1960), pp. 562–571.

:36 to 72:2   Personal communication, 2 April 1976.

:8–23   Associated Press, May 1975. See also *Leaven,* La Leche League International, Franklin Park, Illinois, July–August 1975, p. 21.

:29–32   A. MONTAGU and F. MATSON, *The Dehumanization of Man* (New York: McGraw-Hill, 1983).

:35 to 73:6   *Infant Care* (Washington, D. C.: U.S. Government Printing Office, 1963), p. 16.

:20–24   M. P. MIDDLEMORE, *The Nursing Couple* (London: Cassell, 1941), pp. 18–19.

74:8–13   M. H. KLAUS and J. H. KENNELL, *Parent-Infant Bonding* (St. Louis, Mo.: C. V. Mosby Co., 1982); M. H. Klaus and P. H. Klaus, *The Amazing Newborn* (Reading, Mass.: Addison-Wesley, 1985), pp. 106–107.

:8–10   T. SMITH and R. B. LITTLE, "The Significance of Colostrum to the New-Born Calf," *Journal of Experimental Medicine,* 36 (1922), pp. 181–198.

:10–16   J. A. TOOMEY, "Agglutinins in Mother's Blood, Mother's Milk, and Placental Blood," *American Journal of Diseases of Children,* 47 (1934), pp. 521–528; J. A. Toomey, "Infection and Immunity," *Journal of Pediatrics,* 4 (1934), pp. 529–539.

Page and Line

:16–18   D. B. JELLIFFE and E. F. P. JELLIFFE, *Human Milk in the Modern World* (New York: Oxford University Press, 1978).

77:5–12   G. E. GAULL, "What Is Biochemically Special about Human Milk?" in Dana Raphael (ed.), *Breastfeeding and Food Policy in a Hungry World* (New York: Academic Press, 1979); W. A. STINI, "Errors of a Nutritional Policy to Maximize Growth," ibid., pp. 177–182; JELLIFFE and JELLIFFE, *Human Milk in the Modern World*; H. BAKWIN and R. M. BAKWIN, *Clinical Management of Behavior Disorders in Children* (3rd ed., Philadelphia: Saunders, 1960); J. PITT, "Immunologic Aspects of Human Milk," ibid., pp. 229–232.

78:5–14   M. RIBBLE, *The Rights of Infants* (New York, Columbia University Press, 1965), pp. 17–21.

:20–21   G. C. ANDERSON, "Severe Respiratory Distress in Transitional Newborn Lambs with Recovery Following Nonnutritive Sucking," *Journal of Nurse-Midwifery,* Summer 1975, pp. 24–27.

:21–26   K. HIGGINS and L. VAN ART, *Journal of Nurse-Midwifery,* Summer 1973, pp. 20–28.

:29–31   N. BLURTON JONES, "Comparative Aspects of Mother-Child Contact," in N. Blurton Jones (ed.), *Ethological Studies of Child Behaviour* (Cambridge: The University Press, 1972), pp. 305–328.

:29 to   D. M. BEN SHAUL, "The Composition of the Milk of Wild
79:7   Animals," *International Zoo Yearbook,* 4 (1962), pp. 333–342.

:8–11   R. C. BOELKINS, "Large-Scale Rearing of Infant Rhesus Monkeys *(M. mulatta)* in the Laboratory," *International Zoo Yearbook,* ibid., pp. 286–289.

:15–25   A. PEIPER, *Cerebral Function in Infancy and Childhood* (New York: Consultants Bureau, 1963), pp. 570–571.

:28–32   T. J. CRONIN, "Influence of Lactation upon Ovulation," *The Lancet,* 2 (1968), pp. 422–424; R. Gioiosa, "Incidence of Pregnancy during Lactation in 500 Cases," *American Journal of Obstetrics and Gynecology,* 70 (1955), pp. 162–174; I. C. Udesky, "Ovulation and Lactating Women," *American Journal of Obstetrics and Gynecology,* 59 (1950), pp. 843–851; N. L. Solien de Gonzales, "Lactation and Pregnancy: A Hypothesis," *American Anthropologist,* 66 (1964), pp. 873–878; D. Ra-

Page and Line

phael (ed.), *Breastfeeding and Food Policy in a Hungry World* (New York: Academic Press, 1979).

:32–34　D. B. and E. F. P. JELLIFFE, "Human Milk, Nutrition, and the World Resource Crisis," *Science,* 188 (1975), pp. 557–561.

:36 to
80:7　E. R. KIMBALL, "How I Get Mothers to Breastfeed," OB/GYN's Supplement in *Physician's Management,* June 1968.

:8–16　C. HOEFER and M. C. HARDY, "Later Development of Breast Fed and Artificially Fed Infants," *Journal of the American Medical Association,* 96 (1929), pp. 615–619.

:17–24　S. GOLDBERG and M. LEWIS, "Play Behavior in Year-Old Infant: Early Sex Experimentation," *Child Development,* 40 (1969), p. 21.

:26 to
81:8　J. KRECEK, "Phenotype: Postnatal Development," *Science,* 159 (1968), pp. 658–659.

:9–17　S. BRODY, *Patterns of Mothering* (New York: International Universities Press, 1956); Mary D. S. Ainsworth, *Infancy in Uganda* (Baltimore: The Johns Hopkins Press, 1967), p. 403; W. D. Davidson, "A Brief History of Infant Feeding," *Journal of Pediatrics,* 43 (1953), pp. 74–87; Jelliffe and Jelliffe, *Human Milk in the Modern World,* pp. 406–407.

:21–30　H. E. BATES, *The Vanished World: An Autobiography* (Vol. 1, Columbia: University of Missouri Press, 1969), p. 17.

82:1–3　T. BENEDEK, "Adaptation to Reality in Early Infancy," *Psychoanalytic Quarterly,* 7 (1938), pp. 200–215; Therese Benedek, "The Psychosomatic Implications of the Primary Unit Mother-Child," *American Journal of Orthopsychiatry,* 19 (1949), pp. 642–654.

83:25–28　PHILIP SLATER, *Earthwalk* (New York: Doubleday, 1974), p. 188.

84:11–22　E. ROBIN and E. MA.GITOT, *Gazette Médicale de France,* 1860, p. 251.

:35 to
85:9　F. M. POTTENGER, JR., and B. KROHN, "Influence of Breast Feeding on Facial Development," *Archives of Pediatrics,* 67 (1950), pp. 454–461; F. M. Pottenger, Jr., "The Responsibility of the Pediatrician in the Orthodontic Problem," *California Medicine,* 65 (1946), pp. 169–170.

:9–20　F. M. BERTRAND, "The Relationship of Prolonged Breastfeeding to Facial Features," *Central African Journal of Medicine,* 14 (1968), pp. 226–227.

:21–24　S. ROBINSON and S. R. NAYLOR, "The Effects of Late

Page and Line

Weaning on the Deciduous Teeth," *British Dental Journal,* 115 (1963), p. 250.

:24–26   A. NIZEL, " 'Nursing-Bottle Syndrome': Rampant Dental Caries in Young Children," *Nutrition News,* 38 (1975), p. 1.

86:1–25   F. E. BROAD, "The Effects of Infant Feeding on Speech Quality," *New Zealand Medical Journal,* 76 (1972), pp. 28–31; Frances E. Broad, "Further Studies on the Effects of Infant Feeding on Speech Quality," *New Zealand Medical Journal,* 82 (1975), pp. 373–376; Frances E. Broad, "Suckling and Speech," *Parents Centres Bulletin* 53, November 1972, pp. 4–6.

:32 to 87:19   N. RINGLER, M. A. TRAUSE, M. KLAUS, and J. KENNELL, "The Effects of Extra Postpartum Contact and Maternal Speech Patterns on Children's IQ, Speech, and Language Development," *Child Development,* 49 (1978), pp. 862–865.

88:6–17   D. L. RAPHAEL, "The Lactation-Suckling Process within a Matrix of Supportive Behavior" (Ph.D. diss., Columbia University, 1966), p. 246.

:33–36   W. PAINTER, *The Palace of Pleasure* (London: Tottell and Jones, 1566), I, 43.

89:21–25   See Chapter 2 of the above work for a survey of the ethological evidence.

:28–33   M. WRIGHT, "On the Importance of Skin Contact," *Sounding Board,* 3, 4 (1969), p. 7.

:31–34   For further discussion of this subject, see F. H. Richardson, *The Nursing Mother* (New York: Prentice-Hall, 1953); M. P. Middlemore, *The Nursing Couple* (London: Cassell & Co., 1953); La Leche League International, *The Womanly Art of Breastfeeding* (Franklin Park, Ill., 1963); B. M. Caldwell, "The Effects of Infant Care," in M. L. Hoffman and L. W. Hoffman (eds.), *Review of Child Development Research* (New York: Russell Sage Foundation, 1964), vol. 1, pp. ii–41; A. Montagu and F. Matson, *The Human Connection* (New York: McGraw-Hill, 1979).

:34 to 91:32   M. KING, *Truby King the Man* (London: Allen & Unwin, 1948), pp. 170–178.

92:1–5   H. MOLTZ, R. LEVIN, and M. LEON, "Prolactin in the Postpartum Rat: Synthesis and Release in the Absence of Suckling Stimulation," *Science,* 163 (1969), pp. 1083–1084.

Page and Line

:20–26   S. LORAND and S. ASBOT, "Uber die durch Reizüng der Brustwarze reflektorischen Uterus Kontraktionen," *Zentralblatt für Gynäkologie,* 74 (1952), pp. 345–352.

93:4 to   E. DARWIN, *Zoonomia, or the Laws of Organic Life* (4 vols.,
94:12   3rd ed., London: J. Johnson, 1801), vol. 1, p. 206.

:13 to   R. ST. BARBE BAKER, *Kabongo* (New York: A. S. Barnes,
95:4   1955), p. 18.

:11–13   K. DE SNOO, "Das Trinkende Kind im Uterus," *Monatschrift für Geburtschilfe und Gynäkologie,* 105 (1937), pp. 88–97; A. Montagu, *Prenatal Influences* (Springfield, Illinois: Charles C Thomas, 1962), pp. 106–107.

:13–21   C. K. CROOK and L. P. LIPSITT, "Neonatal Nutritive Sucking: Effects of Taste Stimulation upon Sucking Rhythm and Heart Rate," *Child Development,* 47 (1976), pp. 518–521.

:23–27   T. FIELD and E. GOLDSTON, "Pacifying Effects of Nonnutritive Sucking on Term and Preterm Neonates During Heelstick Procedures," *Pediatrics,* 74 (1984), pp. 1012–1015.

CHAPTER FOUR. TENDER, LOVING CARE

Page and Line

96:1 to   J. L. HALLIDAY, *Psychosocial Medicine: A Study of the Sick*
97:17   *Society,* (New York: Norton, 1948), pp. 244–245.

:30 to   H. D. CHAPIN, "A Plea for Accurate Statistics in Children's
98:12   Institutions," *Transactions of the American Pediatric Society,* 27 (1915), p. 180.

:16–18   F. TALBOT, "Discussion," *Transactions of the American Pediatric Society,* 62 (1941), p. 469.

:29 to   L. E. HOLT, *The Care and Feeding of Children* (15th ed.,
99:5   New York: Appleton-Century, 1935); E. Holt, Jr., *Holt's Care and Feeding of Children* (New York: Appleton-Century, 1948).

:2–25   J. BRENNEMANN, "The Infant Ward," *American Journal of Diseases of Children,* 43 (1932), p. 577.

:25–29   H. BAKWIN, "Emotional Deprivation in Infants," *Journal of Pediatrics,* 35 (1949), pp. 512–521.

100:9–25 M. H. ELLIOTT and F. H. HALL, *Laura Bridgman* (Boston: Little, Brown, 1903); Helen Keller, *The Story of My Life* (New York: Doubleday, 1954); D. Levitsky (ed.),

Page and Line

Nutrition, Environment, and Behavior (Ithaca, N.Y.: Cornell University Press, 1979); R. G. Patton and L. I. Gardner, *Growth Failure and Maternal Deprivation* (Springfield, Ill.: Charles C Thomas, 1963).

:26 to 101:17   K. DAVIS, "Extreme Social Isolation of a Child," *American Journal of Sociology,* 45 (1940), pp. 554–565; K. Davis, "Final Note on a Case of Extreme Isolation," *American Journal of Sociology,* 52 (1947), pp. 432–437; M. K. Mason, "Learning to Speak after Six and One Half Years," *Journal of Speech Disorders,* 7 (1942), pp. 295–304.

:18–19   W. D. STRATTON, "Intonation Feedback for the Deaf Through a Tactile Display," *The Volta Review,* January 1974, pp. 26–35.

:27 to 102:13   The historian Salimbene (13th century), in J. B. Ross and M. M. McLaughlin (eds.), *A Portable Medieval Reader* (New York: Viking Press, 1949), p. 366.

:14–21   H. BAKWIN, "Emotional Deprivation in Infants," *Journal of Pediatrics,* 35 (1949), pp. 512–521.

:22–32   Annotation, "Perinatal Body Temperatures," *The Lancet,* 1 (1968), p. 964; B. D. BOWER, "Neonatal Cold Injury," *The Lancet,* 1 (1962), p. 426.

:37 to 103:14   O. FENICHEL, *The Psychoanalytic Theory of Neurosis* (New York: Norton, 1945), pp. 69–70.

:15–21   Editorial, "At What Temperature Should You Keep a Baby?" *The Lancet,* 2 (1970), p. 556.

:22–28   E. N. HEY and B. O'CONNELL, "Oxygen Consumption and Heat Balance in Cot-Nursed Babies," *Archives of Diseases of Childhood,* 14 (1970), pp. 335–343.

:25–28   K. BRÜCK, "Heat Production and Temperature Regulation," in Uwe Stave (ed.), *Perinatal Physiology* (New York: Plenum, 1978), p. 488.

:34–37   L. GLASS, "Wrapping Up Small Babies," *The Lancet,* 2 (1970), pp. 1039–1040.

104:1–5   J. W. SCOPES, "Control of Body Temperature in Newborn Babies," in *The Scientific Basis of Medicine, Annual Reviews* (London: The Athlone Press, 1970), pp. 31–50.

:6–19   W. AHERNE and D. HULL, "The Site of Heat Production in the Newborn Infant," *Proceedings of the Royal Society of Medicine,* 57 (1964), pp. 1172–1173.

:20–26   C. M. BLATTEIS, "Shivering and Nonshivering Thermogenesis During Hypoxia," *Proceedings of the Interna-*

Page and Line

   tional Symposium on Environmental Psychology, Dublin, 1971, pp. 151–160.

:27–29   F. A. GELDARD, *The Human Senses* (New York: Wiley, 1953), pp. 211–232.

:27–34   T. P. MANN and R. I. K. ELIOT, "Neonatal Cold Injury Due to Accidental Exposure to Cold," *The Lancet,* 1 (1957), pp. 229–234; W. A. Silverman, J. W. Fertig, and A. P. Berger, "The Influence of the Thermal Environment upon the Survival of Newly Born Premature Infants," *Pediatrics,* 22 (1958), pp. 876–886.

105:1–10   E. N. HEY, S. KOHLINSKY, and B. O'CONNELL, "Heat Losses from Babies during Exchange Transfusion," *The Lancet,* 1 (1969), pp. 335–338.

:11–16   C. P. BOYAN, "Cold or Warmed Blood for Massive Transfusions," *Annals of Surgery,* 160 (1964), pp. 282–286.

:32–34   M. S. ELDER, "The Effects of Temperature and Position on the Sucking Pressure of Newborn Infants," *Child Development,* 41 (1970), pp. 94–102.

:34 to
106:5   R. E. COOKE, "The Behavioral Response of Infants to Heat Stress," *Yale Journal of Biology and Medicine,* 24 (1952), pp. 334–340.

:6–18   P. H. WOLFF, "The Natural History of Crying and Other Vocalizations in Infancy," in B. M. Foss (ed.), *Determinants of Infant Behavior* (London: Methuen, 1969), vol. 4, pp. 81–109; P. H. Wolff, *The Causes, Controls, and Organisation of Behaviour* (New York: International Universities Press, 1966).

:27–34   T. SCHAEFER, JR., F. S. WEINGARTEN, and J. C. TOWNE, "Temperature Change: The Basic Variable in the Early Handling Phenomenon?" *Science,* 135 (1962), pp. 41–42.

:31–34   R. ADER, "The Basic Variable in the Early Handling Phenomenon," *Science,* 136 (1962), pp. 580–583; also G. W. Meier, pp. 583–584, and Schaefer et al., "Temperature Change . . . , " *Science,* pp. 584–587.

108:7–9   R. G. PATTON and L. I. GARDNER, *Growth Failure and Maternal Deprivation* (Springfield, Ill.: Charles C Thomas, 1963).

:25–30   R. L. BIRDWHISTELL, "Kinesic Analysis of Filmed Behavior of Children," in B. Schaffner (ed.), *Group Processes* (New York: Josiah Macy, Jr., Foundation, 1956), p. 143; R. L. Birdwhistell, *Kinesics and Context* (Philadelphia:

Page and Line

University of Pennsylvania Press, 1970); J. Fast, *Body Language* (New York: M. Evans, 1970); see also M. Ar-gyle, *Bodily Communication* (New York: International Universities Press, 1975); M. Argyle and M. Cook, *Gaze and Mutual Gaze* (London & New York: Cambridge University Press, 1976).

109:8–21   P. Lacombe, "Du Rôle de la Peau dans l'Attachement Mère-Enfant," *Revue française du Psychanalyse,* 23 (1959), pp. 83–101.

:22 to   P. F. D. Seitz, "Psychocutaneous Conditioning during the
112:2   First Two Weeks of Life," *Psychosomatic Medicine,* 12 (1950), pp. 187–188.

:35 to   M. A. Ribble, "Disorganizing Factors of Infant Personal-
113:11   ity," *American Journal of Psychiatry,* 98 (1941), pp. 459–463.

:12–35   B. Taubman, "Clinical Trial of the Treatment of Colic by Modification of Parent-Infant Interaction," *Pediatrics,* 74 (1984), pp. 998–1003.

114:11–12   L. S. Kubie, "Instincts and Homeostasis," *Psychosomatic Medicine,* 10 (1948), pp. 15–30.

:32–33   D. B. Dill, *Life, Heat, and Altitude* (Cambridge, Mass.: Harvard University Press, 1938).

115:14–17   V. V. Rozanov, *Solitaria* (London: Wishart, 1927).

116:24–29   M. I. Heinstein, "Behavioral Correlates of Breast-Bottle Regimes under Varying Parent-Infant Relationships," *Monographs of the Society for Child Growth and Development,* Serial No. 88, vol. 28, no. 4 (1963); M. I. Heinstein, "Influence of Breast Feeding on Children's Behavior," *Children,* 10 (1963), pp. 93–97.

117:30–35   G. Stanley Hall, "Notes on the Study of Infants," *Pedagogical Seminary,* 1 (1891), pp. 127–138.

:36 to   S. Freud, *Three Essays on the Theory of Sexuality* [1905]
118:16   (London: Imago, 1949), p. 60.

:33   W. Wickler, *The Sexual Code* (New York: Anchor Books, 1973), pp. 169–170.

119:19–23   S. Rado, "The Psychical Effects of Intoxication," *Psychoanalytic Review,* 18 (1931), pp. 69–84.

:30 to   H. F. Harlow and M. K. Harlow, "The Effect of Rearing
120:14   Conditions on Behavior," in John Money (ed.), *Sex Research: New Developments* (New York: Holt, Rinehart & Winston, 1965), pp. 161–175.

:17–20   G. W. Henry, *All the Sexes* (New York: Rinehart, 1955); R. J. Stoller, *Sex and Gender* (New York: Science

Page and Line

House, 1968); S. Brody, *Patterns of Mothering* (New York: International Universities Press, 1956).

:19–25 M. P. MIDDLEMORE, *The Nursing Couple* (London: Cassell, 1941).

:30–36 L. J. YARROW, "Maternal Deprivation: Toward an Empirical and Conceptual Re-valuation," *Psychological Bulletin,* 58 (1961), pp. 459–490; p. 485. See also John Bowlby, *Attachment and Loss,* vol. 1, *Attachment* (New York: Basic Books, 1969).

:35–36 E. GAMPER, "Bau und Leistung eines menschlichen Mittelhirnwesens, II," *Zeitschrift für die Gesammte Neurologie und Psychiatrie,* vol. 104 (1926), pp. 48 et seq.

121:28–32 R. A. SPITZ, *No and Yes* (New York: International Universities Press, 1957), pp. 21–22.

122:4–14 C. A. ALDRICH, "Ancient Processes in a Scientific Age," *American Journal of Diseases of Childhood,* 64 (1942), p. 714; H. Bakwin and R. M. Bakwin, *Clinical Management of Behavior Disorders in Children* (3rd ed., Philadelphia: Saunders, 1966), p. 59.

:16–22 I. DeVORE, "Mother-Infant Relations in Free-Ranging Baboons," in H. L. Rheingold (ed.), *Maternal Behavior in Mammals* (New York: Wiley, 1963), p. 312.

:22–28 Ibid., pp. 314, 317–318.

123:6–19 S. PROVENCE, *Ladies' Home Journal,* March 1976.

:20–24 R. LANG, *The Birth Book* (Palo Alto, California: Science and Behavior Books, 1972); M. H. Klaus and J. H. Kennell, *Maternal-Infant Bonding* (St. Louis, Mo.: C. V. Mosby, 1976), p. 73.

124:24–30 W. ONG, *The Presence of the Word* (New Haven, Conn.: Yale University Press, 1967), pp. 169–170.

:30–33 A. LEVITSKY, quoted by Richard Register, "In Touch with Feeling," *Human Behavior,* 4 (1975), pp. 16–23.

125:11–17 R. M. YERKES, "The Mind of a Gorilla," *Genetic Psychology Monographs,* 2 (1927), p. 147.

:19–32 J. ORTEGA Y GASSET, *Man and People* (New York: Norton, 1957), pp. 72 et seq.

126:11–15 M. A. RIBBLE, *The Rights of Infants* (2nd ed., New York: Columbia University Press, 1965).

:23–26 W. HOFFER, "Mouth, Hand, and Ego-Integration," in A. Freud et al. (eds), *The Psychoanalytic Study of the Child,* vols. 3/4 (New York: International Universities Press, 1949), pp. 49–56; W. Hoffer, "Development of the Body Ego," in *The Psychoanalytic Study of the Child,* vol. 5

Page and Line

(New York: International Universities Press, 1950), pp. 18–23.

:26–28   J. W. WEIFFENBACH (ed.), *Taste and Development* (Bethesda, Maryland: U. S. Department of Health, Education and Welfare, Publication N. NIH 77-1068, 1977); G. H. Nowlis and W. Kessen, "Human Newborns Differentiate Differing Concentrations of Sucrose and Glucose," *Science,* 191 (1976), pp. 865–866.

127:22–30   G. REVESZ, *Psychology and Art of the Blind* (London: Longmans, 1959), pp. 14, 58, 235.

:30–33   SIR C. BELL, *The Hand: Its Mechanism and Vital Endowments as Evincing Design.* Bridgewater Treatise No. 4. (London: Pickering, 1833).

:33–35   F. W. JONES, *The Principles of Anatomy as Seen in the Hand* (2nd ed., London: Balliere & Cox, 1942). See also George Rosen (ed.), The Hand, *Ciba Symposia,* 4 (1942) pp. 1294–1327.

129:21 to   B. BETTELHEIM, "Where Self Begins," *The New York Times*
130:2   *Magazine,* 12 February 1967. Reprinted in *Child and Family,* 7 (1967), pp. 5–9.

132:2 to   R. RUBIN, "Maternal Touch," *Nursing Outlook,* 11 (1963),
133:8   pp. 828–831.

:13–17   R. LANG, "Delivery in the Home," in Marshall H. Klaus, T. Leger, and Mary Anne Trause (eds.), *Maternal Attachment and Mothering Disorders: A Round Table* (New Brunswick, N. J.: Johnson & Johnson, 1975), pp. 45–49.

:30–34   M. PAPOUŠEK, "Discussion," in M. A. Hofer (ed.), *Parent-Infant Interaction* (New York and Amsterdam: Elsevier, 1975), p. 82.

:35 to   M. H. KLAUS, J. H. KENNELL, N. PLUMB, and S. ZUEHLKE,
134:8   "Human Maternal Behavior at the First Contact with Her Young," *Pediatrics,* 46 (1970), pp. 187–192.

:12   C. R. BARNETT, P. H. LEIDERMAN, R. GROBSTEIN, and K. MARSHALL, "Neonatal Separation: the Maternal Side of Interactional Deprivation," *Pediatrics,* 45 (1970), pp. 197–205.

:17–18   C. P. S. WILLIAMS and T. K. OLIVER, JR., "Nursery Routines and Staphylococcal Colonization of the Newborn," *Pediatrics,* 44 (1969), pp. 640–646.

:19 to   Editorial, "Mothers of Premature Babies," *British Medical*
135:6   *Journal,* 6 June 1970, p. 556.

:7–37   S. KITZINGER, *Some Mothers' Experiences of Induced*

Page and Line

Labour (London: The National Childbirth Trust, 1975).

136:1–10   A. M. SOSTEK, J. W. SCANLON, and D. C. ABRAMSON, "Postpartum Contact and Maternal Confidence and Anxiety: A Confirmation of Short-Term Effects," *Infant Behavior and Development*, 5 (1982), pp. 323–329.

:23 to   KLAUS and KENNELL, *Maternal-Infant Bonding*, p. 51.
137:12   Ibid., pp. 93–94.

:19–20   E. FURMAN, in Klaus and Kennell, *Maternal-Infant Bonding*, p. 52.

:21–32   M. J. SEASHORE, A. D. LEIFER, C. R. BARNETT, and P. H. LEIDERMAN, "The Effects of Denial of Early Mother-Infant Interaction on Maternal Self-Confidence," *Journal of Personality and Social Psychology*, 26 (1973), pp. 369–378.

:33 to   P. H. LEIDERMAN, "Mother-Infant Separation: Delayed
138:8   Consequences," in Klaus, Leger, and Trause, *Maternal Attachment and Mothering Disorders: A Round Table*, pp. 67–70.

:15–20   P. DE CHATEAU, "Neonatal Care Routines: Influences on Maternal and Infant Behavior and on Breast Feeding" (Doctoral thesis, Umea University Medical Dissertations, N.S., no. 20), Umea, Sweden, 1976, quoted in Klaus and Kennell, *Maternal Infant-Bonding*, pp. 62–65.

:26 to   M. A. HOFER, "Infant Separation Responses and the Ma-
139:4   ternal Role," *Biological Psychiatry*, 10 (1975), pp. 149–153.

:5–28   M. A. HOFER, "Studies on How Maternal Separation Produces Behavioral Change in Young Rats," *Psychosomatic Medicine*, 37 (1975), pp. 245–264; M. A. Hofer, "Physiological and Behavioural Processes in Early Maternal Deprivation," in D. Hill (ed.), *Physiology, Emotion and Psychosomatic Illness* (London & Amsterdam: Elsevier, 1972), pp. 175–200; M. A. Hofer, "Maternal Separation Affects Infant Rats' Behavior," *Behavioral Biology*, 9 (1973), pp. 629–633.

:29–37   HOFER, "Physiological and Behavioural Processes in Early Maternal Deprivation," p. 185.

140:9–18   M. H. KLAUS and J. H. KENNELL, *Parent-Infant Bonding* (2nd ed., St. Louis, Mo.: C. V. Mosby, 1982), pp. 35–57; Patrick Bateson, "How Do Sensitive Periods Arise and What Are They For?" *Animal Behavior*, 27 (1979), pp. 470–486.

Page and Line

:19–30   KLAUS, LEGER, and TRAUSE, *Maternal Attachment and Mothering Disorders: A Round Table,* p. 43.

:36 to   G. BATESON and M. MEAD, *Balinese Character* (Special
141:13   Publication, New York: New York Academy of Sciences, 1942), p. 30.

:30–37   J. REIS, "Sibling Bonding," *La Leche League News,* May–June 1979, p. 58.

142:18–20   R. S. ILLINGWORTH, *The Development of the Infant and Young Child* (Edinburgh: Livingstone, 1960), pp. 130–132.

:29–31   E. L. THORNDIKE, *Animal Intelligence* (New York: Macmillan, 1911), p. 244. For an account of learning theory see A. Montagu, *The Direction of Human Development* (Revised edition, New York: Hawthorn Books, 1970), pp. 317–345.

:32 to   M. MEAD and F. C. MACGREGOR, *Growth and Culture*
144:2   (New York: G. P. Putnam's Sons, 1951), pp. 42–43.

:2–6   C. MCPHEE, quoted in Mead and Macgregor, *Growth and Culture,* p. 43. See also C. McPhee, *Music in Bali* (New Haven, Conn.: Yale University Press), 1966.

:7–10   B. NETTL, *Ethnomusicology* (New York: Free Press, 1964).

:10–12   J. CHERNOFF, *African Rhythm and African Sensibility* (Chicago: University of Chicago Press, 1979).

145:14–33   A. MONTAGU, "Some Factors in Family Cohesion," *Psychiatry,* 7 (1944), pp. 349–352.

:33 to   J. C. SINGER, *The Child's World of Make-Believe* (New
146:4   York: Academic Press, 1973), p. 238.

:7–13   MEAD and MACGREGOR, *Growth and Culture,* p. 50.

147:5–15   W. WICKLER, *The Sexual Code* (Garden City, N.Y.: Anchor Books, 1973), p. 266.

:29 to   J. ZAHOVSKY, "Discard of the Cradle," *Journal of Pediat-*
148:10   *rics,* 4 (1934), pp. 660–667.

:19 to   L. E. HOLT, *The Care and Feeding of Children* (15th ed.,
149:5   New York: Appleton-Century, 1935).

:21 to   J. B. WATSON, *Psychological Care of Infant and Child* (New
151:31   York: Norton, 1928).

:11   D. COHEN, *J. B. Watson, The Founder of Behaviorism: A Biography* (Boston: Routledge & Kegan Paul, 1979), pp. 196–221, 288.

:34 to   The correspondent who sent me these verses could not re-
152:4   call the name of the author or the source in which they appeared.

:25 to   B. CHISHOLM, *Prescription for Survival* (New York: Colum-
153:33   bia University Press, 1957), pp. 37–38.

154:20–36   E. SYLVESTER, "Discussion," in M. J. E. Senn (ed.), *Prob-*

Page and Line

lems of Infancy (New York: Josiah Macy, Jr., Foundation, 1953), p. 29.

155:8–10   A. B. BERGMAN, J. B. BECKWITH, and C. G. RAY (eds.), *Sudden Infant Death Syndrome* (Seattle: University of Washington Press, 1970).

:14 to   A. MONTAGU, *Touching: The Human Significance of the*
156:33   *Skin,* 2nd ed. (New York: Harper & Row, 1978); "The Origin and Significance of Neonatal and Infant Immaturity in Man," *Journal of American Medical Association,* 178 (1961), pp. 156–157; M. H. Klaus and J. H. Kennell, *Parent-Infant Bonding,* 2nd ed. (St. Louis: Mosby, 1982); T. K. Oliver, Jr. (ed.), *Neonatal Respiratory Adaptation* (Bethesda: National Institutes of Health, 1964); J. A. Comroe, *Transition from Intrauterine to Extrauterine Life* (Bethesda: National Institutes of Health), pp. 95–169; Shaul Harel (ed.), *The At Risk Infant* (Amsterdam: Excerpta Medica, 1980), p. 459; M. H. Klaus, A. A. Faranoff and R. J. Martin, "Respiratory Problems," in M. H. Klaus and A. A. Faranoff (eds.), *Care of the High-risk Neonate,* 2nd ed. (Philadelphia: Saunders, 1979), pp. 173–175; M. A. Valdes-Dapena, "Sudden Infant Death Syndrome: A Review of the Medical Literature 1974–1979," *Pediatrics,* 66 (1980), pp. 597–614; P. M. Farrell and R. H. Perelman, "Respiratory System," in A. A. Faranoff and R. J. Martin (eds.), *Behrman's Neonatal Perinatal Medicine* (St. Louis: Mosby, 1983), pp. 404–413; "General Considerations," in M. A. Avery and H. W. Taeusch, Jr. (eds.), *Schaeffer's Diseases of the Newborn,* 5th ed. (Philadelphia: Saunders, 1984), pp. 110–119; A. Gruen, "Parental Rejection, REM Sleep and Failure to Arouse in the Sudden Infant Death Syndrome: A Theoretical Proposal Based on Retrospective Case Interview Material," in press, 1986.

:33 to   A. GRUEN, "Prior Themes of Death and Rejection Among
157:16   Parents of Sudden Infant Death Victims: Retrospective Accounts and a Proposal Concerning Focusing, REM Sleep and the Failure to Arouse in Such Children," Ms., 1985; R. L. Naeye, "Sudden Infant Death," *Scientific American,* 242 (1980), pp. 56–62.

158:2–7   A. PEIPER, *Cerebral Function in Infancy and Childhood* (New York: Consultants' Bureau, 1963), p. 606.

:11–13   G. R. FORRER, *Weaning and Human Development* (New York: Libra Publishers, 1969).

Page and Line

:23 to   ZAHOVSKY, "Discard of the Cradle," pp. 660–670; see also
159:14   Ashley Montagu, "What Ever Happened to the Cradle?" *Family Weekly* (New York), May 14, 1967.

:31 to   M. A. POWELL, "Riverside Is Rockin' Along With
160:15   Old-Fashioned Rhythm," *Toledo Blade Sun,* February 2, 1958, p. 13.

:21 to   M. NEAL, "Vestibular Stimulation and Developmental Be-
161:2   havior of the Small Premature Infant," *Nursing Research Report,* vol. 3, nos. 1–4 (New York: American Nurses Foundation, 1968).

:3–11   J. M. WOODCOCK, "The Effects of Rocking Stimulation on the Neonatus Reactivity," Purdue University, Lafayette, Indiana, 1969.

:12–37   J. C. SOLOMON, "Passive Motion and Infancy," *American Journal of Orthopsychiatry,* 29 (1959), pp. 650–651.

162:1–23   W. J. GREENE, JR., "Early Object Relations, Somatic, Affective, and Personal," *The Journal of Nervous and Mental Disease,* 126 (1958), pp. 225–253.

:23–29   W. J. GREENE, JR., quoted by A. P. Shasberg, "Of Reading, Rocking, and Rollicking," *New York Times Magazine,* January 5, 1969.

:35 to   D. G. FREEDMAN, H. BOVERMAN, and N. FREEDMAN, "Ef-
163:7   fects of Kinesthetic Stimulation on Weight Gain and Smiling in Premature Infants," paper presented at the meeting of the American Orthopsychiatry Association, San Francisco, April 1960.

:16–24   N. SOKOLOFF, S. YAFFE, D. WEINTRAUB, and B. BLASE, "Effects of Handling on the Subsequent Development of Premature Infants," *Developmental Psychology,* 1 (1969), pp. 765–768.

:25–29   E. G. HASSELMEYER, "The Premature Neonate's Response to Handling," *Journal of the American Nurses Association,* 2 (1964), pp. 14–15.

:30 to   T. M. FIELD and S. M. SCHANBERG et al., "Effects of Tac-
164:13   tile/Kinesthetic Stimulation on Preterm Neonates," *Pediatrics,* May 1986; S. M. Schanberg and T. M. Field, "Sensory Deprivation, Stress and Supplementary Stimulation in the Rat and Preterm Human Neonates," *Child Development,* in press, 1986.

:5–7   T. B. BRAZELTON, *Neonatal Assessment Scale* (London: Heinemann Medical Books, 1973).

:14 to   KLAUS and KENNELL, *Maternal-Infant Bonding,* pp.
165:8   99–166.

:9–11   A. J. SOLNIT, "Comment," ibid., p. 190.

Page and Line

:30 to 166:5 — W. A. MASON and G. BERKSON, "Effects of Maternal Mobility on the Development of Rocking and Other Behavior in Rhesus Monkeys: A Study with Artificial Mothers," *Developmental Psychology,* 8 (1975), pp. 197–211.

167:1–14 — A. F. KORNER, H. C. KRAEMER, E. HEFFNER, and L. M. COSPER, "Effects of Waterbed Flotation on Premature Infants: A Pilot Study," 56 (1975), *Pediatrics,* pp. 361–367.

:15–37 — A. F. KORNER and R. GROBSTEIN, "Visual Alertness as Related to Soothing in Neonates: Implications for Maternal Stimulation and Early Deprivation," *Child Development,* 37 (1966), pp. 867–876; A. F. Korner and E. B. Thoman, "Visual Alertness in Neonates as Evoked by Maternal Care," *Journal of Experimental Child Psychology,* 10 (1970), pp. 67–78; A. F. Korner and E. B. Thoman, "The Relative Efficacy of Contact and Vestibular Stimulation in Soothing Neonates," *Child Development,* 43 (1972), pp. 443–453.

168:1–33 — A. F. KORNER, "Maternal Rhythms and Waterbeds: A Form of Intervention with Premature Infants," in E. B. Thoman (ed.), *Origins of the Infant's Social Responsiveness* (Hillsdale, N.J.: Erlbaum, 1979); A. F. Korner, T. Forrest, and P. Schneider, "Effects of Vestibular-Proprioceptive Stimulation on the Behavioral Development of Preterm Infants: A Pilot Study," *Neuropediatrics,* 14 (1983), pp. 170–175.

169:14–25 — J. J. GIBSON, *The Senses Considered as Perceptual Systems* (Boston: Houghton Mifflin, 1966); J. M. Kennedy, "Haptics," in E. C. Carterette and M. P. Friedman (eds.), *Handbook of Perception* (New York: Academic Press, 1978), pp. 218–318; G. Gordon (ed.), *Active Touch: The Mechanisms of Recognition of Objects by Manipulation: A Multidisciplinary Approach* (Oxford: Pergamon, 1978); William Schiff and Emerson Foulke (eds.), *Tactual Perception: A Sourcebook* (New York: Cambridge University Press, 1982).

:30 to 170:11 — J. L. WHITE and R. C. LABARRA, "The Effects of Tactile and Kinesthetic Stimulation on Neonatal Development in the Premature Infant," *Developmental Psychobiology,* 9 (1976), pp. 569–577.

:12–30 — P. GORSKI et al., "Caring for Immature Infants—A Touchy Subject," in Catherine C. Brown (ed.), *The Many Facets of Touch* (Skillman, N.J.: Johnson & Johnson Baby Products, 1984), pp. 84–89.

Page and Line

:31 to See "Home Care of Premature Infants," in B. Corner, *Pre-*
171:3 *maturity* (Springfield, Ill.: Charles C Thomas, 1960), pp.
     271–276.

170:35 to A. W. GOTTFRIED, "Touch as an Organizer for Learning
171:20 and Development," in Brown (ed.), *The Many Facets of Touch,* pp. 114–120.

:9–15 B. D. SPEIDEL, "Adverse Effects of Routine Procedure on
     Preterm Infants," *Lancet,* 1 (1978), pp. 864–865.

:28–32 D. L. CLARK, J. R. KREUTZBERG, and F. K. W. CHEE,
     "Vestibular Stimulation Influence on Motor Development in Infants," *Science,* 196 (1977), pp. 1228–1229.

172:16–22 L. H. FUCHS, *Family Matters* (New York: Random House,
     1972), p. 57.

:26–30 S. CARRIGHAR, *Home to the Wilderness* (Baltimore: Penguin Books, 1974), p. 37.

:31–33 E. CARPENTER, *Oh, What a Blow the Phantom Gave Me*
     (New York: Holt, Rinehart & Winston, 1973), p. 23.

:34 to L. K. FRANK, "Tactile Communication," *Genetic Psychol-*
173:2 *ogy Monographs,* 56 (1957), p. 227.

:26–33 W. DEVLIN, "Touch Dancing—Where It's At," *Harpers Bazaar,* February 1974, p. 131.

174:3–5 A. P. ROYCE, *The Anthropology of Dance* (Bloomington:
     University of Indiana Press, 1980), p. 199; L. HANNA, *To Dance Is Human: A Theory of Nonverbal Communication* (Austin: University of Texas Press, 1979); S. LONSDALE, *Animals and the Origins of Dance* (New York: Thames and Hudson, 1982); C. SACHS, *World History of Dance* (New York: Norton, 1937); J. Highwater, *Dance: Rituals of Experience* (New York: Alfred van der Marck, 1985).

:18 to L. SALK, "The Effects of the Normal Heartbeat Sound on
175:16 the Behavior of the Newborn Infant: Implications for Mental Health," *World Mental Health,* 12 (1960), pp. 1–8.

:30 to J. A. M. MEERLOO, *The Dance* (Philadelphia: Chilton,
177:7 1960), pp. 13–14.

179:8–14 O. C. IRWIN and L. WEISS, "The Effect of Clothing and
     Vocal Activity of the Newborn Infant," in W. Dennis (ed.), *Readings in Child Psychology* (New York: Prentice-Hall, 1951).

180:22–32 L. WILSON, "Of Babies and Water Beds," *Childbirth and
     Parent Education Association,* Miami, Florida, Newsletter, vol. 8, no. 9, September 1973.

181:14–21 J. C. FLÜGEL, *The Psychology of Clothes* (London: Hogarth
     Press, 1930), p. 87; J. C. FLÜGEL, "Clothes Symbolism

Page and Line

and Clothes Ambivalence," *International Journal of Psychoanalysis,* 10 (1929), p. 205.

:26 to   W. E. HARTMAN, M. FITHIAN, and D. JOHNSON, *Nudist*
182:10   *Society* (New York: Crown, 1970), pp. 289, 293.

:24–28   K. STEWART, *Pygmies and Dream Giants* (New York: Norton, 1954), p. 105.

:37 to   S. R. ARBEIT, B. PARKER, and I. L. RUBIN, "Controlling the
183:12   Electrocution Hazard in the Hospital," *Journal of the American Medical Association,* 220 (1972), pp. 1581–1584.

:13–22   M. L. BIGGAR, "Maternal Aversion to Mother-Infant Contact," in C. C. Brown (ed.), *The Many Facets of Touch* (Skillman, N.J.: Johnson & Johnson Baby Products, 1984), pp. 66–72.

:21–28   G. BATESON, D. JACKSON, J. HALEY, and J. WEAKLAND, "Toward a Theory of Schizophrenia," *Behavioral Sciences,* 1 (1965), pp. 251–264.

184:27–29   A. MONTAGU and F. MATSON, *The Human Connection* (New York: McGraw-Hill, 1979); JOHN BOWLBY, *Attachment and Loss* (3 vols., New York: Basic Books, 1969–1980); A. M. and A. D. B. CLARKE, *Early Experience: Myth and Evidence* (New York: Free Press, 1976).

:32–35   A. M. SOSTEK, J. W. SCANLON, and D. C. ABRAMSON, "Postpartum Contact and Maternal Confidence and Anxiety: A Confirmation of Short-Term Effects," *Infant Behavior and Development,* 5 (1982), pp. 323–329.

185:22–25   H. F. HARLOW, M. K. HARLOW, and E. M. HANSEN, in H. L. RHEINGOLD (ed.), *Maternal Behavior in Mammals* (New York: Wiley, 1963), pp. 254–281; M. NOWAK, *Eve's Rib: A Revolutionary New View of the Female* (New York: St. Martin's Press, 1980), pp. 165–177.

:31 to   J. ROMAINS, *Vision Extra-Rétinienne* (Paris, 1919; English
186:2   translation, *Eyeless Sight,* New York: Putnam, 1924).

:6–8   M. GARDNER, "Dermo-Optical Perception: A Peek Down the Nose," *Science,* 151 (1966), pp. 654–657.

187:8–14   M. R. OSTROW, "Dermographia: A Critical Review," *Annals of Allergy,* 25 (1967), pp. 591–597.

:29 to   P. BACH-Y-RITA, "System May Let Blind 'See with Their
188:2   Skins,'" *Journal of the American Medical Association,* 207 (1967), pp. 2204–2205.

:23–35   F. A. GELDARD, "Body English," *Readings in Psychology Today* (Del Mar, California: CRM Associates, 1969), pp. 237–241; F. A. GELDARD, "Some Neglected Possibilities

Page and Line

of Communication," *Science,* 131 (1960), pp. 1583–1588. See also J. R. HENNESSY, "Cutaneous Sensitivity Communication," *Human Factors,* 8 (1966), pp. 463–469; G. A. GESCHEIDER, "Cutaneous Sound Localization" (Ph.D. diss., University of Virginia, 1964); G. VON BEKESY, "Similarities between Hearing and Skin Sensation," *Psychological Reviews,* 66 (1959), pp. 1–22.

189:1–4   F. TABOR, "Tactile Vision," *Science News,* 114 (1978), p. 387.

:4–12   M. VON SNEDEN, *Space and Sight* (New York: Free Press, 1960).

:16   S. HOCKEN, *Emma and I* (London: Gollancz, 1977).

:20–22   "Replacing Braille?" *Time,* 19 September 1969.

:24 to   B. VON HALLER GILMER AND L. W. GREGG, "The Skin as a
190:19   Channel of Communication," *Etc.,* 18 (1961), pp. 199–209.

:3–5   J. F. HAHN, "Cutaneous Vibratory Thresholds for Square-Wave Electrical Pulses," *Science,* 127 (1958), pp. 879–880.

191:2–16   H. MUSAPH, *Itching and Scratching: Psychodynamics in Dermatology* (Philadelphia: F. A. Davis Co., 1964).

:17–19   P. F. D. SEITZ, "Psychocutaneous Aspects of Persistent Pruritis and Excessive Excoriation," *Archives of Dermatology and Syphilology,* 64 (1951), pp. 136–141; M. E. OBERMAYER, *Psychocutaneous Medicine* (Springfield, Ill.: Charles C Thomas, 1955); S. AYRES, "The Fine Art of Scratching," *Journal of the American Medical Association,* 189 (1964), pp. 1003–1007; J. J. KOPECS and M. ROBIN, "Studies on Itching," *Psychosomatic Medicine,* 17 (1955), pp. 87–95; B. RUSSELL, "Pruritic Skin Conditions," in C. Newman (ed.), *The Nature of Stress Disorder* (Springfield, Ill.: Charles C Thomas, 1959), pp. 40–51.

:20–26   M. A. BEREZIN, "Dynamic Factors in Pruritis Ani: A Case Report," *Psychoanalytic Review,* 41 (1954), pp. 160–172.

192:7–12   O. NASH, *Verses from 1919 On* (Boston: Little, Brown, 1959).

:13–18   B. RUSSELL, "Pruritic Skin Conditions," in Newman, *The Nature of Stress Disorder,* p. 48.

:19–22   E. STERN, "Le Prurit," Étude Psychosomatique, *Acta Psychotherapeutica,* 3 (1955), pp. 107–116.

194:28 to   C. W. SALEEBY, *Sunlight and Health* (London: Nisbet,
195:4   1928), p. 67.

Page and Line

:5   PLATO, *The Republic,* Book 5; G. V. N. DEARBORN, "The Psychology of Clothing," *Psychological Monographs,* 26 (1918/19), no. 1 (1928), p. 64; HILAIRE HILER, *From Nudity to Raiment* (London: Simpkin Marshall, 1930); MAURICE PARMELEE, *The New Gymnosophy* (New York: Hitchcock, 1927); Flügel, *The Psychology of Clothes;* L. E. LANGNER, *The Importance of Wearing Clothes* (New York: Hastings House, 1959).

:14   J. M. KNOX, Symposium on Cosmetics, "The Sunny Side of the Street Is Not the Place to Be," *Journal of the American Medical Association,* 195 (1966), p. 10.

:16–22   A. L. LORINCZ, "Physiological and Pathological Changes in Skin from Sunburn and Suntan," *Journal of the American Medical Association,* 173 (1963), pp. 1227–1231; R. G. FREEMAN, "Carcinogenic Effects of Solar Radiation and Prevention Measured," *Cancer,* 21 (1968), pp. 1114–1120; A. M. KLIGMAN, "Early Destructive Effect of Sunlight on Human Skin," *Journal of the American Medical Association,* 210 (1969), pp. 2377–2380.

196:7–11   C. PINCHER, *Sleep* (London: Daily Express, 1954), pp. 18–19; G. G. Luce and J. Segal, *Sleep and Dreams* (London: Heinemann, 1967).

:12–22   A. FREUD, "Psychoanalysis and Education," *The Psychoanalytic Study of the Child,* vol. 9 (1954), p. 12.

:22 to 197:2   C. M. HEINICKE and I. WESTHEIMER, *Brief Separations* (New York: International Universities Press, 1965), pp. 165, 266.

:3–10   FENICHEL, *The Psychoanalytic Theory of Neurosis,* pp. 120–121.

:14–25   A. ALDRICH, CHIEH SUNG, and C. KNOP, "The Crying of Newly Born Babies," *Journal of Pediatrics,* 27 (1945), p. 95.

CHAPTER FIVE. THE PHYSIOLOGICAL EFFECTS OF TOUCHING

Page and Line

198:1–11   O. WEININGER, personal communication, October 12, 1984.

:11 to 199:25   NOVA, *A Touch of Sensitivity* (Boston: WGBH transcripts, 1980); M. L. REITE, "Touch, Attachment, and Health— Is There a Relationship?" in C. C. Brown (ed.), *The Many Facets of Touch* (Skillman, N.J.: Johnson & John-

Page and Line

son Baby Products, 1984), pp. 58–65; M. L. LAUDEN-SLAGER and M. L. REITE, "Losses and Separations: Immunological Consequences and Health Implications," in P. Shaver (ed.), *Review of Personality and Social Psychology: Emotions, Relationships, and Health* (Beverly Hills: Sage Publications, 1984), pp. 285–312; H. BESEDOVSKY et al., "The Immune Response Evokes Changes in Brain Noradrenergic Neurons," *Science,* 221 (1983), pp. 564–565; J. CUNNINGHAM, "Mind, Body, and Immune Response," in R. Ader (ed.), *Psychoneuroimmunology,* (New York: Academic Press, 1981), pp. 609–617; S. LOCKE et al. (eds.), *Foundations of Psychoneuroimmunology* (New York: Aldine Publishing, 1985).

198:15–21 A. G. CHU et al., "Thymopoietin-like Substance in Human Skin," *Journal of Investigative Dermatology,* 81 (1983), pp. 194–197.

199:5–13 M. L. LAUDENSLAGER, M. REITE, and J. HARBECK, "Suppressed Immune Response in Infant Monkeys Associated with Maternal Separation," *Behavioral and Neural Biology,* 36 (1982), pp. 40–48.

:14–25 M. L. REITE, R. HARBECK, and A. HOFFMAN, "Altered Cellular Immune Response Following Peer Separation," *Life Sciences,* 29 (1981), pp. 1133–1136.

:26 to 200:5 S. R. BUTLER and S. M. SCHANBERG, "Effect of Maternal Deprivation on Polyamine Metabolism in Preweaning Rat Brain and Heart," *Life Sciences,* 21 (1977), pp. 877–884.

:6–19 C. M. KUHN, G. EVONIUK, and S. M. SCHANBERG, "Loss of Tissue Sensitivity to Growth Hormone during Maternal Deprivation in Rats," *Life Sciences,* 25 (1979), pp. 2089–2097.

201:21–32 S. M. SCHANBERG, G. EVONIUK, and C. M. KUHN, "Tactile and Nutritional Aspects of Maternal Care: Specific Regulators of Neuroendocrine Function and Cellular Development," *Proceedings of the Society for Experimental Biology and Medicine,* 175 (1984), pp. 135–146; S. R. BUTLER, M. R. SUSSKIND, and S. M. SCHANBERG, "Maternal Behavior as a Regulator of Polyamine Biosynthesis in Brain and Heart of the Developing Rat Pup," *Science,* 199 (1977), pp. 445–446.

202:13–20 E. M. WIDDOWSON, "Mental Contentment and Physical Growth," *The Lancet,* 1 (1951), pp. 1316–1318; reprinted

Page and Line

              in Ashley Montagu (ed.), *Culture and Human Development: Insights into Growing Human* (Englewood Cliffs, N.J.: Prentice-Hall, 1974), pp. 99–105.

:21–30   G. F. POWELL, J. A. BRASEL, and R. M. BLIZZARD, "Emotional Deprivation and Growth Retardation Simulating Idiopathic Hypopituitarism," *New England Journal of Medicine,* 176 (1967), pp. 1271–1278; G. F. POWELL, J. A. BRASEL, S. RAITI, and R. M. BLIZZARD, "Emotional Deprivation and Growth Retardation Simulating Hypopituitarism: II Endocrinologic Evaluation of the Syndrome," *New England Journal of Medicine,* 176 (1967), pp. 1279–1283, Part I reprinted in Ashley Montagu (ed.), *Culture and Human Development,* pp. 105–106.

:31 to   J. B. REINHART and A. A. DRASH, "Psychosocial Dwarf-
203:3   ism: Environmentally Induced Recovery," *Psychosomatic Medicine,* 31 (1969), pp. 165–172.

CHAPTER SIX. SKIN AND SEX

Page and Line

204:1–6   *Our Bodies, Our Selves* (2nd ed., New York: Simon & Schuster, 1976), p. 41.

205:10–13   A. MONTAGU, *The Human Revolution* (New York: Bantam Books, 1967), pp. 150–151.

:24–28   R. C. KOLODNY, L. S. JACOBS, and W. H. DAGHHADAY, "Mammary Stimulation Causes Prolactin Secretion in Non-Lactating Women," *Nature,* 238 (1972), pp. 284–285.

:28–31   A. BRODAL, *Neurological Anatomy in Relation to Clinical Medicine* (New York: Oxford University Press, 1969), p. 33.

206:8–14   D. GOULD, "Spirits, Doctors and Disease," *New Scientist,* May 17, 1976, pp. 474–475.

:21–26   H. F. HARLOW, M. K. HARLOW, and E. W. HANSEN, "The Maternal Affectional System of Rhesus Monkeys," in H. L. Rheingold (ed.), *Maternal Behavior in Mammals* (New York: Wiley, 1963), pp. 277–278.

:32–36   R. J. STOLLER, *Sex and Gender* (New York: Science House, 1968).

207:12–20   A. FREUD, *Normality and Pathology in Childhood* (New York: International Universities Press, 1965), p. 199.

:28 to   M. H. HOLLENDER, L. LUBORSKY, and T. J. SCARAMELLA,
208:21   "Body Contact and Sexual Excitement," *Archives of*

Page and Line

General Psychiatry, 20 (1969), pp. 188–191; M. H. HOL-
LENDER, "The Wish to Be Held," *Archives of General
Psychiatry,* 22 (1970), pp. 445–453.

:22–23   M. H. HOLLENDER, "Prostitution, the Body, and Human
Relations," *International Journal of Psychoanalysis,* 42
(1961), pp. 404–413.

:25–28   M. G. BLINDER, "Differential Diagnosis and Treatment of
Depressive Disorders," *Journal of the American Medical
Association,* 195 (1966), pp. 8–12.

:29–35   C. P. MALMQUIST, T. J. KIRESUK, and R. M. SPANO, "Personality Characteristics of Women with Repeated Illegitimate Pregnancies: Descriptive Aspects," *American
Journal of Orthopsychiatry,* 36 (1966), pp. 476–484.

:35–36   A. MOLL, *The Sexual Life of the Child* (London: Allen &
Unwin, 1912); H. Graff and R. Mallin, "The Syndrome
of the Wrist Cutter," *American Journal of Psychiatry,*
124 (1967), pp. 36–42.

:37 to   M. H. HOLLENDER, "Women's Wish to Be Held: Sexual
209:6   and Nonsexual Aspects," *Medical Aspects of Human
Sexuality,* October 1971, pp. 12, 17, 19, 21, 25, 26.

:20 to   M. H. HOLLENDER, L. LUBORSKY, and R. B. HARVEY,
210:8   "Correlates of the Desire to Be Held in Women,"
Journal of Psychosomatic Research, 14 (1970), pp.
387–390.

:22–34   M. H. HOLLENDER and J. B. McGHEE, "The Wish to Be
Held during Pregnancy," *Journal of Psychosomatic Research,* 18 (1974), pp. 193–197.

:35 to   M. H. HOLLENDER and A. J. MERCER, "Wish to Be Held
211:8   and Wish to Hold in Men and Women," *Archives of
General Psychiatry,* 33 (1976), pp. 49–51.

:10–20   A. MONTAGU, *The Reproductive Development of the Female:
A Study in the Comparative Physiology of the Adolescent
Organism* (3rd ed., Littleton, Mass.: PSG Publishing
Co., 1979); E. R. MCANARNEY (ed.), *Premature Adoles-
cent Pregnancy and Parenthood* (New York: Grune &
Stratton, 1983).

:21 to   E. R. MCANARNEY, "Touching and Adolescent Sexuality,"
212:4   in C. C. Brown (ed.), *The Many Facets of Touch* (Skillman, N.J.: Johnson & Johnson Baby Products Co.,
1984), pp. 138–145.

:5–18   A. LANDERS, "Sex: Why Women Feel Short-Changed,"
Family Circle, 11 June 1985, pp. 131–132, 134;
A. Landers, "What 100,000 Women Told Ann
Landers," *Reader's Digest,* August 1985, pp. 44–46.

Page and Line

:19 to   L. T. HUANG, R. PHARES, and M. H. HOLLENDER, "The
213:9   Wish to Be Held," *Archives of General Psychiatry,* 33 (1976), pp. 41–43.

:10–26   A. LOWEN, *The Betrayal of the Body* (New York: Collier Books, 1969), p. 102.

:29–33   B. MALIVER, *The Encounter Game* (New York: Stein & Day, 1972), p. 130.

214:7–8   S. FREUD, *An Outline of Psychoanalysis* (New York: Norton, 1949), p. 24.

:8–14   O. FENICHEL, *The Psychoanalytic Theory of Neurosis* (New York: Norton, 1945), p. 70.

:15–27   *Our Bodies, Our Selves,* p. 50.

:35 to   M. FRIEDMAN, *Buried Alive: The Biography of Janis Joplin*
215:15   (New York: William Morrow, 1973), p. 16.

:21–23   E. S. SCHAEFER and N. BAYLEY, "Maternal Behavior, Child Behavior, and Their Intercorrelations from Infancy through Adolescence," *Monographs of the Society for Research in Child Development,* 28, 3 (1963), pp. 1–117.

:26 to   J. RUESCH, *Disturbed Communication* (New York: Norton,
216:3   1957), pp. 31–32.

:4–21   A. MOLL, *The Sexual Life of the Child* (London: Allen & Unwin, 1912), pp. 21–31; H. GRAFF and R. MALLIN, "The Syndrome of the Wrist Cutter," *American Journal of Psychiatry,* 124 (1967), pp. 36–42.

217:5–7   S. BRODY, *Patterns of Mothering* (New York: International Universities Press, 1956), p. 340.

:11–14   S. FREUD, *Introductory Lectures on Psycho-Analysis* (London: Allen & Unwin, 1922), pp. 269–284.

:14–18   L. K. FRANK, "Genetic Psychology and Its Prospects," *American Journal of Orthopsychiatry,* 21 (1951), p. 517.

:29–35   S. BRODY, *Patterns of Mothering,* p. 338.

218:11 to   L. K. FRANK, "The Psychosocial Approach in Sex Re-
219:15   search," *Social Problems,* 1 (1954), p. 134.

:16–24   J. S. PLANT, *Personality and the Cultural Pattern* (New York: The Commonwealth Fund, 1937), p. 22.

:25–27   W. A. WEISSKOPF, *The Psychology of Economics* (Chicago: University of Chicago Press, 1955), p. 147.

:28–35   G. G. LUCE, *Your Second Life* (New York: Delacorte Press, 1979), p. 51.

220:5–18   A. LOWEN, *The Betrayal of the Body,* p. 105.

:19–33   A. BARCLAY, "The Effects of Pregnancy and Childbirth on the Sexual Relationship," *The CEA Philadelphia Chron-*

icler, 11, 8 (December 1975), pp. 6–7, and personal communications from Dr. Barclay.

:34 to
221:6
E. ERIKSON, *Childhood and Society* (New York: Norton, 1950).

:37 to
222:9
J. C. MOLONEY, "Thumbsucking," *Child and Family,* 6 (1967), pp. 29–30.

:9–11
V. LOWENFELD, *Creative and Mental Growth* (New York: Macmillan, 1947).

:24–26
For the gentle touch of the free-living gorilla, see D. Fossey, "More Years with Mountain Gorillas," *National Geographic,* 140 (1971), pp. 574–585; D. Fossey, *Gorillas in the Mist* (Boston: Houghton Mifflin, 1983).

:30 to
223:19
L. K. FRANK, "Tactile Communication," *Genetic Psychology Monographs,* 56 (1957), pp. 209–255; p. 233; Frank, "The Psychosocial Approach in Sex Research," p. 137.

224:9–26
G. M. MCCRAY, "Excessive Masturbation of Childhood: A Symptom of Tactile Deprivation," *Pediatrics,* 62 (1978), pp. 277–279.

:27 to
225:9
H. HARLOW, M. HARLOW, and E. W. HANSEN, "The Maternal Affectional System of Rhesus Monkeys," in H. L. Rheingold (ed.), *Maternal Behavior in Mammals* (New York: Wiley, 1963), pp. 254–281.

:14–21
B. F. STEELE and C. B. POLLOCK, "A Psychiatric Study of Parents Who Abuse Infants and Small Children," in R. Helfer and C. Kempe (eds.), *The Battered Child* (Chicago: University of Chicago Press, 1968).

:21 to
227:2
J. H. PRESCOTT, "Body Pleasure and the Origins of Violence," *The Futurist,* April 1975, pp. 64–65; J. H. Prescott, "Early Somatosensory Deprivation as an Ontogenetic Process in the Abnormal Development of the Brain and Behavior," in E. I. Goldsmith and J. Moor-Jankowski (eds.), *Medical Primatology* (Basel & New York: S. Karger, 1971), pp. 1–20.

:11–13
B. and R. JUSTICE, *The Broken Taboo: Sex in the Family* (New York: Human Sciences Press, 1979).

:18–21
R. VON KRAFFT-EBING, *Psychopathia Sexualis* (New York: Putnam, 1965); G. R. TAYLOR, *Sex in History* (New York: Vanguard Press, 1954).

228:8–15
J. J. ROUSSEAU, *Confessions,* Book 1, 1782.

229:23 to
230:6
TH. VAN DE VELDE, *Ideal Marriage* (New York: Simon & Schuster, 1932), p. 159.

:6–8
H. ELLIS, *Studies in the Psychology of Sex* (New York: Random House, 1936).

Page and Line

:9–15   M. A. OBERMAYER, *Psychocutaneous Medicine* (Springfield, Ill.: Charles C Thomas, 1955), p. 244 et seq.; J. T. MCLAUGHLIN, R. J. SHOEMAKER, and W. B. GUY, "Personality Factors in Adult Atopic Eczema," *Archives of Dermatology and Syphilology,* 68 (1953), p. 506; I. ROSEN (ed.), *The Pathology and Treatment of Sexual Deviation* (New York: Oxford University Press, 1964).

:19–25   I. ROSEN, "Exhibitionism, Scopophilia and Voyeurism," in Rosen, *The Pathology and Treatment of Sexual Deviation,* p. 308.

:29–36   S. FREUD, "Three Essays on the Theory of Sexuality" [1905], in *Complete Psychological Works of Sigmund Freud* (Standard Edition, 24 vols., London: Hogarth Press, 1953), vol. 7, pp. 120–243.

231:35 to   J. K. SKIPPER, JR., and C. H. MCCAGHY, "Stripteasers: The
232:8   Anatomy and Career Contingencies of a Deviant Occupation," *Social Problems,* 17 (1970), pp. 391–405.

:9–16   A. BROYARD, Review of Maureen Green's *Fathering* (New York: McGraw-Hill, 1976), *The New York Times,* 2 April 1976.

:9–15   A. C. KINSEY et al., *Sexual Behavior in the Human Female* (Philadelphia: Saunders, 1953), pp. 570–590, p. 688; J. MONEY, "Psychosexual Differentiation," in J. Money (ed.), *Sex Research: New Developments* (New York: Holt, Rinehart & Winston, 1965), p. 20.

:18–26   E. R. SHIPP, "A Puzzle For Parents: Good Touching or Bad?" *The New York Times,* 3 October 1984, pp. C1, C12.

:37 to   B. MALINOWSKI, *The Sexual Life of Savages in North-West-*
233:3   *ern Melanesia* (London: Routledge, 1932); R. M. and C. M. BERNDT, *Sexual Behavior in Western Arnhem Land* (New York: Viking Fund Publications in Anthropology, No. 16, 1951); C. S. FORD and F. A. BEACH, *Patterns of Sexual Behavior* (New York: Harper, 1951); F. A. BEACH, *Sex & Behavior* (New York: Wiley, 1965).

:24–30   B. FAGOT, "Sex Differences in Toddlers' Behavior and Parental Reaction," *Developmental Psychology,* 10 (1974), pp. 554–555.

:31–37   F. KAHN, *Our Sex Life* (New York: Knopf, 1939), p. 70.

234:4–7   J. MONEY and A. A. EHRHARDT, *Man & Woman: Boy & Girl* (Baltimore: Johns Hopkins University Press, 1972), p. 148.

Page and Line

:29–32　　M. MEAD, *Male and Female* (New York: Morrow, 1949), Chapter 7.

234:32 to　S. GOLDBERG and M. LEWIS, "Play Behavior in the Year-
235:2　　　Old Infant: Early Sex Differences," *Child Development,* 40 (1969), pp. 21–33. See also H. A. MOSS, "Sex, Age, and State as Determinants of Mother-Infant Inter-action," *Merrill-Palmer Quarterly,* 13 (1967), pp. 1936 et seq.

:3–6　　　E. H. ERIKSON, *Childhood and Society* (2nd ed., New York: Norton, 1963), p. 309.

:7　　　　R. R. SEARS, E. E. MACCOBY, and H. LEVIN, *Patterns of Child Rearing* (New York: Row, Peterson, 1957), pp. 56–57, p. 402.

:11–14　　J. L. and A. FISCHER, "The New Englanders of Orchard Town, U.S.A.," in B. B. Whiting (ed.), *Six Cultures* (New York: Wiley, 1963).

:14–18　　V. S. CLAY, "The Effect of Culture on Mother-Child Tac-tile Communication" (Ph.D. diss., Teachers College, Columbia University, 1966), pp. 219 et seq.

:19–22　　R. RUBIN, "Basic Maternal Behavior," *Nursing Outlook,* 9 (1961), p. 684.

:23–25　　C. TAVRIS, and C. OFFIR, *The Longest War: Sex Differences in Perspective* (New York: Harcourt Brace Jovanovich, 1977), p. 44.

:26–27　　G. L. MANGAN, "Personality and Conditioning," *Pavlovian Journal of Biological Science,* 9 (1974), pp. 125–135.

CHAPTER SEVEN. GROWTH AND DEVELOPMENT

Page and Line

237:8–11　L. CASLER, "Maternal Deprivation: A Critical Review of the Literature," *Monographs of the Society for Research in Child Development,* 26, 2 (1961).

:9　　　　J. BOWLBY, *Maternal Care and Mental Health* (Geneva: World Health Organization, 1961).

:15 to　　M. RIBBLE, *The Rights of Infants* (New York: Columbia
238:2　　　University Press, 1943); R. SPITZ, "Hospitalism: An In-quiry into the Genesis of Psychiatric Conditions in Early Childhood," in A. Freud et al. (eds.), *The Psychoanalytic Study of the Child,* vol. 1, 1945, pp. 53–74; A. FREUD and D. BURLINGHAM, *War and Children* (New York: Medi-cal War Books, 1943); W. GOLDFARB, "Variations in

Page and Line

Adolescent Adjustment of Institutionally Reared Children," *American Journal of Orthopsychiatry,* 17 (1947), pp. 449–457; A. MONTAGU, *On Being Human* (New York: Henry Schuman, 1950); A MONTAGU, *The Direction of Human Development* (New York: Harper & Row, 1955); J. ROBERTSON, *Young Children in Hospital* (London: Tavistock Publications, 1958); R. SPITZ, *No and Yes: On the Genesis of Human Communication* (New York: International Universities Press, 1957); Public Health Papers No. 14, *Deprivation of Maternal Care: A Reassessment of Its Effects* (Geneva: World Health Organization, 1962); R. SPITZ "Hospitalism: A Follow-Up Report," *The Psychoanalytic Study of the Child,* vol. 2, 1946, pp. 113–117; R. SPITZ, and K. M. WOLF, "Anaclitic Depression; An Inquiry into the Genesis of Psychiatric Conditions in Childhood," II, *The Psychoanalytic Study of the Child,* vol. 2, 1946, pp. 313–342; R. SPITZ, *The First Year of Life* (New York: International Universities Press, 1965), S. PROVENCE and R. C. LIPTON, *Infants in Institutions* (New York: International Universities Press, 1962); J. BOWLBY, *Attachment and Loss* (3 vols., New York: Basic Books, 1979/73/80); A. M. CLARKE and A. D. B. CLARKE, *Early Experience: Myth and Evidence* (New York: Free Press, 1976); T. BERGMANN, *Children in Hospital* (New York: International Universities Press, 1966); L. CASLER, "Perceptual Deprivation in Institutional Settings," in G. Newton and S. Levene (eds.), *Early Experience and Behavior* (Springfield, Ill.; Charles C Thomas, 1968); A. MONTAGU, "Sociogenic Brain Damage," *American Anthropologist,* 74 (1972), pp. 1045–1061, reprinted in A. Montagu (ed.), *Culture and Human Development,* pp. 44–72.

238:3–10   Cited in G. W. GRAY, "Human Growth," *Scientific American,* 189 (1953), pp. 65–67. The citation is misattributed in this article to Dr. Alfred F. Washburn, when in fact it belongs to Dr. J. D. Benjamin. See. W. R. Ruegamer, L. Bernstein, and J. D. Benjamin, "Growth, Food Utilization, and Thyroid Activity in the Albino Rat as a Function of Extra Handling," *Science,* 120 (1954), p. 314.

:15–20   V. H. DENENBERG and J. R. C. MORTON, "Effects of Environmental Complexity and Social Groupings upon Modification of Emotional Behavior," *Journal of Comparative Psychology,* 55 (1962), pp. 242–246.

Page and Line

:21–23   S. LEVINE, "A Further Study of Infantile Handling and Avoidance Learning," *Journal of Personality*, 25 (1962), pp. 242–246; V. H. Denenberg and C. G. Karas, "Interactive Effects of Age and Duration of Infantile Experience on Adult Learning," *Psychological Reports*, 7 (1960), pp. 313–322.

:22–31   J. T. TAPP and H. MARKOWITZ, "Infant Handling: Effects on Avoidance Learning, Brain Weight, and Cholinesterase Activity," *Science*, 140 (1963), pp. 486–487.

:26–31   L. BERNSTEIN, "A Note on Christie's 'Experimental Naiveté and Experiential Naiveté,'" *Psychological Bulletin*, 49 (1952), pp. 38–40.

:27–35   J. ROSEN, "Dominance Behavior as a Function of Early Gentling Experience in the Albino Rat" (M.A. thesis, University of Toronto, 1957).

:32–35   O. WEININGER, W. J. MCCLELLAND, and K. ARIMA, "Gentling and Weight Gain in the Albino Rat," *Canadian Journal of Psychology*, 8 (1954), pp. 147–151.

239:1   W. R. RUEGAMER, L. BERNSTEIN, and J. D. BENJAMIN, "Growth, Food Utilization, and Thyroid Activity in the Albino Rat as a Function of Extra Handling," pp. 184–185.

:3–7   G. F. SOLOMON, "Early Experience and Immunity," *Nature*, 220 (1968), pp. 821–822.

:10–12   S. LEVINE, M. ALPERT, and G. W. LEWIS, "Infantile Experience and the Maturation of the Pituitary Adrenal Axis," *Science*, 126 (1957), p. 1347.

:12–14   R. W. BELL, G. REISNER, and T. LINN, "Recovery from Electroconvulsive Shock as a Function of Infantile Stimulation," *Science*, 133 (1961), p. 1428.

:18–23   S. LEVINE, "Noxious Stimulation in Infant and Adult Rats and Consummatory Behavior," *Journal of Comparative and Physiological Psychology*, 51 (1958), pp. 230–233.

:21–23   L. BERNSTEIN, "The Effects of Variation in Handling upon Learning and Retention," *Journal of Comparative and Physiological Psychology*, 50 (1957), pp. 162–167.

:24–26   K. LARSSON, "Mating Behavior of the Male Rat," in L. R. Aronson et al. (eds), *Development and Evolution of Behavior* (San Francisco: Freeman, 1970), pp. 337–351.

:27–30   K. LARSSON, "Non-Specific Stimulation and Sexual Behaviour in the Male Rat," *Behaviour*, 20 (1963), pp. 110–114.

:32 to   J. A. KING, "Effects of Early Handling upon Adult Behav-

Page and Line

240:2   ior in Two Subspecies of Deermice, *Peromyscus manicu-latus,*" *Journal of Comparative and Physiological Psychology,* 52 (1959), pp. 82–88.

:2–11   U. BRONFENBRENNER, "Early Deprivation in Mammals: A Cross-Species Analysis," in G. Newton and S. Levine (eds), *Early Experience and Behavior* (Springfield, Ill.: Charles C Thomas, 1968), p. 661; L. Bernstein, "A Note on Christie's 'Experimental Naiveté and Experiential Naiveté,' " *Psychological Bulletin,* 49 (1952), pp. 38–40; L. Bernstein, "The Effects of Variations in Handling upon Learning and Retention," *Journal of Comparative and Physiological Psychology,* 50 (1957), pp. 162–167; V. H. Denenberg, "A Consideration of the Usefulness of the Critical Period Hypothesis as Applied to the Stimulation of Rodents in Infancy," in Newton and Levine, *Early Experience and Behavior,* pp. 42–167.

:19–23   W. R. RUEGAMER, L. BERNSTEIN, and J. D. BENJAMIN, "Growth, Food Utilization, and Thyroid Activity in the Albino Rat," pp. 184–185.

241:5–11   W. VON BUDDENBROCK, *The Senses* (Ann Arbor: The University of Michigan Press, 1958), p. 127.

:17–28   V. S. CLAY, "The Effect of Culture on Mother-Child Tactile Communication" (Ph.D. diss., Teachers College, Columbia University, 1966), p. 308.

:21–23   M. RIBBLE, *The Rights of Infants* (2nd ed., New York: Columbia University Press, 1965), p. 54 et seq.

242 :1–4   G. E. COGHILL, *Anatomy and the Problem of Behavior* (New York & London: Cambridge University Press, 1929; reprinted New York: Hafner Publishing Co., 1964).

:5–19   L. J. YARROW, "Research in Dimension of Early Maternal Care," *Merrill-Palmer Quarterly,* 9 (1963), pp. 101–122.

:20–36   S. PROVINCE and R. C. LIPTON, *Infants in Institutions* (New York: International Universities Press, 1962).

:37to   H. SHEVRIN and P. W. TOUSSIENG, "Vicissitudes of the
243:24   Need for Tactile Stimulation in Instinctual Development," *The Psychoanalytic Study of the Child,* 20 (1965), pp. 310–339; H. SHEVRIN and P. W. TOUSSIENG, "Conflict over Tactile Experiences in Emotionally Disturbed Children," *Journal of the American Academy of Child Psychiatry,* 1 (1962), pp. 564–590.

:12–18   R. SPITZ, *The First Year of Life* (New York: International Universities Press, 1965); RIBBLE, *The Rights of Infants.*

244 :19–26   R. G. PATTON and L. I. GARDNER, *Growth Failure in Ma-*

Page and Line

ternal Deprivation (Springfield, Ill.: Charles C Thomas, 1963).

:26–28   E. M. WIDDOWSON, "Mental Contentment and Physical Growth," *The Lancet,* 1 (1951), pp. 1316–1318; L. J. YARROW, "Maternal Deprivation: Toward an Empirical and Conceptual Revaluation," *Psychological Bulletin,* 58 (1961), pp. 459–490; A. MONTAGU (ed.), *Culture and Human Development* (Englewood Cliffs, N.J.: Prentice-Hall, 1974).

:27–34   G. F. POWELL, J. A. BRASEL, and R. M. BLIZZARD, "Emotional Deprivation and Growth Retardation Simulating Idiopathic Hypopituitarism," *New England Journal of Medicine,* 276 (1967), pp. 1271–1278; G. F. POWELL, J. A. BRASEL, S. RAITI, and R. M. BLIZZARD, "Emotional Deprivation and Growth Retardation Simulating Hypopituitarism," *New England Journal of Medicine,* 276 (1967), pp. 1279–1283; J. B. REINHARDT and A. L. DRASH, "Psychosocial Dwarfism: Environmentally Induced Recovery," *Psychosomatic Medicine,* 31 (1969), pp. 165–172. See also C. Whitten et al., "Evidence that Growth Failure from Maternal Deprivation Is Secondary to Undereating," *Journal of the American Medical Association,* 209 (1969), pp. 1675–1682; Montagu, *Culture and Human Development.*

245:31 to   For a detailed discussion, see W. SCHUMER and R. SPERL-
246:3   ING, "Shock and Its Effect on the Cell," *Journal of the American Medical Association,* 205 (1968), pp. 215–219.

:15–16   M. K. TEMERLIN et al., "Effects of Increased Mothering and Skin Contact on Retarded Boys," *American Journal of Mental Deficiency,* 71 (1967), pp. 890–893.

:16–26   M. McGRAW, *Neuromuscular Maturation of the Human Infant* (New York: Columbia University Press, 1943), p. 102.

:30–33   P. GREENACRE, *Trauma, Growth, and Personality* (New York: Norton, 1952), pp. 12–14; M. SHERMAN and I. C. SHERMAN, "Sensorimotor Response in Infants," *Journal of Comparative Psychology,* 5 (1925), pp. 53–68; A. Thomas et al., *Examen Neurologique du Nourrison* (Paris: La Vie Médicale, 1955); E. H. WATSON and G. H. LOWREY, *Growth and Development of Children* (5th ed., Chicago: Year Book Medical Publishers, 1967).

:33–35   E. DEWEY, *Behavior Development in Infants* (New York: Columbia University Press, 1935).

Page and Line

:35 to   D. SINCLAIR, *Cutaneous Sensation* (New York: Oxford University Press, 1967), p. 38.
247:2

:2–11   H. HEAD, *Studies in Neurology* (Oxford: Oxford University Press, 1922).

:15–27   S. ESCALONA, "Emotional Development in the First Year of Life," in M. J. E. Senn (ed.), *Problems of Infancy and Childhood* (New York: Josiah Macy, Jr., Foundation, 1953), p. 17.

247:27–35   RIBBLE, *The Rights of Infants,* p. 57.

248:3–6   WATSON and LOWREY, *Growth and Development of Children,* pp. 220–221.

:23–30   R. S. LOURIE, "The First Three Years of Life: An Overview of a New Frontier of Psychiatry," *American Journal of Psychiatry,* 127 (1971), pp. 1457–1463.

249:17–33   E. SYLVESTER, "Discussion," in Senn, *Problems of Infancy and Childhood,* p. 29.

:20–35   Ibid.

250:5–10   H. SINCLAIR, "Sensorimotor Action Patterns a Condition for the Acquisition of Syntax," in R. Huxley and E. Ingram (eds.), *Language Acquisition: Models and Methods* (New York: Academic Press, 1971), pp. 121–135; HARRY BEILIN et al., *Studies in the Cognitive Basis of Language Development* (New York: Academic Press, 1975), p. 340.

:31 to   ESCALONA, "Emotional Development in the First Year of Life," in Senn, *Problems of Infancy and Childhood,* p. 25.
252:4

:10–23   SPITZ, *The First Year of Life,* pp. 232–233.

253:10–20   M. S. MAHLER, "On Two Crucial Phases of Integration Concerning Problems of Identity: Separation-Individuation and Bisexual Identity," *Journal of the American Psychoanalytic Association,* 6 (1958), pp. 136–142.

:21 to   E. DARWIN, *Zoonomia, or The Laws of Organic Life* (2 vols., London: J. Johnson, vol. 1, 1794), pp. 109–111.
254:17

:21–34   ESCALONA, "Emotional Development in the First Year of Life," p. 24.

255:3 to   T. K. LANDAUER and J. W. M. WHITING, "Infantile Stimulation and Adult Stature of Human Males," *American Anthropologist,* 66 (1964), pp. 1007–1028.
256:75

:20–22   D. H. WILLIAMS, "Management of Atopic Dermatitis in Children, Control of the Maternal Rejection Factor," *Archives of Dermatology and Syphilology,* 63 (1951), pp. 545–560.

:22–28   F. DUNBAR, *Emotions and Bodily Changes* (4th ed.,

Page and Line

New York: Columbia University Press, 1954), p. 647.

:30–34   D. W. WINNICOTT, "Pediatrics and Psychiatry," *British Journal of Medical Psychology,* 21 (1948), pp. 229–240.

:33–37   SPITZ, *The First Year of Life;* M. E. Allerhand et al, "Personality Factors in Neurodermatitis," *Psychosomatic Medicine,* 12 (1950), pp. 386–390; E. Wittkower and B. Russell, *Emotional Factors in Skin Disease* (New York: Hoeber, 1955).

257:1–6   M. E. OBERMAYER, *Psychocutaneous Medicine* (Springfield, Ill.: Charles C Thomas, 1955).

:6–9   H. C. BETHUNE and C. B. KIDD, "Physiological Mechanisms in Skin Diseases," *The Lancet,* 2 (1961), pp. 1419–1422; J. G. Kepecs et al., "Atopic Dermatitis," *Psychosomatic Medicine,* 13 (1951), pp. 2–9; Dunbar, *Emotions and Bodily Changes,* p. 647.

:11 to   B. BETTELHEIM, *The Empty Fortress: Infantile Autism and*
258:14   *the Birth of Self* (New York: Free Press, 1967), pp. 233–339.

:22–25   G. SCHWING, *A Way to the Souls of the Mentally Ill* (New York: International Universities Press, 1954).

:25 to   N. and E. TINBERGEN, *Autistic Children: New Hope for a*
259:5   *Cure* (London: Allen & Unwin, 1983).

:6 to   M. G. WELCH, "Retrieval from Autism through Mother-
260:8   Child Holding Therapy," in Tinbergen and Tinbergen, pp. 322–336.

:12–14   T. GRANDIN, "My Experience as an Autistic Child and Review of Selected Literature," paper presented at the Third Annual Colloquium for Neurodevelopmental Studies, The Role of the Tactile System, 19–21 March 1982, Phoenix, Arizona.

:15–22   M. RUTTER and E. SCHOPLER, *Autism—A Reappraisal of Concepts and Treatment* (New York: Plenum Press, 1978); G. Victor, *The Riddle of Autism* (Lexington, Mass.: D. C. Heath, 1983).

:23–29   G. O'GORMAN, *The Nature of Childhood Autism* (London: Butterworth, 1970).

:30 to   J. OLDER, *Touching Is Healing* (New York: Stein & Day,
261:2   1984), p. 79.

:3–10   M. ZAPPELLA, "Treating Autistic Children in a Community Setting," in Tinbergen and Tinbergen, pp. 337–348.

:15 to   LOWEN, *The Betrayal of the Body,* pp. 2–3.
262:14

:15–21   O. FENICHEL, *The Psychoanalytic Theory of Neurosis* (New York: Norton, 1945), p. 445.

Page and Line

:27–29   H. WEINER, "Diagnosis and Symptomatology," in L. Bellak (ed.), *Schizophrenia* (New York: Logos Press, 1958), p. 120.

263:35 to   R. J. BEHAN, *Pain: Its Origin, Conduction, Perception and*
264:10   *Diagnostic Significance* (New York: Appleton, 1922); S. RENSHAW and R. J. WHERRY, "Studies on Cutaneous Localization, III. The Age of Onset of Ocular Dominance," *Journal of Genetic Psychology,* 39 (1931), pp. 493–496.

265:11–16   A. F. SILVERMAN, M. E. PRESSMAN, and H. W. BARTEL, "Self-Esteem and Tactile Communication," *Journal of Humanistic Psychology,* 13 (1973), pp. 73–77.

:22 to   J. HOLLAND, "Acute Leukemia: Psychological Aspects of
266:12   Treatment," in B. Elkerbout, P. Thomas, and A. Zwaveling (eds.), *Cancer Chemotherapy* (Leiden, Holland: Leiden University Press, 1971), pp. 199–300. See also J. Holland et al., "Psychological Response of Patients with Acute Leukemia to Germ-Free Environments," *Cancer, Journal of the American Cancer Society,* 40 (1977), pp. 871–879.

:13–24   S. GORDON, *Lonely in America* (New York: Simon & Schuster, 1976); L. Bernikow, *Alone in America* (New York: Harper & Row, 1986).

:29–33   *New York Times,* 15 August 1975, p. 33.

:34 to   R. MAY, *Love and Will* (New York: Norton, 1969),
267:7   p. 69.

:3–8   L. LEIBER et al., "The Communication of Affection between Cancer Patients and Their Spouses," *Psychosomatic Medicine,* 38 (1976), pp. 379–389.

:21–23   Y. VINOKUROV, "Passer-By," trans. Daniel Weissbort, *Poetry,* July 1974, p. 187.

:30 to   K. J. GERGEN, M. M. GERGEN, and W. H. BARTON, "De-
268:16   viance in the Dark," *Psychology Today,* October 1973, pp. 129–130.

:17 to   D. A., "You're Only Allowed to Touch When . . ." (Paper
269:3   written for anthropology class at a California college, 1971).

:14–32   A. F. COPPOLA, "Reality and the Haptic World," *Phi Kappa Phi Journal,* Winter 1970, pp. 14–15.

270:14–31   M. A. MacCULLOCH, "Hand," in J. Hastings (ed.), *Encyclopaedia of Religion and Ethics* (vol. 6, Edinburgh: Clark, 1913), pp. 492–499.

Page and Line

270:13–30   M. BLOCH, *The Royal Touch* (London: Routledge & Kegan Paul, 1973), p. 240.

271:29–36   I. R. MILBERG, "Pinpointing Emotional Factors in Skin Diseases," *Practical Psychology,* 3 (1976), pp. 49–56.

:37 to   "Seventh Son of a Seventh Son," *The Listener* (London), 11
272:9   April 1974, pp. 443–455.

:10–12   G. B. WALKER, in J. Fry, P. S. Byrne, and S. Johnson (eds.), *Textbook of Medical Practice* (Littleton, Mass.: Publishing Sciences Group, 1978), p. 399.

:13–18   E. PANCONESI (ed.), *Stress and Skin Diseases: Psychosomatic Dermatology* (Philadelphia: Lippincott, Clinics in Dermatology, vol. 2, 1984).

:19–28   M. J. ROSENTHAL, "Psychosomatic Study of Infantile Eczema," *Pediatrics,* 10 (1952), pp. 581–593.

:29 to   SPITZ, *The First Year of Life,* p. 24.
273:5

:1–5   R. BERGMAN and C. K. ALDRICH, "The Natural History of Infantile Eczema: A Follow-Up Study," *Psychosomatic Medicine,* 25 (1963), p. 495.

:6–12   E. L. LIPTON, A. STEINSCHNEIDER, and J. B. RICHMOND, "Psychophysiological Disorders in Children," in L. W. and M. L. Hoddman (eds.), *Review of Child Development Research,* vol. 2 (1966), p. 192.

:13–23   H. MUSAPH, "Aggression and Symptom Formation in Dermatology," *Journal of Psychosomatic Research,* 13 (1969), pp. 275–284.

:19–23   J. C. MOLONEY, "Thumbsucking," *Child and Family,* 6 (1967), p. 28.

274:2–3   J. A. M. MEERLOO, "Human Camouflage and Identification with the Environment," *Psychosomatic Medicine,* 19 (1957), pp. 89–98.

275:9–22   LOWEN, *The Betrayal of the Body,* pp. 187–188.

:23–36   M. EUSTIS (ed.), *Players at Work* (New York: Theater Arts, 1937).

276:10–23   E. T. HALL, *The Hidden Dimension* (Garden City, N.Y.: Doubleday, 1966), p. 59.

:24–37   J. BOWLBY, "The Nature of the Child's Tie to His Mother," *International Journal of Psychoanalysis,* 39 (1958), pp. 364–365; J. Bowlby, *Attachment and Loss,* vol. 1, *Attachment* (New York: Basic Books, 1969).

277:1–31   M. BALINT, "Friendly Expanses—Horrid Empty Spaces," *International Journal of Psychoanalysis,* 36 (1955), pp. 225–241.

Page and Line
   :32–36   A. Burton and R. E. Kantor, "The Touching of the
               Body," *Psychoanalytic Review,* 51 (1964), pp. 122–134.
278:2–9   D. Secrest, " 'Catatonics' Cure Is Found," *International
               News Service,* May 27, 1955.
   :9–11   G. Schwing, *A Way to the Souls of the Mentally Ill* (New
               York: International Universities Press, 1954).
   :11–29   N. Waal, "A Special Technique of Psychotherapy with an
               Autistic Child," in G. Caplan (ed.), *Emotional Problems
               of Early Childhood* (New York: Basic Books, 1955), pp.
               443–444.
   :33–36   K. Menninger, *Theory of Psychoanalytic Technique* (New
               York: Basic Books, 1958), p. 40. For an excellent discus-
               sion of the taboo against touching in the psychoanalytic
               situation, see Elizabeth Mintz, "Touch and the Psycho-
               analytic Tradition," *The Psychoanalytic Review,* 56
               (1969), pp. 365–376.
   :37 to   N. Ickeringill, "An Approach to Schizophrenia That Is
279:1   Rooted in Family Love," *New York Times,* 28 April
               1968, p. 44.
   :6 to   B. R. Forer, "The Taboo against Touching in Psychother-
280:11   apy," *Psychotherapy, Theory, Research and Practice,* 6
               (1969), pp. 229–231. See also B. R. Forer, "The Use of
               Physical Contact in Group Therapy," in L. N. Solomon
               and B. Berson (eds.), *New Perspectives on Encounter
               Groups* (San Francisco: Jossey-Bass, 1972), pp.
               195–210.
   :14–21   C. Brenner, *Psychoanalytic Technique and Psychic Conflict*
               (New York: International Universities Press, 1976), p.
               30.
   :23–25   See Freud's letter to Ferenczi in E. Jones, *The Life and
               Works of Sigmund Freud* (New York: Basic Books,
               1955), vol. 3, p. 163.
   :35 to   Forer, "The Taboo against Touching in Psychotherapy,"
281:15   p. 230.
   :16–23   A. Burton and A. G. Heller, "The Touching of the
               Body," *Psychoanalytic Review,* 51 (1964), pp. 122–134.
   :28 to   I. Bartenieff with D. Lewis, *Body Movement: Coping with
282:3   the Environment* (New York: Gordon & Breach, 1980),
               p. 19.
   :13–18   A. Montagu, "On Touching Your Patient," *Practical Psy-
               chology for Physicians,* February 1975, pp. 43–47; J. J.
               Bruhn, "The Doctor's Touch," *Southern Medical Jour-
               nal,* 71 (1978), pp. 1469–1473; M. J. Duttera, "The
               Healer's Hand," *Journal of the American Medical Associ-*

Page and Line

ation, 242 (1979), p. 41; J. Older, "Teaching Touch at Medical School," *Journal of the American Medical Association,* 252 (1984), pp. 931–933.

282:21–27   A. BURTON and A. G. HELLER, "The Touching of the Body," *Psychoanalytic Review,* 51 (1964), pp. 122–134; J. DE AUGUSTINIS, R. S. ISANI, and F. R. KUMLER, "Ward Study: The Meaning of Touch in Inter-Personal Communication," in S. F. Burd and M. A. Marshall (eds.), *Some Clinical Approaches to Psychiatric Nursing* (New York: Macmillan 1963), pp. 271–306: A. CHARLTON, "Identification of Reciprocal Influences of Nurse and Patient Initiated Physical Contact in the Psychiatric Setting" (Master's thesis, University of Maryland, 1959); L. S. MERCER, "Touch: Comfort or Threat?" *Perspectives in Psychiatric Care,* 4 (1966), pp. 20–25; L. CASHAR and B. K. DIXSON, "The Therapeutic Use of Touch," *Journal of Psychiatric Nursing,* 5 (1967), pp. 442–451; E. MINTZ, "Touch and Psychoanalytic Tradition," *Psychoanalytic Review,* 56 (1969), pp. 367–376; M. T. DE THOMASO, "Touch Power," *Perspectives in Psychiatric Care,* 9 (1971), pp. 112–118; A. L. CLARK, *Maternal Tenderness—Cultural and Generational Implications* (Evanston, Ill.: American Nursing Association, No. G. 94, 1973), pp. 98–123; B. UNGER, "Please Touch," *Journal of Practical Nursing,* 24 (1974), p. 29; D. KRIEGER, " 'Therapeutic Touch': An Ancient But Unorthodox Nursing Intervention," Lecture, 12 October 1974, Lake Placid, N.Y.; D. KRIEGER, "The Relationship of Touch, with Intent to Help or to Heal, to Subjects' In-Vivo Hemoglobin Values: A Study in Personalized Interaction," *Proceedings of the American Nurses Association 9th Council of Nurse Researchers* (Kansas City, Mo.: The Association, 1973), pp. 53–76; B. S. JOHNSON, "Meaning of Touch," *Nursing Outlook,* 35 (1965), p. 59; M. S. SALTENIS, "Physical Touch and Nursing Support" (Unpublished master's thesis, Yale University, 1962); J. E. PATTISON, "Effects of Touch on Self-Exploration and the Therapeutic Relationship," *Journal of Consulting and Clinical Psychology,* 40 (1973) pp. 170–175.

:31 to   A. MONTAGU, "The Sensory Influences of the Skin," *Texas*
284:18   *Reports on Biology and Medicine,* 2 (1953), pp. 291–301.

285:12–15   A. M. GARNER and C. WENAR, *The Mother-Child Interac-*

Page and Line

tion in Psychosomatic Disorders (Urbana: University of
Illinois Press, 1959).

:26 to   H. W. NISSEN, K. L. CHOW, and J. SEMMES, "Effects of Re-
286:5   stricted Opportunity for Tactual, Kinesthetic, and
              Manipulative Experience on the Behavior of a Chim-
              panzee," *American Journal of Psychology,* 64 (1951), pp.
              485–507.

:14–15   W. M. MASON, "Early Social Deprivation in the Nonhu-
              man Primates: Implications for Human Behavior," in D.
              C. Glass (ed.), *Environmental Influences* (New York:
              Rockefeller University Press, 1968), pp. 70–101.

:36 to
287:3   D. STEWART, *Outlines of Moral Philosophy* (Edinburgh:
              Creech, 1793), I, X, #87.

289:4–33   M. M. MERZENICH, "Functional 'Maps' of Skin Sensa-
              tions," in Catherine Caldwell Brown (ed.), *The Many
              Facets of Touch* (Skillman, N.J.: Johnson & Johnson
              Baby Products, 1984), pp. 15–29.

290:9–11   J. P. ZUBEK, J. FLYE, and M. AFTANAS, "Cutaneous Sensi-
              tivity after Prolonged Visual Deprivation," *Science,* 144
              (1964), pp. 1591–1593.

:11–13   S. AXELROD, *Effects of Early Blindness* (New York: Ameri-
              can Foundation for the Blind, 1959).

:22–24   D. OGSTON, C. M. OGSTON, and O. D. RATNOFF, "Studies
              on Clot-Promoting Effect of the Skin," *Journal of Labo-
              ratory and Clinical Medicine,* 73 (1969), pp. 70–77.

:32–34   A. BRODAL, *Neurological Anatomy in Relation to Clinical
              Medicine* (2nd ed., New York: Oxford University Press,
              1981).

CHAPTER EIGHT. CULTURE AND CONTACT

Page and Line

296:25 to   R. JAMES DE BOER, "The Netsilik Eskimo and the Origin of
299:14   Human Behavior," MS, 1969, p. 8.

299:15–23   S. MILLET, "When Breastfeeding Declines," *La Leche
              League News,* 21 (1979), pp. 88–89.

:15 to   O. SCHAEFFER, "When the Eskimo Comes to Town," *Nu-
300:3   trition Today,* November–December 1971, pp. 8–16;
              also, "Mental Health and Cultural Change," no refer-
              ence.

:3–15   E. CARPENTER, "Space Concepts of Aivilik Eskimos," *Ex-
              plorations Five,* June 1955, pp. 131–145.

Page and Line

:19–23   S. BURFORD, *One Woman's Arctic* (Boston: Little Brown, 1972), pp. 15, 48.

301:34 to   J. GIBSON, "Pictures, Perspective and Perception," *Dae-*
302:3   *dalus,* Winter 1961.

303:16–17   H. H. ROBERTS and D. JENNESS, *Eskimo Songs, Report of the Canadian Arctic Expedition, 1913–18* (Ottawa), vol. 14 (1925), pp. 9, 12.

:21–36   K. RASMUSSEN, *The Intellectual Culture of the Iglulik Eskimos* (Copenhagen: Gyldendalske boghandel, 1929), p. 27.

304:6–11   V. STEFANSSON, *The Friendly Arctic* (New York: Macmillan, 1943), p. 418; V. Stefansson, *My Life with the Eskimo* (New York: Macmillan, 1915).

:35 to   C. OSGOOD, "Ingalik Social Culture," *Yale University Pub-*
305:9   *lications in Anthropology,* no. 53 (1958), p. 178.

:10–30   E. CARPENTER, F. VARLEY, and R. FLAHERTY, Eskimo: *Explorations Nine* (Toronto: University of Toronto Press, 1959), p. 32.

306:1–28   J. HENRY, *Jungle People* (New York: Vintage Books, 1964), pp. 18–19.

307:1–21   P. DURDIN, "From the Space Age to the Tasaday Age," *New York Times Magazine,* 8 October 1972, p. 14.

:22–23   J. NANCE, *The Gentle Tasaday* (New York: Harcourt Brace Jovanovich, 1975).

:24–26   Y. and R. F. MURPHY, *Women of the Forest* (New York: Columbia University Press, 1974), p. 106.

308:6–19   A. S. MIRKIN, "Resonance Phenomena in Isolated Mechanoreceptors (Pacinian Bodies) with Acoustic Stimulation," *Biofizika,* 2 (1966), pp. 638–645 (in Russian).

:20–25   C. K. MADSEN and W. G. MEARS, "The Effect of Sound upon the Tactile Threshold of Deaf Subjects," *Journal of Music Therapy,* 2 (1965), pp. 64–68.

:26–27   G. A. GESCHEIDER, "Cutaneous Sound Localization" (Ph.D. diss, University of Virginia, 1964; *Dissertation Abstracts,* vol 25 [1964], no. 6, 3701).

:30   B. BERENSON, *Aesthetics and History* (New York: Pantheon,
309:14   1948), pp. 66–70.

:28–37   R. HUGHES, "When God Was an Englishman," *Time,* 1 March 1976, p. 56.

310:1–3   K. CLARK, *The Nude* (New York: Pantheon, 1956), p. 144.

:4–8   M. MCLUHAN and H. PARKER, *Through the Vanishing Point* (New York: Harper & Row, 1969), p. 265.

:10–33   T. KROEBER, *Alfred Kroeber: A Personal Configuration*

Page and Line

　　　　　　　(Berkeley: University of California Press, 1970), pp. 267–268.

:34 to　　　R. BUCKLE, *Jacob Epstein: Sculptor* (New York: World,
311:2　　　　1963).

:3–7　　　　G. LEVINE, *With Henry Moore: The Artist at Work* (New York: Times Books, 1978), p. 48.

:24–29　　　R. CASSIDY, *Margaret Mead: A Choice for Eternity* (New York, Universe Books, 1983), p. 18.

:30 to　　　E. G. SCHACHTEL, "On Memory and Childhood Amnesia,"
312:4　　　　in P. Mullahy (ed.), *A Study of Interpersonal Relations* (New York: Hermitage Press, 1949), pp. 23–24.

:8–11　　　 Ibid., pp. 25–26.

:12–18　　　H. MARCUSE, *Eros and Civilization* (Boston: Beacon Press, 1955), p. 39.

:33 to　　　M. ARGYLE and M. COOK, *Gaze and Mutual Gaze* (New
313:2　　　　York: Cambridge University Press, 1976); F. T. EL-WORTHY, *The Evil Eye* (London: John Murray, 1895, reprinted New York: Julian Press, 1958); E. S. GIFFORD, JR., *The Evil Eye* (New York: Macmillan, 1958).

:4–7　　　　J. GONDA, *Eye and Gaze in the Veda* (Amsterdam & London: North Holland Publishing Co., 1969), p. 16.

:13–21　　　L.-P. LA FARGUE, *Idées,* 1948.

:27–31　　　O. MANDELSTAM, *Entretiens sur Dante.*

314:31–33　 L. MICHAELS and C. RICKS (eds.), *The State of the Language* (Berkeley: University of California Press, 1980), p. xii.

315:13–16　 H. L. PICK, A. D. PICK, and R. E. KLEIN, "Perceptual Integration in Children," in L. P. Lipsitt and C. C. Spiker (eds.), *Advances in Child Behavior and Development,* vol. 3 (New York: Academic Press, 1967), pp. 191–220.

:16–19　　　E. J. GIBSON and R. D. WALK, "The Visual Cliff," *Scientific American,* 202 (1960), pp. 64–71.

:20–26　　　T. G. R. BOWER, "The Object in the World of the Infant," *Scientific American,* 225 (1971), pp. 30–38.

:27–32　　　H. R. SCHAFFER and P. E. EMERSON, "Patterns of Response to Physical Contact in Early Human Development," *Journal of Child Psychology and Psychiatry,* 5 (1964), pp. 1–13.

:33 to　　　R. C. DAVENPORT, C. M. ROGER, and I. A. RUSSELL,
316:4　　　　"Cross Modal Perception in Apes," *Neuropsychologica,* 11 (1973), pp. 21–28.

:5–20　　　　A. V. ZAPOROZHETS, "The Development of Perception in the Preschool Child," in P. H. Mussen (ed.), *European Research in Cognitive Development,* Monographs of the

Page and Line

Society for Research in Child Growth and Development, vol. 30. ser. no. 100 (Chicago: University of Chicago Press, 1965).

:21–25   I. ROCK and C. S. HARRIS, "Vision and Touch," *Scientific American,* 216 (1967), pp. 96–104.

:26 to   S. HOCKEN, "Life at First Sight—The Surprising World of
317:2   Sheila Hocken," *The Listener* (London), June 10, 1976, pp. 730 731.

:3–27   M. D. S. AINSWORTH, *Infancy in Uganda* (Baltimore: Johns Hopkins Press, 1967), p. 451. See also L. K. Fox (ed.), *East African Childhood* (New York: Oxford University Press, 1970).

:33–35   J. ROSCOE, *The Baganda* (London: Macmillan, 1911); L. P. Mair, *An African People in the Twentieth Century* (London: Routledge & Kegan Paul, 1934).

:35 to   A. I. RICHARDS, "Traditional Values and Current Political
318:10   Behavior," in L. A. Fallers (ed.), *The King's Men: Leadership and Status in Modern Buganda* (New York: Oxford University Press, 1964), pp. 297–300.

:11 to   M. GÉBER, "The Psychomotor Development of African
319:15   Children in the First Year and the Influence of Maternal Behavior," *Journal of Social Psychology,* 47 (1958), pp. 185–195; M. GÉBER and R. F. A. DEAN, "The State of Development of Newborn African Children," *The Lancet,* 272 (1957), pp. 1216–1219; M. GÉBER, "Problèmes Posés par le Développement du Jeune Enfant Africain en Fonction de son Milieu Social," *Le Travail Humain,* 23 (1960), pp. 99–111.

:17–25   P. DRAPER, "Crowding Among Hunter-Gatherers: The !Kung Bushmen," *Science,* 182 (1973), pp. 301–303.

:26 to   L. MARSHALL, *The !Kung of Nyae Nyae* (Cambridge,
320:23   Mass.: Harvard University Press, 1976), pp. 315–318.

:24 to   M. J. KONNER, "Aspects of the Developmental Ethology of
321:29   a Foraging People," in N. Blurton Jones (ed.), *Ethological Studies of Child Behaviour* (Cambridge: The University Press, 1972), pp. 285–304; S. R. TULKIN and M. J. KONNER, "Alternative Conceptions of Intellectual Functioning," in K. F. Riegel (ed.), *Intelligence: Alternative Views of a Paradigm* (Basel & New York: Karger, 1973), pp. 33–52; M. J. KONNER, "Maternal Care, Infant Behavior, and Development Among the !Kung," in R. B. LEE and IRVEN DE VORE (eds.), *Kalahari-Hunter Gatherers* (Cambridge, Mass.: Harvard University Press, 1976), pp. 219–245.

466   *References*

Page and Line

321:1–6   A. GESELL and C. AMATRUDA, *Developmental Diagnosis* (New York: Harper & Row, 1947), p. 42.

:30–31   E. M. THOMAS, *The Harmless People* (New York: Knopf, 1959); L. VAN DER POST, *The Lost World of the Kalahari* (New York: William Morrow, 1958); L. VAN DER POST, *The Heart of the Hunter* (New York: William Morrow, 1961); L. VAN DER POST and JANE TAYLOR, *Testament to the Bushmen* (New York: Viking Press, 1984); I. SCHAPERA, *The Khoisan Peoples of South Africa* (London: Routledge & Sons, 1930); L. MARSHALL, "The !Kung Bushmen of the Kalahari Desert," in J. Gibbs (ed.), *Peoples of Africa* (New York: Holt, Rinehart & Winston, 1965); W. D. HAMMOND-TOOKE (ed.), *The Bantu-Speaking Peoples of Southern Africa* (London & Boston: Routledge & Kegan Paul, 1974).

:32 to   M. MEAD, *Sex and Temperament in Three Primitive Socie-*
324:12   *ties* (New York: William Morrow, 1935), pp. 40–41.

:13–25   J. RITCHIE, Review of A. Montagu, *Touching*, Parents Centres *Bulletin* 52, August 1972, p. 22.

:26–32   C. DuBois, *The People of Alor* (Minneapolis: University of Minnesota Press, 1937), p. 152.

325:1 to   T. R. WILLIAMS, "Cultural Structuring of Tactile Experi-
326:16   ence in a Borneo Society," *American Anthropologist,* 68 (1966), pp. 27–39.

:17 to   J. W. PRESCOTT and DOUGLAS WALLACE, "Developmental
327:2   Sociobiology and the Origins of Aggressive Behavior," Paper presented at the XXIst International Congress of Psychology, July 18–25, 1976, Paris.

:3 to   V. S. CLAY, "The Effect of Culture on Mother-Child Tac-
329:19   tile Communication" (Ph.D. diss., Teachers College, Columbia University, 1966).

:12–19   R. RUBIN, "Maternal Touch," *Nursing Outlook,* 11 (1963), pp. 828–831.

:20–30   H. F. HARLOW, M. K. HARLOW, and E. W. HANSEN, "The Maternal Affectional System of Rhesus Monkeys," in H. L. Rheingold (ed.) *Maternal Behavior in Mammals* (New York: Wiley, 1963), pp. 258 et seq.

330:4–23   CLAY, "The Effect of Culture," pp. 201–202.

:24 to   R. E. SEARS, E. E. MACCOBY, and H. LEVIN, *Patterns of*
331:2   *Child Rearing* (New York: Row, Petersen, 1957), pp. 56–57, 402; J. L. FISCHER and A. FISCHER, "The New Englanders of Orchard Town, U. S. A.," in B. B. Whiting (ed.), *Six Cultures* (New York: Wiley, 1963), p. 941.

Page and Line

:7 to
332:14
H. A. Moss, K. S. Robson, and F. Pedersen, "Determinants of Maternal Stimulation of Infants and Consequences of Treatment for Later Reactions to Strangers," *Developmental Psychology,* 1 (1969), pp. 239–246; H. A. Moss and K. S. Robson, "Maternal Influences in Early Social-Visual Behavior," *Child Development,* 38 (1968), pp. 401–408.

331:29 to
332:14
R. H. Walters and R. D. Parke, "The Role of the Distance Receptors in the Development of Social Responsiveness," in L. P. Lipsitt and C. C. Spiker (eds.), *Advances in Child Development and Behavior* (New York: Academic Press, 1965).

:15–21
K. G. Auerbach, "Where Have All the Nursing Mothers Gone?" *Keeping Abreast,* 1 (1976), pp. 222–228; Clay, "The Effect of Culture."

:36 to
333:10
A. Montagu, "Some Factors in Family Cohesion," *Psychiatry,* 7 (1944), pp. 349–352.

:10–26
L. Smith, *Strange Fruit* (New York: Reynal, 1944), p. 74.

:28 to
334:25
W. Caudill and D. W. Plath, "Who Sleeps by Whom? Parent-Child Involvement in Urban Japanese Families," *Psychiatry,* 29 (1966), p. 363.

335:1–11
Takeo Doi, *The Anatomy of Dependence* (New York: Kodansha, 1973); John H. Douglas, "Pioneering a Non-Western Psychology," *Science News,* 113 (1978), pp. 154–158.

:24 to
336:3
E. T. Hall, *Beyond Culture* (Garden City, N.Y.: Anchor Books, Doubleday, 1976), pp. 56–58.

:8–13
See Fischer and Fischer, "The New Englanders," in Whiting, *Six Cultures,* p. 947.

:7–28
E. M. Forster, *Abinger Harvest* (New York: Harcourt, Brace, 1947), p. 8.

337:29–34
D. Sutherland, *The English Gentleman* (London: Debrett's Peerage, 1984), pp. 55–56.

:35 to
338:6
F. Partridge, *Love in Bloomsbury* (Boston: Little, Brown, 1981), pp. 26, 46.

:7–15
J. Austen, *Emma* (London, 1816), Chapter 12.

:16–25
T. Morgan, *Somerset Maugham* (London: Jonathan Cape, 1980).

:27
T. Eden, *The Tribulations of a Baronet* (London: Macmillan, 1933).

:28
R. Hart-Davis, *Hugh Walpole: A Biography* (New York: Macmillan, 1952).

:31–33
W. A. Swanberg, *William Randolph Hearst* (New York: Macmillan, 1961).

Page and Line

:33–35   C. KING, *Strictly Personal* (London: Weidenfeld & Nicolson), 1969.

339:7–13   *The Spectator,* 5 September 1970.

:16–27   M. MEAD, "Cultural Differences in the Bathing of Babies," in K. Soddy (ed.), *Mental Health and Infant Development* (New York: Basic Books, vol. 1, 1956), pp. 170–171.

:32–37   CLAY, "The Effect of Culture," p. 273.

340:13–21   N. M. HENLEY, "The Politics of Touch," in Phil Brown (ed.), *Radical Psychology* (New York: Colophon Books, 1973), pp. 420–433.

341:6–8   S. GOLDBERG and M. LEWIS, "Play Behavior in the Year-Old Infant: Early Sex Differences," *Child Development,* 40 (1966), pp. 21–31; Clay, "The Effect of Culture."

:8–25   S. M. JOURARD, "An Exploratory Study of Body Accessibility," *British Journal of Social and Clinical Psychology,* 5 (1966), pp. 221–231; S. M. Jourard and J. E. Rubin, "Self-Disclosure and Touching: A Study of Two Modes of Interpersonal Encounter and Their Interaction," *Journal of Humanistic Psychology,* 8 (1968), pp. 39–48.

:25 to   HENLEY, "The Politics of Touch," p. 431.
342:2

:6–19   A. FREUD, *Normality and Pathology in Childhood* (New York: International Universities Press, 1965), p. 155.

:35 to   J. JOBIN, "The Family Bed," *Parents,* March 1981, pp.
343:10   57–61.

:22–24   T. THEVENIN, *The Family Bed: An Age Old Concept in Child Rearing,* P. O. Box 16004, Minneapolis, Minn. 55416.

344:8 to   Editorial, "Baby-Care Lambskin Rugs," *Parents Centres*
345:12   (Auckland, N. Z.), Bulletin 38, March 1969, p. 8. See also Bulletin 35, June 1968.

344:22–28   S. SCOTT and M. RICHARDS, "Nursing Low-Birthweight Babies on Lambswool," *The Lancet,* 12 (May 1981), p. 1028; STEPHEN SCOTT and MARTIN RICHARDS, "Lambswool Is Safer for Babies," *The Lancet,* 7 (March 1981), p. 556.

345:1–8   N. F. ROBERTS, "Baby Care Lambskin Rugs," *Parents Centres* (Auckland, N. Z.), Bulletin 39, June 1969, pp. 12–18.

:13–27   R. H. PASSMAN and P. WEISBERG, "Mothers and Blankets as Agents for Promoting Play and Exploration by Young Children in a Novel Environment: The Effects of Social and Nonsocial Attachment Objects," *Develop-*

Page and Line

mental *Psychology,* 11 (1975), pp. 170–177. For earlier studies see D. W. Winnicott, "Transitional Objects and Transitional Phenomena," *International Journal of Psychoanalysis,* 24 (1953); O. Stevenson, "The First Treasured Possession: A Study of the Part Played by Specially Loved Objects and Toys in the Lives of Certain Children," in *The Psychoanalytic Study of the Child,* 9 (1954), pp. 199–217.

:28   R. H. PASSMAN, "The Effects of Mothers and 'Security' Blankets upon Learning in Children (Should Linus Bring His Blanket to School?)," Paper presented at the American Psychological Association Convention, New Orleans, Louisiana, September 1974.

:28–32   R. H. PASSMAN, "Arousal Reducing Properties of Attachment Objects: Testing the Functional Limits of the Security Blanket Relative to the Mother," *Developmental Psychology,* 12 (1976), pp. 468–469.

:33–37   W. A. MASON, "Motivational Factors in Psychosocial Development," in W. A. and M. Page (eds.), *Nebraska Symposium on Motivation* (Lincoln: University of Nebraska, 1970), pp. 35–67.

346:1–8   P. WEISBERG and J. E. RUSSELL, "Proximity and Interactional Behavior of Young Children to Their 'Security' Blanket," *Child Development,* 42 (1971), pp. 1575–1579.

:24–31   P. C. HORTON, *Solace: The Missing Dimension in Psychiatry* (Chicago: University of Chicago Press, 1981).

:35 to 347:2   *Webster's New World Dictionary of the American Language* (New York & Cleveland: World Publishing Co., 1970), p. 1064.

:3–9   B. M. LEVINSON, *Pet-Oriented Child Psychotherapy* (Springfield, Ill.: Charles C Thomas, 1969), p. xiv; B. M. Levinson, *Pets and Human Development* (Springfield, Ill.: Charles C Thomas, 1972).

:14 to 348:5   S. A. CORSON et al., "The Socializing Role of Pet Animals in Nursing Homes: An Experiment in Nonverbal Communication Therapy," in L. Levi (ed.), *Society, Stress and Disease: Aging and Old Age* (New York: Oxford University Press, 1977); S. A. Corson, E. O'L. Corson, and P. H. Gwynne, "Pet-Facilitated Psychotherapy," in R. S. Anderson (ed.), *Pet Animals and Society* (Baltimore: Williams & Wilkins, 1975), pp. 19–35.

:6–8   R. HELFER, "The Relationship between Lack of Bonding

Page and Line

and Child Abuse and Neglect," in M. H. Klaus, T. Leger, and M. A. Trause (eds.), *Maternal Attachment and Mothering Disorders: A Round Table* (New Brunswick, N. J.: Johnson & Johnson, 1975), pp. 21–25.

348:9–14   J. AREHEART-TREICHEL, "Pets: The Health Benefits," *Science News,* 121 (1982), pp. 220–223; R. A. Mugford, *The Social Significance of Pet Ownership* (Leicestershire: Melton Mowbrey, 1978).

:22–28   P. MOHANTI, *My Village, My Life: Portrait of an Indian Village* (New York: Praeger, 1974), pp. 103–107.

:29–33   F. LEBOYER, *Loving Hands: The Traditional Indian Art of Baby Massage* (New York: Knopf, 1976).

:35 to   W. A. CAUDILL and H. WEINSTEIN, "Maternal Care and
349:1–47   Infant Behavior in Japan and America," *Psychiatry,* 32 (1969), pp. 12–43; p. 13.

350:6–13   E. F. VOGEL, *Japan's New Middle Class: The Salary Man and His Family in a Tokyo Suburb* (Berkeley: University of California Press, 1963).

:24–36   CAUDILL and WEINSTEIN, "Maternal Care and Infant Behavior," p. 42. See also W. A. Caudill and C. Schooler, "Child Behavior and Child Rearing in Japan and the United States: An Interim Report," *Journal of Nervous and Mental Disease,* 157 (1973), pp. 323–338.

351:5 to   D. G. HARING, "Aspects of Personal Character in Japan,"
353:4   in D. G. Haring (ed.), *Personal Character and Cultural Milieu* (Syracuse, New York: Syracuse University Press, 1956), p. 416.

356:2–3   Quoted in A. F. COPPOLA, "Reality and the Haptic World," *Phi Kappa Phi Journal,* Winter 1970, p. 29.

:4–12   B. SCHAFFNER, *Father Land* (New York: Columbia University Press, 1948).

357:15–17   G. GREER, *The Female Eunuch* (New York: McGraw-Hill, 1971), p. 112.

:29 to   E. A. DUYCKINCK (ed.), *Wit and Wisdom of the Rev. Sydney*
358:10   *Smith* (New York: Widdleton, 1866), p. 426.

:19–25   J. VAN LAWICK-GOODALL, *In the Shadow of Man* (Boston: Houghton Mifflin, 1971), pp. 241 et seq.

:21   D. FOSSEY, "More Years with Mountain Gorillas," *National Geographic,* October 1971, pp. 574–585; Dian Fossey, *Gorillas in the Mist* (Boston: Houghton Mifflin, 1983).

:29–33   ORTEGA Y GASSET, *Man and People* (New York: Norton, 1957), pp. 192–221.

Page and Line

:33 to   E. WESTERMARCK, *The Origin and Development of the*
359:17   *Moral Ideas* (2 vols., London: Macmillan, 1917), vol. 2, pp. 150–151.

:18–30   A. R. RADCLIFFE-BROWN, *The Andaman Islanders* (Cambridge: University Press, 1933), p. 117.

:31 to   S. F. FELDMAN, *Mannerisms of Speech and Gestures in*
360:10   *Everyday Life* (New York: International Universities Press, 1959), p. 270.

:11–26   H. C. LYON, JR., *Tenderness Is Strength* (New York: Harper & Row, 1977), pp. 17–18.

:27 to   COPPOLA, "Reality and the Haptic World," pp. 30–31.
361:14

:25–33   W. SAFIRE, "Aye, There's the Rub," *The New York Times Magazine,* 30 January 1983.

362:8–22   P. SMITH, *Erasmus: A Study of His Life, Ideals and Place in History* (New York: Harper & Brothers, 1923), p. 60; reprinted New York: Dover Publications, 1962.

:23–27   I. PINCHBECK and M. HEWITT, *Children in English Society,* Vol. 1: *From Tudor Times to the Eighteenth Century* (London: Routledge & Kegan Paul, 1970); L. L. SCHUCKING, *The Puritan Family* (London: Routledge & Kegan Paul, 1970); P. ARIES, *Centuries of Childhood* (New York: Knopf, 1962).

363:1–12   K. W. BACK, *Beyond Words* (New York: Russell Sage Foundation, 1972), p. 154.

:13–14   Ibid., p. 46. For additional works on encounter and sensitivity training, see R. Gustaitis, *Turning On* (New York: Macmillan, 1969); D. Alchen, *What the Hell Are They Trying to Prove, Martha?* (New York: John Day, 1970); J. Howard, *Please Touch* (New York: McGraw-Hill, 1970); B. L. Maliver, *The Encounter Game* (New York: Stein & Day, 1972); L. N. Solomon and B. Berson (eds.), *New Perspectives on Encounter Groups* (San Francisco: Jossey-Bass, 1972).

:15–18   J. R. GIBB, "The Effects of Human Relations Training," in A. E. Bergin and S. L. Garfield (eds.), *Handbook of Psychotherapy and Behavior Change* (New York: Wiley, 1970), pp. 2114–2176.

:18–19   C. R. ROGERS, *Carl Rogers on Encounter Groups* (New York: Harper & Row, 1973), p. 146.

364:7–9   W. E. HARTMAN, M. FIFTHIAN, and D. JOHNSON, *Nudist Society* (New York: Crown, 1970), pp. 278–286. See also Howard, *Please Touch;* M. Shepard and M. Lee, *Marathon 16* (New York: Putnam's, 1970); B. L. Austin, *Sad*

Page and Line

	Nun at Synanon (New York: Holt, Rinehart & Winston, 1970).
:27 to 365:9	M. MEAD and R. MÉTRAUX (eds.), *The Study of Culture at a Distance* (Chicago: University of Chicago Press, 1953), pp. 107–115, 352–353; G. GORER and J. RICKMAN, *The People of Great Russia: A Psychological Study* (New York: Chanticleer Press, 1950).
:11–22	P. H. WOLFF, "The Natural History of Crying and Other Vocalizations in Early Infancy," in E. B. Foss (ed.), *Determinants of Infant Behavior* (vol. 4, London: Methuen, 1969), p. 92.
:28–30	H. ORLANSKY, "Infant Care and Personality," *Psychological Bulletin*, 46 (1949), pp. 1–48.
365:34 to 367:5	MEAD and MÉTRAUX, *The Study of Culture at a Distance*, p. 163.
366:4 to 367:5	V. DAL, *The Dictionary of the Living Great Russian Language* [*Tolkovyi slovar Velikomusskavo Yazkaya*] (St. Petersburg, 1903).
:16–17	N. LEITES, *The Operational Code of the Politburo* (New York: McGraw-Hill, 1951).
:17 to 368:3	L. H. HAIMSON, "Russian 'Visual Thinking,'" in Mead and Métraux, p. 247.
:36 to 369:2	D. LEIGHTON and C. KLUCKHOHN, *Children of the People* (Cambridge, Mass.: Harvard University Press, 1947), pp. 24–25.
:13–16	R. E. RITZENTHALER and P. RITZENTHALER, *The Woodland Indians* (New York: The Natural History Press, 1970), p. 29.
:33–34	Quoted by LEIGHTON and KLUCKHOHN, *Children of the People*, pp. 29–30.
370:3–6	W. DENNIS, *The Hopi Child* (New York: Appleton-Century, 1940), p. 101.
:7–13	Quoted by LEIGHTON and KLUCKHOHN, Margaret Fries on swaddling, pp. 29–30.
:16–30	L. CALLEY, "A Baby on a Cradle Board," *Child and Family*, 5 (1966), pp. 8–10.
371:16–31	B. LOZOFF and G. BRITTENHAM, "Infant Care: Cache or Carry," *The Journal of Pediatrics*, 95 (1979), pp. 478–483.
:32 to 372:16	N. CUNNINGHAM and E. ANISFIELD, "Baby Carriers and Infant Development," manuscript, November 1982; Nicholas Cunningham, "The Influence of Early Carrying on Infant Development," manuscript, January 1983.

Page and Line

372:36 to   J. E. RITCHIE, "The Husband's Role," Parents Centres
373:7   (Auckland, N. Z.), *Bulletin* 38, March 1969, pp. 4–7.

374:8–25   R. D. PARKE, "Father-Infant Interaction," in Klaus, Leger,
           and Trause, *Maternal Attachment and Mothering Disor-
           ders,* pp. 61–63. See also M. H. Klaus and J. H. Kennell,
           Maternal-Infant Bonding (St. Louis, Mo.: C. V. Mosby,
           1976).

:26–32   D. W. WINNICOTT, "The Theory of Parent-Infant Relation-
           ship," *International Journal of Psychoanalysis,* 41 (1958),
           p. 591.

375:13–16 G. GREENE, *A Sort of Life* (New York: Simon & Schuster,
           1971), p. 64.

376:12–22 L. K. FRANK, "The Psychological Approach in Sex Re-
           search," *Social Problems,* 1 (1954), pp. 133–139.

:28–32   CLAY, "The Effect of Culture," p. 278.

:30–32   L. M. STOLZ, *Influences on Parent Behavior* (Stanford,
           Calif.: Stanford University Press, 1967), p. 141.

377:21–23 R. E. HAWKINS and J. A. POPPLESTONE, "The Tattoo as an
           Exoskeletal Defense," *Perceptual and Motor Skills,* 19
           (1964), p. 500; J. A. Popplestone, "A Syllabus of Exo-
           skeletal Defenses," *Psychological Record,* 13 (1963), pp.
           15–25; H. EBERSTEIN, *Pierced Hearts and True Love*
           (London: Derek Verschoyle, 1953).

:27–32   F. ROME, *The Tattooed Men* (New York: Delacorte Press,
           1975), p. 54.

378:2–14   J. H. BURMA, "Self-Tattooing among Delinquents," *Sociol-
           ogy and Social Research,* 43 (1959), pp. 341–345.

:15–18   S. FISHER, *Body Consciousness* (Englewood Cliffs, N. J.:
           Prentice-Hall, 1973), p. 91.

:19–22   A. M. HOCART, "Tattooing and Healing," in his *The Life-
           Giving Myth* (New York: Grove Press, n.d.) pp.
           169–172.

:22–33   For a good survey see W. G. SUMNER and A. G. KELLER,
           The Science of Society (New Haven, Conn.: Yale Uni-
           versity Press, 1929), vol. 3, pp. 2130–2135. See also
           C. Jenkinson, "Tatuing," in J. Hastings (ed.), *Encyclo-
           paedia of Religion and Ethics* (New York: Scribners,
           1920), vol. 12, pp. 208–214; Henry Field, "Body-Mark-
           ing in Southwestern Asia," *Papers of the Peabody Mu-
           seum of Archaeology and Ethnology,* Harvard University,
           45, (1958), pp. xiii–162.

379:7–12   A. VIRÉL, *Decorated Man: The Human Body as Art*
           (New York: Abrams, 1980); M. KIRK and ANDREW
           STRATHERN, *Man as Art* (New York: Viking Press,

Page and Line

1981); ANGELA FISHER, *Africa Adorned* (New York: Abrams, 1984); J. ANDERSON BLACK, MADGE GARLAND, and FRANCES KENNETT, *A History of Fashion* (New York, William Morrow, 1980); J. C. FLÜGEL, *The Psychology of Clothes* (London: Hogarth Press, 1930); JOHN M. VINCENT, *Clothes and Conduct* (Baltimore: The Johns Hopkins Press, 1935); JOHN BULWER, *Anthropometamorphosis: Man Transformed* (London: William Hunt, 1653).

:13–16   A. MONTAGU, "Clothes and Behavior," *Johnson and Johnson Profiles,* 2 (July 1964), pp. 9–11.

:30–32   These studies are summarized in Klaus and Kennell, *Maternal-Infant Bonding,* pp. 2–3.

:33 to 380:3   H. KEMPE, "Detecting Child Abuse," *Intercom* (Washington, D.C.) 4, 11 (1976), p. 5.

:4–12   R. HELFER, "The Relationship between Lack of Bonding and Child Abuse and Neglect," in Klaus, Leger, and Trause, *Maternal Attachment and Mothering Disorders,* pp. 21–25.

:13–27   S. FRAIBERG, in Kempe.

381:2–4   F. DUNBAR, *Psychosomatic Diagnosis* (New York: Hoeber, 1943), pp. 86–87; J. G. KEPECS, "Some Patterns of Somatic Displacement," *Psychosomatic Medicine,* 15 (1953), pp. 425–432.

:8–13   C. E. BENDA, *The Image of Love* (New York: Free Press, 1961), p. 162.

:19–29   J. G. KEPECS, M. ROBIN, and M. J. BRUNNER, "Relationship between Certain Emotional States and Exudation into the Skin," *Psychosomatic Medicine,* 13 (1951), pp. 10–17.

382:1–3   J. G. KEPECS, A. RABIN, and M. ROBIN, "Atopic Dermatitis: A Clinical Psychiatric Study," *Psychosomatic Medicine,* 13 (1951), pp. 1–9; H. C. BETHUNE and C. B. KIDD, "Psychophysiological Mechanisms in Skin Diseases," *The Lancet,* 2 (1961), pp. 1419–1422.

:5–9   H. F. HARLOW and M. K. HARLOW, "Learning to Love," *American Scientist,* 54 (1966), pp. 244–272, and numerous other papers.

:10–14   H. F. HARLOW, "Primary Affectional Patterns in Primates," *American Journal of Orthopsychiatry,* 30 (1960), pp. 676–677; M. K. HARLOW and H. F. HARLOW, "Affection in Primates," *Discovery,* 27 (January 1966).

383:2–5   HARLOW, "Primary Affectional Patterns in Primates."

Page and Line

:10 to   CLAY, "The Effect of Culture," pp. 281–282.
384:10

:11–16   H. F. HARLOW and M. K. HARLOW, "Learning to Love,"
American Scientist, 54 (1966), p. 250.

:18 to   A. KULKA, C. FRY, and F. J. GOLDSTEIN, "Kinesthetic
385:2   Needs in Infancy," *American Journal of Orthopsychiatry,*
30 (1960), pp. 562–571.

:4 to   H. F. HARLOW, "Development of the Second and Third
386:13   Affectional Systems in Macaques Monkeys," in T. T.
Tourlentes, S. L. Pollack, and H. E. Himwich (eds.), *Research Approaches to Psychiatric Problems* (New York:
Grune & Stratton, 1962), pp. 209–229.

:14 to   CLAY, "The Effect of Culture," p. 290.
387:30

:5–8   See also C. LOIZOS, "Play Behavior in Higher Primates: A
Review," in D. Morris (ed.), *Primate Ethology* (Chicago:
Aldine, 1967), pp. 176–218; O. Aldis, *Play Fighting* (New
York: Academic Press, 1975); P. A. Jewell and C. Loizos
(eds.), *Play, Exploration and Territory in Mammals* (New
York: Academic Press, 1966); S. Miller, *The Psychology
of Play* (Baltimore: Penguin Books, 1968).

:20–25   T. R. WILLIAMS, "Cultural Structuring of Tactile Experience in a Borneo Society," *American Anthropologist,* 68
(1966), pp. 27–39.

:31–36   A. TSUMORI, "Newly Acquired Behavior and Social Interactions of Japanese Monkeys," in S. A. Altmann (ed.),
Social Communication among Primates (Chicago: University of Chicago Press, 1967), pp. 207–219.

:34–36   K. R. L HALL, "Observational Learning in Monkeys and
Apes," *British Journal of Psychology,* 54 (1963), pp.
201–206; K. R. L. Hall, "Social Learning in Monkeys,"
in P. Jay (ed.), *Primates* (New York: Holt, Rinehart &
Winston, 1969), pp. 383–397.

388:6–23   H. L. RHEINGOLD and C. O. ECKERMAN, "The Infant Separates Himself from His Mother," *Science,* 168 (1970), pp.
78–83.

:16–18   R. HELD and A. HEIN, "Movement-Produced Stimulation
in the Development of Visually Guided Behavior,"
Journal of Comparative and Physiological Psychology, 56
(1963), pp. 872–876.

389:30–31   D. STERN, *The First Relationship: Mother and Infant* (Cambridge, Mass.: Harvard University Press, 1977), p. 46.

:36 to   C. DARWIN, *The Expression of the Emotions in Man and
390:2   the Animals* (London: John Murray, 1872), pp. 201–202.

Page and Line
390:13–15   N. B. BLACKMAN, "Pleasure and Touching: Their Significance in the Development of the Preschool Child—An Exploratory Study."

391:4–32   CLAY, "The Effect of Culture," pp. 308, 322.

CHAPTER NINE. TOUCH AND AGE

Page and Line
396:12–18   See A. MONTAGU, *Growing Young* (New York: McGraw-Hill, 1981).

:19–24   C. A. FANSLOW, "Touch and the Elderly," in Catherine Caldwell Brown (ed.), *The Many Facets of Touch* (Skillman, N. J.: Johnson and Johnson Baby Products, 1984), pp. 183–189.

:22–24   R. RUBIN, "Maternal Touch," *Nursing Outlook,* 11 (1963), pp. 828–831; see also S. J. Tobiason, "Touching Is for Everyone," *American Journal of Nursing,* 81 (1981), pp. 728–730; K. E. Barnett, *The Development of a Theoretical Construct of the Concepts of Touch as They Relate to Nursing. Final Report to U. S. Department of Health, Education and Welfare,* Project No. 0-G-027, 1972.

:27 to   D. SWANSON, "Minnie Remembers," in Janice Grana
398:19   (compiler), *Images* (Winona, Minn.: St. Mary's College Press, 1977).

:23 to   R. McCORKLE and M. HOLLENBACH, "Touch and the
399:35   Acutely Ill," in Brown (ed.), *The Many Facets of Touch,* pp. 175–183.

APPENDIX 1

Page and Line
404:4 to   D. KRIEGER, *The Therapeutic Touch: How to Use Your*
405   *Hands to Help or to Heal* (Englewood Cliffs, N. J.: Pren-
:28   tice-Hall, 1982), p. 13.

:29–35   D. KRIEGER, "The Relationship of Touch, with Intent to Help or Heal to Subjects' In-Vivo Hemoglobin Values: A Study in Personalized Interaction," in E. M. Jacobi and L. E. Netter (eds.), *American Nurses Association Ninth Research Conference* (San Antonio, Texas, 1973), pp. 39–58; R. M. SCHLOTFELDT, "Critique of Dr. Krieger's Paper," ibid., pp. 59–65; D. KRIEGER, "Rejoinder," ibid., pp. 67–71; G. B. UJHELY, "Nursing Im-

Page and Line

plications," ibid., pp. 73–77; D. KRIEGER and D. KUNZ (1973), described by Marie-Thérèse Connelly in "Therapeutic Touch: The State of the Art," in Brown (ed.), *The Many Facets of Touch,* p. 150; D. KRIEGER, "Therapeutic Touch: The Imprimatur of Nursing," *American Journal of Nursing,* 5 (1975), pp. 784–787.

:36 to J. F. QUINN, "An Investigation of Therapeutic Touch Done
406:9   Without Physical Contact on State of Anxiety of Hospitalized Cardiovascular Patients" (PhD dissertation, New York University, 1981).

:10–34 E. PEPER and S. ANCOLI, "The Two Endpoints of an EEG Continuum of Meditation—Alpha/Theta and Fast Beta," in E. Peper, S. Ancoli and M. Quinn, *Mind/Body Integration* (New York: Plenum Press, 1979), pp. 141–148.

407:3–7 M.-T. CONNELLY, "Therapeutic Touch: The State of the Art," p. 155.

:15–17 M. D. BORELLI and P. HEIDT (eds.), *Therapeutic Touch* (New York: Pringer Publishing Co., 1981), pp. 3–39.

:18–20 I. S. WOLFSON, "Therapeutic Touch and Midwifery," in Brown (ed.), *The Many Facets of Touch,* pp. 166–172.

:21–33 J. A. SMITH, "A Critical Appraisal of Therapeutic Touch," in Brown (ed.), *The Many Facets of Touch,* pp. 151–165; see also Jules Older, *Touching Is Healing* (New York: Stein & Day, 1982), pp. 156–157, 282.

:25   J. D. FRANK, *Persuasion and Healing* (Baltimore: The Johns Hopkins University Press, 1961).

408:27–30 G. M. SHEPHERD, *The Synaptic Organization of the Brain* (2nd ed., New York: Oxford University Press, 1979); RICHARD M. RESTAK, *The Brain* (New York: Bantam Books, 1984); JOHN BODDY, *Brain Systems and Psychological Concepts* (New York, Wiley, 1978); HUGH BROWN, *Brain & Behavior* (New York: Oxford University Press, 1976).

409:2–7 R. MILLER, *Meaning and Purpose in the Intact Brain* (New York: Oxford University Press, 1981), p. 70.

410:7–10 H. JOST and LESTER W. SONTAG, "The Genetic Factor in Autonomic System Function," *Psychosomatic Medicine,* 6 (1944), pp. 308–310; see also Herbert Athenstaedt, Helge Clausen, and Daniel Schaper, "Epidermis of Human Skin: Pyroelectric and Pizoelectric Sensor Layer," *Science,* 216 (1982), pp. 1018–1020.

Page and Line

:11 to   G. J. TORTORA and NICHOLAS P. ANAGNOSTAKOS, *Princi-*
411:5   *ples of Anatomy and Physiology* (3rd ed., New York:
            Harper & Row, 1981), p. 341; ARTHUR C. GUYTON,
            Textbook of Medical Physiology (6th ed., Philadelphia,
            1981).

:7–12   C. GUJA, "Propriétés Bio-Electrique de l'Envelope Cutanée
            Humaine: Résultats de Quelques Recherches Experi-
            mentales," *Bulletin et Mémoires de la Société d'Anthro-*
            pologie de Paris, series 13 (1980), pp. 205–220.

:19–25   R. ADER (ed.), *Psychoneuroimmunology* (New York: Aca-
            demic Press, 1981); STEVEN LOCKE et al. (eds.), *Founda-*
            tions of Psychoneuroimmunology (New York: Aldine,
            1985).

INDEX

ABOUT THE AUTHOR

Ashley Montagu is one of the few experts on just about everything to do with people. He is, at last count, the author or editor of over sixty books on such varied subjects as anatomy and physiology, psychology, anthropology, race, evolution and heredity, love, aggression and touching, human development, sexuality, the history of science, the dangers of pollution, the anatomy of swearing, and the dolphin in human history. Among his classic works are *The Natural Superiority of Women, Man's Most Dangerous Myth: The Fallacy of Race, Human Evolution, The Elephant Man, Touching, Anthropology and Human Nature, Life Before Birth, On Being Human, Growing Young,* and *The Nature of Human Aggression.* He is co-author with Floyd Matson of *The Human Connection* and *The Dehumanization of Man.* He is the writer and director of the film "One World or None," described as one of the best documentaries ever made. Ashley Montagu has taught at Harvard, New York University, University of California, Rutgers University, and Princeton University.

> The times call for the social scientist who controls at a good level the many different sciences that deal with human nature. In this area Ashley Montagu is our, and the world's, best man.
>
> —John Dollard,
> Yale University
> *The New York Times Book Review*

ANGela

angela bautista tirona